THE CULINARY CHRONICLE

As regards the recipes in English, the metric weights and
measures (grams, liters, etc.) have been converted to imperial
and, wherever suitable, to American measures. Due to inevitable
rounding off, these measures may deviate from the original.
For these deviations no responsibility whatsoever is taken.

Photography and Design

Bruno Hausch

THE CULINARY CHRONICLE

Text

Hans-Albert Stechl (Hong Kong and London)
Dr. Barbara Schweighofer, Ludwig Riepl (Morocco · Marokko)

Editorial director and recipe editor

Christine Messer Hausch

Translation from the German

John Smith

FOOD FOR FRIENDS

CONTENTS · INHALT

Editorial 6

Hong Kong 8

Restaurant Yü, The Regent 22
Restaurant Plume, The Regent 40
Restaurant Lai Ching Heen, The Regent 44
Sun Tung Lok Shark's Fin Restaurant 60
East Ocean Seafood Restaurant 68
Tai Woo Restaurant 89
Wan Loong Court Restaurant, The Kowloon Hotel 96
Hunan Garden Restaurant 108
Snow Garden Restaurant 115
Golden Island Bird's Nest Chiu Chau Restaurant 126
Yung Kee Restaurant 134
Forum Restaurant 144
Restaurant Petrus, Island Shangri-La 158
Gaddi's Restaurant, The Peninsula 172
Felix, The Peninsula 183

Morocco · Marokko 198

La Gazelle d'Or, Taroudannt 216
La Roseraie, Val d'Ouirgane 255
Le Tivoli, Agadir 273
Villa Maroc, Essaouira 278
La Mamounia, Marrakech 282
Restaurant El Yacout, Marrakech 322

London 356

Mosimann's London 354
The Dorchester 362
The Stafford 408
Restaurant Zafferano 423
Restaurant Aubergine 446
Restaurant Pied-à-Terre 468

Addresses · Adressen 486
Acknowledgements · Danksagung 487
Illustration credits · Bildnachweis 487
Recipe Index 490
Rezeptverzeichnis 493

Food is culture.

This concept is the basis of the present book and the idea behind a series of volumes to follow. The aim of THE CULINARY CHRONICLE is to document the wealth of food culture from all over the world – each year anew, with painstakingly researched articles on regions supposedly well-known, but worth discovering afresh. The purpose of the book is to explore a new dimension: it wants to document the times we live in, offering plenty of culinary information for the eye and the mind, while at the same time, with its modern design, generous series of illustrations and high-quality production, providing enjoyment and stimulating the senses.

The first volume picks out the focal points of three totally heterogeneous locations. The cuisine of Hong Kong is illuminated in depth, from the most renowned gastronomies of the international hotels to the best Chinese specialty restaurants. The city in which money is the number-one topic is also impressive in its bustling, hectic wok kitchens with their flame-belching stoves, the clearly defined recipes for success of the individual establishments, the multicultural, cosmopolitan top-class addresses, but also in the perfection of its service.

A world away lies Morocco, whose southern region represents a counterpart that could not be richer in contrasts. The tranquility of the country, the carefully nurtured traditions, the light and colors, the arabesques of the architecture and design create an atmosphere of receptiveness for pleasure. Morocco's unspoilt natural surroundings, simple life-style and the genuine hospitality of the people harmonize with the luxurious cordiality of the hotels and restaurants into a multi-faceted unison.

London, finally, represents the modern age. Having awoken from its long culinary torpor, the city can today claim its place in the avantgarde. Both camps – the champions and supporters of the latest success cuisine as well as the young, extremely creative cooks who achieve their high aims and novel ideas with incredible perfection and professionalism – are portrayed in this book.

For the fist time, in THE CULINARY CHRONICLE, a comprehensive documentation is dedicated to the globally cultivated and celebrated art of cooking. As experienced and multiple prize-winning book publishers we regard it as our special challenge to go a step beyond the usual forms of presentation and to acclaim the world's food culture at the highest level. This is what the readers of THE CULINARY CHRONICLE may also expect in the future: a new volume each year, which literally appeals to all the senses.

We wish all our readers much epicurean pleasure and sensual enjoyment.

Essen ist Kultur.

Auf dieser Erkenntnis basiert das vorliegende Buch und die Idee zu einer Reihe von Folgebänden. THE CULINARY CHRONICLE hat zum Ziel, das globale Gut der Eßkultur zu dokumentieren – jedes Jahr aufs Neue, mit sorgfältig aufgearbeiteten Beiträgen zu entdeckungswürdigen und nur vermeintlich bekannten Regionen. Das Buch wagt sich mit seinem Konzept an eine neue Dimension heran: es will Zeitdokument sein, es will viel kulinarische Information für Augen und Kopf bieten und gleichzeitig mit der modernen Gestaltung, den großzügigen Bildstrecken und der hochwertigen Verarbeitung Genuß vermitteln und die Sinne beflügeln.

Der erste Band setzt die Schwerpunkte in drei völlig gegensätzlichen Gegenden. Die Hong Kong-Küche wird eingehend beleuchtet, von den renommiertesten Gastronomiebetrieben der internationalen Hotels bis zu den besten chinesischen Spezialitäten-Restaurants. Die Stadt, in der Geld das Thema Nummer eins ist, beeindruckt durch die quirligen, hektischen Wok-Küchen mit ihren feuerspeienden Kochstellen, die klaren Erfolgsrezepte der einzelnen Betriebe, die multikulturellen, kosmopolitischen Lokale auf höchstem Niveau, aber auch durch die Perfektion der Dienstleistung.

Ganz anders Marokko, dessen Süden ein Pendant abgibt, das kontrastreicher nicht sein könnte. Die Beschaulichkeit des Landes, die gepflegte Tradition, Licht und Farben sowie das Arabeske von Architektur und Design vermitteln Behaglichkeit und die Bereitschaft zum Genuß. In Marokko verschmelzen die intakte Natur, das schlichte Leben und die natürliche Gastfreundschaft der Bevölkerung mit der luxuriösen Gastlichkeit in den Hotels und Restaurants zu einer facettenreichen Harmonie.

London schließlich repräsentiert die Moderne. Aus dem langen kulinarischen Dornröschenschlaf erwacht, kann die Stadt für sich in Anspruch nehmen, heute die gastronomische Avantgarde zu bilden. Beide Lager – die Vorkämpfer und Stützen der aktuellen Erfolgsgastronomie wie auch die jungen, äußerst kreativen Köche, die ihre hochgesteckten Ziele und neuartigen Konzepte mit unglaublicher Perfektion und Professionalität umsetzen, – sind im vorliegenden Buch porträtiert.

Der weltweit gepflegten und zelebrierten Kunst des Kochens wird mit THE CULINARY CHRONICLE erstmals eine umfassende Dokumentation gewidmet. Als professionelle und mehrfach ausgezeichnete Büchermacher sehen wir die besondere Herausforderung darin, über gewohnte Darstellungsformen hinauszugehen und das Weltkulturgut „Essen" auf höchstem Niveau umzusetzen. Dies dürfen die Leser des Chronicle auch in Zukunft erwarten: jedes Jahr einen Band, der alle Sinne anspricht.

Wir wünschen Ihnen bei der Lektüre viel lukullischen Spaß und sinnlichen Genuß.

Hong Kong

Hong Kong is – among an infinite number of other things – primarily one great culinary festival, it is like a huge 24-hour restaurant with several thousand highly pleasurable departments. This multicultural melting pot is simultaneously a multi-culinary cooking pot. Here you can hear the sizzle of Italian and French food that is just as good as in the best kitchens of Rome or Paris. You can dine in Spanish, Thai, Indonesian, Japanese, Vietnamese, and probably also Kirghiz, Turkoman or Saudi-Arabian style.

What is incomparable, however, is a trip right through the endless variety of Chinese cuisine, a submersion in the secrets of Chinese culinary and alimentary culture. To embark on such a culinary as well as cultural adventure, there are basically just two choices open to the gourmet. Either he buys a year's ticket on the Chinese state railway and travels across the giant Middle Kingdom, or he takes a room for a week in Hong Kong (bearing in mind that the latter – with accommodation in first-class hotels – would scarcely come any cheaper).

The advantage that Hong Kong offers the epicure is obvious, however: having had your fill of Peking duck and with an appetite for the chili-laden piquancy of Hunan, there is no need to travel thousands of miles: just stroll around the corner. For a mid-morning snack you can slurp a dollar-fifty noodle soup from an open stand in the street, for lunch enjoy a sweet-and-sour Shanghai meal in a middle-class restaurant with a similar price range, and in the evening plunder your bank account for a $300 abalone dish or tureen of shark's fin soup.

You can play it safe and order fried rice or pluck up courage and visit a restaurant specialising in snake dishes. As solace to the faint-hearted, let it be said that visually and tastewise the soup of snake meat is reminiscent of a regular tripe soup. In a Hunan restaurant you can get the taste buds dancing with ultra-hot chilis. Or taste the gentle spices of Canton cuisine.

The very contrasts are what fascinate. At a street corner you can dine in the open air under bamboo mats. Out of the wok come stir-fried vegetables with chicken, to go with this a pot of tea, and all for the price of a hamburger. Fifty yards away, a 600-foot façade of glass soars to the sky. The penthouse restaurant is at the top – in every respect (the luxury tax on imported wines is merciless).

And then the fish markets. "If it swims, we have it" could be their slogan. You stroll past endless rows of tanks of live fish and seafood, buying a few oysters here, a few whelks there, then a lobster, next door a sea bream and a little further beyond a something-or-other. "It will taste excellent", promises the fishwife with a smile that has to be believed. No fish could be fresher than the fish here. You then hand over the five purchases to the waiter at the market restaurant that has been set up for this purpose, giving rough instructions as to how you would like them prepared (strong or mild seasoning, steamed or deep-fried) and wait to see what turns out. A short time later the table is groaning under innumerable plates and dishes, and you can only marvel at what has become of those few fishes. Fresh, delicious, tasty, and every one spiced a little differently, often mysteriously: quality and variety without end.

Kong Bixia, the inscrutable genius of a cook in Lu Wenfu's novel "The Gourmet" wanted to invite guests to a grand dinner. She had to cross off the menu an eel steamed in soy sauce because the eel bought from the fishmonger would have had to be specially fed for a whole week beforehand, and she did not have so much time. And to serve it in any other way was out of the question, for quality was of paramount importance. When you have eaten your way through Hong Kong's leading Chinese restaurants, you can begin to understand Kong Bixia.

Hong Kong

Hong Kong, das ist – neben unendlich vielen anderen Dingen mehr – vor allem auch ein einziges großes kulinarisches Fest. Das ist wie riesiges, rund um die Uhr geöffnetes Restaurant mit einigen tausend höchst vergnüglichen Unterabteilungen. Dieser multikulturelle Schmelztiegel ist gleichzeitig ein mulitkulinarischer Kochtopf. Da wird italienisch und französisch gebrutzelt, so gut wie bei den besten Köchen in Rom oder Paris. Man kann sich spanisch, thailändisch, indonesisch, japanisch, vietnamesisch und vermutlich auch kirgiesisch, turkmenisch oder saudi-arabisch verkstigen.

Unvergleichlich aber ist ein Trip quer durch die unendliche Vielfalt der chinesischen Küche, ein Eintauchen in die Geheimnisse der chinesischen Koch- und Eßkultur. Für ein derartiges kulinarisches wie kulturelles Abenteuer hat der Gourmet im Grunde nur zwei Möglichkeiten. Entweder er bucht ein Jahresticket mit der chinesischen Staatsbahn und reist quer durchs riesige Reich der Mitte, oder er quartiert sich für eine Woche in Hong Kong ein (wobei letzteres – die Übernachtung in erstklassigen Hotels vorausgesetzt – kaum billiger sein dürfte).

Der Vorteil, den Hong Kong dem Feinschmecker bietet, liegt aber auf der Hand: Wer sich an der Peking-Ente sattgegessen hat und Lust auf die Chili-Schärfe Hunans hat, muß nicht x-tausend Kilometer fahren, sondern nur um die Ecke biegen. Man kann zum zweiten Frühstück eine Zweimarkfünfzig-Nudelsuppe am offenen Stand auf der Straße schlürfen, zum Mittagessen Süß-Saures aus Shanghai in einem ordentlichen Restaurant der Mittelklasse zu ebensolchen Preisen verspeisen und am Abend beim Fünfhundert-Mark-Abalone-Teller oder einer Terrine Haifischflossensuppe sein Konto plündern. Man kann sich auf die sichere Seite begeben und fried rice ordern, oder Mut beweisen und ein auf Schlangengerichte spezialisiertes Restaurant aufsuchen. Zur Beruhigung für alle Mutlosen: die Suppe mit Schlangenfleisch erinnert optisch wie geschmacklich stark an eine ordentliche Kuttelsuppe. Man kann in einem Hunan-Restaurant die Geschmackspapillen auf der Zunge mit ultrascharfen Chilis zum Tanzen bringen. Oder die sanfte Würze der Kanton-Küche schmecken.

Es sind gerade die Kontraste, die faszinieren. Da wird an einer Ecke unter Bambusmatten im Freien getafelt. Aus dem Wok kommt kurzgebratenes Gemüse mit Hühnerfleisch, dazu ein Topf Tee und das alles in der Preislage eines Hamburger-Klopses. Fünfzig Meter nebenan recken sich 200 Meter Glasfassade in den Himmel. Das Restaurant im obersten Stockwerk ist on the top – und das in jeder Beziehung (die Luxussteuer schlägt bei den importierten Weinen gnadenlos zu).

Und dann diese Fischmärkte. „If it swims – we have it" könnte deren Losung sein. Man schlendert an unzähligen Aquarien mit lebenden Fischen und Meeresfrüchten vorbei, kauft hier ein paar Austern, dort einige Schnecken, dann einen Hummer, nebenan eine Dorade und etwas weiter hinten einen Ich-weiß-nicht-was. Daß er exzellent schmecken wird, versichert die Verkäuferin mit einem Lächeln, dem man glauben muß. Frischer als hier kann Fisch nicht sein. Die fünf Tüten drückt man dann dem Kellner des eigens darauf eingerichteten Markt-Restaurants in die Hände, gibt grobe Anweisungen über die Art und Weise der gewünschten Zubereitung (scharf oder nicht, gedämpft oder fritiert) und wartet auf die Dinge, die da kommen werden. Schon kurze Zeit später biegt sich der Tisch unter einer Unzahl von Tellern und Platten und man kann sich nur noch wundern, was aus den paar Fischen alles geworden ist. Frisch, lecker, schmackhaft, immer wieder ein bißchen anders gewürzt, oft geheimnisvoll, Qualität und Vielfalt ohne Ende.

Kong Bixia, die unergründlich-geniale Köchin aus Lu Wenfus amüsantem Roman „Der Gourmet", wollte zu einem großen Essen einladen. Einen in Soja-Sauce geschmorten Aal mußte sie wieder von der Speisekarte streichen, da der beim Händler gekaufte Aal eine ganze Woche auf spezielle Weise hätte gefüttert werden müssen, und so lange hatte sie nicht mehr Zeit. Und anders wollte sie ihn nicht servieren, denn Qualität ging ihr über alles. Wer sich durch Hong Kongs führende China-Restaurants gefuttert hat, fängt an, Kong Bixia zu verstehen.

THE REGENT

Restaurant Yü

*T*he star performers of the restaurant ogle the guest as soon as he enters the bright dining room overlooking the harbor: in a huge, over 45-foot long aquarium with gently curved glass sides, parrot fish, tiger garoupa, coral trout, rainbow trout, hung yau, mandarin fish, lun pun, so mei, maori, pomfret, red garoupa and eastern star garoupa silently glide up and down between computer-controlled streams of dancing air bubbles. In this gigantic, turquoise shimmering wall of water, custom-built in Japan, a purification system without chemicals ensures water quality the like of which these fish would scarcely find in their native south-east Asian Pacific. On one

side, oysters lie on a bed of ice. A few steps further there are bubbling aquariums for lobsters, langoustes, scampi and shrimp. All this tells the guest at every step just one thing: nowhere can the choice of fish and fruits de mer be fresher and more varied than in the seafood restaurant Yü in the Regent Hotel. Here, every delicacy that swims arrives on the plate fresh from the ocean and without long transportation.

The first-class range of basic produce available is paralleled by the variety of preparation methods: in Chinese and European style, food is boiled, steamed, fried and broiled, hot-spiced or more moderately so, depending on your instructions to the waiters in their gaily colored fish-motif neckties. And if you prefer to take advice, you are in the best of hands with this friendly and professional team. The kitchen is open; there are no secrets withheld from the guest. And as a special attraction, a huge copper cauldron of seething, highly concentrated fish bouillon stands in the room, in which in a matter of seconds lobster, langouste and garoupa are poached to a succulent turn. A few yards away, an oyster bar invites you to sample the best quality oysters that are cultivated anywhere on the globe.

These efforts soon found recognition: already in 1994, a year after the Yü opened, it was chosen on site by the American Board of Trade as Hong Kong's best seafood restaurant. Hotel journals regularly list it among the ten best hotel restaurants in the world. To "blame" for all this is Jürg Blaser (together with his right-hand man Christof Syré), a Swiss original from Berne with decades of Asia experience, who has kept the total of five restaurants of the Regent Hotel (Plume, Yü, Lai Ching Heen,

The Steakhouse Bar & Grill and the Harbourside) in culinary top form since their opening in 1980. The kitchens employ a staff of 186, whom he directs and motivates with a cool superiority acquired in hotels and restaurants in Basle, Lucerne and Flims and over a period of 13 years at the Hong Kong Peninsula Hotel, just 300 yards away.

The pauses between courses are devoted to the harbor view, the skyline of Hong Kong, which can from nowhere be as spectacular as from here, from the Kowloon side. Even the just-finished mouse garoupa, the fragrance of lemon grass and fresh market vegetables and the glittering Sancerre are forgotten for a brief moment. But only for a brief moment. For also the desserts, perhaps the Yü apple tart or the kirsch-flavored ice soufflé with fresh fruits and chocolate chips have every chance of upstaging the harbor view.

Restaurant Yü

$\mathcal{D}$ie Hauptdarsteller des Restaurants beäugen den Gast gleich beim Betreten des hellen, zum Hafen hin ausgerichteten Gastraumes: In einem riesigen, deckenhohen und über 45 Feet langen Aquarium mit sanft geschwungenen Glasscheiben schweben Parrot Fish, Tiger Garoupa, Coral Trout, Rainbow Trout, Hung Yau, Mandarin Fish, Lun Pun, So Mei, Maori, Pomfret, Red Garoupa und Eastern Star Garoupa zwischen

computergesteuert tanzenden Luftbläschen in einem lautlosen Auf und Ab. In dieser gigantischen, blau-grün schimmernden Wasserwand, einer japanischen Spezialanfertigung, sorgt ein Reinigungssystem ohne jede Chemikalie für Wasserqualitäten, wie sie die Fische in den Weiten ihres Süd-Ost-Asiatischen Pazifiks kaum besser hatten. Daneben liegen Austern auf Eis. Einige Schritte weiter sprudelt es in den Aquarien für Hummer, Langusten, Gambas und Krevetten. All das soll dem Gast auf Schritt und Tritt nur das eine signalisieren: frischer und vielfältiger als im Seafood-Restaurant Yü im Regent-Hotel kann die Auswahl an Fischen und Meeresfrüchten gar nicht sein. Alles, was schwimmt und delikat ist – im Yü kommt es fangfrisch und ohne Umwege auf den Teller. Dem erstklassigen Angebot an Grundprodukten entspricht die Variationsbreite bei den Zubereitungsarten: es wird chinesisch und europäisch gekocht, gedämpft, gebraten und gegrillt, scharf oder eher verhalten, ganz so wie man es den Kellnern mit ihren frech-bunten Fisch-Motiv-Krawatten in Auftrag gibt. Und wer sich lieber beraten läßt, ist bei dieser ebenso freundlichen wie professionellen Mannschaft in den besten Händen. Die Küche ist offen, Geheimnisse vor dem Gast gibt es nicht. Und als besondere Attraktion steht ein riesiger Kupferkessel mit wallender, hoch konzentrierter Fischboullion im Raum, in der in Sekundenschnelle Hummer, Languste und Garoupa saftig und auf den Punkt poschiert werden. Ein paar Meter daneben lädt eine Austernbar ein, die besten Austernqualitäten, die rund um den Globus gezüchtet werden, zu verkosten.

Bei so viel Aufwand konnte die Anerkennung nicht ausbleiben: Bereits 1994, ein Jahr nach der Eröffnung des Yü, wurde es von der örtlichen amerikanischen Handelskammer zum besten Seafood-Restaurant von Hong Kong gewählt. Hotel-Zeitschriften listen es regelmäßig unter die zehn besten Hotel-Restaurants der Welt. „Schuld" an alledem ist Jürg Blaser (zusammen mit seiner rechten Hand, Christof Syré), ein Schweizer Urgestein aus Bern mit jahrzehntelanger Asienerfahrung, der die insgesamt fünf Restaurants des Regent-Hotels (Plume, Yü, Lai Ching Heen, The Steakhouse Bar & Grill und das Harbourside) seit der Eröffnung im Jahre 1980 kulinarisch in Bestform hält. 186 Mitarbeiter zählt die Küchencrew, die er dirigiert und motiviert mit jener gelassenen Souveränität, die er sich in Hotels und Restaurants in Basel, Luzern und Flims sowie 13 Jahre lang im 300 Meter nebenan gelegenen Peninsula-Hotel in Hong Kong angeeignet hat.

Die Pausen zwischen den Menü-Gängen gehören der Harbourview, dem Blick auf die Skyline von Hong Kong, der kaum irgendwo spektakulärer ist als von hier, von der Kowloon-Seite aus. Dann geraten selbst der gerade zuvor genossene Mouse Garoupa, der Duft von Zitronengras und frischem Marktgemüse und der funkelnde Sancerre für einen kurzen Augenblick in Vergessenheit. Aber nur für einen kurzen Augenblick. Denn auch die Nachspeisen, etwa die Yü Apple Tart oder das mit Kirschwasser aromatisierte Eis-Soufflé mit frischen Früchten und Schokoladenstückchen haben alle Chancen, der Harbourview die Show zu stehlen.

At the Regent

OYSTERS

Blue Point (USA)	$30.00 per oyster	**Sydney Rock (Australia)**	$30.00 per oyster
Belon 0000 (France)	$60.00 per oyster	**Pacific (Canada)**	$26.00 per oyster
Fine de Claire No 1 (France)	$30.00 per oyster	**Imperial 0000 (Netherlands)**	$48.00 per oyster

served on ice • gratinated with fine herbs • glazed with Champagne sauce

Kilpatrick • Rockerfeller

or with Bloody Mary as an Oyster Shooter

Due to the seasonality of Oysters we apologize if your selection is unavailable

STARTERS

The Regent Seafood Platter

small $730.00 (for 2 persons) • medium $1,460.00 (for 4 persons) • large $2,080.00 (for 6 persons)

Lobster Salad $220.00   **Scallop and Salmon Carpaccio** $160.00   **Garden Salad** $85.00

Deepfried Squid $125.00   **YÜ Sushi Selection** $200.00   **Iranian Caviar** (30gr.) $520.00

Mussel Chowder $102.00   **Lobster Bisque** $110.00   **Seafood Ravioli in Crab Bouillon** $105.00

MAIN COURSES

YÜ Paella $210.00

Crystal Prawns in Chilli-Lemongrass Sauce $250.00

Assorted Seafood in Crustacean Sauce $230.00

Poached Turbot in Court-Bouillon Served with Hollandaise $380.00

Grilled Dover Sole $340.00

Sautéed Boston Lobster with Black Beans and Fine Noodles $350.00

Scallops and Marrons gratinated with Herbs and Truffled Mashed Potatoes $260.00

Seagrass Shell Pasta with Grilled Tiger Prawns $190.00

Light Mango Flavoured Yabbie Curry $220.00

LIVE FISH & SEAFOOD

Select your fish from our special Fish Menu   at market price

South China Sea Basket

Prawns, Jumping Shrimps, Yabbie, Baby Abalone, Mussels, Baby Geoduck $390.00

We prepare your favourite seafood   at market price

steamed • poached in our bouillon pot • grilled

Jumping Shrimp	**Yabbie**	**Large Clams**
King or Tiger Prawns	**Boston Lobster**	**Cherrystone Clams**
Green or Red Crab	**Spiny Lobster**	**Baby Geoduck**
Rock Lobster	**Baby Abalone**	**Green Mussels**

*All hot main courses are served with your choice of fresh market vegetables and
steamed rice • fried rice • wild rice • parsley potatoes*

DESSERTS

Iced Soufflé YÜ $85.00

Glazed Apple Cake $80.00   **Fresh Fruit Salad** $78.00

Macaroon Crème Brulée $55.00   **Calamansi Sherbet** $55.00

Red Berry Compote with homemade Vanilla Sauce $80.00

Grand Marnier Soufflé Tart with Berries $80.00

Plus 10% Service Charge

At the Regent

SEAFOOD PAELLA "YÜ"

For 6 persons:

For the rice:
400 g/14 oz/2 cups short-grain rice, 2 tbsp olive oil,
1 small onion, finely chopped,
1.2 liters/2 pints 3 fl oz/ 5 cups chicken broth,
1 knife-tip saffron, 1 bay leaf,
salt, pepper from the mill

60 g/2 oz/¹/₄ cup green peas,
60 g/2 oz/¹/₄ cup Chinese broccoli, sliced,
60 g/2 oz/¹/₄ cup carrot, cut into diamond shapes

350 g/12 oz/1¹/₂ cups breast of chicken, cubed,
2 tbsp olive oil,
1 white onion, cut into fine strips,
1 garlic clove, finely chopped,
a little fresh thyme and rosemary, chopped,
1 tbsp butter

4 tiger prawns, halved,
6 fillets of bass of about 50 g/2 oz each,
6 baby squid, 2 tbsp olive oil, salt, pepper,
12 mussels, 18 cockles, 12 scallops,
240 ml/8 fl oz/1 cup vegetable broth,
smooth-leaved parsley

For the rice: Heat the oil in an oven-proof dish. Add the rice and onions and sauté until transparent, stirring. Boil the chicken broth with the saffron and the bay leaf and use this to quench the rice. Season with salt and pepper.
Cover the dish and place in the oven preheated to 190° C/375° F. Cook for about forty minutes, leaving the rice al dente.
Cook the vegetables in salt water until barely done and drain through a sieve.
Fry the breast of chicken in olive oil. Add the onion, garlic and herbs and fry briefly, then turn down the heat and braise.
Mix the vegetables and chicken with the cooked rice, adding a little hot chicken broth if necessary, season and stir in the butter.
Fry the prawns, fish and squid in olive oil and season lightly with salt and pepper. Steam the mussels in the vegetable broth, in a covered pot, until they open.
To serve: Pile the rice on a large platter (or, if available, a paella pan). Decorate with the seafood, garnish with parsley and serve.

MEERESFRÜCHTE-PAELLA „YÜ"

Für 6 Personen:

Für den Reis:
400 g Halbkornreis, 2 EL Olivenöl,
1 kleine Zwiebel, fein geschnitten,
1,2 Liter Hühnerbrühe,
1 Msp. Safran, 1 Lorbeerblatt,
Salz, Pfeffer aus der Mühle

60 g grüne Erbsen,
60 g chinesischer Broccoli, in Scheiben geschnitten,
60 g Karotte, rautenförmig geschnitten

350 g Hühnerbrust, in Würfel geschnitten,
2 EL Olivenöl,
1 weiße Zwiebel, in feine Streifen geschnitten,
1 Knoblauchzehe, fein geschnitten,
etwas frischer Thymian und Rosmarin, gehackt,
1 EL Butter

4 Riesengarnelen, halbiert,
6 Filetstücke vom Wolfsbarsch, je ca. 50 g,
6 Baby-Tintenfische, 2 EL Olivenöl, Salz, Pfeffer,
12 Pfahlmuscheln, 18 Herzmuscheln,
12 Jakobsmuscheln,
240 ml Gemüsebrühe, glatte Petersilie

Für den Reis: In einem feuerfesten Topf das Öl erhitzen. Reis und Zwiebel zugeben und unter Rühren glasig dünsten. Hühnerbrühe mit dem Safran und dem Lorbeerblatt aufkochen, den Reis damit ablöschen. Mit Salz und Pfeffer würzen und den Topf zugedeckt in den auf 190° C vorgeheizten Ofen stellen. Ungefähr vierzig Minuten garen lassen, der Reis soll noch Biß haben.
Die Gemüse in Salzwasser knapp gar kochen, durch ein Sieb abgießen.
Hühnerbrust im Olivenöl anbraten, Zwiebel, Knoblauch und Kräuter kurz mitbraten, dann Hitze zurückstellen und dünsten. Gemüse und Hühnerfleisch unter den fertigen Reis mischen, wenn nötig, etwas heiße Hühnerbrühe zugeben, abschmecken und die Butter einrühren.
Garnelen, Fisch und Tintenfische in Olivenöl braten, mit Salz und Pfeffer würzen. Muscheln in der Gemüsebrühe zugedeckt dünsten, bis sie sich öffnen.
Zum Servieren: Reis auf eine grosse Platte (oder, wenn vorhanden, in eine Paellapfanne) anrichten, mit den Meeresfrüchten belegen und mit der Petersilie garniert servieren.

For 4 persons:

For the broth:
150 g/5 oz crab carcasses, 100 g/3¹/₂ oz white soup
vegetables (fennel, celeriac, leek, onion),
2 cloves garlic, sliced,
1 bay leaf, 3 tbsp olive oil,
2 liters/3¹/₂ pints/8 cups chicken broth,
20 g/²/₃ oz Chinese Yunnan ham (raw ham),
thyme, rosemary, parsley

For the won ton:
12 sheets of won ton pastry, each about 10 x 10 cm/
4 x 4 in (or normal noodle dough as a substitute),
60 g/2 oz/¹/₄ cup lobster flesh,
120 g/4 oz/¹/₂ cup scallop flesh,
60 g/2 oz/¹/₄ cup bamboo shoots from a can,
1 spring onion, coriander leaves, salt, pepper,
12 prawns peeled

60 g/2 oz/¹/₄ cup crab meat,
60 g/2 oz/¹/₄ cup Chinese broccoli, sliced and cooked,
60 g/2 oz/¹/₄ cup blanched spinach, coarsely chopped

For the bouillon: Fry the carcasses and soup vegetables in the olive oil. Pour over the chicken broth and boil down to 1.2 liters/2 pints 3 fl oz/ 5 cups. Fifteen minutes before the end of the cooking, add the ham and the herbs. Strain the broth through a cloth.
For the filling: Finely chop the lobster, scallops, bamboo and spring onion. Season with coriander leaves, salt and pepper and mix well.
Spread out the pastry sheets and coat with this filling. Place one prawn on each and fold into small parcels. Simmer in the bouillon on a low heat until the won tons float on the surface.
To serve: Place a little crab meat, broccoli and spinach in each dish. Add three won tons and pour over the hot broth.

Für 4 Personen:

Für die Bouillon:
150 g Krebskarkassen, 100 g weißes Suppengemüse
(Fenchel, Sellerie, Lauch, Zwiebel),
2 Knoblauchzehen, in Scheiben geschnitten,
1 Lorbeerblatt, 3 EL Olivenöl,
2 Liter Hühnerbrühe,
20 g chinesischer Yunnan-Schinken (Rohschinken),
Thymian, Rosmarin, Petersilie

Für die Won-Ton:
12 Won-Ton Teigblätter, je ca. 10 x 10 cm
(ersatzweise normaler Nudelteig),
60 g Hummerfleisch,
120 g Jakobsmuschelfleisch,
60 g Bambussprossen aus der Dose,
1 Frühlingszwiebel, Koriandergrün, Salz, Pfeffer,
12 Garnelen, geschält

60 g Krebsfleisch, 60 g chinesischer Broccoli,
in Scheiben geschnitten und gekocht,
60 g blanchierter Spinat, grob geschnitten

Für die Bouillon: Karkassen und Suppengemüse im Olivenöl anbraten. Mit Hühnerbrühe aufgießen und bis auf 1,2 Liter einkochen lassen. Fünfzehn Minuten vor Kochende den Schinken und die Kräuter zugeben. Brühe durch ein Tuch passieren.
Für die Füllung: Hummer, Jakobsmuscheln, Bambus und Frühlingszwiebel fein hacken. Mit Korianderblättchen, Salz und Pfeffer würzen und gut vermischen. Teigblätter ausbreiten und mit dieser Füllung belegen. Je eine Garnele darauf setzen und zu kleinen Paketen verschließen. In der Bouillon bei kleiner Hitze sieden lassen, bis die Won-Tons an der Oberfläche schwimmen.
Zum Servieren in jede Schale etwas Krebsfleisch, Broccoli und Spinat füllen, drei Won-Tons zugeben und mit der heißen Brühe aufgießen.

PRAWNS
IN LEMON-GRASS CHILI SAUCE

GARNELEN
IN ZITRONENGRAS-CHILISAUCE

For 4 persons:

650 g/1 lb 7 oz fresh prawns,
60 g/2 oz/¹/₄ cup cornstarch,
90 g/3 oz/²/₅ cup corn oil,
salt, pepper

For the sauce:
¹/₂ chicken,
500 ml/1 pint/2 cups chicken broth,
80 g/2²/₃ oz lemon grass,
split lengthwise,
2 fresh red chilis,
halved and seeded,
50 g/1²/₃ oz lemon grass,
cut into fine slices,
3 tbsp cornstarch,
150 ml/5 fl oz/²/₃ cup Chinese
white wine (Hua Diao),
smooth-leaved parsley,
finely chopped

Garnish:
Coriander leaves,
lemon grass, cut into fine strips

Für 4 Personen:

650 g frische Garnelen,
60 g Maisstärke,
90 g Maiskeimöl,
Salz, Pfeffer

Für die Sauce:
¹/₂ Huhn,
500 ml Hühnerbrühe,
80 g Zitronengras, der Länge
nach halbiert,
2 frische rote Chili, halbiert,
entkernt,
50 g Zitronengras, in feine
Scheiben geschnitten,
3 EL Maisstärke,
150 ml chinesischer Weißwein
(Hua Diao),
glatte Petersilie,
fein geschnitten

Garnitur:
Koriandergrün, Zitronengras, in
feine Streifen geschnitten

Place the half chicken in the broth in a pot, and bring to the boil. Cover and cook for thirty minutes. Add the lemon grass and chili and continue cooking until 200 ml/7 fl oz/⁴/₅ cup of broth remains. Pass through a fine sieve. Blend the cornstarch into a little wine and use this for binding the sauce. Add the remaining wine, lemon-grass strips and parsley and set aside.
Season the prawns with salt and pepper and roll them in cornstarch.
Fry on all sides in the wok, in hot oil, turning constantly. Remove with a slotted spoon and mix with the hot sauce. Transfer to a serving dish.
Decorate with coriander sprigs and lemon grass, and serve.

Das halbe Huhn mit der Brühe in einem Topf zum Kochen bringen. Abgedeckt 30 Minuten kochen lassen. Zitronengras und Chili zugeben und weiterkochen, bis 200 ml Brühe übrigbleiben. Durch ein feines Sieb abgießen. Maisstärke mit etwas Wein anrühren und die Sauce damit binden. Restlichen Wein, Zitronengrasstreifen und Petersilie zufügen, beiseite stellen.
Garnelen mit Salz und Pfeffer würzen, in der Stärke wenden. Im Wok im heißen Öl unter ständigem Wenden rundum braten. Mit einer Lochkelle herausheben und mit der heißen Sauce vermischen.
In eine Servierschüssel füllen, mit Korianderzweiglein und Zitronengras dekoriert servieren.

FRIED LOBSTER
WITH BLACK-BEAN SAUCE

GEBRATENER HUMMER
AN SCHWARZER BOHNENSAUCE

For 4 persons:

4 American lobsters (Boston) of
about 500 g/1 lb each,
2 tbsp cornstarch, 2 whites of egg

For the sauce:
2 tbsp corn oil,
2 tbsp black bean paste,
1 garlic clove, pressed,
1 tsp finely chopped red chili,
400 ml/13 fl oz /1²/₃ cups clear
chicken broth,
1 dash of dark soy sauce,
salt, pepper,
2 tbsp Chinese white wine,
1 spring onion, sliced,
1 tbsp chopped coriander leaves

300 g/10 oz thin Chinese
egg noodles,
sprigs of coriander

Boil the lobsters in salted water
for one minute. Remove from
the water. Allow to cool and
break out the flesh.
Save the carapaces of the lobster
tails for decoration. Cut the
flesh into walnut-sized pieces.
Roll them first in the cornstarch, then in the beaten egg
white.
For the sauce: Heat the oil in
the wok. Fry the bean paste,
garlic and chili. Pour in the
chicken broth and season with
soy sauce, salt, and pepper. Add
the spring onion and simmer
the sauce for two minutes. Place
the coated pieces of lobster in
the sauce and simmer for two
more minutes, stirring. Finally
mix in the chopped coriander
leaves.
Boil the noodles in salted water,
drain through a sieve and transfer to warmed plates.
Serve the lobster with the sauce,
garnishing each portion with a
lobster tail and coriander sprigs.

Für 4 Personen:

4 amerikanische Hummer
(Boston) von je ca. 500 g,
2 EL Maisstärke, 2 Eiweiß

Für die Sauce:
2 EL Maiskeimöl,
2 EL schwarze Bohnenpaste,
1 Knoblauchzehe, durchgedrückt,
1 TL feingehackter roter Chili,
400 ml klare Hühnerbrühe,
1 Spritzer dunkle Sojasauce,
Salz, Pfeffer,
2 EL chinesischer Weißwein,
1 Frühlingszwiebel,
in Scheiben geschnitten,
1 EL gehacktes Koriandergrün

300 g dünne chinesische
Eiernudeln,
Koriandergrün

Hummer in kochendem Salz-
wasser eine Minute kochen. Aus
dem Wasser nehmen, abkühlen
lassen, das Fleisch ausbrechen.
die Hummerschwanzschalen zur
Dekoration aufheben.
Das Fleisch in walnußgroße
Stücke schneiden, dann zuerst in
der Stärke und anschließend im
verquirlten Eiweiß wenden.
Für die Sauce: Im Wok das Öl
erhitzen. Bohnenpaste, Knoblauch und Chili anbraten. Mit
Hühnerbrühe aufgießen, mit
Sojasauce, Salz und Pfeffer würzen. Frühlingszwiebeln zugeben
und zwei Minuten köcheln lassen. Hummerstücke in die Sauce
geben und unter Rühren weitere
zwei Minuten köcheln lassen.
Zum Schluß das gehackte
Koriandergrün unterziehen.
Die gekochten Nudeln auf
vorgewärmte Teller verteilen.
Hummer mit der Sauce anrichten, mit je einem Hummer-
schwanz und Korianderzweiglein garnieren.

SHELL NOODLES WITH GRILLED TIGER PRAWNS

MUSCHELNUDELN MIT GEGRILLTEN RIESENGARNELEN

For 4 persons:

300 g/10 oz baby squid,
1 garlic clove, pressed,
1 tbsp olive oil,
salt, pepper,
8 tiger prawns,
1 tbsp olive oil,
300 g/10 oz three-color shell-shaped
noodles, boiled,
200 g/7 oz/⁷/₈ cup tomato concassé
(tomatoes skinned, seeded and cubed),
40 g/1¹/₃ oz dried seaweed,
parmesan shavings,
smooth-leaved parsley

Für 4 Personen:

300 g Baby-Tintenfische,
1 Knoblauchzehe, durchgedrückt,
1 EL Olivenöl,
Salz, Pfeffer,
8 Riesengarnelen (Tiger prawns),
1 EL Olivenöl,
300 g dreifarbige, muschelförmige
Nudeln, gekocht,
200 g Tomaten concassé (Tomaten enthäutet,
entkernt und in Würfel geschnitten),
40 g getrocknete Algen,
Parmesan, in Späne geschnitten,
glatte Petersilie

Fry the baby squid and garlic in hot olive oil on all sides. Season with salt and pepper and set aside.

Salt and pepper the tiger prawns and fry on both sides on the griddle for two minutes. Heat the olive oil in the wok. Fry the shell noodles, add the tomato concassé and the squid and sprinkle with the seaweed. Stir until hot, season and ladle into deep plates or dishes. Place two grilled prawns on each plate and garnish with Parmesan shavings and parsley.

Baby-Tintenfische und Knoblauch im Olivenöl heiß anbraten. Mit Salz und Pfeffer würzen, beiseite stellen.

Riesengarnelen salzen, pfeffern und auf dem Grill von beiden Seiten zwei Minuten rösten. Olivenöl im Wok erhitzen. Muschelnudeln anbraten, Tomaten concassé und Tintenfische zugeben und mit den Algen bestreuen. Unter Rühren heiß werden lassen, abschmecken und in tiefe Teller oder Schalen füllen. Mit je zwei gegrillten Garnelen belegen, mit Parmesanspänen und Petersilie garnieren.

STEAMED GROUPER

For 4 persons:

*1 whole grouper of about 1.3 kg/3 lb, kitchen-ready
and scaled,
3 spring onions,
cut into fine juliennes,
20 g/²/₃ oz/2 tbsp root ginger, finely chopped,
2 red chilis, sliced,
coriander leaves*

*For the soy sauce:
60 ml/2 fl oz/¹/₄ cup dark soy sauce,
90 ml/3 fl oz/²/₅ cup light soy sauce,
60 ml/2 fl oz/¹/₄ cup strong chicken broth*

*500 g/1 lb pak choi (or baby Swiss chard),
coriander leaves,
60 ml/2 fl oz/¹/₄ cup peanut oil*

Lay the fish in a large pot over a steamer insert. Surround with spring onions, ginger, chili and a little coriander, pour in a little water and steam the fish for about fifteen minutes.
For the sauce: Bring the soy sauces and broth to the boil and reduce to half the quantity.
Cook the pak choi whole in salt water.
To serve: Carefully lift out the fish onto a large platter. Surround with pak choi, spring onions. Sprinkle with ginger and chili.
Garnish with fresh coriander leaves and pour over the sauce.
Finally, drizzle with the hot peanut oil and serve immediately.
(Photo: page 35).

GEDÄMPFTER ZACKENBARSCH

Für 4 Personen:

*1 ganzer Zackenbarsch von ca. 1,3 kg (Grouper),
küchenfertig und geschuppt,
3 Frühlingszwiebeln, in feine Streifen
geschnitten (Julienne),
20 g Ingwerwurzel, fein geschnitten,
2 rote Chilischoten, in Scheiben geschnitten,
Koriandergrün*

*Für die Sojasauce:
60 ml dunkle Sojasauce,
90 ml helle Sojasauce,
60 ml kräftige Hühnerbrühe*

*500 g Pak Choi (oder Babymangold),
Koriandergrün,
60 ml Erdnußöl*

Den Fisch über einem Dämpfeinsatz in einen großen Topf legen. Mit Frühlingszwiebeln, Ingwer, Chili und etwas Koriandergrün umlegen, etwas Wasser einfüllen und den Fisch so über Dampf ungefähr fünfzehn Minuten garen.
Für die Sauce: Sojasaucen mit der Brühe zum Kochen bringen und auf die halbe Menge reduzieren.
Das Pak Choi-Gemüse im Ganzen in Salzwasser gar kochen. Zum Servieren den Fisch vorsichtig auf eine große Platte heben. Mit dem Gemüse umlegen, die Frühlingszwiebeln, Ingwer und Chili darüber geben, mit frischem Koriandergrün garnieren und mit der Sauce begießen. Zum Schluß mit dem heißen Erdnußöl besprenkeln und sofort servieren.
(Foto: Seite 35).

SEAFOOD PLATE

For 4 persons:

*The ingredients are variable according
to market supply, personal taste and season:
2 lobsters, 4 yabbies (crayfish),
4 tiger prawns, 18 prawns, 2 giant crabs,
vegetable broth, 1 garlic clove, finely chopped,
1 shallot, finely chopped,
200 ml/7 fl oz/⁷⁄₈ cup white wine, parsley,
4 hard clams, 4 mussels, 4 oysters*

*Soy sauce:
60 ml/2 fl oz/¹⁄₄ cup dark soy sauce,
90 ml/3 fl oz/²⁄₅ cup light soy sauce,
60 ml/2 fl oz/¹⁄₄ cup strong chicken broth*

*Chili-tomato sauce:
200 ml/7 fl oz/⁷⁄₈ cup tomato concassé,
¹⁄₂ onion, finely chopped,
1 chili, finely chopped,
1 tbsp olive oil, salt, sugar*

*White-wine sauce:
2 shallots, finely chopped, 1 tbsp butter,
60 ml/2 fl oz/¹⁄₄ cup white wine,
60 ml/2 fl oz/¹⁄₄ cup cream, salt, pepper*

60 ml/2 fl oz/¹⁄₄ cup garlic mayonnaise

*Garnish:
Green (vine) leaves, fresh seaweed,
lobster shell (head), sufficient ice,
3 limes, cut into wedges,
3 lemons, cut into wedges*

In the vegetable broth, cook in turn the lobsters, crayfish and prawns. Remove them from the liquid and allow to go cold.

Briefly fry the garlic and the shallot in a wok in olive oil, pour in the white wine, add the parsley and bring to the boil. Add the mussels according to size and cook on a low heat until done. Strain through a sieve and allow to go cold.

For the soy sauce: Bring the soy sauces and the broth to the boil and reduce to half the quantity.

For the chili-tomato sauce: Sauté the onion and chili in the olive oil, add the tomatoes and cook until liquefied. Season with salt and a pinch of sugar.

For the white-wine sauce: Sauté the shallots in butter, add the white wine, boil down, add the cream. Boil down again and finally season with salt and pepper.

To serve: Make a heap of ice on a large serving platter. Decorate with the prepared seafood, lemon and lime wedges, and leaves or seaweed. Serve the sauces separately.

MEERESFRÜCHTE-PLATTE

Für 4 Personen:

*Die Zutaten sind je nach Marktangebot,
persönlichem Geschmack und Saison variabel:
2 Hummer, 4 Yabbies (Flußkrebs), 4 Riesengarnelen,
18 Garnelen, 2 Taschenkrebse, Gemüsebrühe,
1 Knoblauchzehe, fein geschnitten,
1 Schalotte, fein geschnitten, 200 ml Weißwein,
Petersilie, 4 Venusmuscheln,
4 Pfahl- oder Miesmuscheln, 4 Austern*

*Sojasauce:
60 ml dunkle Sojasauce,
90 ml helle Sojasauce
60 ml kräftige Hühnerbrühe*

*Chili-Tomatensauce:
200 ml Tomaten concassé,
¹⁄₂ Zwiebel, fein geschnitten,
1 Chilischote, fein geschnitten,
1 EL Olivenöl, Salz, Zucker*

*Weißweinsauce:
2 Schalotten, fein geschnitten, 1 EL Butter,
60 ml Weißwein, 60 ml Sahne,
Salz, Pfeffer*

60 ml Knoblauchmayonnaise

*Garnitur:
Grüne (Wein-) Blätter, frische Algen,
Hummerschale (Kopf), genügend Eis,
3 Limonen, in Schnitze geschnitten,
3 Zitronen, in Schnitze geschnitten*

In der Gemüsebrühe die Hummer, Krebse und Garnelen nach und nach garen. Aus dem Sud nehmen und erkalten lassen. In einem Wok den Knoblauch und die Schalotte in Olivenöl kurz anbraten, mit Weißwein aufgießen, Petersilie zugeben und zum Kochen bringen. Muscheln der Größe nach zugeben und bei kleiner Hitze schmoren, bis sie gar sind. Durch ein Sieb abgießen und erkalten lassen.

Für die Sojasauce: Sojasaucen mit der Brühe zum Kochen bringen und auf die Hälfte reduzieren.

Für die Chili-Tomatensauce: Zwiebel und Chili im Olivenöl dünsten, Tomaten zugeben und einkochen lassen. Mit Salz und einer Prise Zucker würzen.

Für die Weißweinsauce: Schalotten in Butter dünsten, Weißwein zugeben, einkochen lassen, Sahne zugeben, erneut einkochen lassen, zum Schluß mit Salz und Pfeffer würzen.

Zum Servieren: Auf einer großen Servierplatte einen Berg von Eis häufen. Mit den vorbereiteten Meeresfrüchten dekorativ belegen, mit Zitronen- und Limonenschnitzen und Blättern oder Algen dekorieren. Die Saucen separat dazureichen.

Plume

PLUME CLASSICS

FRENCH GOOSELIVER PARFAIT FLAVOURED
WITH PEACH AND PARMESAN

CLEAR OX-TAIL BROTH WITH SEMOLINA AND LOVAGE

PANFRIED VENISON MEDALLIONS AND
KUMQUAT SCENTED RED CABBAGE
WITH BREAD DUMPLINGS

QUARK CHEESE STRUDEL WITH BLUEBERRIES,
THYME AND WHITE CHOCOLATE ICE CREAM

MOCHA
PETITS FOURS

HK$720.00 PER PERSON

—— ◆ ——

SEAFOOD MENU

TIGER PRAWN IN WASABI MOUSSE TERRINE
WITH SAUCE REMOULADE

BOUILLABAISSE WITH SAUTÉED BABY SQUID
AND VIRGIN OLIVE OIL

CRISPY PANFRIED POMFRET ON
THAI EGGPLANT RISOTTO WITH KALE

CHILLED POMELO SOUP WITH GREEN GRAPE SHERBET

MOCHA
PETITS FOURS

HK$740.00 PER PERSON

—— ◆ ——

MEDITERRANEAN MENU

SCALLOP AND RED TUNA TARTAR
WITH OVEN TOMATO AND BALSAMIC SABAYON

HERBED DOVER SOLE AND
BELLPEPPER COULIS WITH STEAMED WILD RICE

ROASTED LAMB LOIN WITH VEGETABLE
SPRING ROLL 'FOUGASS' AND PEARL POTATO

GRATINATED FIGS IN PISTACHIO CREAM
WITH BLOSSOM HONEY

MOCHA
PETITS FOURS

HK$710.00 PER PERSON

—— ◆ ——

AUTUMN MENU

MARINATED COHO SALMON AND
BELUGA CAVIAR WITH POTATO SALAD

GOLDEN NUGGET PUMPKIN SOUP
WITH STUFFED BUTTON SQUASH

STEAMED HUNG YAU ON LOTUS ROOT AND CHOI SUM
WITH SOYA SAUCE AND RICE NOODLE

BRESSE PIGEON BREAST ON TRUFFLED VEGETABLES
WITH COUSCOUS WRAPPED IN CORN LEAF

CARAMELIZED PASSION FRUIT FLAN
WITH DARK BITTER CHOCOLATE SHERBET

MOCHA
PETITS FOURS

HK$840.00 PER PERSON

APPETIZERS

FRENCH GOOSELIVER PARFAIT FLAVOURED
WITH PEACH AND PARMESAN $240.00

TIGER PRAWN IN WASABI MOUSSE TERRINE
WITH SAUCE REMOULADE $215.00

SCALLOP AND RED TUNA TARTAR
WITH OVEN TOMATO AND BALSAMIC SABAYON $230.00

MARINATED COHO SALMON AND
BELUGA CAVIAR WITH POTATO SALAD $260.00

SWEETBREAD ESCALOPES AND CEPES
ON ROMAINE LETTUCE
WITH JUNIPER BERRY SAUCE $195.00

SOUPS

CLEAR OX-TAIL BROTH
WITH SEMOLINA AND LOVAGE $105.00

BOUILLABAISSE WITH SAUTÉED BABY SQUID
AND VIRGIN OLIVE OIL $105.00

GOLDEN NUGGET PUMPKIN SOUP
WITH STUFFED BUTTON SQUASH $100.00

DELICATE CREAM OF ARTICHOKE AND BELUGA $105.00

SEAFOOD

CRISPY PANFRIED POMFRET ON
THAI EGGPLANT RISOTTO WITH KALE $320.00

HERBED DOVER SOLE AND
BELLPEPPER COULIS WITH STEAMED WILD RICE $380.00

STEAMED HUNG YAU ON LOTUS ROOT AND CHOI SUM
WITH SOYA SAUCE AND RICE NOODLE $320.00

WHOLE EASTERN STAR GAROUPA 'EN PAPILLOTE'
WITH SUNDRIED TOMATO GNOCCHI $460.00

AUSTRALIAN ROCK LOBSTER ON BAMBOO SHOOTS
AND ROQUEFORT CRUSTACEAN SAUCE $610.00

MEAT

PANFRIED VENISON MEDALLIONS AND
KUMQUAT SCENTED RED CABBAGE
WITH BREAD DUMPLINGS $240.00

ROASTED LAMB LOIN WITH VEGETABLE
SPRING ROLL 'FOUGASS' AND PEARL POTATO $340.00

BRESSE PIGEON BREAST ON TRUFFLED VEGETABLES
WITH COUSCOUS WRAPPED IN CORN LEAF $380.00

U.S. BEEF TENDERLOIN TOPPED WITH ONION
AND POTATO ON TRUFFLED CANDY BEET CANE
AND WHITE TURNIP $340.00

WHOLE OVEN ROASTED GUINEA FOWL
WITH CREAMY SAVOY CABBAGE
SERVED FOR TWO PERSONS   ($270 per person)

DESSERTS

QUARK CHEESE STRUDEL WITH BLUEBERRIES,
THYME AND WHITE CHOCOLATE ICE CREAM $100.00

CHILLED POMELO SOUP
WITH GREEN GRAPE SHERBET $90.00

GRATINATED FIGS IN PISTACHIO CREAM
WITH BLOSSOM HONEY $95.00

CARAMELIZED PASSION FRUIT FLAN
WITH DARK BITTER CHOCOLATE SHERBET $100.00

COCONUT MOUSSE WITH SAGO
ON PANAMANIAN PINEAPPLE RAGOUT $100.00

SELECTION OF HOT SOUFFLES $100.00

PLUS 10% SERVICE CHARGE

PRAWN WASABI TERRINE WITH DEEP-FRIED PRAWN BALLS

GARNELEN-WASABI-TERRINE MIT FRITIERTEN GARNELENBÄLLCHEN

For 4 persons:

200 g/7 oz salmon fillet,
250 ml/8¹/₃ fl oz/1 cup chicken broth,
5 white peppercorns, crushed, 1 sheet gelatin,
100 ml/3¹/₂ fl oz/²/₅ cup whipped cream,
wasabi paste (Japanese horseradish,
quantity according to taste), salt,
150 ml/5 fl oz/²/₃ cup strong lobster fumet, jellied,
3 fresh tiger prawns, shelled and cooked

90 g/3 oz prawns, peeled, cooked and finely chopped,
50 g/2 oz mango, finely chopped,
1 tbsp chopped coriander leaves,
100 g/3¹/₂ oz/²/₅ cup purée of cooked white fish fillet,
100 g/3¹/₂ oz/²/₅ cup freshly grated white bread
(without crust)

120 g/4 oz mixed leaf salads,
40 ml/1¹/₃ fl oz/¹/₆ cup balsamic vinegar dressing
(aceto balsamico, olive oil, salt, pepper),
sprigs of chervil, edible blossoms

For the wasabi mousse: Bring the chicken broth to the boil with the white pepper. Poach the salmon fillet in this for three minutes, then finely purée in a blender. Stir in the softened gelatin, pass the mixture through a sieve and allow to cool. Fold in the stiffly whipped cream and season with the wasabi paste and a little salt.

For the terrine: Warm the lobster fumet; coat a terrine mold with this and allow it to set in the refrigerator. Then spoon in half of the wasabi mousse, lay the tiger prawns in lengthwise and cover with the remaining wasabi mousse. Smooth the surface with a knife. Allow to set for several hours in the refrigerator.

For the prawn balls: Mix the prawns with the mango, coriander leaves and fish purée. Lightly salt and pepper and form into small balls. Roll in the grated white bread and just before serving fry in hot oil.

To serve: Wet the salad leaves with a little balsamic vinegar dressing and distribute on the plates. Turn the terrine out of the mold, cut into slices, arrange on the plates.

Add the fried prawn balls and garnish with sprigs of chervil and edible blossoms.

Für 4 Personen:

200 g Lachsfilet,
250 ml Hühnerbrühe,
5 weiße Pfefferkörner, zerstoßen, 1 Blatt Gelatine,
100 ml geschlagene Sahne,
Wasabipaste (japanischer grüner Meerrettich,
Menge nach Geschmack), Salz,
150 ml kräftiger Hummerfond, geliert,
3 frische Riesengarnelen, geschält und gekocht

90 g Garnelen, geschält, gekocht und fein gehackt,
50 g Mango, feingeschnitten,
1 EL gehacktes Koriandergrün,
100 g Püree von einem weißen, gekochten Fischfilet,
100 g frischgeriebenes Weißbrot
(ohne Rinde)

120 g bunt gemischte Salatblätter,
40 ml Balsamicodressing (Aceto Balsamico, Olivenöl,
Salz, Pfeffer),
Kerbelzweiglein, eßbare Blüten

Für die Wasabimousse: Hühnerbrühe mit dem weißen Pfeffer zum Kochen bringen. Lachsfilet darin drei Minuten pochieren, anschließend im Mixer fein pürieren. Eingeweichte Gelatine einrühren, die Masse durch ein Sieb streichen und abkühlen lassen. Steifgeschlagene Sahne unterziehen und mit der Wasabipaste und etwas Salz würzen.

Für die Terrine: Den Hummerfond erwärmen. Eine Terrinenform damit ausgießen und im Kühlschrank festwerden lassen. Dann die Hälfte der Wasabimousse einfüllen, die Riesengarnelen der Länge nach einlegen und mit der restlichen Wasabimousse bedecken. Die Oberfläche mit einem Messer glatt streichen. Im Kühlschrank einige Stunden fest werden lassen.

Für die Garnelenbällchen: Garnelen mit Mango, Koriandergrün und Fischmus vermengen, leicht salzen, pfeffern und aus diesem Teig kleine Bällchen formen. Im geriebenen Weißbrot wenden und kurz vor dem Servieren in heißem Öl ausbacken.

Zum Servieren: Die Salatblätter mit etwas Balsamicodressing benetzen und auf Teller verteilen. Terrine aus der Form stürzen, in Scheiben schneiden, anrichten, die fritierten Bällchen dazugeben und mit Kerbelzweiglein und Blüten garnieren.

STEAMED HUNG YAU ON LOTUS ROOT AND BROCCOLI

GEDÄMPFTER HUNG YAU AUF LOTOSWURZEL UND BROCCOLI

For 4 persons:

4 hung yau fillets (bream) of 150 g/5 oz each
250 g/8¹/₂ oz Chinese broccoli, cut into pieces,
100 g/3¹/₂ oz lotus root, sliced,
1 tbsp corn oil,
1 red chili, cut into diamonds,
30 g/1 oz/3 tbsp Yunnan ham,
finely cubed (raw ham),
Chinese yellow chives
(or normal chives as a substitute), finely chopped
For the sauce:
1 tbsp finely chopped white onion, 2 tsp root ginger, grated,
1 tbsp peanut oil, 150 ml/5 fl oz/³/₅ cup strong chicken broth,
1 tsp sugar, 1 tbsp finely chopped Yunnan ham (raw ham)
1 tbsp light soy sauce
Accompaniment: Chinese rice noodles, Garnish: coriander leaves

For the sauce: Sauté the onion and ginger in the oil. Pour on the chicken broth, add the sugar and ham and boil the sauce down to half the quantity. Pass through a sieve, then season with soy sauce. Lightly season the fish fillets with salt and pepper, then steam. Fry the broccoli and lotus slices in corn oil in the wok over a low heat until almost done. Finally add the chili diamonds, ham cubes, and chives. Cook the rice noodles through in salted water and drain through a sieve.
To serve: Arrange the vegetables and noodles on plates, lay the fish fillets on top and pour over the sauce. Decorate with coriander leaves.

Für 4 Personen:

4 Hung Yau Filets (Brasse), von je 150 g
250 g chinesischer Broccoli, in Stücke geschnitten,
100 g Lotoswurzel, in Scheiben geschnitten,
1 EL Maiskeimöl,
1 rote Chilischote, in Rauten geschnitten,
30 g Yunnan Schinken, in feine Würfel
geschnitten (Rohschinken),
chinesischer gelber Schnittlauch (ersatzweise
normaler Schnittlauch), fein geschnitten
Für die Sauce:
1 EL feingeschnittene Gemüsezwiebel, 2 TL Ingwerwurzel, gerieben,
1 EL Erdnußöl, 150 ml kräftige Hühnerbrühe, 1 TL Zucker,
1 EL feingeschnittener Yunnan Schinken (Rohschinken)
1 EL helle Sojasauce,
Beilage: Chinesische Reisnudeln, Garnitur: Koriandergrün

Für die Sauce: Zwiebel und Ingwer im Öl anschwitzen. Mit Hühnerbrühe aufgießen, Zucker und Schinken zufügen und die Sauce auf die halbe Menge einkochen lassen. Durch ein Sieb passieren, dann mit Sojasauce würzen. Die Fischfilets mit Salz und Pfeffer leicht würzen und über Dampf garen. Broccoli und Lotosscheiben im Wok in Maiskeimöl bei kleiner Hitze knapp gar braten. Zum Schluß die Chili, Schinkenwürfel und Schnittlauch zugeben. Reisnudeln in Salzwasser gar kochen, durch ein Sieb abgießen.
Zum Servieren: Gemüse und Nudeln auf Teller anrichten, Fischfilets darüberlegen und mit Sauce begießen. Mit Koriandergrün garnieren.

COCONUT MOUSSE WITH SAGO ON PINEAPPLE

KOKOSNUSS-MOUSSE MIT SAGO AUF ANANAS

For 4 persons:

For the mousse:
360 ml/12 fl oz/2¹/₂ cups coconut milk from a can,
50 g/1²/₃ oz/¹/₄ cup sugar, 3 g/1 tsp gelatin powder,
200 ml/7 fl oz/⁷/₈ cup whipped cream, 25 g/1 oz/2 tbsp pearl sago, cooked
For the pineapple ragout: 160 ml/5¹/₂ fl oz/²/₃ cup pineapple juice,
3 - 4 threads of saffron, ¹/₂ pod vanilla,
2 tsp confectioners' sugar, 1 tsp cornstarch, flesh of 2 baby pineapples

For the mousse: Slightly warm the coconut milk with the sugar. Soften the gelatin powder in a little water and dissolve it in the milk. Allow the mixture to cool and stir in the cream and the pearl sago. Pour into little molds and allow to set in the refrigerator for a few hours. For the pineapple ragout: Heat the pineapple juice and stir in the threads of saffron, the scraped out vanilla pith and the confectioners' sugar. Blend the cornstarch with a little water and use this to bind the juice. Allow to cool. Finely cube the pineapple and fold into the sauce. To serve: Turn the mousse out of the molds onto plates, surround with pineapple ragout and garnish with chocolate decorations and mint leaves.

Für 4 Personen:

Für die Mousse:
360 ml Kokosmilch aus der Dose, 50 g Zucker,
3 g Gelatinepulver, 200 ml geschlagene Sahne,
25 g Sagoperlen, gekocht
Für das Ananasragout:
160 ml Ananassaft, 3-4 Safranfäden, ¹/₂ Vanillestange,
2 TL Puderzucker, 1 TL Maisstärke, Fruchtfleisch von 2 Babyananas

Für die Mousse: Kokosmilch mit dem Zucker leicht erwärmen. Gelatinepulver in wenig Wasser einweichen und in der Milch auflösen. Masse abkühlen lassen und mit der Sahne und den Sagoperlen verrühren. In Förmchen füllen und im Kühlschrank einige Stunden festwerden lassen.
Für das Ananasragout: Ananassaft erhitzen, Safranfäden, ausgeschabtes Vanillemark und Puderzucker einrühren. Maisstärke in wenig Wasser anrühren und den Saft damit binden. Abkühlen lassen. Die Ananas fein würfeln und mit der Sauce vermischen.
Zum Servieren: Die Mousse auf Teller stürzen. Mit Ananasragout umgießen, mit Schokoladedekor und Minzeblättchen garnieren.

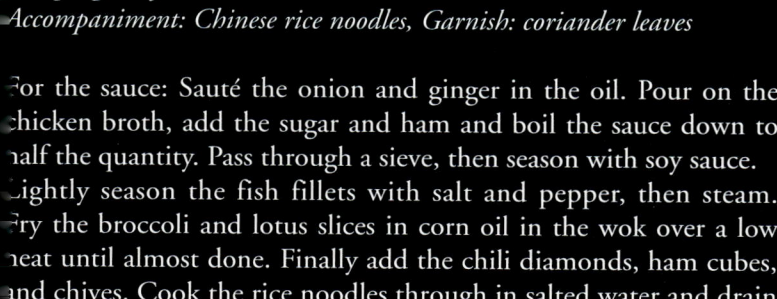

Cheung Kam Chuen
Chan Yan Tak

Restaurant
Lai Ching Heen

"Lai Ching" is the Chinese name for the Regent Hotel. "Heen" can have various meanings: an elegant dining room is thus designated; it is used as a synonym for happy and carefree; moreover it can mean balcony or pavilion. The Regent managers could not have found a more fitting name for this special-class Cantonese restaurant. Its location with a view of the harbor befits the description balcony or pavilion. Happy and carefree is the way some of the world's best Cantonese cuisine is served. Only the title "elegant dining room" is a gentle understatement.

Let us commence with the elegance. The restaurant radiates clarity, is as elegant as it is simple, without unnecessary decoration; it seems quite unpretentious, but in the appointment of the tables it reaches a standard of tasteful extravagance that is incomparable. The silver-framed place-setting plate of jade is engraved with the logo of Lai Ching Heen: two fishes tied together with bands, a symbol that goes back to seventh-century China and conveys wishes for a good future. This motif is found again embroidered in silk on the finest table linen. The chopsticks, carved from ivory and silver-tipped, are works of art in themselves. No less the jade chopstick rests – hand crafted like all the other accessories. A silver-inlaid jade spoon completes the set, of perfect harmony and Asiatic gracefulness. The green jade used exclusively here is for the Chinese a symbol of purity and perfection. The other appointments of the room are in pale gray and pink, two colors that harmonize particularly well with the green of the jade.

The dining room is suffused with soft light. Chef de cuisine Cheung Kam Chuen and his right-hand man at the wok, Chan Yan Tak, together with the brigade of 70 cooks begin to put on a culinary firework display for the 130 guests, the maximum capacity of the restaurant. Cheung Kam Chuen, Chinese-born from Guangzhou, son of a well-known Chinese cook, has raised Cantonese cuisine to unsuspected heights. Each guest is welcomed with an amuse-gueule representing yin and yang, the positive and negative principles of universal life. A small plate of hors d'oeuvres is composed of two fishes, a silvery one symbolizing light. The other, darkened by vinegar and spices, represents darkness. The composition signifies equilibrium, harmony and wishes for a happy future. At each new moon, Cheung Kam Chuen and Chan Yan Tak put together a new sequence of courses oriented toward the specialties of the season. With it the flowers of the table decorations change as does the large flower arrangement by the entrance on the 17th-century zi-tan table. You see and feel it: a lunchtime or an evening in the Lai Ching Heen is more than a culinary journey of discovery at the highest level. It is a far more comprehensive immersion in Chinese culture, into its sphere of feelings and thoughts, embracing all aspects of life, and hence of course food as well. To pick up the spoon, the chopsticks, is to understand a work of art.

What always remains is the selection of dim sum and its sophisticated and subtle varieties and fillings of meat, fish and shellfish, which all in all claim a quality category for themselves. Then the sauces in which they are dipped – spicy, fiery, sour, robust. All together a spectrum of taste impressions that last.

Lai Ching ist der chinesische Name für das Regent Hotel. Heen hat eine Vielzahl von Bedeutungen: ein eleganter Speiseraum wird so bezeichnet; als Synonym für fröhlich und unbeschwert wird es gebraucht; ebenso kann es Balkon oder Pavillon heißen. Einen passenderen Namen hätten die Regent-Manager für dieses kantonesische Restaurant der Extra-Klasse nicht finden können. Seine Lage mit Blick auf den Hafen löst die Bedeutung des Balkons oder Pavillons ein. Fröhlich und unbeschwert wird eine des besten kantonesischen Küchen weltweit serviert. Nur die Bezeichnung „eleganter Speiseraum" ist eine gelinde Untertreibung.

Beginnen wir bei der Eleganz. Das Restaurant strahlt Klarheit aus, ist ebenso elegant wie schlicht, ohne Schnörkel, wirkt ganz unprätentiös, erreicht aber bei der Ausstattung der Tische ein Niveau von geschmackvoller Extravaganz, die ihresgleichen sucht. In die silbergefassten Platzteller aus Jade ist das Logo von Lai Ching Heen eingraviert: zwei mit Bändern zusammengehaltene Fische, ein Symbol, das ins siebte Jahrhundert von China zurückreicht und Wünsche für eine gute Zukunft beinhaltet. In Seide gestickt wiederholt sich dieses Motiv in der Tischwäsche aus feinstem Leinen. Die Ess-Stäbchen – aus Elfenbein geschnitzt und mit Silber armiert – sind ein Kunstwerk für sich. Die Jadebänkchen für ihre Ablage – handgefertigt wie alle anderen Accessoires – nicht minder. Ein Jadelöffel mit Silbereinlage komplettiert das Set von vollendeter Harmonie und asiatischer Anmut. Der grüne Jadestein, der ausschließlich hierfür verwendet wird, ist für Chinesen ein Zeichen von Reinheit und Vollkommenheit. Die übrige Ausstattung des Raumes ist in hellgrau und rosa gehalten, zwei Farben, die mit dem Jadegrün besonders harmonieren.

Der Speiseraum ist in sanftes Licht getaucht, Chefkoch Cheung Kam Chuen und seine rechte Hand am Wok, Chan Yan Tak sowie die Brigade von 70 Köchen beginnen, ein kulinarisches Feuerwerk für die 130 Gäste, die das Restaurant maximal faßt, zu inszenieren. Cheung Kam Chuen, gebürtiger Chinese aus Guangzhou, Sohn eines bekannten chinesischen Kochs, hat die kantonesische Küche in ungeahnte Höhen geführt. Jeder Gast wird mit einem amuse gueule empfangen, das Yin und Yang darstellt, die positiven und negativen Prinzipien eines universellen Lebens. Ein kleiner Vorspeiseteller wird aus zwei Fischen komponiert; einem silberfarbenen, der das Licht symbolisiert, der andere, mit Essig und Gewürzen dunkel gebeizt, veranschaulicht die Dunkelheit. Die Komposition versinnbildlicht Gleichgewicht, Harmonie und Wünsche für eine glückliche Zukunft. Mit jedem Mondwechsel stellen Cheung Kam Chuen und Chan Yan Tak einen neues, an den saisonalen Spezialitäten orientiertes Menü zusammen. Mit ihm wechseln auch die Blumen der Tischdekoration ebenso wie das große Blumengesteck am Eingang auf dem Zi-Tan-Tisch aus dem 17. Jahrhundert. Man sieht und man spürt es: ein Mittag oder ein Abend im Lai Ching Heen ist mehr als eine kulinarische Entdeckungsreise auf höchstem Niveau. Es ist ein viel umfassenderes Eintauchen in die chinesische Kultur, in deren Gefühls- und Gedankenwelt, die alle Lebensbereiche, und damit natürlich auch das Essen, umfaßt. Der Griff zum Löffel, zu den Stäbchen, wird zum Begreifen eines Kunstwerkes.

Was immer bleibt, ist die Auswahl an Dim Sum und deren raffiniert-subtile Varianten und Füllungen aus Fleisch, Fisch und Schalentieren, die allesamt eine Qualitätskategorie für sich markieren. Dazu die Saucen, in die sie gestippt werden – würzig, scharf, sauer, kräftig. Alles zusammen eine Bandbreite von geschmacklichen Anmutungen, die sich einprägt.

PRAWNS WITH GARLIC AND HONEY

GARNELEN MIT KNOBLAUCH UND HONIG

For 4 persons:

12 tiger prawns,
salt, 1 white of egg, flour,
4 tbsp peanut oil

1 garlic clove,
3 tbsp strong chicken stock,
3 tbsp honey

200 g/7 oz mange-tout, cooked,
1 red chili,
cut into very fine strips

Für 4 Personen:

12 Riesengarnelen,
Salz, 1 Eiweiß, Mehl,
4 EL Erdnußöl

1 Knoblauchzehe,
3 EL starker Hühnerfond,
3 EL Honig

200 g Zuckerschoten, gekocht,
1 rote Chilischote,
in sehr feine Streifen geschnitten

Peel, wash and dry the prawns and split lengthwise. Salt lightly and roll first in egg white, then in flour.
Fry in the hot oil, turning constantly until they are done. Remove and keep in a warm place.
Briefly fry the garlic in the wok. Then add the stock and the honey, and bring to the boil.
Add the prawns and heat them in the sauce, stirring.
Arrange on plates. Lay the mange-tout on top and decorate with strips of chili.

Garnelen schälen, waschen, trocknen und der Länge nach halbieren. Leicht salzen, dann zuerst im Eiweiß und dann im Mehl wenden. Im heißen Öl unter ständigem Wenden braten, bis sie gar sind. Herausnehmen und warmstellen. Knoblauch im Wok kurz anbraten, den Fond und den Honig zugeben und zum Kochen bringen. Garnelen dazugeben und in der Sauce unter Rühren heiß werden lassen.
Auf Teller anrichten, mit Zuckerschoten und Chilistreifen dekorieren.

SCALLOPS WITH BELL PEPPERS

JAKOBSMUSCHELN MIT PAPRIKA

For 4 persons:

*12 scallops, shucked,
salt, pepper, flour*

*1 red, 1 green
and 1 yellow bell pepper*

*peanut oil for deep-frying,
1 garlic clove, finely chopped,
3 tbsp poultry stock*

Lightly salt and pepper the scallops and dust with flour.

Clean and wash the bell peppers and cut into strips, 5 to 6 cm/2 to 2¹/₂ in long. Cut a hole in each scallop and stick three differently colored pieces of bell pepper in the hole.

Heat the oil in the wok. Fry the scallops in the deep oil until done. Remove and drain.

Heat a little oil in the wok. Briefly fry the garlic and pour in the poultry stock.

Once again, boil up the scallops in this jus. Serve immediately.

Für 4 Personen:

*12 Jakobsmuscheln, ausgelöst,
Salz, Pfeffer, Mehl*

*je eine rote, eine grüne
und eine gelbe Paprika*

*Erdnußöl zum Fritieren,
1 Knoblauchzehe, fein gehackt,
3 EL Geflügelfond*

Jakobsmuscheln leicht salzen, pfeffern und mit Mehl bestäuben.

Die Paprika putzen, waschen und in 5 bis 6 cm lange Streifen schneiden. In jede Jakobsmuschel ein Loch schneiden und drei verschiedenfarbige Paprikastäbchen durchstecken.

Erdnußöl im Wok erhitzen. Die Jakobsmuscheln darin schwimmend backen, bis sie gar sind. Herausnehmen und abtropfen lassen. Wenig Öl im Wok erhitzen. Knoblauch kurz anbraten und mit Geflügelfond aufgießen. Jakobsmuscheln in dieser Jus noch einmal aufkochen lassen. Sofort servieren.

BRAISED GROUPER

GESCHMORTER ZACKENBARSCH

For 4 persons:

*600 g/1 lb 5 oz fillet of red grouper,
salt, 1 white of egg, flour,
4 tbsp peanut oil*

*500 g/1 lb 2 oz pak choi (or as a substitute
young Swiss chard or Chinese cabbage)*

*200 g/7 oz shredded pork,
200 g/7 oz mushrooms (button
mushrooms or shiitake), sliced,
2 tbsp finely chopped root ginger,
200 ml/7 fl oz/⁷⁄₈ cup chicken broth,
oyster sauce,
dark soy sauce,
1 tsp cornstarch,
coriander leaves*

Für 4 Personen:

*600 g Garoupafilet (braunroter
Zackenbarsch), Salz, 1 Eiweiß, Mehl,
4 EL Erdnußöl*

*500 g Pak Choi (ersatzweise junger
Mangold oder Chinakohl)*

*200 g geschnetzeltes Schweinefleisch,
200 g Pilze (Champignons oder
Shiitake), in Scheiben geschnitten,
2 EL fein geschnittene Ingwerwurzel, 200
ml Hühnerbrühe,
Austernsauce (oyster sauce),
dunkle Sojasauce,
1 TL Maisstärke,
Koriandergrün*

Cut the fish fillets into pieces about 6 x 6 cm/2¹⁄₃ x 2¹⁄₃ in, salt lightly, roll in egg white, then flour. Heat the oil in the wok and fry the fillets on both sides until golden. Remove and keep in a warm place.

Blanch the vegetables in salted water for five minutes, then braise in a little oil in the wok, over a low heat.

Fry the pork, mushrooms and ginger in a little oil in the hot wok, turning frequently.

Add the pieces of fish, then pour in the chicken stock. Season with oyster sauce and dark soy sauce. Simmer for three minutes. Lightly bind with cornstarch, stirred with a little water, and arrange on deep plates.

Garnish with the fried vegetables and coriander leaves.

Fischfilets in ca. 6 x 6 cm große Stücke schneiden, leicht salzen, anschließend im Eiweiß und im Mehl wenden. Öl im Wok erhitzen und die Filets von beiden Seiten goldbraun anbraten. Herausnehmen und warmstellen.

Gemüse in Salzwasser fünf Minuten blanchieren, anschließend im Wok bei kleiner Hitze in etwas Öl schmoren.

Schweinefleisch, Pilze und Ingwer im heißen Wok in wenig Öl unter ständigem Wenden anbraten.

Die Fischstücke zugeben, dann mit dem Hühnerfond aufgießen. Mit Austernsauce und dunkler Sojasauce würzen, drei Minuten köcheln lassen. Mit angerührter Maisstärke leicht binden und in tiefe Teller anrichten.

Mit dem gebratenen Gemüse und etwas Koriandergrün garnieren.

FRIED BREAST OF DUCK WITH DRIED CHILI IN BLACK-BEAN SAUCE

GEBRATENE ENTENBRUST MIT CHILI IN SCHWARZER BOHNENSAUCE

For 4 persons:

600 g/1 lb 5 oz breast of duck, salt, pepper,
4 tbsp peanut oil,
2 garlic cloves, 1 shallot, 1 onion,
1 tsp root ginger, finely chopped,
4 dried chilis, cut into coarse pieces,
1 tsp black-bean paste,
250 ml/8¹/₃ fl oz/1 cup poultry stock,
salt, pepper, sugar,
¹/₂ tbsp dark soy sauce,
¹/₂ tbsp oyster sauce,
¹/₂ tbsp cornstarch,
chives, coriander leaves

Für 4 Personen:

600 g Entenbrust, Salz, Pfeffer,
4 EL Erdnußöl,
2 Knoblauchzehen, 1 Schalotte, 1 Zwiebel,
1 TL Ingwerwurzel, fein gehackt,
4 getrocknete Chilischoten, grob gehackt,
1 TL schwarze Bohnenpaste,
250 ml Geflügelfond,
Salz, Pfeffer, Zucker,
¹/₂ EL dunkle Sojasauce,
¹/₂ EL Austernsauce (oyster sauce),
¹/₂ EL Maisstärke,
Schnittlauch, Koriandergrün

Cut the breast of duck into slices and season with salt and pepper.
Heat the oil in the wok and fry the duck meat, turning frequently.
Thinly slice the garlic, shallot and onion, and add.
Stir in the ginger, chili and bean paste, and fry.
Pour in the poultry stock and season with salt, pepper, sugar, soy sauce, and oyster sauce.
Stir the cornstarch in water and use this to bind the sauce. Finally, add the herbs, bring to the boil and serve hot.

Die Entenbrust in Scheiben schneiden, mit Salz und Pfeffer würzen. Öl im Wok erhitzen, und das Entenfleisch unter Wenden anbraten.
Den Knoblauch, die Schalotte und die Zwiebel in dünne Scheiben schneiden, zugeben. Ingwer, Chili und Bohnenpaste unterrühren und ebenfalls mitbraten. Mit Geflügelfond aufgießen und mit Salz, Pfeffer, Zucker, Sojasauce und Austernsauce würzen. Maisstärke in Wasser anrühren, die Sauce damit binden. Zum Schluß die Kräuter zugeben, einmal zum Kochen bringen und heiß servieren.

STRIPS OF FILLET STEAK IN A CRISPY BASKET

RINDERFILETSTREIFEN IM KNUSPRIGEN KÖRBCHEN

For 4 persons:

600 g/1 lb 5 oz fillet beef steak, 1 tsp chili sauce,
1 tsp chopped chili and garlic, mixed,
salt, pepper, 1 white of egg, flour, peanut oil for deep-frying

Batter: 90 g/3 oz/¹/₃ cup flour, ¹/₂ egg, ¹/₂ tsp salt,
20 ml/²/₃ fl oz/4 tsp water
To garnish: about 20 fine leaves of spinach

Preparation of the batter: Sift the flour into a bowl and mix with the egg and the salt. Gradually add the water and knead the mixture for five minutes to form a smooth, firm dough. Pack this in cling film and allow to rest in the refrigerator overnight.

Cut the fillet steak into strips and mix well with chili sauce, chili-garlic mixture, a little salt and pepper and the white of egg. Cover and allow to stand in the refrigerator for one hour.

Heat sufficient oil for deep-frying in the wok. Roll the strips of meat in flour and then fry in the hot oil until they begin to change color (about three minutes).

For the baskets: Roll out the prepared dough very thinly on a floured surface. Line a mold with the dough. Press a second mold into this and fry in the hot oil. Fry the spinach leaves in the hot oil.

To serve: Place the baskets on plates, fill with the meat and decorate all around with the fried spinach leaves.

Für 4 Personen:

600 g Rinderfilet, 1 TL Chilisauce,
1 TL gehackter Chili und Knoblauch gemischt,
Salz, Pfeffer, 1 Eiweiß, Mehl, Erdnußöl zum Fritieren

Teig: 90 g Mehl, ¹/₂ Ei, ¹/₂ TL Salz,
20 ml Wasser
Garnitur: ca. 20 schöne Spinatblätter

Vorbereitung für den Teig: Mehl in eine Schüssel sieben und mit Ei und Salz vermengen. Nach und nach das Wasser zugeben und die Masse fünf Minuten zu einem glatten, festen Teig kneten. In Frischhaltefolie packen und im Kühlschrank über Nacht ruhen lassen.

Rinderfilet in Streifen schneiden und mit Chilisauce, Chili-Knoblauchgemisch, etwas Salz und Pfeffer und dem Eiweiß gut vermischen. Zugedeckt im Kühlschrank eine Stunde ziehen lassen. Im Wok genügend Öl zum Fritieren erhitzen. Fleischstreifen in Mehl wälzen und dann im heißen Öl fritieren, bis sie anfangen Farbe anzunehmen (ca. drei Minuten).

Für die Körbchen: Vorbereiteten Teig auf einer gemehlten Oberfläche sehr dünn auswallen. Je ein Förmchen mit dem Teig ausschlagen und mit einem zweiten Förmchen befestigt im heißen Öl ausbacken. Spinatblätter im heißen Öl fritieren.

Zum Servieren: Die Körbchen auf Teller legen, das Fleisch einfüllen und rundum mit den fritierten Spinatblättern dekorieren.

FRIED LOTUS ROOT CAKES IN BLACK-BEAN SAUCE

GEBRATENE LOTOSWURZELKUCHEN IN SCHWARZER BOHNENSAUCE

For 4 persons:

500 g/1 lb 2 oz/2 cups ground pork, salt, pepper,
2 dried black mushrooms, soaked,
4 water chestnuts, peeled, chives,
1 tbsp flour, 1 lotus root,
200 ml/7 fl oz/⁷/₈ cup peanut oil for deep-frying

1 garlic clove, finely chopped,
¹/₂ tsp black soy-bean paste,
100 ml/3¹/₂ fl oz/²/₅ cup poultry stock,
1 tsp oyster sauce, 1 tsp soy sauce,
1 tsp flour, coriander leaves

Season the ground meat with salt and pepper. Dry the mushrooms and chop finely, together with the water chestnuts. Finely chop the chives and knead everything together with the flour and the meat. Wash the lotus root and cut into 5-mm/¹/₅ in slices. Fill two slices of lotus with meat mixture and press firmly together. Heat the oil in the wok and, over a medium heat, fry the lotus cakes one at a time until they are done. Keep in a warm place.
Heat a little oil in the wok and add the chopped garlic and the bean paste. Add the stock, oyster sauce, and soy sauce and season. Stir the flour into a little water and use this to bind the sauce.
Heat the lotus cakes once again in this sauce and arrange on plates. Garnish with coriander leaves and serve.

Für 4 Personen:

500 g Schweinehackfleisch, Salz, Pfeffer,
2 getrocknete, schwarze Pilze, eingeweicht,
4 Wasserkastanien, geschält, Schnittlauch,
1 EL Mehl, 1 Lotoswurzel,
200 ml Erdnußöl zum Fritieren

1 Knoblauchzehe, fein gehackt,
¹/₂ TL schwarze Sojabohnenpaste,
100 ml Geflügelfond,
1 TL Austernsauce (oyster sauce), 1 TL Sojasauce,
1 TL Mehl, Koriandergrün

Hackfleisch mit Salz und Pfeffer würzen. Pilze abtrocknen und mit den Wasserkastanien fein hacken. Schnittlauch fein schneiden und alles zusammen mit dem Mehl und dem Hackfleisch verkneten. Lotoswurzeln waschen und in 5 mm dicke Scheiben schneiden. Jeweils zwei Lotosscheiben mit Hackfleischmasse füllen, gut zusammendrücken. Im Wok das Öl erhitzen und bei mittlerer Hitze nach und nach die Lotosküchlein braten, bis sie gar sind. Warmstellen.
Wenig Öl im Wok erhitzen und den Knoblauch und die Bohnenpaste zugeben. Fond, Austernsauce und Sojasauce zugeben, abschmecken. Mehl in etwas Wasser anrühren und die Sauce damit binden. Lotosküchlein in dieser Sauce nochmals aufkochen und auf Teller anrichten. Mit Koriandergrün garnieren.

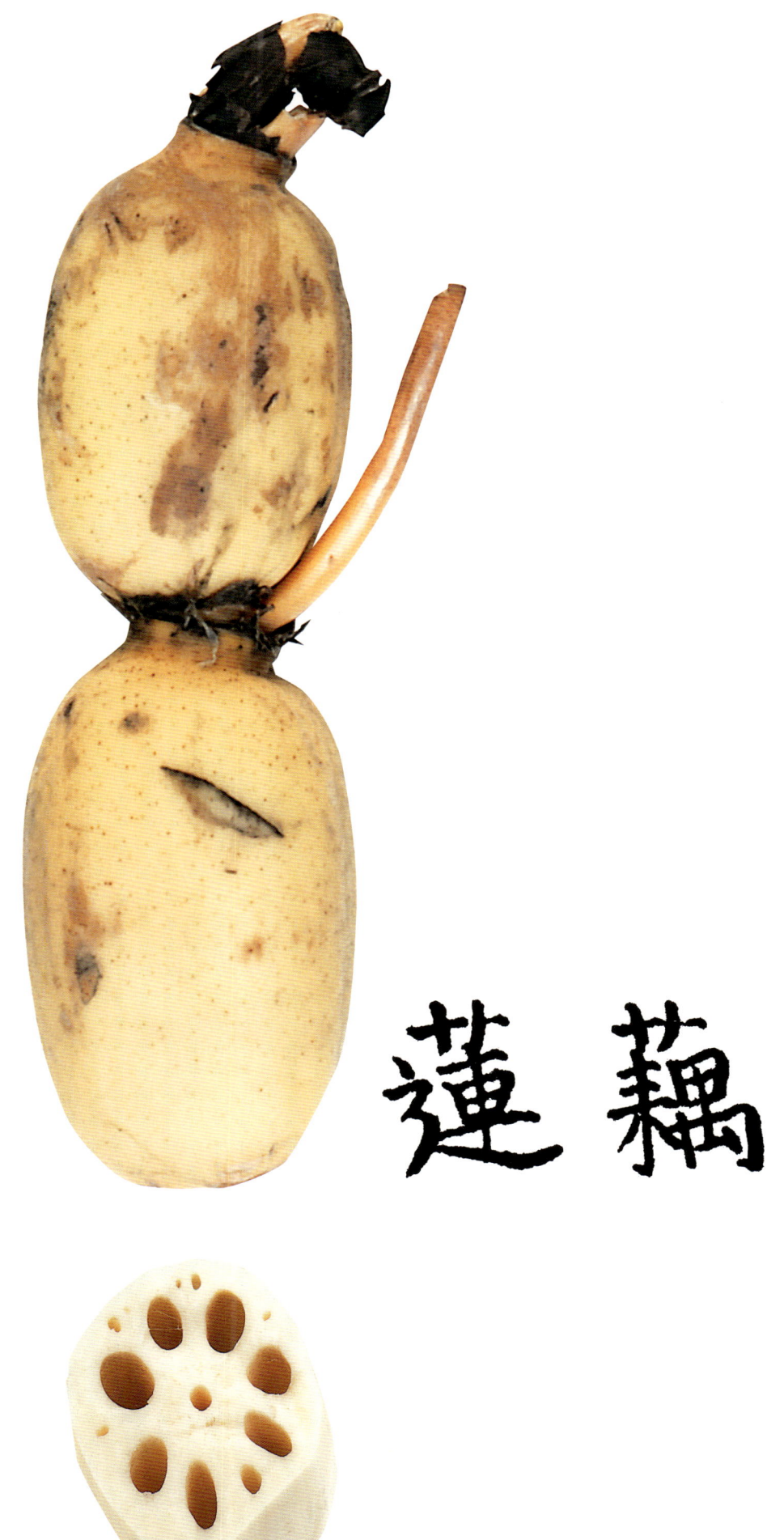

蓮藕

Lotus Root
Lotoswurzel

So Mei

蘇 眉

Chelinus undulatus

Maori

芝 麻 班

Coris lineolatus

Eastern Star Garoupa

東 星 班

Plectropomus leopardus

Red Garoupa

紅 班

Epinephelus morio

Coral Trout

瓜 子 班

Variola louti

Hung Yau

紅 鮋

Lutjanus argentimaculatus

Pomfret

倉 魚

Stomateoides sinensis

Mouse Garoupa

老 鼠 班

Cromileptes altivelis

Rainbow Trout

彩 虹 魚

Oncorhynchus mykiss

Parrot Fish

紅 頭

Labrichthys psittacula

Mandarin Fish

桂 魚

Siniperca chuatsi

Lun Pun

冧 蚌

Lutjanus

Shark's Fin
フカのヒレ

HK$

紅燒招牌群翅皇
フカのヒレの煮込みブラウンソースかけ（特上）
Braised Shark's Fins Supreme in Brown Sauce

每位 Each 720

竹笙燉大群翅
キヌガサタケとフカのヒレの蒸しスープ
Double Boiled Shark's Fins Superlative with Bamboo-mushrooms

每位 Each 630

蟹黃扒大群翅
フカのヒレの煮込みカニの卵かけ（上）
Braised Shark's Fins Superlative with Crab Roe

每位 Each 680

蟹肉扒大群翅
フカのヒレの煮込みカニ肉かけ（上）
Braised Shark's Fins Superlative with Crab Meat

每位 Each 630

雞絲扒大群翅
フカのヒレと鶏肉の細切りの煮込み（上）
Braised Shark's Fins Superlative with Shredded Chicken

每位 Each 600

紅燒大群翅
ブラウンリー人煮込み極上フカヒレ
Braised Superlative Shark's Fin in Brown Sauce

每位 Each 580

清湯大群翅
煮込み極上フカヒレスープ
Braised Superlative Shark's Fin in Clear Soup

每位 Each 580

乾燒排翅
フカのヒレの煮込み（上）
Braised Shark's Fins Superlative (Szechuen Style)

每位 Each 550

紅燒中鮑翅
フカのヒレの煮込みブラウンソースかけ（並）
Braised Shark's Fins Premier in Brown Sauce

每位 Each 300

紅燒蟹肉翅
フカのヒレの煮込みカニ肉かけ
Braised Shark's Fins with Crab Meat

HK$

每位 Each 260

紅燒雞絲翅
フカのヒレと鶏肉の細切りの煮込み
Braised Shark's Fins with Shredded Chicken

每位 Each 260

大群翅燉雞
フカのヒレと鶏肉の蒸しスープ（上）
Double Boiled Shark's Fins Superlative with Chicken

壹隻 Whole（20兩翅）4200
半隻 Half（10兩翅）2100

中鮑翅燉雞
フカのヒレと鶏肉の蒸しスープ（並）
Double Boiled Shark's Fins Premier with Chicken

壹隻 Whole（16兩翅）2400
半隻 Half（8兩翅）1200

原盅雞燉鮑翅
フカのヒレと鶏肉の蒸しスープ（並）（一人前）
Double Boiled Shark's Fins Premier with Chicken

每位 Each 350

原隻肘子燉大群翅
フカのヒレとハムの蒸しスープ
Double Boiled Shark's Fins with Chinese Ham

歡迎預定 Advance Order

新同楽

Sun Tung Lok
Shark's Fin Restaurant

Shark's Fin Restaurant

Haifischflossen Restaurant

So this is shark's fin soup. Shark's fin soup, we have been told, is an expensive Chinese specialty. Fins of a few particular kinds of shark, notably the hammerhead and the tiger shark, are salted and dried. In this dried state, middle-yellow triangles are stacked in the kitchens of those restaurants that have specialized in this extravagant dish. There are not very many, for even in capitalist Hong Kong, shark's fin soup is not something one can afford every day. And moreover it is a delicacy that is surrounded by a certain nimbus of reputation or mythology, and something like that cannot simply be shoveled down one's throat. This myth states (formulated in a nutshell so that it can be understood by the European ignorant of the ultimate secrets of Asian cuisine): an incredible lot of protein, therefore incredibly healthy, therefore incredibly good for the potency, therefore incredibly expensive.

Well then: shark's fin soup lies to a great extent beyond the faculties of assessment of a restaurant critic who has blown in from Europe. Therefore this attempt at an objective description. After a lengthy soaking and boiling procedure in the kitchen, the fin of the shark has reverted from the dried state to its original soft state, and then some time later has resolved itself into its individual fibers. These are all the more valuable, the longer and stronger they are. The fibers are yellowish, and of a slightly glassy consistency, which is why they remind us of noodles. A pile of these is first placed in the center of a soup-plate. The size of the pile depends on how much you want to spend on the soup. This commences at 260 Hong Kong dollars for a small pile of medium quality fin, and does not end at 4000 Hong Kong dollars for a large pile of first-class fin.

Over these shark's fin fibers, whose consistency is quite comparable to that of al dente noodles, the waiter pours highly concentrated, brownish, not excessively pungent but very spicy and boiling-hot broth, a kind of tasty chicken-fish stock of the very best quality. One may add a few drops of sesame oil for aroma. All together this tastes very rich, and the fin fibers have a most interesting feel.

Hong Kong – among a thousand other things, this is the city of plagiarism – copied wrist-watches and stolen designer labels. Hong Kong would not be Hong Kong if there were not also a kind of poor man's shark's fin soup. This can be found in the small, outdoor food stalls on the appropriate night markets. The broth does not taste anywhere near as fine as the real thing, rather somewhat austere. The pile in the middle of the plate is not the fibers of shark's fin, but honest-to-goodness noodles. The lot for a dollar fifty. It is the same difference as that between the Rolex and the pirated Rolex. Both show the time. But one a hundred times better.

Das also nun ist Haifischflossensuppe. Haifischflossensuppe, so hat man uns gesagt, ist eine kostspielige chinesische Spezialität. Flossen von einigen besonderen Haifischarten, vor allem vom Hammer- und vom Tiger-Hai, werden gesalzen und getrocknet. Und diese im getrockneten Zustand mittelgelben Dreiecke stapeln sich denn auch in den Küchen jener Restaurants, die sich auf diese extravagante Speise spezialisiert haben. Es sind nicht eben viele, denn eine Haifischflossensuppe gehört selbst im kapitalkräftigen Hong Kong zu jenen Gerichten, die man sich nicht alle Tage leistet.

Es ist zudem eine Speise, der ein gewisser Ruf, ja ein Mythos, vorausgeht, und so etwas futtert man erst recht nicht gerade mal so. Und dieser Mythos lautet (auf eine ebenso kurze wie griffige, gegenüber den letzten Geheimnissen der asiatischen Küche europäisch-ignorante Formel gebracht): unglaublich viel Protein, deshalb unglaublich gesund, deshalb unglaublich gut für die Potenz, deshalb unglaublich teuer.

Also: Haifischflossensuppe entzieht sich weitgehend der Beurteilung eines aus Europa hereingeschmeckten Gastrokritikers. Deshalb hier der Versuch einer sachlichen Beschreibung. Die Flosse des Haifisches hat sich, nach einer langwierigen Einweich- und Kochprozedur, in der Küche vom getrockneten Zustand wieder in ihren ursprünglich weichen zurückverwandelt und nochmals einige Zeit später in ihre einzelnen Fasern aufgelöst. Diese sind umso wertvoller, je länger und kräftiger sie sind. Die Fasern sind gelblich und von leicht glasiger Konsistenz, weshalb sie uns an Nudeln erinnern. Von diesen kommt nun ein Häufchen in die Mitte eines Suppentellers. Die Größe des Häufchens hängt davon ab, wieviel Geld wir für die Suppe ausgeben wollen. Das fängt bei 260 Hong-Kong-Dollar für ein kleines Häufchen mittlerer Flossenqualität an und hört – für ein großes Häufchen in First-Class-Qualität – bei 4000 Hong-Kong-Dollar noch nicht auf.

Auf diese Haifischflossenfasern, deren Konsistenz einer al-dente gekochten Nudel durchaus entspricht, gießt der Kellner eine überaus konzentrierte, bräunliche, nicht übertrieben scharfe aber sehr würzige und siedendheiße Brühe, so eine Art schmackhafter Hühner-Fisch-Fond allererster Güte. Ein paar Tropfen Sesamöl zum Aromatisieren kann man obendrauf geben. Das alles schmeckt dann sehr kräftig, die Flossenfasern sind haptisch recht interessant.

Hong Kong – neben tausend anderem ist es auch die Stadt der Plagiate, der Copy-Armbanduhren und der geklauten Designer-Labels. Hong Kong wäre nicht Hong Kong, gäbe es nicht auch eine Art Copy-Haifischflossensuppe. Diese findet man in den kleinen, offenen Garküchen auf den entsprechenden nächtlichen Märkten. Die Brühe dort schmeckt lange nicht so fein wie die echte, eher etwas streng. Das Häufchen in der Mitte des Tellers besteht nicht aus den Fasern der Haifischflosse, sondern aus veritablen Nudeln. Das ganze für Zweimarkfünfzig. Es ist wie der Unterschied zwischen Rolex und Copy-Rolex. Beide zeigen die Zeit an. Die eine aber hundertmal besser als die andere.

魚翅

Shark's Fin
Haifischflosse

SHARK'S FIN SOUP

HAIFISCHFLOSSENSUPPE

For 6 persons:

250 g/8¹/₂ oz dried shark's fin,
softened and cleaned as described

For the soup:
1 small chicken, 450 g/1 lb lean pork,
300 g/10 oz Yunnan ham
(lean Chinese raw ham), salt

Cut the chicken and meat into pieces, place in a large pot with 2 liters/4 pints/8 cups of cold water, bring to the boil, and simmer over a low heat for three hours. Finely slice the ham and set aside a little of it for garnishing. Put the rest of the ham in the broth and simmer for another hour.
Strain the soup through a sieve, season with salt, and allow to stand for half an hour to clear it.
Ladle out the concentrated broth, heat the prepared shark's fin fibers in it and transfer to deep plates. Serve sprinkled with the very finely cut strips of ham.

Für 6 Personen:

250 g getrocknete Haifischflosse,
eingeweicht und gereinigt wie beschrieben

Für die Suppe:
1 kleines Huhn, 450 g mageres Schweinefleisch,
300 g Yunnan Schinken (magerer chinesischer
Rohschinken), Salz

Huhn und Fleisch in Stücke schneiden. In einem großen Topf mit zwei Liter kaltem Wasser aufsetzen, zum Kochen bringen und bei kleiner Hitze drei Stunden sieden lassen. Schinken fein schneiden, ein bisschen davon für die Garnitur beiseite stellen. Restlichen Schinken zu der Brühe geben und eine weitere Stunde köcheln lassen. Suppe durch ein Sieb abgießen, mit Salz abschmecken und zum Klären eine halbe Stunde stehen lassen.
Die Brühe abschöpfen, vorbereitete Haifischflossenfasern darin erwärmen und in tiefe Teller anrichten. Mit den Schinkenstreifen bestreut servieren.

SHARK'S FIN IN BROWN SAUCE

HAIFISCHFLOSSE IN BRAUNER SAUCE

For 6 persons:

250 g/8¹/₂ oz dried shark's fin,
softened and cleaned as described,
250 g/8¹/₂ fl oz/1 cup chicken broth

1 tbsp corn oil, 2 tbsp dark soy sauce,
1 tbsp light soy sauce, 1 tbsp sweet rice wine,
600 ml/1 pint 1 fl oz/2¹/₂ cups chicken broth,
¹/₂ tsp salt, ¹/₂ tsp monosodium glutamate,
¹/₂ tsp sugar, white pepper, 1¹/₂ tbsp cornstarch

Bring the chicken broth to the boil in the wok. Add the softened and cleaned shark's fin and simmer on a low heat for four minutes. Pass through a sieve. Heat the oil in the wok and add the soy sauces, wine and chicken broth. Season with salt, glutamate, sugar and a little white pepper. Bind with the cornstarch, blended with a little water, and add the shark's fin. Simmer for a further four minutes and serve in deep plates.

Für 6 Personen:

250 g getrocknete Haifischflosse,
eingeweicht und gereinigt wie beschrieben,
250 ml Hühnerbrühe

1 EL Maiskeimöl, 2 EL dunkle Sojasauce,
1 EL helle Sojasauce, 1 EL süßer Reiswein,
600 ml Hühnerbrühe,
¹/₂ TL Salz, ¹/₂ TL Glutamat, ¹/₂ TL Zucker,
weißer Pfeffer, 1¹/₂ EL Maisstärke

Hühnerbrühe im Wok zum Kochen bringen. Eingeweichte und geputzte Haifischflossen zugeben und vier Minuten bei kleiner Hitze köcheln lassen. Durch ein Sieb abschütten. Öl im Wok erhitzen und Sojasaucen, Wein und Hühnerbrühe zugeben. Mit Salz, Glutamat, Zucker, und etwas weißem Pfeffer würzen. Mit der angerührten Maisstärke binden und die Haifischflossen zugeben. Weitere vier Minuten köcheln lassen und in tiefen Tellern servieren.

To prepare the shark's fin:
Soak the dried shark's fin
in a pot of cold water for
two to three hours.
Set the pot on the stove,
bring to the boil and cook
for half an hour.
Drain through a sieve,
fill up with fresh water
and soak again. Repeat
this procedure two to
three times until the fin is
completely soft. Carefully
clean the fibers under
running cold water.

Vorbereitung der
Haifischflosse: Die
getrocknete Haifischflosse
in einem Topf in kaltem
Wasser zwei bis drei
Stunden einweichen. Topf
auf den Herd setzen, zum
Kochen bringen und eine
halbe Stunde sieden
lassen. Durch ein Sieb
abgießen, mit frischem
Wasser auffüllen und
erneut einweichen lassen.
Diesen Vorgang zwei-
dreimal wiederholen, bis
die Flosse völlig
aufgeweicht ist.
Unter fließendem kalten
Wasser die Fasern
sorgfältig reinigen.

Charles Cheung, Robert Ko

As its name indicates, the East Ocean Seafood Restaurant offers a wide variety of delicacies from the depths of the sea. These include tender squid with garlic and bean paste, which are given a quite special touch by the celery sticks cooked in chicken broth. But the restaurant is really well-known for two other reasons. On the one hand the skilled art of decorative vegetable carving is practised and developed here.

How nimble hands – and considering the filigree delicacy of the carved patterns – a surprisingly large knife can, with a flick of the wrist, turn a thick carrot into a Chinese dragon, a bird or a mythical figure amazes the onlooker every time. In Asia, and especially in China, such carvings do not have a merely decorative character, but are also symbols and bringers of good luck. So it is not surprising that for wedding feasts and christenings, when the table is specially laden, entire carved scenarios of carrots, celeriac and other vegetables decorate the table, plates and dishes.

And the second reason: Charles Cheung, the right-hand man of chef Eric Chow, is a past master in the preparation of Peking duck. With the Peking duck it is a little like other specialties from around the world: there is more than one recipe, but every cook claims to have the only original one. It is the same with Marseilles bouillabaisse and not much different with Black Forest cherry gâteau. It therefore tastes a little different each time, and there is sometimes a note of disappointment when eating, along the lines of: this is supposed to be this world-famous special treat?

The Peking duck of Charles Cheung is however really a classic, and if after three or four attempts you perhaps were on the point of resignation – here you should in any event give it another try. Crispily tender skin, juicy and flavorful meat, plus the best ingredients and accompaniments, a classic comme il faut.

East Ocean Seafood Restaurant

Das East Ocean Seafood Restaurant hat, wie schon der Name sagt, vielfältige Leckereien aus den Tiefen des Meeres anzubieten. Dazu gehören auch die zarten Tintenfische mit Knoblauch und Bohnenpaste, denen in Hühnerbrühe gekochter Stangensellerie den ganz besonderen Pfiff geben. So richtig bekannt ist das Restaurant jedoch aus zwei anderen Gründen.

Zum einen wird hier die hohe Schule der dekorativen Gemüseschnitzerei gepflegt und weiterentwickelt. Wie hier unter flinken Händen und mit – in Anbetracht der filigranen Schnitzmuster – erstaunlich großen Messern aus einer dicken Möhre im Handumdrehen ein chinesischer Drache, ein Vogel oder eine andere mythologische Figur entsteht, verblüfft den Zuschauer jedesmal aufs neue. Solche Schnitzereien haben in Asien und besonders in China nicht nur rein dekorativen Charakter, es sind vielmehr Symbole und Glücksbringer. Und so verwundert es nicht, daß gerade für Hochzeitsfeiern und bei Taufen, wenn die Küche besonders üppig anrichtet, ganze geschnitzte Szenarien aus Möhren, Sellerieknollen und anderen Gemüsen die Tische, Teller und Platten verzieren.

Der zweite Grund: Charles Cheung, rechte Hand des Chefkochs Eric Chow, ist ein wahrer Meister im Zubereiten der Peking-Ente. Mit der Peking-Ente ist es ein bißchen so wie mit den Spezialitäten in anderen Ländern dieser Welt: Es gibt meist mehr als nur ein Rezept, aber jeder behauptet, das einzig originale zu haben. Das ist bei der Marseiller Bouillabaisse nicht viel anders als bei der Schwarzwälder Kirschtorte.

Und deshalb schmeckt es auch
jedesmal ein bißchen anders, und
manchmal schwingt beim Essen dann
auch ein bißchen Enttäuschung
mit nach dem Motto:
Und das soll nun diese weltberühmte
Besonderheit sein?!
Die Peking-Ente von Charles Cheung
ist nun wirklich ein Klassiker,
und wer nach womöglich drei oder
vier Versuchen schon aufgeben
wollte – hier sollte man es auf jeden
Fall noch mal probieren.
Knusperzart die Haut, noch saftig
und hocharomatisch das Fleisch,
dazu beste Zutaten und Beilagen – ein
Klassiker also comme il faut.

東海 海鮮酒家

East Ocean Seafood Restaurant

乳鴿崧
生菜包

Fried Minced Pigeon Served w/Lettuce

夏
SUMMER

冬
WINTER

醬燒化皮
乳豬

Roasted Suckling Pig (Whole)

GIANT CRAB IN YELLOW RICE-WINE SAUCE

TASCHENKREBS IN GELBER REISWEINSAUCE

For 1 person:

1 giant crab of about 600 g/1 lb 5 oz

*70 ml/2¹/₃ fl oz/¹/₄ cup Chinese yellow wine
(or as a substitute dry sherry or Shao Hsing wine),
70 g/2¹/₃ oz/¹/₃ cup poultry fat,
1 egg, beaten,
1 tsp granular chicken broth*

Für 1 Person:

1 Taschenkrebs von ca. 600 g

*70 ml chinesischer gelber Wein
(ersatzweise trockener Sherry oder Shao Hsing Wein),
70 g Geflügelfett,
1 Ei, verquirlt,
1 TL gekörnte Hühnerbrühe*

Carefully wash the crab under running cold water and fast-boil in a large pot of salted water for one minute. Remove and drain well.
Place on a grid in a pot and steam together with the wine and the fat, sprinkled with the granular chicken broth, for ten minutes. Baste occasionally with the cooking liquid.
Pour the sauce into a small bowl and beat in the egg. Pour this mixture over the crab and steam for about ten seconds more.
As an accompaniment serve grated white radish, coloured with beetroot juice, and grated ginger with Chinkiang vinegar.

Krebs unter fließendem kalten Wasser sorgfältig waschen und in einem großen Topf in sprudelnd kochendem Salzwasser eine Minute kochen. Herausnehmen und abtropfen lassen. Auf einen Gitterboden in einem Topf legen, Wein und Fett zugeben, mit der gekörnten Hühnerbrühe bestreuen und zehn Minuten über Dampf garen. Zwischendurch mit der Garflüssigkeit begießen. Die Sauce in eine kleine Schüssel abgießen und mit dem Ei verrühren. Diese Masse über den Krebs gießen und erneut ca. zehn Sekunden dämpfen. Als Beilage passen geriebener, in rote Bete Saft gefärbter Rettich und geriebener Ingwer mit Chinkiang Essig.

FRIED SQUID

TINTENFISCH

For 4 persons:

*600 g/1 lb 5 oz squid, washed,
skinned, and cleaned, without tentacles,
oil for deep-frying*

*¹/₂ liter/1 pt/2 cups chicken broth, 1 tbsp corn oil, salt,
600 g/1 lb 5 oz celery, cleaned
and cut into 3-cm/1¹/₅ in pieces*

*2 tsp finely chopped garlic,
¹/₂ tsp hot soy-bean paste,
1 tbsp yellow rice wine, 1 tsp cornstarch,
¹/₂ tsp finely chopped chili
To garnish: mint leaves, watercress*

Cut the squid into 2 - 3 cm/1 in squares. Boil in salted water for ten to fifteen minutes, then drain and dry well. Deep-fry in hot oil until golden brown, then drain.
In a pot, bring the chicken broth to the boil. Add oil and salt and cook the celery in it for two minutes. Drain through a sieve.
Heat a little oil in the wok. Briefly fry the garlic and bean paste, then add the celery and the squid and, over a strong heat, stir-fry for thirty seconds. Add the rice wine, season with salt, and bind with the cornstarch, blended with a little water. Add the chopped chili, mix well, and fry for ten seconds more. Arrange on plates and decorate with the mint and cress.

Für 4 Personen:

*600 g Tintenfisch, gewaschen,
gehäutet und geputzt, ohne Fangarme,
Öl zum Fritieren*

*¹/₂ Liter Hühnerbrühe, 1 EL Maiskeimöl, Salz,
600 g Stangensellerie, geputzt,
in 3 cm große Stücke geschnitten*

*2 TL feingehackter Knoblauch,
¹/₂ TL scharfe Sojabohnenpaste,
1 EL gelber Reiswein, 1 TL Maisstärke,
¹/₂ TL fein gehackte Chilischote
Garnitur: Minzeblätter, Brunnenkresse*

Tintenfisch in 2 bis 3 cm große Quadrate schneiden. In Salzwasser zehn bis fünfzehn Minuten kochen, anschließend abgießen und gut trocknen. In heißem Öl goldbraun fritieren, abtropfen lassen.
In einem Topf die Hühnerbrühe zum Kochen bringen. Öl und Salz zugeben und den Sellerie zwei Minuten darin kochen. Durch ein Sieb abgießen und abtropfen lassen. Etwas Öl im Wok erhitzen. Knoblauch und Bohnenpaste kurz anbraten, dann den Sellerie und den Tintenfisch zugeben und bei starker Hitze unter Wenden dreißig Sekunden braten. Mit Reiswein und Salz würzen und mit der angerührten Stärke binden. Chili unterrühren und weitere zehn Sekunden braten. Auf Teller anrichten, mit der Minze und der Kresse dekorieren.

JIANGNAN SPARE RIBS

For 4 persons:

1.2 kg/2²/₃ lb spare ribs,
oil for deep-frying

120 g/4 oz fresh broad beans

1 tbsp rice-wine vinegar,
2 tbsp hoisin sauce (sauce made from red beans,
soy beans, sugar, and spices,
sold in cans and jars),
dark soy sauce,
sugar,
salt,
2 tbsp peanut oil

Cut the spare ribs into square pieces. Deep-fry for a few seconds in hot oil and drain well.
Lay the beans on a greased baking tray and cook in the hot oven until done.
Place the sauces and spices in the wok, add the meat and, turning constantly, cook over a low heat until the meat is tender.
To serve: Scatter the baked beans over the ribs.
A suitable accompaniment would be braised pak choi (Chinese mustard cabbage) or as a substitute Chinese cabbage or young Swiss chard.

Für 4 Personen:

1,2 kg Spare-ribs,
Öl zum Fritieren

120 g frische dicke Bohnen

1 EL Reisweinessig,
2 EL Hoisin-Sauce (Sauce aus roten Bohnen,
Sojabohnen, Zucker und Gewürzen,
wird in Dosen und Gläsern verkauft),
dunkle Sojasauce,
Zucker,
Salz,
2 EL Erdnußöl

Spare-ribs in viereckige Stücke schneiden. In heißem Öl einige Sekunden fritieren; gut abtropfen lassen. Bohnen auf ein gefettetes Backblech geben und im heißen Ofen backen, bis sie gar sind.
Saucen und Gewürze in den Wok geben, Fleisch dazu geben und unter ständigem Wenden bei kleiner Hitze garen, bis das Fleisch zart ist.
Zum Servieren: Die gebackenen Bohnen über die Rippchen streuen. Als Beilage paßt gedünsteter Pak Choi (chinesischer Senfkohl, ersatzweise Chinakohl oder junger Mangold).

PEKING DUCK

PEKING ENTE

For 8 - 10 persons:

1 duck of about 3 kg/6 - 7 lb
¹/₂ liter/1 pt/2 cups water, 200 g/7 oz/⁴/₅ cup maltose,
2 tbsp dark soy sauce,
1 bunch spring onions, 1 cucumber

pancakes:
600 g/20 oz/2¹/₂ cups wheat flour, 600 g/20 oz/2¹/₂ cups
boiling water, salt, peanut oil, hoisin sauce

Wash the duck and dry well with a cloth. Make a slit in the skin of the neck and inflate with a pump to detach the skin from the body (in this way, the skin becomes crispy during cooking). Stitch up the slit. In the wok, bring the water to the boil with the maltose and the soy sauce. Dip the duck in the boiling syrup for five seconds on each side so that the syrup also reaches the inside. Then hang the bird in a warm, airy place for four to five hours to dry.
Preheat the oven to 190° C/375° F and roast the duck, if possible hanging, for about one hour until crispy.
Cut the spring onions and cucumber into 10-cm/4-in sticks.
For the pancakes: Sift the flour into a bowl. Gradually add the water and mix to a smooth dough. Salt lightly. Allow the mixture to stand for twenty minutes, covered with a damp cloth. Then knead well once again. Form small balls from the dough and roll them out paper-thin.
Heat an omelette pan on the stove. Paint with a little oil and fry the pancakes on both sides until the dough blisters.
To serve: Detach the skin from the duck and cut into pieces. Then carve the bird and serve the meat on a separate platter. Serve separately hoisin sauce for dipping the pancakes and the vegetables.

Für 8 bis 10 Personen:

1 Ente von ca. 3 kg
¹/₂ Liter Wasser, 200 g Maltose (Malzzucker),
2 EL dunkle Sojasauce,
1 Bund Frühlingszwiebeln, 1 Salatgurke

Pfannkuchen:
600 g Weizenmehl, 600 g kochendes Wasser,
Salz, Erdnußöl, Hoi Sin Sauce

Ente waschen und mit einem Tuch gut abtrocknen. Im Nacken die Haut einschneiden und mit einer Pumpe aufblasen, so daß sich die Haut vom Körper löst (so wird die Haut beim Garprozess knusprig), Schnittstelle gut vernähen. Wasser, Maltose und Sojasauce im Wok zum Kochen bringen. Ente von allen Seiten je fünf Sekunden in den kochenden Sirup halten, so daß er auch in das Innere gelangen kann. Anschließend das Tier an einem warmen, luftigen Ort vier bis fünf Stunden zum Trocknen aufhängen. Ofen auf 190° C vorheizen und die Ente, wenn möglich hängend, darin ungefähr eine Stunde knusprig braun braten. Frühlingszwiebeln und Gurke in 10 cm lange Stifte schneiden.
Für die Pfannkuchen: Mehl in eine Schüssel sieben. Wasser nach und nach zufügen und zu einem glatten Teig verarbeiten, leicht salzen. Zwanzig Minuten mit einem feuchten Tuch zugedeckt stehen lassen, anschließend nochmals gut kneten. Aus dem Teig kleine Kugeln formen und diese papierdünn auswallen. Eine Omelettpfanne auf dem Herd heiß werden lassen, mit etwas Öl bepinseln, und die Küchlein von beiden Seiten braten, bis der Teig Blasen wirft.
Zum Servieren: Die Haut der Ente ablösen und in Stücke schneiden. Dann das Tier zerteilen und das Fleisch auf einer Platte servieren. Hoi Sin Sauce zum Dippen der Pfannkuchen und der Gemüse separat anrichten.

叉　燒　酥

Barbecued Pork Rolls
Fritierte Rollen mit gegrilltem Schweinefleisch

Dim Sum

春 黄 蝦 筒

Deep-fried Shrimps
Fritierte Garnelen

糯　米　鷄

Glutinous Rice in Lotus leaf
Klebereis im Lotosblatt

魚 翅 灌 湯 餃

Shark's Fin Dumpling
Haifischflossenklöße

黃 橋 燒 餅

Baked Minced Meat Pie
Gebackene Hackfleischküchlein

酥 皮 蛋 撻

Mini Egg Tart
Eiertörtchen

香 杧 布 甸

Mango Dessert

Dried squid
Getrockneter Tintenfisch

鹹魚

乾瑤柱

Dried scallops, conpoi
Getrocknete Jakobsmuscheln

Dried salted fish
Getrockneter, gesalzener Fisch

鹹魚

太湖海鮮城

Tai Woo Restaurant

Every afternoon in the Tai Woo Restaurant, fresh fish is delivered. There are usually 30 different species swimming in the aquarium behind the entrance. Here the fish is primarily served steamed, a light and practically fat-free method of preparation. The style of the restaurant's cuisine is oriented toward that of Canton, the great province in the south of China. It is a Chinese cuisine that is familiar to us. For the first emigrants, who then opened the first Chinese restaurants in the capital cities of the western world, came from this region. Cantonese cuisine, which is rather more sparing with hot seasoning, is held to be one of the best in China, the haute cuisine of the Middle Kingdom, so to speak – which is saying something, considering the culinary variety and tradition of this country.

Im Tai Woo Restaurant wird jeden Nach-mittag frischer Fisch angeliefert. Meist schwimmen dreißig verschiedene Sorten im Aquarium hinter dem Eingang. Steamed, also leicht und praktisch ohne Fett zubereitet, kommt er hier vorzugsweise auf den Tisch. Der Küchenstil des Restaurants orientiert sich an Kanton, der großen Provinz im Süden Chinas. Es ist eine Chinaküche, die uns vertraut ist. Denn die ersten Emigranten, die auch die ersten China-Restaurants in den Hauptstädten der westlichen Welt eröffneten, kamen aus dieser Gegend. Kantonesische Küche, die sich bei der Schärfe eher zurückhält, gilt als eine der besten in China, sozusagen als die Haute Cuisine im Reich der Mitte – was bei der kulinarischen Vielfalt und Tradition dieses Landes einiges bedeutet.

Thousand-year-old Chinese Eggs

Why this is so is explained by taking a look back into history: in the 17th century, when the Ming dynasty was deposed, the imperial court of Peking fled south to the province of Canton. The out-of-work courtiers had time and leisure to devote their entire attention to preparing food. And so it came about that the time-consuming art of filling, rolling, twisting and parceling of dim sum snacks was developed to perfection.

In the Tai Woo this tradition is upheld at a high standard. Incessantly the waiter brings in the small, round wood-chip boxes, in which the dim sum are steamed. There is no end to the variety. Chicken, pork, duck, fish and shellfish, finely chopped or minced, with all kinds of spices and wrapped in a wide variety of pastry types, and then all dipped in various sauces – hot, mild or sweet-and-sour, results in such multifarious nuances of taste that one is amazed over and over again. As a dessert, the whole dim sum range of shapes is available as sweets.
The favorite wrapping is then a yeast dough, which makes the dim sum balls look like miniature versions of grandmother's steamed dumplings.

Warum dies so ist, zeigt ein Blick in die Geschichte: Im 17. Jahrhundert, als die Ming-Dynastie gestürzt wurde, floh der Kaiserliche Hof von Peking nach Süden, in die Provinz Kanton. Der arbeitslose Hofstaat hatte Zeit und Muße, der Essenszubereitung seine ganze Aufmerksamkeit zu widmen. Und so wurde nicht zuletzt das zeitauf-wendige Füllen, Rollen, Drehen und Verpacken der Dim-Sum-Häppchen zur Perfektion entwickelt.

Im Tai Woo wird diese Tradition auf hohem Niveau gepflegt. Unablässig bringt der Kellner die kleinen runden Holzspanschachteln heran, in denen die Dim Sum über Dampf gegart werden. Der Vielfalt sind keine Grenzen gesetzt. Huhn, Schwein, Ente, Fisch und Krustentiere, kleingehackt oder durch den Fleischwolf gedreht, mit Gewürzen aller Art und in die unterschiedlichsten Teigsorten gehüllt, und das alles dann noch in verschiedene Saucen – scharf, mild oder süßsauer – gedippt, das ergibt eine Vielfalt an Geschmacksnuancen, die immer wieder verblüfft. Und als Nachspeise gibt es die gesamte Dim-Sum-Palette auch in süß. Dann favorisiert man als Hülle einen Hefeteig, der die Dim-Sum-Bällchen aussehen läßt wie Großmutters Dampfnudeln im Miniformat.

Liu Che Lik, the chef of this establishment, a Cantonese by birth, who learned his trade in a seafood restaurant in the New Territories, serves, however, yet another specialty of the cuisine that is the diametric opposite of the ultra-fresh fish dishes and the à point dim sum snacks: the famous, nay legendary, thousand-year-old Chinese eggs.

If you have never dared to try them, here is your chance. A little courage is necessary, even if the eggs – they are always duck-eggs – are really only one or two months old. Even so, for us European fresh-egg fetishists this is a small eternity. The eggs are packed, raw, in a firm, half-inch thick crust of ash, clay and rice-straw husks, then stored for at least 28 days in a cool place.

What chemical processes occur inside the eggshell during this time, we do not know. The result is in any case fascinating to see: the egg-white has become firm, dark and glassy. The yolk is still slightly moist and shimmers in opalescent colors between emerald green, brown and dark ochre yellow. Of the smell, the less said the better. And even the Chinese seem not to be too happy about the taste. For only with a goodly piece of pickled ginger with its tart, pungent bite – the obligatory accompaniment to the thousand-year-old egg – does the whole become, after all, a surprising gustatory experience.

Liu Che Lik, der Chefkoch des Hauses, gebürtiger Kantonese, der in einem Seafood-Restaurant in den New Territories gelernt hat, bringt jedoch noch eine andere Spezialität der Küche auf den Tisch, die zu den top-frisch zubereiteten Fischgerichten und den à point gegarten Dim-Sum-Häppchen in krassem Gegensatz steht: die berühmten, ja legendären tausendjährigen chinesischen Eier.

Wer es noch nie gewagt hat, sie zu probieren: hier ist die Gelegenheit. Mut gehört allemal dazu, auch wenn die Eier – es sind immer solche von der Ente – lediglich ein bis zwei Monate alt sind. Dennoch: für uns europäische Frischei-Fetischisten das eine kleine Ewigkeit. Die Eier werden roh in eine feste, etwa einen Zentimeter starke Hülle aus Asche, Lehm und Reisstrohspelzen gepackt und dann für mindestens 28 Tage an einem kühlen Platz gelagert.

Was sich in dieser Zeit in der Eischale chemisch abspielt, wissen wir nicht. Das Ergebnis ist zumindest optisch faszinierend: das Eiweiß ist fest und dunkel-glasig geworden. Das Eigelb ist noch etwas feucht und opalisiert in den schönsten Farben zwischen smaragdgrün, braun und dunkelockergelb. Über den Geruch schweigen die Götter. Und dem Geschmack trauen wohl auch die Chinesen – zumindest pur genossen – nicht so recht über den Weg. Denn erst ein schönes Stück eingelegter Ingwer mit seiner ganzen rezenten Schärfe – die obligatorische Beilage zum tausendjährigen Ei – macht alles zusammen zu einem immerhin erstaunlichen Geschmackserlebnis.

A "thousand-year-old" egg ripens for about 28 days
in a crust of ash, clay and rice-straw husks.

Ein „tausendjähriges" Ei reift ca. 28 Tage
in einer Hülle aus Asche, Lehm und Reisstrohspelzen.

皮蛋

SCALLOPS WITH VEGETABLES

JAKOBSMUSCHELN MIT GEMÜSE

FRIED CRAB
WITH GINGER AND BELL PEPPER

GEBRATENER KREBS
MIT INGWER UND PAPRIKA

For 4 persons:

400 g/13 oz scallops, shucked
(in the original recipe
conpoy is used,
a related species),
1 tbsp corn oil,
200 g/7 oz celery sticks,
cut into pieces,
200 g/7oz mange-tout, halved,
100 g/3¹/₂ oz lotus root, sliced,
100 g/3¹/₂ oz carrot,
cut into sticks,
20 g/²/₃ oz/2 tbsp root ginger,
finely grated,
1 tsp oyster sauce,
¹/₂ tsp sugar,
¹/₂ tsp salt,
250 ml/8 fl oz/1 cup chicken broth,
2 tsp cornstarch

Fry the scallops on all sides in
the wok, in oil, over a medium
heat. Add the vegetables and
ginger and fry for about two
minutes.
Season with the oyster sauce,
sugar and salt and pour in the
chicken broth.
Finally, bind the sauce with
the cornstarch, blended with a
little water.

Für 4 Personen:

400 g ausgelöste Jakobsmuscheln
(im Originalrezept wird
Conpoy verwendet, eine
verwandte Kammuschelart),
1 EL Maiskeimöl,
200 g Stangensellerie,
in Stücke geschnitten,
200 g Zuckerschoten, halbiert,
100 g Lotoswurzel,
in Scheiben geschnitten,
100 g Karotte,
in Stifte geschnitten,
20 g Ingwer, fein gerieben,
1 TL Austernsauce (oyster sauce),
1/2 TL Zucker,
1/2 TL Salz,
250 ml Hühnerbrühe,
2 TL Maisstärke

Die Jakobsmuscheln im Wok
im Öl bei mittlerer Hitze unter
Rühren rundum anbraten.
Gemüse und Ingwer zugeben
und ungefähr zwei Minuten
mitbraten.
Mit der Austernsauce, Zucker
und Salz würzen, mit der Hühnerbrühe aufgießen.
Zum Schluß die Sauce mit der
angerührten Maisstärke binden.

For 4 persons:

1 giant crab
of 800 - 1000 g/1¹/₂ to 2 lb,
oil for deep-frying,
2 spring onions,
cut into 2-cm/1-in pieces,
2 tbsp grated root ginger,
1 red bell pepper,
cut into fine strips,
¹/₂ tsp salt, 1 tsp sugar,
1 tsp oyster sauce, 2 tbsp rice wine,
250 ml/8 fl oz/1 cup chicken broth,
1 tbsp cornstarch

Thoroughly wash the crab.
Place in fast boiling salted
water, cover, and cook for one
to two minutes. Remove, cut
into pieces, and fry in hot oil
for one to two minutes.
Heat a little oil in the wok. Add
the pieces of crab, spring onions,
ginger and bell pepper and fry for
one minute, turning occasionally.
Add the salt, sugar, oyster sauce
and rice wine, and continue to
fry for one minute.
Pour in the chicken broth and
bind with the cornstarch,
blended with a little water.

Für 4 Personen:

1 Taschenkrebs von 800 - 1000 g,
Öl zum Fritieren,
2 Frühlingszwiebeln, in 2 cm
lange Stücke geschnitten,
2 EL geriebene Ingwerwurzel,
1 rote Paprikaschote, in feine
Streifen geschnitten,
¹/₂ TL Salz, 1 TL Zucker,
1 TL Austernsauce (oyster sauce),
2 EL Reiswein,
250 ml Hühnerbrühe,
1 EL Maisstärke

Den Krebs gründlich waschen,
dann in sprudelnd kochendem
Wasser zugedeckt ein bis zwei
Minuten kochen. Herausnehmen, in Stücke schneiden und in
heißem Öl ein bis zwei Minuten
fritieren.
Etwas Öl im Wok erhitzen. Die
Krebsstücke, Frühlingszwiebeln,
Ingwer und Paprika zugeben
und eine Minute unter Wenden
braten. Salz, Zucker, Austernsauce und Reiswein zugeben,
eine Minute weiterbraten. Die
Hühnerbrühe zugießen und mit
der angerührten Stärke binden.

FRIED LOBSTER WITH NOODLES

GEBRATENER HUMMER AUF NUDELN

For 4 persons:

*2 lobsters of about 500 g/1 lb each,
oil for deep-frying*

400 g/13 oz Chinese egg noodles

*1 tbsp butter,
2 spring onions,
cut into fine strips,
2 tbsp finely chopped root ginger,
50 g/1²/₃ oz/¹/₅ cup Thai crab sauce,
100 ml/3¹/₂ fl oz/²/₅ cup fish fumet,
salt, pepper*

Thoroughly wash the lobster. Place in fast boiling salted water, cover, and cook for one minute.
Then remove, cut into coarse pieces, and deep-fry in hot oil for two minutes.
Cook the noodles in salted water. Strain through a sieve, and fry them in a little oil in the wok until they begin to change color.
Melt the butter in the wok, add the pieces of lobster, spring onions and ginger, and fry for five minutes over a medium heat, turning frequently.
Add the crab paste and fish fumet and mix well with the ingredients. Season with salt and pepper.
To serve: On a serving platter, make a bed of fried noodles and top with the lobster and sauce.

Für 4 Personen:

*2 Hummer von ca. 500 g,
Öl zum Fritieren*

400 g chinesische Eiernudeln

*1 EL Butter,
2 Frühlingszwiebeln, in feine
Streifen geschnitten,
2 EL fein gehackte Ingwerwurzel,
50 g thailändische Krebssauce,
100 ml Fischfond,
Salz, Pfeffer*

Hummer gründlich waschen und in sprudelnd kochendem Salzwasser zugedeckt eine Minute kochen. Anschließend herausnehmen, in grobe Stücke teilen und in heißem Öl zwei Minuten fritieren. Nudeln in Salzwasser gar kochen, durch ein Sieb abgießen und im Wok in etwas Öl braten, bis sie anfangen, Farbe anzunehmen. Butter im Wok schmelzen lassen. Hummerstücke, Frühlingszwiebeln und Ingwer zugeben und fünf Minuten unter ständigem Wenden bei mittlerer Hitze braten. Krebssauce und Fischfond zugeben und gut mit den Zutaten vermischen. Mit Salz und Pfeffer abschmecken.
Zum Servieren: Auf eine Servierplatte ein Bett von gebratenen Nudeln anrichten, den Hummer mit der Sauce darübergeben.

The Kowloon Hotel

Cantonese cuisine is regarded as the best in China. Connoisseurs of Chinese culinary variety confirm this. It is fresh and spicy, without fieriness, yet at the same time far from insipid. Leung Chun Wah, chef at the Wan Loong Court Chinese Restaurant of the Kowloon Hotel, was born in Hong Kong. Canton province lies at the gates of Hong Kong (or vice-versa), so it was only natural for Leung Chun Wah to look into the pots and pans here. Since he has learned and worked in renowned restaurants in Peking, Taiwan, Singapore and Hong Kong, and the motto of his life and work is "to learn and work until the last day", it is no wonder that the Wan Loong Court Chinese Restaurant is one of the best for Cantonese cuisine.

The Cantonese love soups above all. And someone who likes clear, strong soups of course abhors mushy sauces. The sauces of Canton are therefore thickened by reduction, and not by creamy or other dubious additives. And the Cantonese love one other thing: dim-sum. These little snacks are a specialty of Cantonese cuisine – no wonder, for these – usually steamed – delicacies have everything that characterizes a clever, light cuisine: fresh, varied ingredients, clear and strong flavors and gentle preparation. Leung Chun Wah would not be Chinese if food were not also a delight to the eye. His twisted, folded, spun and rolled dim sum creations are, visually, small works of art. They taste out of this world: whether of fish, of meat or vegetarian – even after dipping for the nth time into the little round chip baskets they never get boring, not least because he encourages his 26 cooks to be creative. It may be traditional, it should be creative, but in any case it must taste good and look attractive. With this culinary philosophy he has so far made every guest happy.

Die kantonesische Küche gilt als die beste Chinas. Intime Kenner der chinesischen Küchenvielfalt sagen: Es ist die beste. Sie ist frisch und würzig, ohne gnadenlose Schärfe und doch gleichzeitig fern jeder Langeweile. Leung Chun Wah, Chefkoch im Wan Loong Court Chinese Restaurant des Kowloon-Hotels, ist in Hong Kong geboren. Die Provinz Kanton liegt vor den Toren Hong Kongs (oder umgekehrt), und so war es für Leung Chun Wah naheliegend, in die dortigen Töpfe und Pfannen zu schauen. Da er in renommierten Restaurants in Peking, Taiwan, Singapore und Hong Kong gelernt und gearbeitet hat und „to learn and work until the last day" sein Lebens- und Arbeitsmotto ist, verwundert es nicht mehr, daß das Wan Loong Court Chinese Restaurant zu einem der besten in Sachen kantonesischer Küche gehört.

Der Kantonese liebt Suppen über alles. Und wer klare, kräftige Suppen mag, dem sind pampige Saucen logischerweise ein Greuel. Deshalb sind in Kanton die Saucen vom Reduzieren sämig, und nicht von cremigen oder anderen zweifelhaften Zusätzen. Und ein zweites liebt der Kantonese: Dim Sum. Die kleinen Häppchen sind eine Spezialität der kantonesischen Küche – kein Wunder, denn die in der Regel über Dampf gegarten Leckereien haben alles, was eine kluge, leichte Küche auszeichnet: frische, abwechslungsreiche Zutaten, klare und kräftige Aromen nebst einer schonenden Zubereitung. Leung Chun Wah wäre nicht Chinese, würde bei ihm nicht auch das Auge mitessen. Seine gedrehten, gefalteten, gezwirbelten und gerollten Dim-Sum-Kreationen sind schon optisch kleine Kunstwerke. Geschmacklich sind sie umwerfend: ob fischig, fleischig oder vegetarisch – auch beim x-ten Griff in die kleine runde Spanschachtel kommt keine Langeweile auf, und das liegt nicht zuletzt daran, daß er seine 26 Köche zur Kreativität ermuntert. Traditionell kann es sein, kreativ sollte es sein, gut schmecken und schön aussehen muß es sowieso. Mit dieser Küchenphilosophie hat er hier noch jeden Gast glücklich gemacht.

DEEP-FRIED PRAWN ROLLS

FRITIERTE GARNELENRÖLLCHEN

For 4 - 6 persons:

18 prawns, peeled, 12 thin strips of celeriac,
6 thin slices of Chinese Yunnan ham (or raw ham),
6 thin strips of carrot, cut lengthwise, 1 tsp salt,
1/2 tsp sugar, 2 tsp cornstarch, 1 egg, 3 tbsp white bread crumbs,
peanut oil for deep-frying

100 g/3 1/2 oz/2/5 cup Chinese sweet-and-sour sauce (from a jar)
200 g/7 oz broccoli, 200 ml/7 fl oz/4/5 cup chicken broth

Wrap each of six prawns first in a strip of celeriac, then in a slice of ham. The next six prawns first in a slice of celeriac, then in a strip of carrot. Sprinkle with salt, sugar, and cornstarch. Coat in beaten egg and fry until golden. Drain well and keep in a warm place.
Poach the remaining prawns in the sweet-and-sour sauce with a little oil, for two minutes.
Fry the broccoli rosettes in very little oil in the wok. Add the chicken broth, season with salt and sugar, and cook for two minutes.
Using a slotted spoon, remove them from the wok and arrange them in a circle on a pre-warmed serving platter. Place the poached prawns in the middle and surround the broccoli with the deep-fried prawn rolls

Für 4 - 6 Personen:

18 Garnelen, geschält, 12 dünne Streifen Sellerie,
6 dünne Scheiben chinesischer Yunnan Schinken (oder Rohschinken),
6 dünne, längs geschnittene Karottenstreifen,
1 TL Salz, 1/2 TL Zucker, 2 TL Maisstärke, 1 Ei, 3 EL Semmelbrösel,
Erdnußöl zum Fritieren

100 g chinesische süßsaure Sauce (aus dem Glas)
200 g Broccoli, 200 ml Hühnerbrühe

Sechs Garnelen zuerst je in eine Sellerie-, dann in eine Schinkenscheibe wickeln, die nächsten sechs Garnelen zuerst in eine Selleriescheibe, dann in einen Karottenstreifen wickeln. Mit Salz, Zucker und Maisstärke bestreuen, im verquirlten Ei wenden und in Semmelbröseln wälzen. Öl im Wok erhitzen, die Garnelenröllchen goldgelb ausbacken. Gut abtropfen lassen und warmstellen.
Die restlichen Garnelen in der süßsauren Sauce mit etwas Öl zwei Minuten pochieren. Broccoliröschen in wenig Öl im Wok anbraten. Hühnerbrühe zugießen, mit Salz und Zucker würzen und zwei Minuten kochen lassen. Mit einer Lochkelle aus dem Wok nehmen und kreisförmig auf eine vorgewärmte Servierplatte arrangieren. Die pochierten Garnelen in die Mitte geben, mit den fritierten Garnelenröllchen den Broccoli umlegen.

FRIED SEAFOOD

ON CHILI SAUCE

IN A TARO BASKET

MEERESFRÜCHTE

AN CHILISAUCE

IM TAROKÖRBCHEN

For 4 persons:

1 taro tuber of about 300 g/10 oz
(or sweet potato as a substitute)
for the basket,
peanut oil for deep-frying

For the X.O. chili sauce:
50 g/1²/₃ oz dried conpoi and shrimps,
2 red chili peppers, dried,
50 g/1²/₃ oz Yunnan ham
(raw ham),
1 tbsp oil, 2 tbsp rice vinegar,
200 ml/7 fl oz/⁴/₅ cup chicken broth,
¹/₂ tsp monosodium glutamate,
¹/₂ tsp salt, ¹/₂ tsp sugar

200 g/7 oz broccoli stems,
cut into 3-cm/1¹/₅-in pieces
(Chinese broccoli consists practically
entirely of stems; green asparagus
may be used as a substitute),
300 ml/10 fl oz/1¹/₄ cups chicken broth,
1 tsp finely chopped root ginger,
2 tbsp rice wine, ¹/₂ tsp salt, ¹/₂ tsp sugar

300 g/10 oz mixed seafood,
without shells
(e.g. scallops, hard clams, crab meat),
1 tbsp corn oil,
¹/₂ garlic clove, finely chopped,
¹/₂ shallot, finely sliced

Für 4 Personen:

1 Taro-Knolle von ca. 300 g
(ersatzweise Süßkartoffel)
für das Körbchen,
Erdnußöl zum Fritieren

Für die X.O. Chilisauce:
50 g getrocknete Conpoi und Shrimps,
2 rote Chilischoten, getrocknet,
50 g Yunnan Schinken
(Rohschinken),
1 EL Öl, 2 EL Reisessig
200 ml Hühnerbrühe
¹/₂ TL Glutamat
¹/₂ TL Salz, ¹/₂ TL Zucker

200 g Broccolistengel,
in 3 cm lange Stücke geschnitten
(chinesischer Broccoli besteht
praktisch nur aus Stengeln,
ersatzweise eignet sich grüner Spargel),
300 ml Hühnerbrühe,
1 TL feingeschnittene Ingwerwurzel,
2 EL Reiswein, ¹/₂ TL Salz, ¹/₂ TL Zucker

300 g gemischte Meeresfrüchte,
ohne Schalen (z. B. Jakobsmuscheln,
Venusmuscheln, Krebsfleisch),
1 EL Maiskeimöl,
¹/₂ Knoblauchzehe, fein gehackt,
¹/₂ Schalotte, fein geschitten

Peel the taro tuber, cut it into long thin strips and cook these half through in salted water, then drain. Weave a basket from the strips and deep-fry in hot oil until golden.
For the X.O. sauce: Finely slice the conpoi, shrimps, chilis, and ham and lightly fry in the oil. Add the remaining ingredients and simmer for ten minutes.
On a low heat, cook the broccoli, together with the chicken broth, ginger, rice wine, salt and sugar in the wok until barely done.
Cut the seafood into slices and poach for two minutes in boiling salted water. Drain in a sieve.
In the wok, heat the oil, garlic, shallot and two teaspoon of the X.O. chili sauce.
Add the seafood and fry over a strong heat for half a minute.
To serve: Lay the broccoli in the basket and cover with the seafood.
Serve the remaining chili sauce as a separate accompaniment.

Taro-Knolle schälen, in lange dünne Streifen schneiden und diese in Salzwasser halbgar kochen, abgießen. Aus den Streifen ein Körbchen flechten und dieses in heißem Öl goldbraun fritieren.
Für die X.O. Sauce: Conpoi, Shrimps, Chilischoten und Schinken fein schneiden, dann im Öl anbraten. Die restlichen Zutaten beigeben und zehn Minuten köcheln lassen.
Broccoli mit der Hühnerbrühe, Ingwer, Reiswein, Salz und Zucker im Wok fünf Minuten bei kleiner Hitze knapp gar kochen. Meeresfrüchte in Scheiben schneiden und zwei Minuten in siedendem Salzwasser pochieren. Im Sieb abtropfen lassen.
Im Wok das Öl, Knoblauch, Schalotte und zwei Teelöffel von der X.O. Chilisauce erhitzen. Die Meeresfrüchte zugeben und bei starker Hitze eine halbe Minute braten.
Zum Servieren: Den Broccoli und darüber die Meeresfrüchte in das Körbchen füllen. Restliche Chilisauce separat dazu auftragen.

For 4 persons:

*400 ml/13 fl oz/1²/₃ cups coconut milk
from a can, 200 g/6¹/₂ oz/⁴/₅ cup milk,
1 egg, 150 g/5 oz/³/₅ cup soft butter,
100 g/3¹/₂ oz/²/₅ cup sugar*

*150 g/5 oz/³/₅ cup rice flour,
sticky variety (not starch),
40 g/1¹/₃ oz/¹/₆ cup custard powder
(unsweetened),
50 g/1²/₃ oz/¹/₅ cup sugar*

In the blender, mix half of the coconut milk with the milk, the egg, the butter and the sugar. Pour into a metal mixing bowl and heat in a bain-marie, stirring constantly until the mixture thickens. Blend the rice flour with the custard powder, the sugar and the remaining coconut milk and knead to form a dough. Line oval molds with the dough, leaving enough overlap to seal; fill with the egg cream, then seal the dough to cover. Cook over steam for about ten minutes in a steamer insert or Chinese wood-chip basket.
To serve: Turn out the molds and decorate as desired.

STEAMED DOUGHBALLS WITH COCONUT-EGG CREAM

GEDÄMPFTE TEIGBÄLLCHEN MIT KOKOSNUSS-EIERCREME

Für 4 Personen:

*400 ml Kokosmilch aus der Dose,
200 g Milch, 1 Ei,
150 g weiche Butter, 100 g Zucker*

*150 g Reismehl, klebrige Sorte
(keine Stärke),
40 g Puddingpulver (ungesüßt),
50 g Zucker*

Im Mixer die Hälfte der Kokomilch mit der Milch, dem Ei, der Butter und dem Zucker verrühren. In eine Rührschüssel aus Metall umfüllen und im Wasserbad unter ständigem Rühren erhitzen, bis die Masse fest wird. Das Reismehl mit dem Puddingpulver, dem Zucker und der restlichen Kokosmilch verarbeiten und zu einem Teig verkneten. Ovale Förmchen mit dem Teig auslegen, mit der Eiercreme füllen und oben den Teig wieder verschließen. In einem Sieb-einsatz oder chinesischen Bastkörbchen über Dampf ungefähr zehn Minuten garen. Zum Servieren: Teigbällchen aus den Förmchen stürzen und nach Be-lieben dekorieren.

STEAMED DUMPLINGS WITH SCALLOPS

TEIGTASCHEN MIT JAKOBSMUSCHELN

For 4 persons:

150 g/5 oz scallops, shucked,
1 black Chinese mushroom
(mu-err), steeped,
1 tbsp coriander leaves,
¹/₂ tsp salt,
1 tsp sugar

120 g/4 oz/¹/₂ cup flour,
40 g/1¹/₃ oz/¹/₆ cup custard
powder (unsweetened),
160 ml/5¹/₃ fl oz/²/₃ cup water

Für 4 Personen:

150 g Jakobsmuscheln, ausgelöst,
1 schwarzer chinesischer Pilz
(Mu-err), eingeweicht,
1 EL Korianderblättchen,
¹/₂ TL Salz,
1 TL Zucker

120 g Mehl,
40 g Puddingpulver
(ungesüßt),
160 ml Wasser

Slice the scallops thinly and mix with the finely chopped mushroom, coriander leaves, salt and sugar, and allow to stand in the refrigerator for half an hour.
For the dough: Sift the flour into a bowl, add the custard powder, then gradually work in the hot water. Knead the mixture well for five minutes.
Roll out the dough as thinly as possible, cut into pieces, coat with the filling, and form into elongated rolls.
Steam for about ten minutes in a steamer insert or Chinese wood-chip basket.

Jakobsmuscheln in dünne Scheiben schneiden und mit dem feingeschnittenen Pilz, Korianderblättchen, Salz und Zucker vermengen und im Kühlschrank eine halbe Stunde ziehen lassen. Für den Teig: Mehl in eine Schüssel sieben, Puddingpulver beifügen, dann nach und nach das heiße Wasser einarbeiten, fünf Minuten gut kneten. Den Teig so dünn wie möglich ausrollen, in Stücke schneiden, mit der Füllung belegen und zu Rollen formen. In einem Siebeinsatz oder chinesischen Bastkörbchen über Dampf ca. zehn Minuten garen.

STEAMED DUMPLINGS WITH SQUID

TEIGTASCHEN IM DAMPF MIT TINTENFISCH

For 4 persons:

150 g/5 oz squid meat,
finely chopped,
20 g/²/₃ oz scallop coral,
¹/₂ tsp salt,
1 tsp sugar,
1 tsp sesame oil

80 g/2²/₃ oz/¹/₃ cup flour,
80 g/2²/₃ oz/¹/₃ cup cornstarch,
130 ml/4¹/₃ fl oz/¹/₂ cup water,
pinch of salt

Für 4 Personen:

150 g Tintenfischfleisch,
fein gehackt,
20 g Corail von der
Jakobsmuschel,
¹/₂ TL Salz, 1 TL Zucker,
1 TL Sesamöl

80 g Mehl,
80 g Maisstärke,
130 ml Wasser,
1 Prise Salz

Finely purée the squid, coral, salt, sugar, and sesame oil in the blender.
For the dough: Sift the flour and starch into a bowl. Bring the water to the boil with a pinch of salt and pour into the bowl. Immediately work with the flour, to form a stiff dough, cover with a damp cloth and allow to stand for 30 minutes. Knead again until the dough is smooth and elastic. Roll out as thinly as possible, cut out squares, about 20 x 20 cm/ 8 x 8 in, and coat with the filling.
Fold and seal into square parcels, and steam these for ten minutes in a steamer insert or Chinese wood-chip basket.

Tintenfisch, Corail, Salz, Zucker und Sesamöl im Mixer fein pürieren.
Für den Teig: Mehl und Stärke in eine Schüssel sieben. Wasser mit einer Prise Salz zum Kochen bringen und in die Schüssel gießen. Sofort mit dem Mehl zu einem festen Teig verarbeiten und mit einem feuchten Tuch bedeckt dreißig Minuten ruhen lassen. Erneut kneten, bis der Teig glatt und elastisch ist. So dünn wie möglich ausrollen, Quadrate von ca. 20 x 20 cm ausschneiden und mit der Füllung bestreichen. Zu quadratischen Päckchen verschließen und diese in einem Siebeinsatz oder chinesischen Bastkörbchen über Dampf 10 Minuten garen.

DUMPLINGS WITH PRAWNS AND LIME
TEIGTASCHEN MIT GARNELEN UND LIMONE

For 4 persons:

*150 g/5 oz prawns, peeled, ¹/₂ lime,
100 ml/3 ¹/₂ fl oz/²/₅ cup water,
¹/₂ tsp monosodium glutamate,
1 tsp salt, 1 tsp sugar,
150 g/5 oz spinach, 30 g/1 oz
broccoli, 100 g/3¹/₂ oz/²/₅ cup flour,
100 g/3¹/₂ oz/²/₅ cup cornstarch*

For the filling: Finely chop the prawns. Thinly peel the lime, finely dice the peel, and finely cut the lime flesh. Bring the water to the boil with the lime flesh and sugar, and boil down to a teaspoonful. Mix with the chopped prawns, the strips of lime peel, the glutamate, and the salt. Boil the spinach and broccoli in salted water for one minute. Save and measure out 160 ml/ 5¹/₃ fl oz/²/₃ cup from the cooking broth. Bring to the boil again. Sift the flour and starch into a bowl. Pour over the hot green cooking water, and immediately work into a stiff dough. Cover with a damp cloth and allow to stand for 30 minutes. Knead again until the dough is smooth and elastic. Roll out as thinly as possible, cut out oblongs of about 15 x 20 cm/ 6 x 8 in, and coat with the filling. Form envelopes in a mange-tout shape, and steam these for five to ten minutes in a steamer insert or a Chinese wood-chip basket.

Für 4 Personen:

*150 g Garnelen, geschält,
¹/₂ Limone, 100 ml Wasser,
¹/₂ TL Glutamat, 1 TL Salz,
1 TL Zucker,
150 g Spinat, 30 g Broccoli,
100 g Mehl,
100 g Maisstärke*

Für die Füllung: Garnelen fein hacken. Limone dünn abschälen, Schale fein würfeln, Limonenfleisch fein schneiden. Wasser mit dem Limonenfleisch und Zucker zum Kochen bringen und bis auf einen Eßlöffel einkochen lassen. Mit Garnelen, Limonenschalenstreifen, Glutamat und Salz vermischen.
Spinat und Broccoli eine Minute in Salzwasser kochen. Vom Kochsud 160 ml abmessen. Mehl und Stärke in eine Schüssel sieben. Den heißen grünen Kochsud dazugießen und sofort zu einem festen Teig verarbeiten. Mit einem feuchten Tuch bedeckt dreißig Minuten ruhen lassen. Erneut kneten, bis der Teig glatt und elastisch ist. So dünn wie möglich ausrollen, Rechtecke von ca. 15 x 20 cm ausschneiden und mit der Füllung belegen. Zuckerschotenförmige Taschen formen und diese in einem Siebeinsatz oder chinesischen Bastkörbchen über Dampf fünf bis zehn Minuten garen.

ICED MANGO DESSERT

GEEISTER MANGO PUDDING

Für 4 - 6 Personen:

4 reife Mango,
300 ml Sahne,
150 ml Milch,
35 g Gelatine,
300 g Zucker,
600 ml Wasser

Das Fruchtfleisch von zwei Mangos mit der Sahne und der Milch im Mixer pürieren. Die übrigen Mangos in feine Würfel schneiden.
Gelatine einweichen und mit dem Zucker in 600 ml heissem (nicht kochendem) Wasser auflösen, abkühlen lassen. Alle Komponenten gut verrühren und in Dessertschalen füllen. Im Eisfach leicht gefrieren lassen.

For 4 - 6 persons:

4 ripe mangoes,
300 ml/10 fl oz/1 1/4 cups cream,
150 ml/5 fl oz/3/5 cup milk,
35 g/1 oz gelatin,
300 g/10 oz/1 1/4 cups sugar,
600 ml/20 fl oz/2 1/2 cups water

Purée the flesh of two mangoes together with the cream and the milk in the blender.
Slice the other mangoes into fine cubes.
Dissolve the softened gelatin and sugar in 600 ml/20 fl oz/ 2 1/2 cups hot (but not boiling) water, and allow to cool. Mix all ingredients together and pour into dessert bowls. Lightly freeze in the freezing compartment.

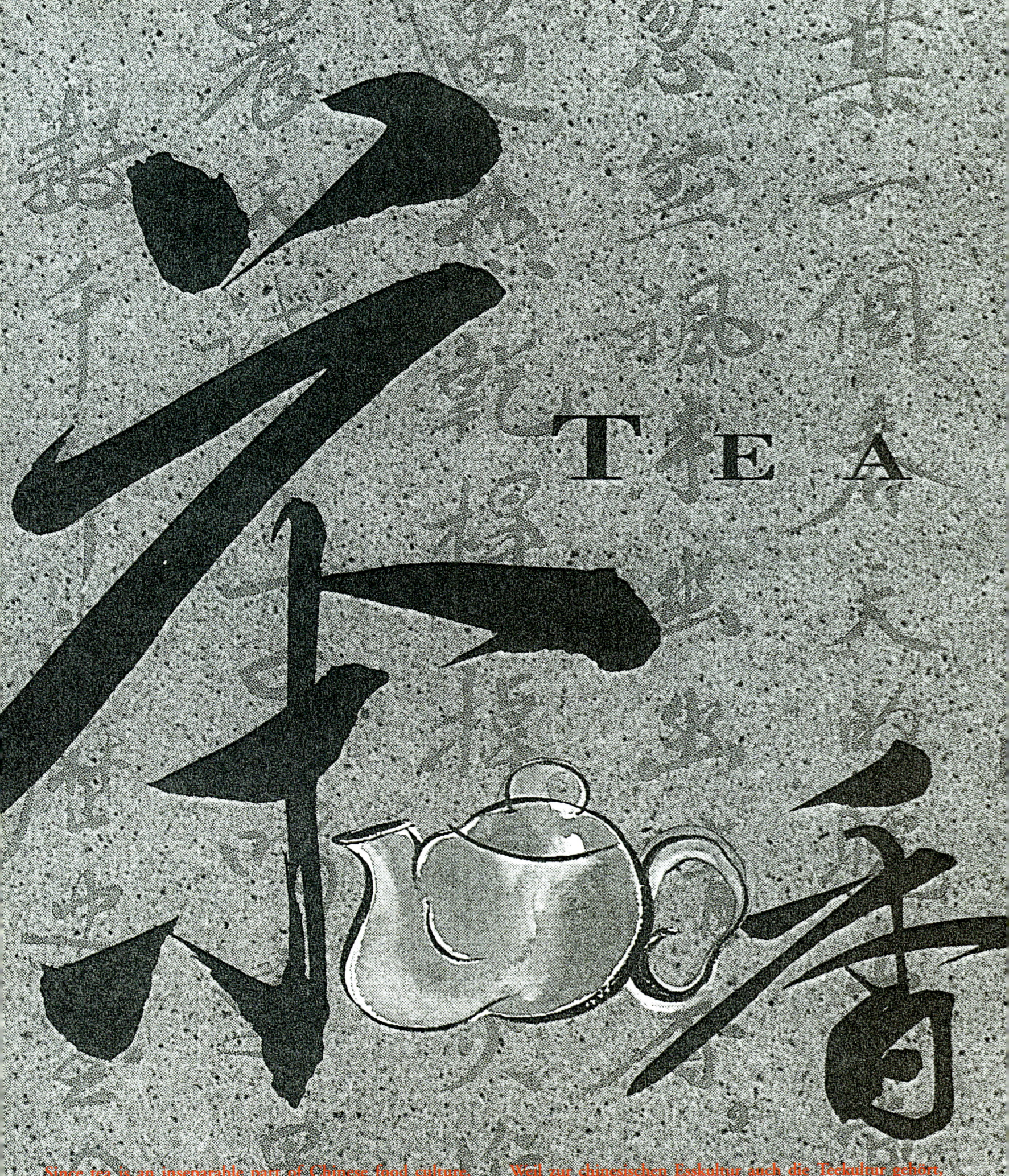

T E A

THE STORY OF TEA

Legend has it that tea - the 'sweet dew' - was first
enjoyed in China in the third millennium B.C..
"One evening in spring, Emperor Shen Nung was relaxing
under a camellia tree, by a fire place,
when leaves dried up due to the heat and drifted down
into the pot of water boiling in front of him.
Intrigued by the delicate aroma, the Emperor took a sip,
the flavour was astringent, clean, refreshing....."
This art of tea-drinking, a centuries-old yet popular
custom in China, is now revived at The Kowloon Hotel.
Premium Chinese tea leaves selections are specially
introduced by the Wan Loong Court, wishing to share
with guests this local culinary experience.

「茶」之典故

傳說中「茶」早源於公元前三千年的中國⋯⋯
⋯⋯「某一個春天的晚上,當神農氏正於茶花樹下生火
休息時,忽然飄來陣陣幽香,仰頭一望,原來是茶樹
葉子遇熱乾旱,掉進火堆上燙熱的水瓶內而飄來的。
神農氏試了一口,味道果然清甜,甘香⋯⋯」
數千年的歷史至今,茗茶風尚已遍全球,
要瞭解及領略箇中文化及學問確不簡單,
而傳統茗茶藝術更極盡細緻優雅。
九龍酒店環龍閣現特設一系列中國特級香茗,
誠與嘉賓共分享。

AGE UNKNOWN LIU AN

"Age Unknown Liu An" is a kind of Black Tea grown in
the mountain area of Hwo Shan. Similar to Pu Er ,
it is blackish coral red. Aromatic beta flavour and
smooth, helps to dissolve the excess oil in food.

「不知年舊六安」屬後發酵茶,產於霍山的一種黑茶,
其特性與普洱相似,越陳越佳,茶湯深紫紅色,
帶檳榔香氣,性溫和,去膩有幫助消化之功用。

WHITE PEONY

This precious tea is a kind of White Tea
from Fujian. The tea is golden yellow colour,
fragrant and fresh in taste.

白牡丹屬輕發酵茶,產於福建的一種名貴白茶,
茶湯黃亮明靜,湯味鮮醇,毫香明顯,有退熱驅暑之功。

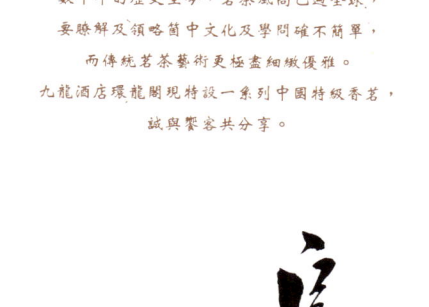

TAIWAN DONGDING OOLONG

"Taiwan Dongding Oolong" is a Dark Green Tea from
Dongding mountain in Taiwan. The tea is golden in
colour, with a full fragrance and riped fruit flavour.

「凍頂烏龍」屬半發酵茶,產於台灣凍頂山的一種青茶,
茶湯色金黃明亮,茶湯溢味濃厚,有熟果香味。

NANYAN SUPREME "TI GUAN YIN"

This premier "Ti Guan Yin" is a Dark Green Tea
from its original location in Nan Yan. Leaves are heavy
and in pale green, tea is golden yellow with fruity,
floral fragrance and fresh full liquorice taste.

鐵觀音屬半發酵茶,產於福建省安溪縣的一種青茶
(烏龍茶類),茶湯金黃,入口回甘帶蘭花味,
醇厚甜鮮,香氣馥郁。

HANGZHOU PRE-CHING MING "LONG JIN"

Supreme quality "Long Jin" is picked 3 days
before Ching Ming. The tea is translucent pale green
with a taste of fresh liquorice and little green peas.

「杭州龍井」屬無發酵茶,在綠茶中最負盛名,
極品乃清明前三天所採者,茶湯翠綠明亮,
湯味甘醇鮮爽,香氣鮮嫩馥郁,清新悅鼻。

WUYI SHU XIAN

"Wuyi Shu Xian" is the highest quality tea among
Wuyi Tea family. Refreshing, light,
smooth with strong fragrance.

「武夷翠數水仙」屬半發酵茶,產於閩北崇安縣武夷山岩
的一種青茶,茶湯清澈橙黃,香氣濃郁,
具蘭花清香,滋味醇厚回甘。

GINSENG TI GUAN YIN

"Ginseng Ti Guan Yin" is a mixture of Supreme Ginseng
& Nan Yan Ti Guan Yin. It has a strong aroma of fresh
ginseng and floral fragrance of the Ti Guan Yin,
and contains high nutritional value.

「觀音參茶」乃精選優質人參及南岩鐵觀音茶而成的。
茶湯有鐵觀音的甘香及人參甘甜味,
品嘗者莱得參與茶的營養成份和保健療效。

AGE UNKNOWN PU ER

"Pu Er" is a Black Tea from Yunan and
becomes smooth after preserving. The tea is red coral
colour with smoked pine fragrance, mellow smooth,
full and famed for its medicinal value.

「不知年舊普洱」,產於雲南著名的一種黑茶,
保存愈久茶愈醇,茶湯橙黃帶紅,
茶性溫和並且有健身療效,能止渴解酒消肥膩。

ZHEJIANG JASMINE TEA

Leaves of "Zhejiang Jasmine Tea" are fresh green with
white sprouts, tight and delicate. Tea is in orange with
fresh floral and aromatic smooth taste.

「茉莉毛峰」屬無發酵茶,採用浙江省特種毛峰綠茶混合上等
茉莉花焙製而成,茶湯橙黃色,味醇濃鮮爽。

PRE-CHING MING "BI LOU CHUN"

"Bi Lou Chun" is grown in eastern & western mountains
of Tong Tiang Lake and the best are picked before
Ching Ming. The tea has a particularly strong
aromatic fragrance.

「碧螺春」屬無發酵茶,產於江蘇洞庭山的一種
著名綠茶,以春分至清明前採製的品質最佳,
茶湯碧綠清澈;湯味幽香鮮雅,茶芳味醇回甘鮮爽。

One story higher than the Wan Loong Court restaurant the cooking is done by Alex Brand, who risks a balancing act between Italian and Chinese cooking. This sometimes sounds rather adventurous, but does in fact taste astonishingly good. For example, his pizza may not be covered with Parma ham, but with finely sliced breast of Peking duck, and not sprinkled with cheese but with a fine sweet-and-sour plum sauce. Or his risotto may be intermixed with pieces of mango and pineapple and slices of lotus root. And lemon grass with spaghetti frutti di mare obviously also does no harm, as one can see for oneself.

Ein Stockwerk über dem Wan Loong Court Restaurant kocht Alex Brand, und er wagt den Spagat zwischen italienischer und chinesischer Küche. Das klingt ab und zu zwar abenteuerlich, schmeckt dann aber doch erstaunlich lecker. Etwa dann, wenn er eine Pizza nicht mit Parma-Schinken belegt, sondern mit der fein aufgeschnittenen Brust einer Peking-Ente und obendrauf kein Käse kommt, sondern eine feine süß-saure Pflaumensauce oder wenn er unter den Risotto Mango- und Ananas-Stückchen nebst Scheibchen von der Lotos-Wurzel mischt. Und Zitronengras an Spaghetti frutti di mare schadet, wie man hier unschwer feststellen kann, offensichtlich auch nicht.

For 4 persons:

600 g/20 oz pizza dough (Italian bread dough),
80 g/2²/₃ oz/¹/₃ cup pesto (from a jar)

400 g/13 oz broiled breast of duck, sliced,
80 g/2²/₃ oz/¹/₃ cup Chinese plum sauce,
(from a jar), 1 mango, peeled and sliced,
¹/₂ spring onion, cut into fine strips

Preheat the oven to 250° C/485° F. Roll out the dough on a floured surface to about 5 mm/ ¹/₅ in thickness and line a baking mold with it. Coat the dough base with pesto and bake the pizza until the edges are golden and the base is crispy.
Coat the slices of duck with the plum sauce and arrange them in a fan-like pattern on the pizza. Lay the slices of mango on top and bake for a further three to five minutes.
Before serving, sprinkle with the strips of spring onion.

Für 4 Personen:

600 g Pizzateig (italienischer Brotteig),
80 g Pestosauce (aus dem Glas)

400 gegrillte Entenbrust, in Scheiben geschnitten,
80 g chinesische Pflaumensauce (aus dem Glas),
1 Mango, geschält und in Scheiben geschnitten,
¹/₂ Frühlingszwiebel, in feine Streifen geschnitten

Backofen auf 250° C vorheizen. Den Teig auf bemehlter Oberfläche ca. 5 mm dick auswallen und eine Backform damit auslegen. Den Teigboden mit Pestosauce bestreichen und die Pizza backen, bis die Ränder goldbraun und der Boden knusprig sind. Die Entenscheiben mit der Pflaumensauce bestreichen und die Pizza fächerartig damit belegen. Mangoscheiben darüberlegen und die Pizza weitere drei bis fünf Minuten backen.
Vor dem Servieren mit Frühlingszwiebelstreifen bestreuen.

Pierre C. H. Tang

Hunan Garden Restaurant

At the latest after studying the menu it becomes clear without any doubt what you are letting yourself in for here: glowing red chili peppers, in some dishes one, in others even two, indicate like threatening exclamation marks that you have entered a restaurant where the cuisine of the Chinese province Hunan is served. Scarcely anywhere else in China is the food so highly seasoned.
Among the classical Chinese regional cuisines, such as Shanghai, Canton and Peking it is without compare. And since the Hunan Garden is regarded as the only really authentic Hunan restaurant in Hong Kong, the fiery seasoning is original here too. This means for the European palate: dishes without the chili pepper warning-signal bring beads of sweat to the brow. Those with one chili pepper practically paralyse our taste nerves. With two chili peppers only the fire extinguisher can help.

Senior chef Pierre C.H. Tang puts his finger on it: "Hunan cooking is like fire." And his chef Lai Wai Keung rejoices that he only ever uses original chili peppers directly imported from Hunan, which are simply more fiery than the ones that grow here.

Together with Szechuan, Hunan belongs to China's western region, without a coastline and cut off from the rest of the country by high mountains. Chicken, pork, ham, bacon and beans dominate the range of comestibles of this region. If there are fish, then only those from the rivers Han and Yangtze. Beef and veal are seldom: cattle are working animals and not meat providers.

Why such hot spicing? Tang explains it in terms of the climate. Summers in Hunan are hot, the winters relatively mild. All over the world in the hotter regions, food is more highly spiced. Garlic, onions, ginger, and of course the famous red chilis are consumed in masses. This is healthy and stimulates the circulation. Tang, a charming elderly gentleman, beams and philosophizes over the link between European and Chinese cooking, which have in common a widespread use of pork, and encourages us to sample his extra-hot pork.
And hands us a cup of green tea to quench the flames.

Spätestens beim Studium der Speisekarte wird einem unmißverständlich klar gemacht, auf was man sich hier eingelassen hat: leuchtend rote Pfefferschoten – bei manchen Gerichten eine – bei anderen gar deren zwei, weisen wie drohende Ausrufungszeichen darauf hin, daß man ein Restaurant betreten hat, in dem die Küche aus der chinesischen Provinz Hunan gepflegt wird. Schärfer als dort wird in China sonst kaum irgendwo gekocht. Unter den klassischen chinesischen Küchenregionen wie Shanghai, Kanton und Peking ist sie ohne Vergleich. Und weil das Hunan Garden als das einzige wirklich authentische Hunan-Restaurant in Hong Kong gilt, ist hier auch die Schärfe original. Das bedeutet für europäische Gaumen: Gerichte ohne Pfefferschoten-Warnsignal treiben den Schweiß auf die Stirn. Solche mit einer Pfefferschote legen unsere Geschmacksnerven weitgehend lahm. Bei zwei Pfefferschoten hilft nur noch der Feuerlöscher.

Senior-Chef Pierre C. H. Tang bringt es auf den Punkt: „Hunan-Küche ist wie Feuer." Und sein Chefkoch Lai Wai Keung frohlockt, daß er immer nur die direkt aus Hunan importierten Original-Pfefferschoten verwendet, die einfach rassiger sind als die, die hier wachsen.

Hunan gehört zusammen mit Szechuan zur westlichen Region Chinas; ohne Küste und vom restlichen Land durch hohe Berge abgeschnitten. Huhn, Schwein, Schinken, Speck und Bohnen dominieren das Lebens- mittelangebot dieser Region. Wenn es Fische gibt, dann nur solche aus den Flüssen Han und Yangtze. Rind- und Kalbfleisch gibt es kaum: die Kühe sind hier Arbeitstiere und keine Fleischlieferanten.

Warum man hier so scharf ißt? Tang erklärt es mit dem Klima. Die Sommer in Hunan sind heiß, die Winter relativ mild. Überall auf der Welt wird in den heißeren Regionen auch schärfer gegessen. Knoblauch, Zwiebeln, Ingwer und eben die berühmten red chillies werden bergeweise verarbeitet. Das ist gesund und regt den Kreislauf an. Tang, der liebenswürdige ältere Herr, strahlt, philosophiert über die Verbundenheit der europäischen und der chinesischen Küche wegen der gemeinsamen weitverbreiteten Verwendung von Schweinefleisch, ermuntert uns, von seinem extrascharfen Schweinefleisch zu kosten. Und reicht als Feuerlöscher eine Tasse vom grünen Tee.

BRAISED BRISKET OF BEEF

For 4 persons:

600 g/20 oz brisket of beef,
2 tbsp oil, 2 slices of root ginger,
1 tsp soy-bean paste, 2 star anise,
1 small stick of cinnamon,
3 garlic cloves, 2 tbsp chili oil,
3 tbsp dark soy sauce, 1 tsp sugar

3 tsp cornstarch,
1.2 liters/2 pints 2 fl oz/5 cups chicken broth,
1 kg/2 lb 3 oz white cabbage

Slice the meat. Heat the oil in a wok and fry the slices of ginger. Add the soy-bean paste and season with star anise, cinnamon, finely chopped garlic, chili oil and soy sauce. Stir the starch into the chicken broth and blend in. Boil the sauce for a few minutes, stirring constantly. Season and pass through a sieve.
Cut up the white cabbage finely. Heat a little oil in the wok and fry the cabbage over a medium heat, stirring. Place it in a pot (preferably earthenware). Lay the beef in layers on top and pour the sauce over it.
Cover the pot with a lid and cook everything over a low heat for three to four hours.

GESCHMORTE RINDERBRUST

Für 4 Personen:

600 g Rinderbrust,
2 EL Öl, 2 Scheiben Ingwerwurzel,
1 TL Sojabohnenpaste, 2 Sternanis,
1 kleines Stück Zimtstange,
3 Knoblauchzehen, 2 EL Chiliöl,
3 EL dunkle Sojasauce, 1 TL Zucker

3 TL Stärkemehl,
1,2 Liter Hühnerbrühe,
1 kg Weißkohl

Fleisch in Scheiben schneiden. Öl in einem Wok heiß werden lassen und Ingwerscheiben darin anbraten. Sojabohnenpaste zugeben und mit Sternanis, Zimt, feingeschnittenem Knoblauch, Chiliöl, Sojasauce und Zucker würzen. Die Stärke mit der Hühnerbrühe anrühren und unterrühren. Die Sauce unter Rühren einige Minuten kochen lassen, abschmecken und dann durch ein Sieb passieren.
Weißkohl feinschneiden. Etwas Öl im Wok heißwerden lassen und den Kohl unter Wenden bei mittlerer Hitze darin anbraten. In einen Topf (möglichst aus Steingut) geben, Fleischscheiben darüberschichten und mit der Sauce begießen. Zugedeckt bei kleiner Hitze drei bis vier Stunden garen.

CHICKEN AND CASHEW NUTS IN SOY SAUCE

For 4 persons:

600 g/20 oz breast of chicken,
cut into strips,
100 g/3¹/₂ oz/¹/₂ cup cashew nuts, peanut
oil, 1 tbsp soy-bean paste, 1 tbsp chili oil,
1 tbsp Chinese white wine, salt

Fry the chicken and cashew kernels in hot oil. Add the soy-bean paste, chili oil and white wine and continue to fry, stirring, until everything is well mixed. Season with salt.

HÜHNERFLEISCH UND CASHEWNÜSSE IN SOJASAUCE

Für 4 Personen:

600 g Hühnerbrust,
in Streifen geschnitten,
100 g Cashewnüße, Erdnußöl,
1 EL Sojabohnenpaste, 1 EL Chiliöl,
1 EL chinesischer Weißwein, Salz

Hühnerfleisch und Cashewkerne in heißem Öl anbraten. Sojabohnenpaste, Chiliöl und Weißwein beigeben und unter Rühren weiterbraten, bis sich alles gut vermischt hat. Mit Salz abschmecken.

FRIED GREEN BEANS

For 4 persons:

800 g/1³/₄ lb green beans, 2 tbsp peanut
oil, 200 ml/7 fl oz/⁴/₅ cup chicken broth,
1 garlic clove, finely chopped,
1 tsp dried, pulverized chili
(as desired),
2 tbsp plucked coriander leaves,
light soy sauce

Blanch the beans in salted water. Drain and fry in the wok in hot oil over a medium heat. Add the chicken broth and cook, stirring, until almost all the broth has evaporated. Add the garlic, chili and coriander, and braise. Season with soy sauce.

GEBRATENE GRÜNE BOHNEN

Für 4 Personen:

800 g grüne Bohnen, 2 EL Erdnußöl,
200 ml Hühnerbrühe,
1 Knoblauchzehe, feingehackt,
1 TL getrocknete, zerriebene Chili,
(nach Geschmack),
2 EL gezupfte Korianderblättchen,
helle Sojasauce

Bohnen in Salzwasser blanchieren. Abgießen und im Wok im heißen Öl bei mittlerer Hitze braten. Hühnerbrühe zugeben und unter Rühren kochen, bis fast alle Brühe verdampft ist. Knoblauch, Chili und Koriander zugeben und mitdünsten. Mit Sojasauce abschmecken.

FRIED PRAWNS WITH CHILI

For 4 persons:

500 g/1 lb 2 oz peeled prawns, peanut oil
As desired, dried red chili
and/or bell peppers,
2 cloves garlic, pressed,
2 spring onions, finely chopped,
2 tbsp chili sauce,
1 tsp hot bean paste,
1 tbsp white Chinese vinegar,
100 ml/3 1/2 fl oz/2/5 cup chicken broth,
1 tsp cornstarch,
soy sauce

Briefly fry the prawns in the hot oil. Remove with the skimming ladle and set aside. Pour away the oil and again heat one tablespoon of oil. Fry the dried chilis or bell peppers. Add the garlic, spring onions, chili sauce and bean paste and fry. Quench with vinegar and chicken broth and boil briefly. Stir the cornstarch into a little water and use to bind the sauce. Season with soy sauce. Add the prawns and cook over a medium heat for one minute.

GEBRATENE GARNELEN MIT CHILI

Für 4 Personen:

500 g geschälte Garnelen, Erdnußöl,
Nach Belieben: getrocknete rote
Chili- und/oder Paprikaschoten,
2 Knoblauchzehen, durchgedrückt,
2 Frühlingszwiebeln,
feingeschnitten,
2 EL Chilisauce,
1 TL scharfe Bohnenpaste,
1 EL weißer chinesischer Essig,
100 ml Hühnerbrühe,
1 TL Maisstärke,
Sojasauce

Garnelen im heißen Öl kurz anbraten, mit der Schaumkelle entnehmen und beiseite stellen. Öl weggießen und einen Eßlöffel Öl erneut erhitzen. Getrocknete Chili- oder Paprikaschoten anbraten. Knoblauch, Frühlingszwiebeln, Chilisauce und scharfe Bohnenpaste zugeben und mitbraten.
Mit Essig und Hühnerbrühe ablöschen und kurz kochen lassen. Maisstärke anrühren und die Sauce damit binden. Mit Sojasauce abschmecken. Garnelen zugeben und bei mittlerer Hitze eine Minute kochen.

蝦、帶子 海老、貝柱
PRAWN & SCALLOP

🌶️🌶️ **左宗棠明蝦**
揚げ車海老の唐辛子ソースかけ
Fried Prawns with Chilli ..... HK$ 168

生煎蝦排
焼車海老のにんにくソース合え（3尾)
Fried Prawns in Shell with Garlic Sauce (3 pieces) 172

蒜苗蝦仁
芝海老のにんにく苗炒め
Sauteed Shrimps with Garlic Stem 172

🌶️ **宮爆明蝦**
揚げ車海老の唐辛子ソースかけ
Fried Prawns with Chilli Sauce 172

香糟鳳尾蝦
車海老の酒粕入りあんかけ
Prawns in Rice Wine Sauce with Vegetables 172

🌶️ **貴妃鮮貝**
貝柱と唐辛子の炒めもの
Sauteed Scallops with Pepper 172

豆酥鮮貝
貝柱の大豆ソース炒め
Scallops with Fried Minced Bean 172

🌶️ **酸辣鮮貝**
炒め貝柱の辛い酸味ソースかけ
Sauteed Scallops with Hot & Sour Sauce 172

翡翠鮮貝
貝柱と野菜の炒めもの
Sauteed Scallops with Vegetables 172

湖南佳餚
湖南割烹料理
Hunan Cuisine

🌶️ 微辣 Moderate Hot からい
🌶️🌶️ 辣 Hot とてもからい

Shanghai is China's largest city, and its harbor the busiest in the whole country. This is where the mighty Yangtze ends in a valley of vast width. This is an incredibly fertile plain that is the fruit and vegetable garden of the country. It is no wonder then that Shanghai cuisine has such an excellent reputation among vegetarians. Chinese wok cooking with its short frying times is definitely the most ideal way of preparing vegetables. And since it would be hard to conceive of a more imaginative and varied way of cooking fresh vegetables, it is also highly prized by gourmets. Rice too grows here in abundance, so that the both popular and supra-regionally renowned fried rice with vegetables belongs to the standard repertoire of good cuisine.

Its reputation is augmented by Chingkiang, which is made here and is held to be the best vinegar in the whole country. Chinese epicures are also filled with praise for the soy sauce of Shanghai and its surrounding district. Both the soy sauce and the vinegar are used for seasoning as well as separately as a dip. And since sugar cane grows profusely in the Yangtze plain, Shanghai is the center for the ubiquitously popular sweet-and-sour Chinese cuisine. Hot seasonings are mainly avoided. Cooking must be brisk, leaving the ingredients fresh and crisp. This is especially good for fish dishes, for which only first-class produce is used, thanks to the proximity of the coast.

In the Snow Garden restaurant all these principles of Shanghai cuisine are taken to heart at a high level. For example, a whole fish is slit scale-wise, so that leaves of flesh remain attached to the backbone. It is then briefly marinated in the famous Chingkiang vinegar, lightly dusted with cornstarch and fried for barely five minutes in hot oil. To this is added a sweet-and-sour balanced sauce of tomatoes, garlic and carrot cubes, a dash of rice vinegar, and hey presto! We have a beautifully fresh sweet-and-sour dish that makes us wonder why the Chinese restaurants back home rarely get it right.

Shanghai ist die größte Stadt Chinas, ihr Hafen der umtriebigste im ganzen Land. Hier endet der riesige Yangtze in einem unendlich weiten Tal. Es ist eine unwahrscheinlich fruchtbare Ebene, es ist der Obst- und Gemüsegarten des Landes. Kein Wunder also, daß die Shanghai-Küche gerade bei Vegetariern einen exzellenten Ruf genießt. Die chinesische Wok-Küche mit ihren kurzen Garzeiten ist für die Gemüsezubereitung ohnehin ideal. Und da man sich eine einfalls- und abwechslungsreichere Zubereitung als hier von frischen Gemüsen nur schwerlich vorstellen kann, steht sie auch bei Gourmets hoch im Kurs. Auch Reis wächst hier reichlich, und so gehört der ebenso beliebte wie über die Grenzen der Region hinaus bekannte fried rice mit Gemüsen zum Standard-Repertoire der guten Küche.

Zu ihrem Ruf trägt auch der Chingkiang bei, der hier hergestellt wird und als der beste Essig im ganzen Lande gilt. Auch über die Soja-Sauce aus Shanghai und Umgebung sind chinesische Feinschmecker nur des Lobes voll. Beides, Soja-Sauce wie Essig, werden sowohl als Gewürze wie auch pur als Dip verwendet, und da in der Ebene des Yangtze auch Zuckerrohr in Unmengen gedeiht, ist Shanghai die Hochburg der überall so beliebten süß-sauren chinesischen Küche. Rassige Schärfe wird eher vermieden. Die Zubereitung muß frisch, kurz und knackig sein. Das tut vor allem Fischgerichten gut, für die es hier dank der Küstennähe nur erstklassige Zutaten gibt.

Snow Garden Restaurant

Im Snow-Garden-Restaurant werden all diese Grundsätze der Shanghai-Küche auf hohem Niveau beherzigt. Ein ganzer Fisch beispielweise wird schuppenförmig so eingeschnitten, daß die Fleischstücke noch an der Rückengräte hängenbleiben. Es folgt ein kurzes Marinade-Bad im berühmten Chingkiang-Essig, sodann leichtes Einstäuben mit Maismehl und knappe fünf Minuten Garen in heißem Fett. Dazu kommt eine süß-sauer abgeschmeckte Sauce aus Tomaten, Knoblauch und Karottenwürfeln, ein Schuß Reisessig und fertig ist ein herrlich frisches süß-saures Gericht, bei dem man sich nur noch fragt, warum das China-Restaurants bei uns so meist nicht hinbekommen.

SWEET-AND-SOUR FRIED CARP

For 4 persons:

1 Yellow River carp of about 800 g/1 lb 12 oz

For the marinade:
1 tsp root ginger, finely grated,
1 spring onion, finely chopped, salt, pepper,
100 ml/3 1/2 fl oz/2/5 cup rice wine

cornstarch, oil for deep-frying

For the sauce:
150 g/5 oz peeled, cubed tomatoes,
1 spring onion, finely chopped,
1 garlic clove, finely chopped,
1 carrot, finely cubed,
1 tbsp tomato purée, 4 tbsp white rice vinegar,
100 ml/3 1/2 fl oz/2/5 cup chicken broth, sugar, salt,
1/2 tsp monosodium glutamate,
1 tsp sesame oil, 1 tsp cornstarch

To garnish:
pine kernels, deep-frozen garden peas, thawed

Preparation: Scale and clean the carp and carefully wash under running cold water. Lay the fish flat and halve lengthwise, inserting the knife directly below the head on the belly side, piercing the backbone and making a vigorous cut right to the tail. Remove the head. Lay the halves skin side down and cut out the backbone as well as possible. Make four to five oblique cuts in the flesh without damaging the skin.
For the marinade: Stir together the ginger, spring onions, salt, pepper, and rice wine. Pour over the fish halves and allow to stand in the refrigerator for about half an hour.
Take out the fillets, dry them and liberally dust with cornstarch. Heat enough oil in the wok and fry the fish halves for about five minutes.
For the sauce: Fry the tomato cubes, spring onions, garlic and carrots in the wok in a little oil. Add the tomato purée and quench with rice vinegar and chicken broth.
Season with sugar, salt, glutamate and sesame oil, and finally bind with the cornstarch blended with a little water.
To serve: Lay the fried fish halves on a serving platter and pour over the sauce.
Sprinkle with pine kernels and briefly scalded peas and serve.

KARPFEN SÜSS-SAUER

Für 4 Personen:

1 Flußkarpfen von ca. 800 g (Yellow River carp)

Für die Marinade:
1 TL Ingwerwurzel, fein gerieben,
1 Frühlingszwiebel, fein geschnitten, Salz, Pfeffer,
100 ml Reiswein

Maisstärke, Öl zum Fritieren

Für die Sauce:
150 g Würfel von geschälten Tomaten,
1 Frühlingszwiebel, fein geschnitten,
1 Knoblauchzehe, fein geschnitten,
1 Karotte, in kleine Würfel geschnitten,
1 EL Tomatenmark, 4 EL weißer Reisessig,
100 ml Hühnerbrühe, Zucker, Salz,
1/2 TL Glutamat,
1 TL Sesamöl, 1 TL Maisstärke

Garnitur:
Pinienkerne, tiefgekühlte Gartenerbsen, aufgetaut

Vorbereitung: Karpfen schuppen, ausnehmen und unter fließendem, kalten Wasser sorgfältig waschen. Den Fisch flach hinlegen und der Länge nach halbieren, indem man das Messer von der Bauchseite her direkt hinter dem Kopf ansetzt, durch die Wirbelsäule sticht und dann in einem kräftigen Schnitt bis zu Schwanz durchschneidet. Kopf entfernen. Fischhälften mit Hautseite nach unten legen, nach Möglichkeit die Wirbelsäule herausschneiden. Das Fleisch je vier bis fünf mal quer einschneiden, ohne dabei die Haut zu verletzen.
Für die Marinade: Ingwer, Frühlingszwiebel, Salz, Pfeffer und Reiswein verrühren und die Fischhälften darin ungefähr eine halbe Stunde im Kühlschrank ziehen lassen. Herausnehmen, abtrocknen und großzügig mit Maisstärke bestäuben. Im Wok genügend Öl erhitzen und den Fisch darin fünf Minuten fritieren. Für die Sauce: Tomatenwürfel, Frühlingszwiebel, Knoblauch und Karotten im Wok in etwas Öl anbraten. Tomatenmark zugeben, mit Reisessig und Hühnerbrühe ablöschen. Mit Zucker, Salz, Glutamat und Sesamöl würzen, zum Schluß mit der angerührten Stärke binden.
Zum Servieren: Die gebratenen Fischhälften auf eine Servierplatte legen und mit der Sauce übergießen. Mit Pinienkernen und kurz überbrühten Erbsen bestreut servieren.

STIR-FRIED SHRIMPS WITH SPRING ONIONS

For 4 persons:

600 g/1 lb 5 oz shrimps, peeled, 2 whites of egg, 3 tbsp flour, salt

1 tbsp peanut oil, 4 spring onions, ¹/₂ tsp salt, ¹/₂ tsp sugar,
1 tsp monosodium glutamate, 1 tsp rice vinegar, 4 tbsp rice wine,
1 tbsp soy sauce, 1 tbsp sesame oil

1 tbsp dark brown rice vinegar for drizzling

For the shrimps: Mix the egg whites with flour, salt lightly, and turn the shrimps in the mixture by hand until they are thinly coated with batter.
Heat the oil in the wok. First fry the chopped spring onions. Then add the shrimps and, stirring, add the remaining ingredients. Arrange on plates, drizzle with a little dark brown rice vinegar and serve.

KURZ GEBRATENE KRABBEN MIT FRÜHLINGSZWIEBELN

Für 4 Personen:

600 g Krabben, geschält, 2 Eiweiß, 3 EL Mehl, Salz

1 EL Erdnußöl, 4 Frühlingszwiebeln, ¹/₂ TL Salz, ¹/₂ TL Zucker,
1 TL Glutamat, 1 TL Reisessig, 4 EL Reiswein,
1 EL Sojasauce, 1 EL Sesamöl

1 EL dunkelbrauner Reisessig zum Beträufeln

Für die Krabben: Eiweiß mit Mehl verrühren, leicht salzen und die Krabben darin mit den Händen wenden, bis sie dünn mit dem Teig überzogen sind.
Das Öl im Wok erhitzen. Zuerst die kleingeschnittenen Frühlingszwiebeln darin anbraten. Dann die Krabben mitbraten und unter ständigem Wenden die restlichen Zutaten zugeben. Auf Teller verteilen und mit etwas dunkelbraunem Reisessig beträufelt servieren.

VEGETABLES WITH BAMBOO SHOOTS

For 4 persons:

120 g/4 oz button mushrooms, 120 g/4 oz carrots,
120 g/ 4 oz kohlrabi, 120 g/4 oz bamboo shoots,
120 g/4 oz broad beans, 80 g/2²/₃ oz gingko nuts (available in a jar)

250 ml/8¹/₂ fl oz/1 cup strong chicken broth,
2 tsp rice starch, salt, pepper

Clean the mushrooms and peel the carrots, kohlrabi and bamboo shoots. Cut all vegetables into pieces about 2 x 1 cm/ ⁴/₅ x ²/₅ in.
In the wok, bring the chicken broth to the boil and cook the vegetables and the nuts for about five minutes.
Bind with the starch, blended with a little water, season with salt and pepper and serve.

GEMÜSETOPF MIT BAMBUSSCHOTE

Für 4 Personen:

120 g Champignons, 120 g Karotten,
120 g Kohlrabi, 120 g Bambusschote,
120 g dicke Bohnen, 80 g Gingko-Nüsse (im Glas erhältlich)

250 ml kräftige Hühnerbrühe,
2 TL Reisstärke, Salz, Pfeffer

Champignons putzen, Karotten, Kohlrabi und Bambusschote schälen. Alle Gemüse in ca. 1 x 2 cm große Stücke schneiden. Die Hühnerbrühe im Wok zum Kochen bringen und die Gemüse und Nüsse ungefähr fünf Minuten kochen.
Mit der angerührten Stärke binden, mit Salz und Pfeffer abschmecken und servieren.

Shanghai Street
Food Market

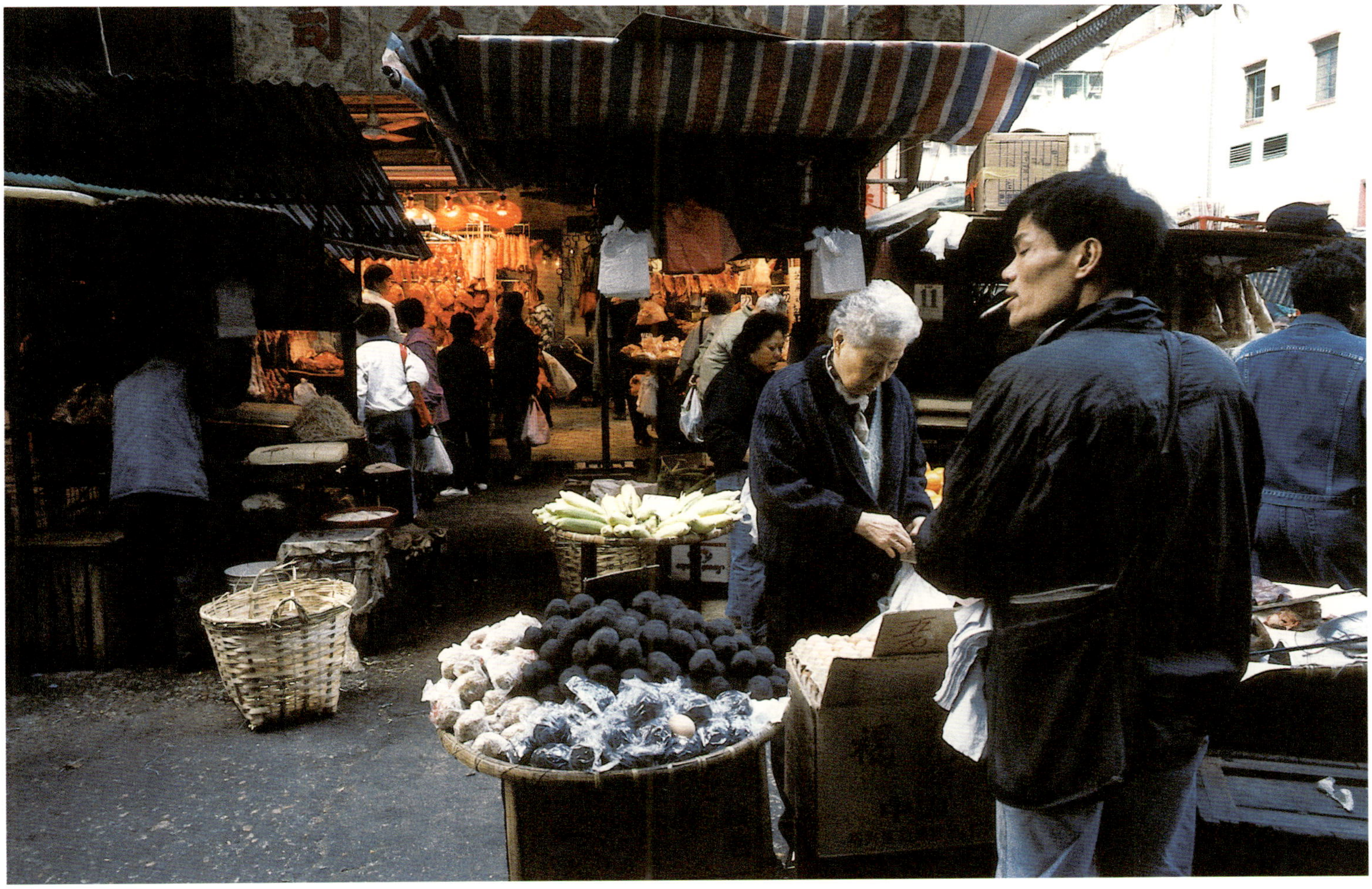

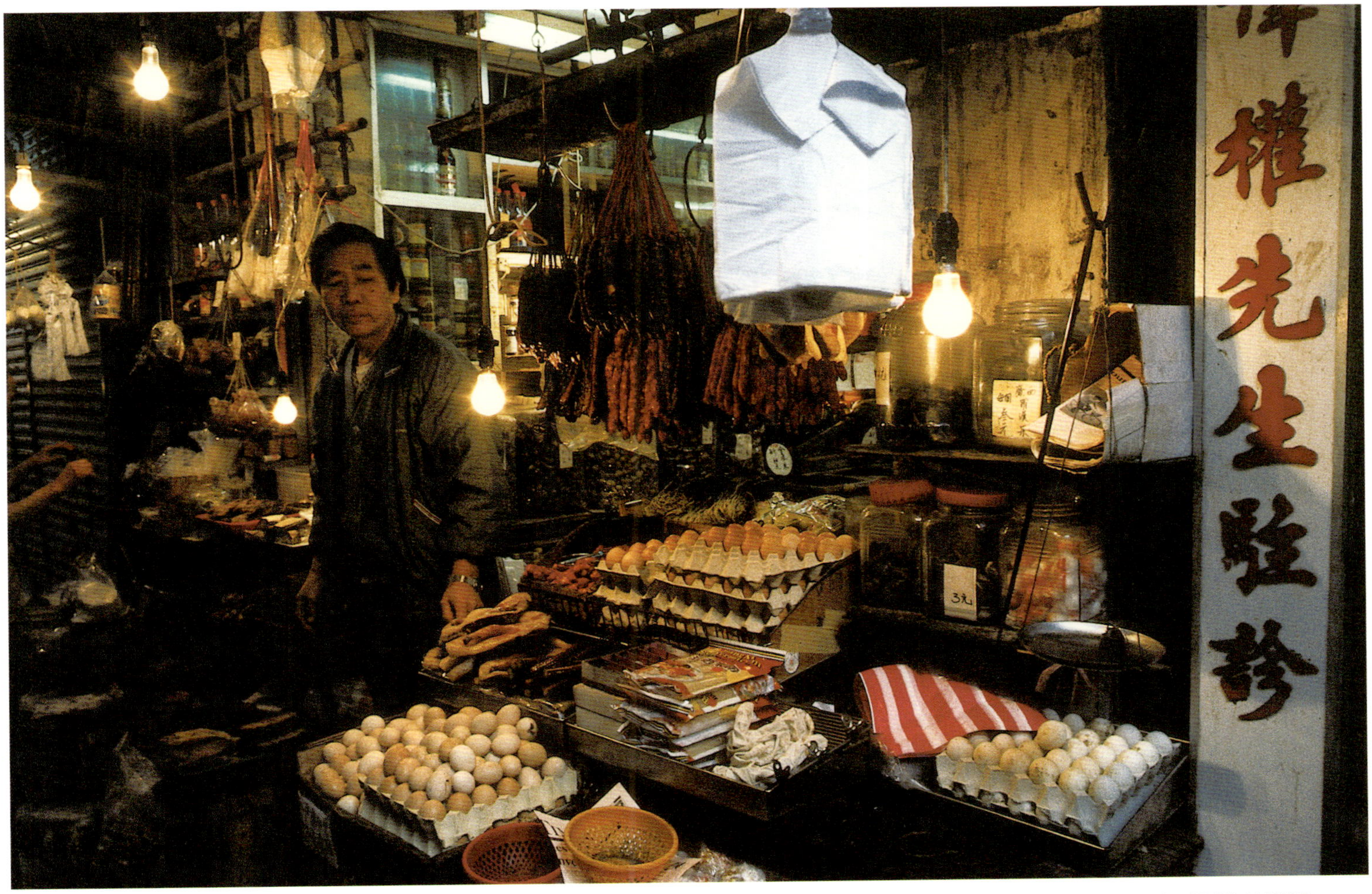
權先生駐診

臘腸

臘肉

Dried Pork Sausages
Luftgetrocknete Schweinewürstchen

Dried Bacon
Getrockneter Speck

臘鴨

Dried Leg of Duck
Getrocknete Entenkeule

Golden Island Bird's Nest Chiu Chau Restaurant

Chiu Chau is a coastal region in the north-east of China that is known for its fresh, simple and healthy cuisine. Using little oil or fat, seafood and vegetables of all kinds are turned into light, easily digestible dishes. Here in particular the gentle steam cooking method is traditional. Deep-fried food is less liked. Hot spices are kept in restraint. This is partly for climatic reasons. Chili-seasoned food is preferred mainly in the warmer regions of China. In the cooler north, much less use is made of fiery condiments. Here food is mainly seasoned with fish sauce, very popular in Asian cooking, also with a hearty bean sauce, derived from fermented yellow beans.

Part of the old tradition here is the continual serving of extremely strong, yet at the same time stomach-friendly and drinkable tea, which is sipped from small bowls before, during and after the meal, as an appetizer and digestif in one.

The province Chiu Chau has a reputation not only as a culinary region in China. It is also a center for the art of vegetable carving, producing the cleverest of table decorations from all kinds of vegetables. In practically no other country but China is the decoration of dishes so highly rated. The chef Ng Muk Hing is a master of this art. With a flick of the wrist he can turn a carrot into a Buddha figure or a hissing dragon. And when a wedding is to be celebrated and the table decorations must be something really special, the dragon also gets tiny, battery-powered lamps for eyes, which flash benignly at the newly-weds.

Chiu Chau ist eine Küsten-
region im Nordosten von China,
die für ihre frische, einfache und
gesunde Küche bekannt ist. Mit
wenig Öl und Fett werden Meeresfrüchte und Gemüse aller Art zu
leichten, bekömmlichen Gerichten
komponiert. Hier hat vor allem das
schonende Garen über Dampf
Tradition. Fritiertes dagegen wird
weniger geschätzt. Mit der Schärfe
hält man sich zurück. Das hat nicht
zuletzt klimatische Gründe.
Chilischarfes Essen wird in China
vor allem in den heißen Regionen
bevorzugt. Im kälteren Norden
geht man mit den Scharfmachern
wesentlich behutsamer um.
Gewürzt wird vor allem mit der in
der asiatischen Küche sehr beliebten
Fischsauce, ferner mit einer herz-
haften Bohnensauce, die aus
fermentierten gelben Bohnen
gewonnen wird.

Zur guten Tradition gehört
hier auch das ständige Servieren
eines außergewöhnlich starken, aber
gleichwohl magenfreundlichen und
bekömmlichen Tees, der aus
winzigen Schälchen vor, während
und nach dem Essen geschlürft
wird; als Appetitanreger und
die Verdauung förderndes
Getränk in einem.

Die Provinz Chiu Chau hat
jedoch nicht nur als kulinarische
Region einen guten Namen in
China, sie ist auch eine Hochburg
jener Schnitzkunst, die aus allen
möglichen Gemüsen die
raffiniertesten Tischdekorationen
werden läßt. In kaum einem
anderen Land hat das Verzieren und
Dekorieren von Speisen einen
solchen Stellenwert wie in China.
Chef-Koch Ng Muk Hing
beherrscht auch diese Kunst meister-
haft. Im Handumdrehen wird bei
ihm aus einer Möhre eine Buddha-
Figur oder ein fauchender Drache.

Wenn eine Hochzeit ansteht
und die Tischdekoration ganz
besonders aufwendig sein muß,
dann bekommt der Drache noch
zusätzlich kleine, von einer Batterie
gespeiste Lämpchen als Augen,
die das Hochzeitspaar freundlich
anblinken....

MIXED HORS D'OEUVRES "DELICIOUS COMBINATION"

GEMISCHTE VORSPEISE „DELICIOUS COMBINATION"

For 4 - 6 persons:

Shrimp rolls:
300 g/10 oz large shrimp tails, peeled,
salt, pepper, monosodium glutamate, soy-bean paper

Scallops:
250 g/8 oz scallops, shucked,
oil for deep-frying, 1 tsp starch, 2 tbsp chicken stock,
1 tbsp very finely chopped vegetables
(celery, chili, and garlic)

Shrimp dumplings:
200 g/7 oz shrimps, peeled,
80 g/3 oz water chestnuts, peeled, salt, pepper,
1/2 tsp monosodium glutamate, oil for deep-frying

Jellyfish:
250 g/8 oz jellyfish, salted, 2 tbsp corn oil,
1 stick of celery, cut into fine strips,
1/2 chili, finely chopped,
2 tbsp fish stock, 1 tbsp sesame oil

Decoration:
white radish, red food coloring, parsley

Für 4 bis 6 Personen:

Krabbenrollen:
300 g große Krabbenschwänze, geschält,
Salz, Pfeffer, Glutamat, Sojabohnenpapier

Jakobsmuscheln:
250 g Jakobsmuscheln, ausgelöst,
Öl zum Fritieren, 1 TL Stärke, 2 EL Hühnerfond,
1 EL sehr fein gehacktes Gemüse
(Stangensellerie, Chili und Knoblauch)

Krabbenklöße:
200 g Krabben, geschält,
80 g Wasserkastanien, geschält,
Salz, Pfeffer, 1/2 TL Glutamat, Öl zum Fritieren

Qualle:
250 g Qualle, eingesalzen, 2 EL Maiskeimöl,
1 Stück Stangensellerie, in feine Streifen geschnitten,
1/2 Chilischote, fein geschnitten,
2 EL Fischfond, 1 EL Sesamöl

Dekoration:
Weißer Rettich, rote Lebensmittelfarbe, Petersilie

Purée the shrimp tails in the blender and season with salt, pepper and glutamate. Roll the mixture in soy-bean paper (edible, similar to wafers) to form a stick. Steam for five minutes, then cut into pieces.

Immerse the scallop flesh briefly in boiling water, drain, and dry. Fry for five seconds in hot oil. Pour off the oil and lightly bind the clams with the cornstarch, blended with chicken stock. Sprinkle with the finely chopped vegetables.

Purée the shrimps in the blender. Finely chop the water chestnuts and mix with the shrimp purée. Season with salt, pepper and glutamate. Shape by hand walnut-sized dumplings and fry in the hot oil for about five minutes until golden.

Cut the jellyfish into thin strips. Place in a sieve and immerse for two seconds in boiling water. Then immerse the sieve in cold water and soak for four hours, changing the water every thirty minutes, or allow it to trickle throughout the soaking period.

Drain the soaked jellyfish. Heat a little oil in a wok and fry the celery and the chili. Add the fish stock and sesame oil. Remove from the heat and carefully mix with the jellyfish.

To serve: Arrange all preparations on a large serving platter. Decorate with carved and colored radish figures and sprigs of parsley.

Krabbenschwänze im Mixer pürieren und mit Salz, Pfeffer und Glutamat würzen. Die Masse in Sojabohnenpapier (eßbar, ähnlich wie Oblaten) zu einer Stange rollen. Über Dampf fünf Minuten garen und dann in Stücke schneiden.

Jakobsmuschelfleisch kurz in kochendes Wasser tauchen, abgießen und abtrocknen. Fünf Sekunden im heißen Öl fritieren. Öl abgießen, Muscheln mit der mit Hühnerfond angerührten Stärke binden. Mit dem feingehackten Gemüse bestreuen.

Krabben im Mixer pürieren. Wasserkastanien fein hacken und unter die Krabbenmasse mischen. Mit Salz, Pfeffer und Glutamat würzen. Von Hand walnußgroße Klöße formen und im heissen Öl ca. fünf Minuten goldgelb ausbacken.

Qualle in dünne Streifen schneiden. In ein Sieb geben und zwei Sekunden in kochendes Wasser tauchen. Dann das Sieb in kaltes Wasser tauchen und vier Stunden wässern; Wasser alle dreißig Minuten austauschen.

Eingeweichte Qualle abtropfen lassen. Im Wok etwas Öl erhitzen und den Sellerie und den Chili anbraten. Fischfond und Sesamöl zugeben. Vom Feuer nehmen und vorsichtig mit der Qualle vermischen.

Zum Servieren: Alle Gerichte auf eine große Servierplatte anrichten. Dekorieren mit geschnitzten und eingefärbten Rettichfiguren und Petersiliesträußchen.

CHICKEN-SPINACH CRÈME "YIN YANG"

HÜHNERFLEISCH-SPINATCREME „YIN YANG"

For 4 persons:

1 kg/2 lb 3 oz fresh spinach, cleaned,
¹/₂ liter/1 pint/2 cups chicken broth,
salt, ¹/₂ tsp monosodium glutamate,
1 tsp cornstarch

150 g/5 oz chicken meat,
1 white of egg,
250 ml/8 fl oz/1 cup chicken broth,
salt, ¹/₂ tsp monosodium glutamate

Für 4 Personen:

1 kg frischer Spinat, geputzt,
¹/₂ Liter Hühnerbrühe,
Salz, ¹/₂ TL Glutamat,
1 TL Maisstärke

150 g Hühnerfleisch,
1 Eiweiß,
250 ml Hühnerbrühe,
Salz, ¹/₂ TL Glutamat

For the green crème: Boil the spinach in the broth for one minute, then finely purée in the blender. Season with salt and glutamate and lightly bind with the cornstarch blended with a little water.
For the white crème: Purée the chicken meat in the blender and mix well with the white of egg. Bring the broth to a boil and stir in the mixture. Season with salt and glutamate and simmer for one minute.
To serve: Fill deep plates or bowls with the spinach crème. On each plate cover half with the chicken crème and with a small spoon draw the corners into the other color. Complete the Yin Yang sign (symbolizing the harmony of all things in Chinese philosophy) with a circular spot in the middle of each half.

Für die grüne Creme: Den Spinat in der Brühe eine Minute kochen, und im Mixer fein pürieren. Mit Salz und Glutamat würzen, mit der angerührten Stärke leicht binden.
Für die weiße Creme: Hühnerfleisch im Mixer pürieren und mit dem Eiweiß gut verrühren. Brühe zum Kochen bringen und das Gemisch einrühren. Mit Salz und Glutamat würzen und eine Minute köcheln lassen.
Zum Servieren: Tiefe Teller oder Schalen mit der Spinatcreme füllen. Jeweils eine Hälfte mit der Hühnercreme bedecken, mit einem kleinen Löffel die Ecken in die andere Farbe ziehen. Mit je einem kreisrunden Tupfen als Dekoration das Yin-Yang-Zeichen (Symbol für das Gleichgewicht der Dinge in der chinesischen Philosophie) vervollständigen.

VEGETABLE PLATTER WITH MUSHROOMS

GEMÜSEPLATTE MIT PILZEN

For 6 - 8 persons:

12 large dried pink mushrooms,
1 kg/2 lb 3 oz Chinese cabbage,
1 liter/1 pint 14 fl oz/4 cups chicken broth,
500 g/1 lb 2 oz Chinese broccoli or green asparagus,
500 g/1 lb 2 oz carrots

150 ml/5 fl oz/³/₅ cup chicken stock, 1 tbsp chicken fat,
150 g/5 oz Yunnan ham (Chinese air-dried ham
or lean raw ham as a substitute),
1 tsp cornstarch, 2 tbsp corn oil,
100 ml/3¹/₂ fl oz/²/₅ cup fish stock (or Chinese fish
sauce made from dried fish)

Preparation: Place the mushrooms in cold water. Boil the whole Chinese cabbage in chicken broth for about twenty minutes until soft but crisp. Remove and allow to go cold. Cut the vegetables into approx. 12-cm/5 in lengths and taper to a point. Boil the green vegetables and carrots in salted water with a little oil for two minutes, then drain through a sieve.

To finish: In the wok, or in a pot, bring the chicken stock together with the chicken fat to the boil. Steam the softened mushrooms in a sieve insert or in a wood-chip basket for one hour. Using the same system but over water, cook the ham for one hour. Then cut the ham into thin slices. Bind the ham-cooking liquid lightly with cornstarch, blended with a little water, and season with salt and pepper.

Briefly fry the green vegetables and the carrots in the wok, in a little oil, and quench with the fish stock. Allow to boil down briefly. Heat the Chinese cabbage over steam.

To serve: Arrange the vegetables in a star pattern on a serving platter. Place the mushrooms in the center and surround with slices of ham. Pour over the sauce and serve immediately.

Für 6 - 8 Personen:

12 große, getrocknete rosa Champignons,
1 kg Chinakohl,
1 Liter Hühnerbrühe,
500 g chinesischer Broccoli oder grüner Spargel,
500 g Karotten

150 ml Hühnerfond, 1 EL Hühnerfett,
150 g Yunnan Schinken (chinesischer luftgetrockneter
Schinken, ersatzweise magerer Rohschinken),
1 TL Maisstärke, 2 EL Maiskeimöl,
100 ml Fischfond (oder chinesische Fischsauce, wird
aus getrocknetem Fisch hergestellt)

Vorbereitung: Champignons in kaltem Wasser einlegen. Chinakohl im Ganzen in Hühnerbrühe etwa zwanzig Minuten knackig-weich kochen. Herausnehmen und erkalten lassen. Die Gemüse ca. 12 cm lang und spitz zuschneiden. Grünes Gemüse und Karotten in Salzwasser mit etwas Öl zwei Minuten kochen, dann durch ein Sieb abgießen.

Fertigstellung: Im Wok oder in einem Topf den Hühnerfond mit dem Hühnerfett zum Kochen bringen. Eingeweichte Champignons in einem Siebeinsatz oder im Bastkörbchen über Dampf eine Stunde garen. Mit dem gleichen System, jedoch nur über Wasser, den Schinken eine Stunde garen. Anschließend den Schinken in dünne Scheiben schneiden. Den entstandenen Schinkensud mit angerührter Maisstärke leicht binden und mit Salz und Pfeffer abschmecken.

Die grünen Gemüse und die Karotten im Wok in etwas Öl kurz anbraten und mit dem Fischfond ablöschen. Kurz einkochen lassen. Den Chinakohl über Dampf erwärmen.

Zum Servieren: Die Gemüse sternförmig auf eine Servierplatte auslegen. Champignons in die Mitte geben und mit den Schinkenscheiben umlegen. Mit der Sauce begießen und sofort servieren.

Birds' nests

Birds' nests are regarded as an absolute delicacy in China and are almost unaffordably expensive. They come mainly from Thailand and consist principally of the saliva of salangane swiftlets which, in this way, build the framework of their nests on the rocky coast. The high price is justified by the practically inaccessible rocky ledges to which the nests are attached.

Preparation:
Per person: 8 g dried bird's nest
Place the birds' nests in hot water and soak for two hours. Then wash them and carefully remove any residues (down feathers, dirt). Heat a little water in a small pot and lay the birds' nests over the water on a fine grid. Cover and steam the nests over a low heat for about fifty minutes. Serve the birds' nests either hot in a poultry consommé or as a sweet just with syrup.

Schwalbennester

Schwalbennester gelten als absolute Delikatesse in China und sind fast unerschwinglich teuer. Sie kommen meistens aus Thailand und bestehen hauptsächlich aus dem Speichel der Schwalben, die sie an der Felsküste als eigentliches Gerüst für ihre Nester bauen. Der hohe Preis rechtfertigt sich durch die praktisch unzugänglichen Felsvorsprünge, an denen die Nester kleben.

Zubereitung:
Pro Person: 8 g getrocknetes Schwalbennest
Schwalbennester in heißem Wasser zwei Stunden einweichen lassen. Anschließend waschen und sorgfältig von eventuellen Rückständen befreien (Federchen, Schmutz). In einem kleinen Topf etwas Wasser erhitzen und die Schwalbennester auf einem feinen Gitter darüber legen. Zudecken und die Nester so über Dampf bei kleiner Hitze etwa fünfzig Minuten garen. Schwalben-nester entweder heiß in einer Geflügelconsommé oder als Süß-speise, nur mit Zuckerwasser, servieren.

記酒家於公元一九四二年由甘穗煇先生創立。

數十年來群策群力，不斷改進，本酒家從一小店發展成具實力雄厚全球一流食府。一九六八年為美國「幸福雜誌」評為全球十五大最佳食府中唯一中菜館。

數十年來，本酒家應邀香港旅遊協會及局、海外各地美食比賽之白金獎、金獎及其他各項榮譽。

其中榮獲美食，讓與本酒家經埋垂詢。

Starting at the year of 1941, from a young and penniless restaurant appreciate to become the owner of Yung Kee Restaurant, Mr Kam Shui Fai, has been acclaimed as a legendary figure for his success by foreign and local press.

In 1968, we have been named by the American FORTUNE MAGAZINE to be one of the Top Fifteen Restaurant in the world, the only Chinese restaurant on the list.

Our restaurant has been participating in the food competitions organized by the Hong Kong Tourist Association Hong Kong Trade Development Council and overseas international contest for many years. We have won a lot of awards from our unique and tasteful dishes. You may wish to taste the following award-winning dishes, please contact our managers to make arrangement.

YEAR	AWARD	
1968	Top Fifteen Best Restaurants in the World 世界十五大最佳食府	Fortune Magazine (America) 美國幸福雜誌
1986	Shark's Fin Soup with Crab Meat 美點金特	HK Food Festival Gold Award 黃金獎
1986	Pork Roll Stuffed with Ham & Vegetable 玉捲珠簾	HK Food Festival Gold Award 黃金獎
1986	Meat Collation in Phoenix Patter 鳳閣瓊樓	HK Food Festival Gold Award 黃金獎
1986	The Never Ending Story – Crispy Citron Finger & Steamed Green Pear Cake 蓬池仙果・佛手蟠桃	HK Food Festival Platinum Award 白金獎
1986	Roasted Goose In Five Delightful Varieties 五福鵝亭	Chinese Culinary Arts Exposition By Hong Kong Top Chef 世紀之宴會
1987	Pigeon Egg And Superlative Bird's Nest 月映妙資	Chinese Culinary Arts Exposition By Hong Kong Top Chef 世紀之宴會
1987	Lobster's Head & Leg with Rice In Soup 龍皇御賜	Golden Flower Party Award (Canada) 加國金花宴獎
1989	Poached Fillet Of Lobster In Soup 龍蝦過橋	HK Food Festival Platinum Award 白金獎
1989	Sautéed Bone Of Frogs & Seafood Combination 櫻桃仙子	HK Food Festival Platinum Award 白金獎
1989	Smoked Fragrant Goose 虹鵝添香	HK Food Festival Gold Award 黃金獎
1989	A Combination of Custard Pastries & Steamed Date Dumplings 祝福	HK Food Festival Gold Award 黃金獎
1989	Vegetarian Platter 鱸蘿濫門	HK Food Festival Silver Award 銀獎
1991	Roasted Chicken with Chicken Liver Medallions 雞舞金錢	HK Food Festival Platinum Award 白金獎
1991	Steamed Egg-Plant with Chinese Mushroom 蒞峰翠玉	HK Food Festival Platinum Award 白金獎
1991	Leg Of Lamb accompanied by Four Dishes – Spring, Summer, Autumn and Winter 春夏狄冬它假案	HK Food Festival Gold Award 黃金獎
1991	The Best Restaurant 最佳服務獎	American Express 美國運通
1992	The Best Restaurant 最佳服務獎	American Express 美國運通
1993	The Best Cuisine 最佳食府	Hong Kong Tourist Association 香港旅遊協會
1993	Stir-fried Lobster-Meat with Dried Garoupa Skin 雙龍銀獎	HK Food Festival Gold Award 黃金獎
1993	Fragrant Rice In Lobster Bouillon 龍騰麗映	HOFEX 93 Golden Award 貿易發展局黃金獎
1993	The Best Cuisine 最佳服務獎	American Express 美國運通
1993	The Best Service 最佳服務獎	Diners Club 大來信用證
1993	The Commanderie des Cordons Bleus de France 藍帶勳章	France Cuisine Association 法國美食協會
1994	Les Disciples D'Auguste Escoffier officer Commanderie 美食 officer 勳章	France Cuisine Association 法國美食協會
1994	The Best Food Award 最佳廚藝大獎	Diners Club 大來信用証
1995	The General Taking Off His Helmet 霸王卸甲	HK Food Festival Platinum Award 白金獎
1995	The Three Treasures Of Shunde 順德三寶	HK Food Festival Platinum Award 白金獎
1995	White Jade And Golden Duck 白玉金搭鴨	HK Food Festival Gold Award 黃金獎
1995	Stewed Lamb 大漠手抓羊	HK Food Festival Gold Award 黃金獎
1995	Assorted Pork In Five Delightful Varieties 華亭聚五福	Icon of the Great Chef (Japan) 料理職人獎
1996	Roasted Goose In Five Delightful Varieties (New Style) 金裝伍福鵝亭	Golden Party Award 金殿之夜獎

Yung Kee Restaurant

雞鴨類 Chicken and Duck

			HK$ Half	HK$ Whole
76	生扣鴛鴦雞 Chicken with Ham and Mushrooms			
77	金華玉樹雞 Steamed Sliced Chicken with Ham and Vegetable		$130.00	$260.00
78	脆皮炸子雞 Roasted Chicken Cantonese Style		130.00	260.00
79	正式鹽焗雞 Baked Chicken with Salt		100.00	200.00
80	蠔油手撕雞 Shredded Chicken with Oyster Sauce		110.00	220.00
81	豉葱生抽雞 Soyed Chicken with Spring Onion		110.00	220.00
82	菜胆上湯雞 Boiled Chicken and Vegetable		110.00	220.00
83	原粒豆豉雞 Sautéed Chicken with Salted Beans		110.00	220.00
84	蠔油炆雞 Chicken with Oyster Sauce		110.00	220.00
85	腰果雞丁 Diced Chicken with Cashewnuts			62.00
86	辣椒雞絲 Shredded Chicken with Chilli			62.00
87	菜遠雞球 Chicken Meat and Vegetable			62.00
88	清蒸滑雞 Steamed Chicken			62.00
89	西芹雞柳 Shredded Chicken with Celery			62.00
90	酥炸珍肝 Fried Chicken Giblet			62.00
91	廣式片皮鵝（晚市供應）Roasted Crispy Skin Goose (Served at dinner)			35.00
92	北菇扒鴨 Braised Duck with Mushrooms			360.00
93	八珍扒鴨 Braised Duck with Chop Suey		100.00	200.00
94	時菜扒鴨 Braised Duck with Vegetable		100.00	

Mr. Kam Kin Shing, the general manager, and Mr. Leung Wai Kee, the chef, are the uncrowned kings for roast goose in Hong Kong. Each and every day, 300 of these birds, on holidays sometimes 400, are served at 800 seats on four floors to an international clientele that is amazed every time. 80 cooks toil in the kitchen, of whom 16 are concerned solely with trimming, smoking, roasting, carving and serving these geese. Five cooks attend to nothing but the noodles that are traditionally eaten as an accompaniment. Six work from morning until night crafting the dim sum parcels that people like to order for starters. The remainder clean vegetables, slicing and finely chopping, wiping, checking the large grill, always with a weather eye on the giant pot in which – full to the brim – the chicken soup simmers away. A kitchen like an adventure playground – steaming and hissing.

A stay in Asia without eating goose is like a trip to Salzburg without the eponymous "Nockerln". Well then: the Yung Kee restaurant is almost a must for the visitor to Hong Kong. For despite the size of the restaurant and its impressive turnover, no corners are cut where quality is concerned. On the contrary: fast turnover of produce guarantees freshness; the crispy goose does not lie around until the skin becomes limp and tough.

Father Kam Shui Kai, the founder of the restaurant, brought back from a trip to China all the traditional recipes that are adhered to until this day, and will be in the future, we are reliably assured. And for this reason the heart of the kitchen includes not only the row of wok stoves, obligatory in Asia and always impressive. At least equal in importance at the Yung Kee are the man-high, barrel-like, stainless steel vessels, a yard in diameter. In these the geese are suspended from a rack, so that the smoke from the small fire smouldering in the base of the steel vessel can evenly brown and flavor the birds from all sides and give the skin the coveted crisp consistency. We can reveal only so much: the smoke comes from the charcoal which, however, is given all kinds of aromatic additives. People speak of dried mandarin orange peel and of cinnamon and of 16 or 17 other ingredients, which are all part of a spice mixture that is a closely guarded secret of the establishment.

In order that the skin of the goose – a delicacy in itself – gets especially crisp, it must not be attached to the flesh while the bird is in the smoke chamber. A needle is therefore used to force compressed air under the skin to detach it. In this way the hot air reaches it from both sides – the delicious result has made Yung Chee famous.

Kam Shui Kai, the senior chef, eats every day in his restaurant. Except on Sundays. Then he stays home, where there are fish and vegetables.

Kam Kin Shing
Leung Wai Kee

Glazed Goose

Glacierte Gans

Mister Kam Kin Shing, der General-Manager, und Mister Leung Wai Kee, der Chefkoch, sind die ungekrönten Könige für gebratene Gänse in Hong Kong. 300 dieser Federtiere, an Feiertagen auch mal 400, werden hier Tag für Tag an 800 Plätzen auf vier Etagen einem internationalen, immer wieder staunenden Publikum aufgetischt. 80 Köche werkeln in der Küche, davon sind allein 16 mit nichts anderem beschäftigt, als eben jene Gänse zu parieren, zu räuchern, zu braten, zu tranchieren und anzurichten. Fünf Köche kümmern sich um nichts anderes als die Nudeln, die es traditionsgemäß dazu gibt. Sechs basteln von morgens bis abends Dim-Sum-Päckchen, die man gerne als Vorspeise bestellt. Der Rest putzt Gemüse, schnippelt und hackt es klitzeklein, wischt, kontrolliert den großen Grill, ein Auge immer auf den riesengroßen Topf gerichtet, in dem – randvoll – die Hühnersuppe vor sich hin köchelt. Eine Küche wie ein Abenteuerspielplatz – dampfend, fauchend.

Ein Asien-Aufenthalt ohne ein Gänseessen ist wie eine Salzburg-Reise ohne die gleichnamigen Nockerln. Also: Yung Kee Restaurant ist für den Hong-Kong-Reisenden fast ein Muß. Denn bei aller Größe des Restaurants und trotz beeindruckender Umsatzzahlen: an der Qualität werden hier keinerlei Abstriche gemacht. Im Gegenteil: flotter Umschlag der Ware garantiert Frische, die knusprige Gans liegt nicht herum bis die Haut wieder schlaff und zäh ist.

Vater Kam Shui Kai, der Gründer des Restaurants, hat von einer China-Reise alle diejenigen traditionellen Rezepte mitgebracht, an die man sich hier bis heute hält – und auch in Zukunft halten wird, wie man glaubhaft versichert. Deshalb gehört zum Herzstück der Küche nicht nur die in Asien obligatorische und immer wieder beeindruckende Reihe von Wok-Kochstellen. Mindestens ebenso wichtig sind bei Yung Kee die mannshohen, faßartigen Edelstahlgefäße mit fast einem Meter Durchmesser. In diese werden die Gänse an einem Gestell freischwebend gehängt, damit der Rauch des kleinen Feuerchens, das am Boden des Stahlbehälters glimmt, die Tiere von allen Seiten schön gleichmäßig bräunen und aromatisieren kann und der Haut zur begehrten knusprigen Konsistenz verhilft. Verraten wird nur so viel: der Rauch kommt von der Holzkohle, der jedoch allerlei aromatische Zutaten mitgegeben werden. Da ist von getrockneter Mandarinenschale und von Zimt die Rede und von 16 bis 17 weiteren Zutaten, die aber allesamt unter die streng geheimgehaltene Würzmischung des Hauses fallen.

Damit die Haut der Gans – eine Delikatesse für sich – besonderes knusprig wird, darf sie, wenn sich das Tier in der Räucherkammer befindet, nicht fest anliegen. Deshalb wird mit einer Nadel Druckluft unter die Haut gepresst, damit sie sich vom Fleisch löst. So kommt von zwei Seiten die heiße Luft an sie heran – das leckere Ergebnis hat Yung Kee berühmt gemacht.

Kam Shui Kai, der Senior-Chef, ißt jeden Tag in seinem Restaurant. Nur nicht am Sonntag, dann bleibt er zuhause, wo es Fisch und Gemüse gibt.

GLAZED ROAST GOOSE

For 6 - 8 persons:

1 goose of about 3 kg/6 lb

1 tsp grated root ginger,
1 tsp star anise, finely ground in the mortar,
1 tsp Szechuan pepper, finely ground in the mortar,
1 tsp yellow soy-bean paste, salt,
2 tbsp sugar, boiled to a syrup with 2 tbsp water

GEBRATENE GLACIERTE GANS

Für 6 - 8 Personen:

1 Gans von ca. 3 kg/6 lb

1 TL geriebene Ingwerwurzel,
1 TL Sternanis, im Mörser fein zerstossen,
1 TL Sechuanpfeffer, im Mörser fein zerstossen,
1 TL gelbe Sojabohnenpaste, Salz,
2 EL Zucker, mit 2 EL Wasser zu Sirup gekocht

Wash the goose and dry it well. Mix the spices and carefully rub them into the inside of the goose. Make a slit in the skin of the neck and inflate the goose with a pump to detach the skin from the body.
Seal the cut. Paint the goose with the syrup and hang it up to dry in an airy place for three to four hours.
Preheat the oven to 180° C/360° F and roast the goose for 1 to 1¼ hours. Turn it from time to time.

Gans waschen und gut abtrocknen. Gewürze vermischen und das Innere der Gans damit sorgfältig einreiben. Im Nacken die Haut einschneiden und die Gans mit einer Pumpe aufblasen, so daß sich die Haut vom Körper trennt. Die Schnittstelle verschließen. Die Gans mit dem Sirup bepinseln und an einem luftigen Ort drei bis vier Stunden zum Trocknen aufhängen.
Im vorgeheizten Ofen bei 180° C eine bis eineinviertel Stunden braten. Von Zeit zu Zeit wenden.

Forum Restaurant

forum
restaurant (1977) ltd.

485, LOCKHART RD,
CAUSEWAY BAY,
HONG KONG.
2891 2516-7
2891 2555

Yeung Koon Yat

abalone

Mr. Yeung Koon Yat is Mr. Abalone. For under Yeung Koon Yat's direction, abalone becomes the delicacy of delicacies for crowned and uncrowned heads of state and for all those who can afford it. A picture gallery of well-known faces from all over the world is the impressive proof of this. Of his 25 years' experience as a cook, Yeung has spent the last 14 years solely on perfecting the preparation of abalone. This has brought him the title Ah Yat, Number One.

What is it about this abalone that commands, per specimen (assuming top quality), prices even on the market of 4000 Hong Kong dollars? Abalone is a sea snail, and that only the very best are served in the Restaurant Forum is a matter of course. They come from Japan, are about seven years old and have grown in the open sea, i.e. are not cultured. These fine specimens, as big as the palm of the hand, must first be dried for 50 days, so as to concentrate their taste. Then they are boiled non-stop for fifteen hours in a broth together with chicken and pork. When this laborious procedure is over, the master himself takes over, namely before the very eyes of the guests. In a porcelain dish it is heated in a concentrated sauce and served at table. This royal dish (or hors d'oeuvre) costs 5000 Hong Kong dollars. Being good for diabetics and purifying the kidneys are just pleasant side-effects. In consistency and taste it reminds us long-noses of a plump escargot with a slightly fishy flavor. Even an original Chinese cookbook can only describe the taste as an undefinable sea flavor, the consistency as firm and almost a little slippery.

Abalone – similarly to shark's fin soup – is one of those Asian culinary secrets that you have to think your way into and live with, in order to be able – perhaps – one day to understand and enjoy them. The third extraordinary specialty in this round is bird's nest soup, which Yeung prepares like no-one else. He only uses nests from Indonesia, which are cleaner and therefore better than any others. They are steeped in cold water for five hours, then the master himself prepares them before the guests. Following sixteen different recipes created by him, they are heated and seasoned with all kinds of ingredients and spices, some even as sweet desserts. In appearance and consistency they are reminiscent of glass noodles; their inherent flavor is very unprepossessing. And the high protein content makes them healthy for body and soul.

Meeresschnecke

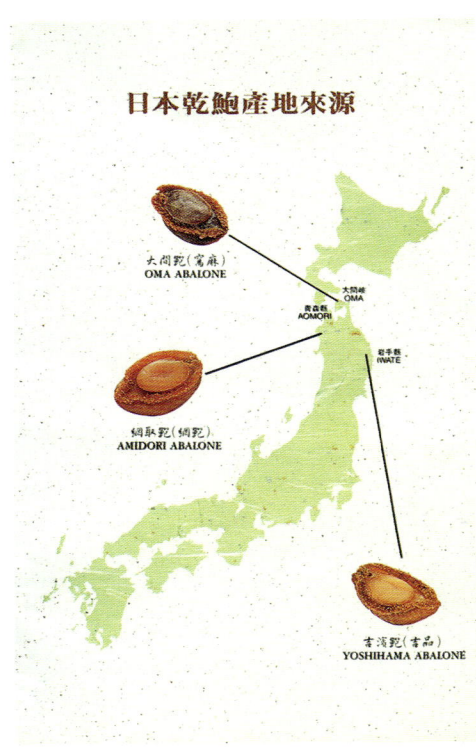

日本乾鮑產地來源

大間鮑（宮麻）
OMA ABALONE

大間崎
OMA

青森縣
AOMORI

岩手縣
IWATE

網取鮑（網鮑）
AMIDORI ABALONE

吉濱鮑（吉品）
YOSHIHAMA ABALONE

Mister Yeung Koon Yat ist Mister Abalone.
Denn unter Yeung Koon Yats Regie wird die Abalone zur
Delikatesse schlechthin für gekrönte und ungekrönte
Staatsoberhäupter und für all jene, die sie sich leisten
können. Eine Foto-Galerie mit bekannten Gesichtern aus
aller Welt ist der beeindruckende Beleg hierfür.
Von den 25 Jahren Erfahrung als Koch hat Yeung alleine
die letzten 14 Jahre ganz der Perfektionierung der
Abalone-Zubereitung gewidmet. Das hat ihm den Titel
Ah Yat, die Nummer Eins, eingebracht.

Was hat es mit dieser Abalone auf sich, die pro Stück
(First-Class-Qualität vorausgesetzt), schon im Einkauf
4000 Hong-Kong-Dollar kostet? Abalone ist eine
Meeresschnecke, und daß im Restaurant Forum nur die
besten serviert werden, versteht sich von selbst. Diese
kommen aus Japan, sind etwa sieben Jahre alt und frei
aufgewachsen, also nicht gezüchtet. Die dann fast
handtellergroßen Prachtexemplare müssen zunächst
50 Tage lang getrocknet werden, damit sich ihr
Geschmack konzentriert. Dann werden sie fünfzehn
Stunden ununterbrochen gekocht, und zwar in einer
Brühe zusammen mit Hühner- und Schweinefleisch.
Wenn diese aufwendige Prozedur vorbei ist, legt der
Meister selbst Hand an, und dies vor den Augen der
Gäste. In einer Porzellanschüssel wird sie am Tisch in einer
konzentrierten Sauce erwärmt und serviert. 5000 Hong-
Kong Dollar kostet diese königliche (Vor)Speise.
Daß sie gut ist für Diabetiker und die Nieren reinigt, ist
ein angenehmer Nebeneffekt. In Konsistenz und
Geschmack erinnert sie uns Langnasen an eine ordentliche
Weinbergschnecke mit leicht fischigem Aroma. Selbst
ein original chinesisches Kochbuch kann den Geschmack
nur als undefinierbares Meeresaroma beschreiben,
die Konsistenz als fest und fast ein bißchen glitschig.

Abalone ist – ähnlich wie die Haifischflossensuppe –
eines jener asiatischen Küchengeheimnisse, in die
man sich hineindenken und hineinleben muß,
um sie – vielleicht – verstehen und genießen zu können.
Die dritte außergewöhnliche Spezialität in dieser Runde
ist die Schwalbennester-Suppe, die Yeung ebenfalls wie
kaum ein Zweiter zubereitet. Er verwendet nur Nester aus
Indonesien, die sauberer und damit besser sind als alle
anderen. Fünf Stunden werden sie im kalten Wasser
eingeweicht, dann bereitet sie der Meister selbst direkt
am Tisch zu. Nach von ihm kreierten sechzehn
verschiedenen Rezepturen werden sie erwärmt und
mit allerlei unterschiedlichen Zutaten und Gewürzen
abgeschmeckt, manche sogar süß als Dessert.
In Optik und Konsistenz erinnern sie an Glasnudeln,
ihr Eigengeschmack ist sehr zurückhaltend. Der hohe
Proteingehalt macht sie gesund für Leib und Seele.

乾　鮑

Dried Abalone
Getrocknete Meeresschnecke

SEA SNAILS

For 6 persons:

6 whole dried sea snails (abalone)
of about 120 g/4 oz each,
300 g/10 oz lean pork,
½ chicken

½ tsp sugar,
250 ml/8 fl oz/1 cup broth,
boiled from chicken and pork,
2 slices of raw ham, softened in water,
1 tsp light soy sauce,
2 tsp cornstarch, blended with a little water,
500 g/1 lb Chinese broccoli, cooked in salted water

Soak the abalone in cold water overnight. Scrub with a small brush under running water. Lay a wooden grid in a large earthenware pot (or crisscross four wooden spoons or chopsticks).
Place first the pork, then the abalone and finally the half chicken in the pot. Fill with water to cover the chicken, bring slowly to the boil, cover, and simmer on a low heat for sixteen hours. Check the liquid level from time to time, topping up with water when necessary.
After the cooking time, take out the abalone and allow to cool on a plate.
In a small earthenware pot, bring about six tablespoons of the broth to a boil.
Add the abalone, sprinkle with sugar, and cook for five to six minutes, stirring constantly in a clockwise direction.
Pour over the chicken broth, add the sliced ham, and stir for a further four minutes until cooked. Remove the ham, season with soy sauce.
Mix in the starch and stir well until the abalone are covered on all sides with a thick juice.
Serve the abalone on a bed of vegetables. Pour over the remaining cooking juice.

MEERESSCHNECKEN

Für 6 Personen:

6 ganze, getrocknete Meerschnecken (Abalone)
von je ca. 120 g,
300 g mageres Schweinefleisch,
½ Hähnchen

½ TL Zucker,
250 ml Brühe, von Huhn und
Schweinefleisch gekocht,
2 Scheiben Rohschinken, in Wasser eingeweicht,
1 TL helle Sojasauce,
2 TL Stärkelösung (mit Wasser angerührte Maisstärke),
500 g chinesischer Broccoli, in Salzwasser gegart

Die Meeresschnecken über Nacht in kaltem Wasser einweichen. Mit einer kleinen Bürste unter fließendem Wasser säubern. In einen großen Tontopf einen Gitterboden aus Holz legen (oder vier Holzlöffel oder -Stäbchen über Kreuz legen). In diesen Topf zuerst das Schweinefleisch, dann die Schnecken und zum Schluß das halbe Hühnchen legen. Mit Wasser auffüllen, bis alles bedeckt ist, langsam zum Kochen bringen und zugedeckt bei kleiner Hitze sechzehn Stunden sieden lassen. Von Zeit zu Zeit den Flüssigkeitsstand kontrollieren, bei Bedarf etwas Wasser nachgießen. Nach der Kochzeit die Schnecken herausnehmen und auskühlen lassen.
In einem kleinen Tontopf ca. sechs Eßlöffel von dem Kochsud erhitzen. Schnecken zugeben, mit Zucker bestreuen und unter ständigem Rühren im Uhrzeigersinn fünf bis sechs Minuten garen. Mit der Brühe aufgießen, Schinken hineinlegen und unter Rühren weitere vier Minuten garen. Schinken entfernen, mit Sojasauce würzen. Stärkelösung zugeben und weiterrühren, bis die Schnecken rundum von dem dicken Saft überzogen sind.
Meeresschnecken auf einem Gemüsebett auf Teller anrichten. Mit restlichem Kochsaft übergießen.

FRIED BIRD'S-NESTS WITH EGG-WHITE

GEBRATENES SCHWALBENNEST MIT EIWEISS

For 4 persons:

50 g/1²/₃ oz dried birds' nests (salangane)

1 tbsp oil, 2 whites of egg, 60 g/2 oz crab meat,
1 tbsp coral of giant crab
(the orange-colored part),
1 tbsp ham juice (from boiled raw ham),
¹/₄ tsp salt,
2 tsp cornstarch, blended with a little water

100 g/3¹/₂ oz slender rice noodles, boiled, then fried
and broken into small pieces,
1 tsp raw ham, finely chopped

Soak the birds' nests for about two hours in cold water. Then carefully remove any nest residues.
Heat the oil in an earthenware pot. Drain the birds' nests and sauté over a low heat for about five minutes, stirring constantly.
Add the beaten eggwhite and stir for a further ten minutes over a low heat. Add the crab meat, coral, ham juice and salt. Stir in the cornstarch-water blend to thicken the dish.
To serve: Form a small nest of fried noodles on each plate.
Ladle the birds'-nest mixture over this and sprinkle with ham cubes before serving.

Für 4 Personen:

50 g getrocknetes Schwalbennest

1 EL Öl, 2 Eiweiß, 60 g Krebsfleisch,
1 EL Corail vom Taschenkrebs
(der orangefarbene Teil),
1 EL Schinkensaft (von ausgekochtem Rohschinken),
¹/₄ TL Salz,
2 TL Stärkelösung (mit Wasser angerührte Stärke)

100 g dünne Reisnudeln, gekocht, anschließend
gebraten und in kleine Stücke gebrochen,
1 TL Rohschinken, fein geschnitten

Schwalbennest zwei Stunden in kaltem Wasser einlegen. Anschließend sorgfältig von eventuellen Nestrückständen befreien und abtropfen lassen.
In einem Tontopf das Öl erhitzen. Das abgetropfte Schwalbennest bei kleiner Hitze unter ständigem Rühren fünf Minuten anschwitzen. Verquirltes Eiweiß zugeben und weitere zehn Minuten auf kleiner Hitze rühren. Krebsfleisch, Corail, Schinkensaft und Salz zugeben. Mit der angerührten Stärke binden.
Zum Servieren: Mit den gebratenen Nudeln auf den Tellern jeweils ein kleines Nest auslegen.
Die Schwalbennestspeise darüber schöpfen und mit Schinkenwürfeln bestreut servieren.

LOTUS SOUP WITH DATES

For each person:

8 whole dried lotus seeds, 8 whole dried red dates,
brown rock candy

Steam the lotus seeds and dates for two hours. Place
in a small earthenware pot, cover with water, add
rock candy, replace the lid and simmer for about one
hour. Ladle into serving dishes and allow to go cold.

LOTOSSÜPPCHEN MIT DATTELN

Pro Person:

8 ganze, getrocknete Lotossamen,
8 ganze, getrocknete rote Datteln, brauner Kandiszucker

Lotossamen und Datteln zwei Stunden im Wasserdampf garen. In einen kleinen Tontopf umfüllen, mit
Wasser bedecken, Kandiszucker zugeben und zugedeckt ungefähr eine Stunde köcheln lassen. In
Servierschalen füllen und erkalten lassen.

Dried Black Fungus
Getrockneter schwarzer Pilz

木耳

Dried Yellow Fungus
Getrockneter gelber Pilz

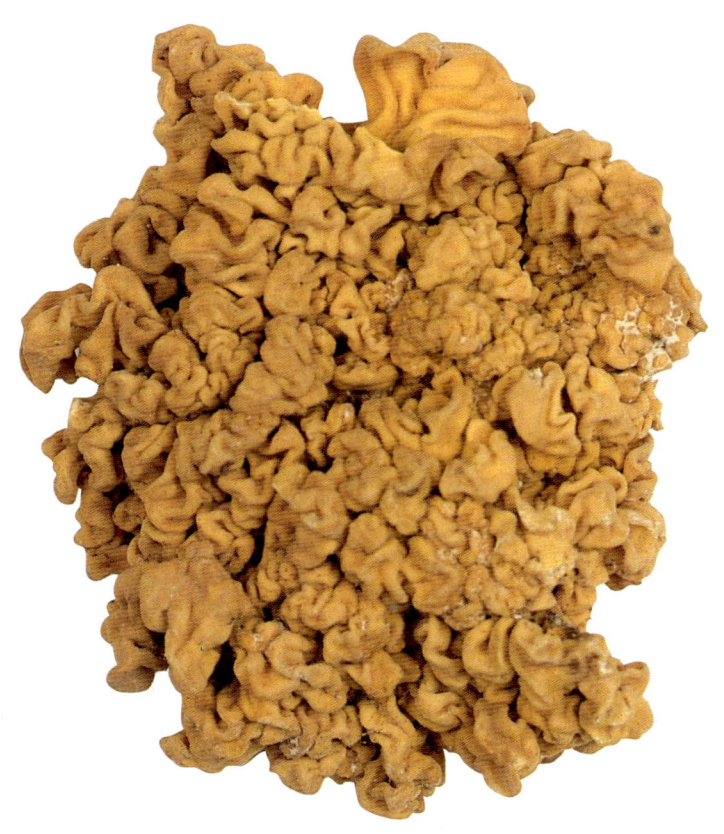

Dried Mushroom
Getrockneter Champignon

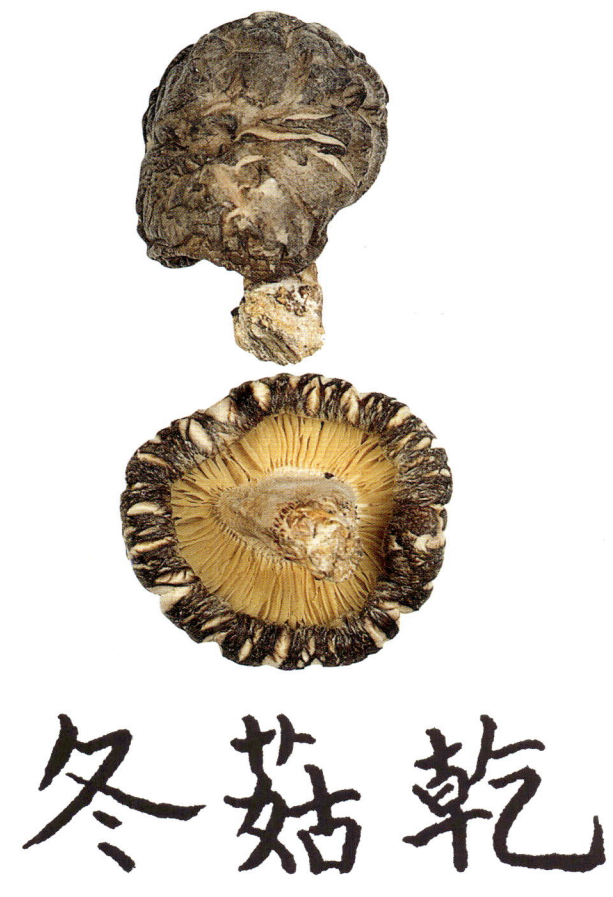

冬菇乾

Water Chestnut
Wasserkastanie

馬蹄

竹筍

Bamboo Shoot
Bambusschote

粽

Rice and meat, wrapped in a lotus leaf
Reis und Fleisch im Lotosblatt

Restaurant Petrus

The way up to the top floor of the Island Shangri-La hotel, to the Restaurant Petrus, is itself spectacular: the glass cabin of the elevator swishes 166 breathtaking feet (past 16 floors) in the hotel atrium past the world's biggest hand-painted Chinese landscape. 166 feet high, 45 feet wide; 40 artists from the Institute of Arts and Handicrafts in Peking labored for six months on this monumental work. Like in a time-lapse film, the huge country floats past: the Huangguoshu waterfalls, the Great Wall, Peking, the Yellow River. Breathtaking landscapes and views – a moment ago as an artistic painting, minutes later in the original: in the Restaurant Petrus on the 56th floor of the Shangri-La hotel, Hong Kong lies at our feet. Kowloon on the opposite side of the harbor has shrunk to the size of toys, the Star Ferry is just a nutshell. Only the tower of the Central Plaza and the bold Bank of China are a match for height.

Restaurant Petrus: the name is a program. We are not only high above the canyon-like streets of Hong Kong, we have also landed in the seventh heaven of wine. Beside much more of that which has renown and esteem in the international wine world, a more complete collection of Château Petrus wines than up here would be difficult to find – even in France.
The list begins with a magnum of 1906. One can, of course, also order such a large bottle of the legendary and rare vintages 1929, 1945, 1959 or 1961. The last one alone, however, would strain our bank account to the tune of 92,800 Hong Kong dollars. In levying duty on foreign luxury products the authorities here know no mercy. But the wine list of over 500 items means that we shall not die of thirst, even if we have tighter purse-strings.

That a wise hotel management does not only invest in the wine cellar, but also in the kitchen and not least in the chef of the same, has been demonstrated here by engaging Alain Verzeroli, a Frenchman born 31 years ago in Vietnam. After graduating from school, he studied at the Ecole Supérieure de Cuisine Française and then ascended the ladder step by step, only under first-class masters: he worked for Guy Savoy, Taillevent, Arpège, and to crown this, for three years as sous-chef with the Paris three-star king Joël Robuchon. Maître d'hôtel Eric Desgouttes and food and beverage manager Michael Hendler show how proud they are to have him: "Verzeroli brings us the Michelin three-star status and supplements it by his own creative style".

His own creative style, this means for Verzeroli a sublime marriage of Asiatic and French flavors, products and preparation methods, adapting the French cuisine in Asia and not vice-versa. So he has no inhibitions about using cream and butter – albeit only in finely controlled amounts, of course.
The two-hundred percent accuracy of his handicraft – it is a joy to watch him – identifies him without a doubt as an attentive disciple of Robuchon. His culinary art, the quality of the produce he uses, and the spectacular wine cellar are the three pillars of the pleasures of the table at the Petrus.

Huangguoshu waterfalls

Der Weg ins oberste Stockwerk des Island Shangri-La Hotels, hinauf zum Restaurant Petrus, ist schon ein Spektakel für sich: die Glaskabine des Aufzuges rauscht im Atrium des Hotels 51 atemberaubende Meter (oder genau über 16 Stockwerke hinweg) am weltgrößten chinesischen handgemalten Landschaftsbild vorbei. 51 Meter hoch, 14 Meter breit: 40 Künstler vom Institut für Kunst und Handwerk in Peking haben sechs Monate lang an diesem Monumentalwerk gearbeitet. Im Zeitraffer schwebt das riesige Land an einem vorbei: die Huangguoshu-Wasserfälle, die Große Mauer, Peking, der Gelbe Fluß. Atemberaubende Landschaften und Ausblicke – soeben noch als kunstvolles Gemälde, Minuten später im Original: im Restaurant Petrus im 56. Stockwerk des Shangri-La Hotels liegt uns Hong Kong zu Füßen. Kowloon auf der gegenüberliegenden Seite ist auf Spielzeuggröße geschrumpft, die Star-Ferry gerade noch eine Nußschale. Nur der Turm des Central Plaza und die kühne Bank of China halten mit.

Restaurant Petrus: der Name ist Programm. Wir sind nicht nur hoch über den Straßenschluchten von Hong Kong, wir sind auch im siebten Wein-Himmel gelandet. Neben vielem anderen, was in der internationalen Weinwelt Rang und Namen hat: eine vollständigere Kollektion von Château-Petrus-Weinen als hier oben wird man lange suchen müssen – selbst in Frankreich. Mit einer Magnum von 1906 beginnt die Liste. Selbstverständlich kann eine solche Groß-Bouteille auch von den legendären und raren Jahrgängen 1929, 1945, 1959 oder 1961 geordert werden. Alleine die letztere würde jedoch unser Konto mit 92'800,00 Hongkong-Dollar belasten. Bei Zollabgaben auf ausländische Luxusprodukte kennen die Behörden hier kein Pardon. Aber die über 500 Positionen umfassende Weinkarte läßt uns auch bei einem schmaleren Budget nicht verdursten.

Daß ein kluges Hotelmanagement nicht nur in den Weinkeller investiert, sondern auch in die Küche und dort nicht zuletzt in den Chef derselben, hat man hier bewiesen mit der Verpflichtung von Alain Verzeroli, einem Franzosen, der vor 31 Jahren in Vietnam das Licht der Welt erblickt hat. Nach dem Abitur absolvierte er die Ecole Supérieure de Cuisine Française, danach ging es Schritt für Schritt und nur bei erstklassigen Lehrmeistern nach oben: Stationen bei Guy Savoy, Taillevent, Arpège und, als Krönung, drei Jahre als Sous-Chef beim Pariser Drei-Sterne-König Joël Robuchon. Bei Maître d'hôtel Eric Desgouttes und bei Food & Beverage-Manager Michael Hendler schwingt denn auch einiger Stolz mit: „Verzeroli bringt das Drei-Sterne-Michelin-Niveau zu uns und erweitert es mit seinem eigenen kreativen Stil".

Eigener kreativer Stil, das bedeutet bei Verzeroli eine sublime Vermählung von asiatischen und französischen Aromen, Produkten und Zubereitungsarten, wobei er die französische Küche in Asien adaptiert und nicht umgekehrt. So hat er überhaupt keine Scheu, auch Sahne und Butter – selbstverständlich nur in fein dosierten Maßen – zu verwenden. Die zweihundertprozentige handwerkliche Akuratesse – es ist ein Genuß, ihm zuzuschauen – weist ihn ohne jeden Zweifel als gelehrigen Robuchon-Schüler aus. Seine Kochkunst, die Qualität der verwendeten Produkte und das spektakuläre Weinangebot sind die drei Säulen der Tafelfreuden im Petrus.

Alain Verzeroli

MENU DEGUSTATION

SALADE DE HOMARD EN BOLERO
Boston lobster salad served with a creamy Xeres vinegar dressing
and vegetable pearls

* * *

TRANCHE FOIE GRAS DE CANARD POELEE AUX NAVETS CONFITS
REDUCTION DE VIEUX PORTO
Sautéed slice of duckliver with candied turnips and vintage Port reduction

* * *

SOUPE DE TRUFFES NOIRES DU PERIGORD
AUX ASPERGES VERTES ET SALSIFIS
Black Perigord truffle soup with green asparagus and salsify

* * *

LOTTE GLACEE AUX EPICES DOUCES, ETUVE DE CHOU VERT
BEURRE DE SAUGE
Glazed monkfish fillet with fragrant spices, sage and lemon butter

* * *

CARRE D'AGNEAU EN ROBE DE NOIX, SAUCE LEGERE AU CARVI,
CROUSTILLANT DE CELERI
Gratinated Australian rack of lamb in walnut crust served with deepfried celery
and a light caraway seed sauce

* * *

FROMAGES DE LA FERME CENERI
Selection of Céneri cheeses

* * *

MILLE-FEUILLES DE POMMES AUX AMANDES
ACCOMPAGNE D'UNE GLACE AU BOURBON
Apple and almond mille-feuilles served with a Bourbon ice cream

* * *

MOCCA
Coffee or tea

HK$820.00 per person
(Minimum two persons)

Subject to 10% service charge

TUNA FISH TARTARE ON SESAME OIL SAUCE WITH WHITE-RADISH SALAD

THUNFISCHTATAR AN SESAMÖLSAUCE MIT RETTICHSALAT

For 4 persons:

500 g/1 lb 2 oz best quality fresh tuna,
80 ml/2²/₃ fl oz/¹/₃ cup mayonnaise,
4 tsp Worcestershire sauce, 1 dash Tabasco,
1 tbsp finely chopped shallots, 1 piece of lemon

Sesame oil dressing:
75 ml/2¹/₂ fl oz/¹/₃ cup sesame oil,
75 ml/2¹/₂ fl oz/¹/₃ cup peanut oil,
4 tbsp dark soy sauce, 2 tbsp aceto balsamico,
salt, pepper

To garnish:
100 g/3 oz carrot, 200 g/7 oz white radish,
100 g/3 oz celeriac,
1 knife-tip saffron, a little ruccola,
20 g/²/₃ oz fresh coriander leaves,
Chinese chives,
2 edible yellow blossoms (kiku)

Stir the ingredients for the sesame oil dressing well; season with salt and pepper.
Cut the tuna into 1-cm/²/₅-in cubes. Mix well with the mayonnaise, the spices, a little lemon juice and 60 ml/2 fl oz/¹/₄ cup sesame oil dressing, and season with salt and pepper. Allow to stand in the refrigerator for about one hour.
Cut the carrot, white radish and celeriac into fine juliennes. Lay half of the white-radish juliennes in a small bowl with ice-water and color with the saffron. Lay the remaining white radish in clear ice-water.
Divide the tartare into four portions and arrange in a circle in the center of the plates. Wet the vegetable juliennes with the dressing and spread loosely over the tartare. Decorate with ruccola leaves, coriander leaves and Chinese chives and finally scatter with the plucked blossom petals.

Für 4 Personen:

500 g frischer Thunfisch bester Qualität,
80 ml Mayonnaise,
4 TL Worcestershire Sauce, 1 Spritzer Tabasco,
1 EL feingeschnittene Schalotten, 1 Stück Zitrone

Sesamöldressing:
75 ml Sesamöl,
75 ml Erdnußöl,
4 EL dunkle Sojasauce, 2 EL Aceto Balsamico,
Salz, Pfeffer

Garnitur:
100 g Karotte, 200 g Rettich,
100 g Sellerie,
1 Msp. Safran, etwas Ruccola,
20 g frisches Koriandergrün,
chinesischer Schnittlauch,
2 eßbare gelbe Blüten (Kiku)

Zutaten für das Sesamöldressing gut verrühren, mit Salz und Pfeffer abschmecken.
Thunfisch in 1 cm große Würfel schneiden. Mit der Mayonnaise, den Gewürzen, etwas Zitronensaft und 60 ml Sesamöldressing gut vermengen und mit Salz und Pfeffer abschmecken. Im Kühlschrank etwa eine Stunde ziehen lassen. Karotte, Rettich und Sellerie in feine Streifen (Julienne) schneiden. Die Hälfte der Rettichjulienne in eine kleine Schale mit Eiswasser legen und mit Safran einfärben. Den restlichen Rettich in klares Eiswasser legen.
Tatar in vier Portionen teilen und jeweils kreisförmig in die Mitte der Teller anrichten. Die Gemüsejulienne mit dem Dressing benetzen und locker über das Tatar verteilen. Mit Ruccolablättern, Koriandergrün und chinesischem Schnittlauch dekorieren und zum Schluß mit den gezupften gelben Blütenblättern bestreuen.

STUFFED GLAZED TOMATOES WITH ORANGE SYRUP

GEFÜLLTE GLACIERTE TOMATEN AN ORANGENSIRUP

For 6 persons:

For the orange syrup:
300 ml/10 fl oz/1¼ cups freshly pressed orange juice,
300 g/10 oz/1¼ cups sugar, 1 vanilla pod,
3 star anise, 3 cloves

For the tomato filling:
150 g/5 oz red apple, 150 g/5 oz pear,
50 g/1⅔ oz pineapple, 50 g/1⅔ oz mango,
2 g/½ tsp fresh root ginger, 3 mint leaves,
1 tsp raisins, 1 tsp pistachios,
1 knife-tip ground cinnamon, 2 tsp butter,
1 tsp finely chopped orange zest,
1 tsp finely chopped lemon zest,
2 tsp sugar

6 tomatoes of 60 g/2 oz each,
1 piece of lemon, vanilla ice-cream

Für 6 Personen:

Für den Orangensirup:
300 ml frischgepreßter Orangensaft,
300 g Zucker, 1 Vanillestengel,
3 Sternanis, 3 Gewürznelken

Für die Tomatenfüllung:
150 g roter Apfel, 150 g Birne,
50 g Ananas, 50 g Mango,
2 g frische Ingwerwurzel, 3 Minzeblätter,
1 TL Rosinen, 1 TL Pistazien,
1 Msp Zimt gemahlen, 2 TL Butter,
1 TL feingehackte Orangenschale,
1 TL feingehackte Zitronenschale,
2 TL Zucker

6 Tomaten von je 60 g,
1 Stück Zitrone, Vanilleeis

For the orange syrup: Boil the orange juice with sugar, scraped-out vanilla pith and the spices in a small pot for three to four minutes. Set aside.

For the filling: Cut the apple, pear, pineapple and mango into small cubes (Brunoise); finely chop the ginger, mint, raisins, and pistachios.

Heat the butter in a skillet, add the prepared fruit and spices, stir in the sugar, and over a strong heat boil for about one minute, stirring. Then remove the skillet from the stove and allow to cool.

Immerse the tomatoes in boiling water for ten seconds and skin them. Cut out the stalk root and, through this hole, use a small spoon to carefully remove the seeds. Stuff the tomatoes with the filling, place on a baking tray and cook for eight to nine minutes in a 200° C/390° F preheated oven. During the cooking time, baste frequently with the syrup.

To serve: Transfer the tomatoes to plates, surround with orange syrup and squeeze a few drops of lemon juice over each one.

Place a large ball of vanilla ice-cream on each plate and serve.

Für den Orangensirup: Orangensaft mit Zucker, ausgeschabtem Vanillemark und den Gewürzen in einem kleinen Topf drei bis vier Minuten kochen lassen. Beiseite stellen.

Für die Füllung: Apfel, Birne, Ananas und Mango in feine Würfel (Brunoise) schneiden; Ingwer, Minze, Rosinen und Pistazien fein hacken. Butter in einer Pfanne erhitzen, die vorbereiteten Früchte und Gewürze zugeben, den Zucker untermischen und alles bei grosser Hitze ca. eine Minute unter Rühren kochen lassen. Pfanne vom Herd nehmen und auskühlen lassen. Die Tomaten zehn Sekunden in kochendes Wasser tauchen und enthäuten. Stielansatz wegschneiden und durch dieses Loch mit einem kleinen Löffel vorsichtig die Kerne herauslösen. Tomaten mit der Füllung versehen, auf ein Blech setzen und im auf 200° C vorgeheizten Ofen acht bis neun Minuten garen. Während der Garzeit öfters mit dem Sirup besprenkeln.

Zum Servieren: Die Tomaten auf Teller geben, mit Orangensirup umgießen und jeweils einige Tropfen Zitronensaft darüber ausdrücken. Eine große Kugel Vanilleeis daneben setzen und servieren.

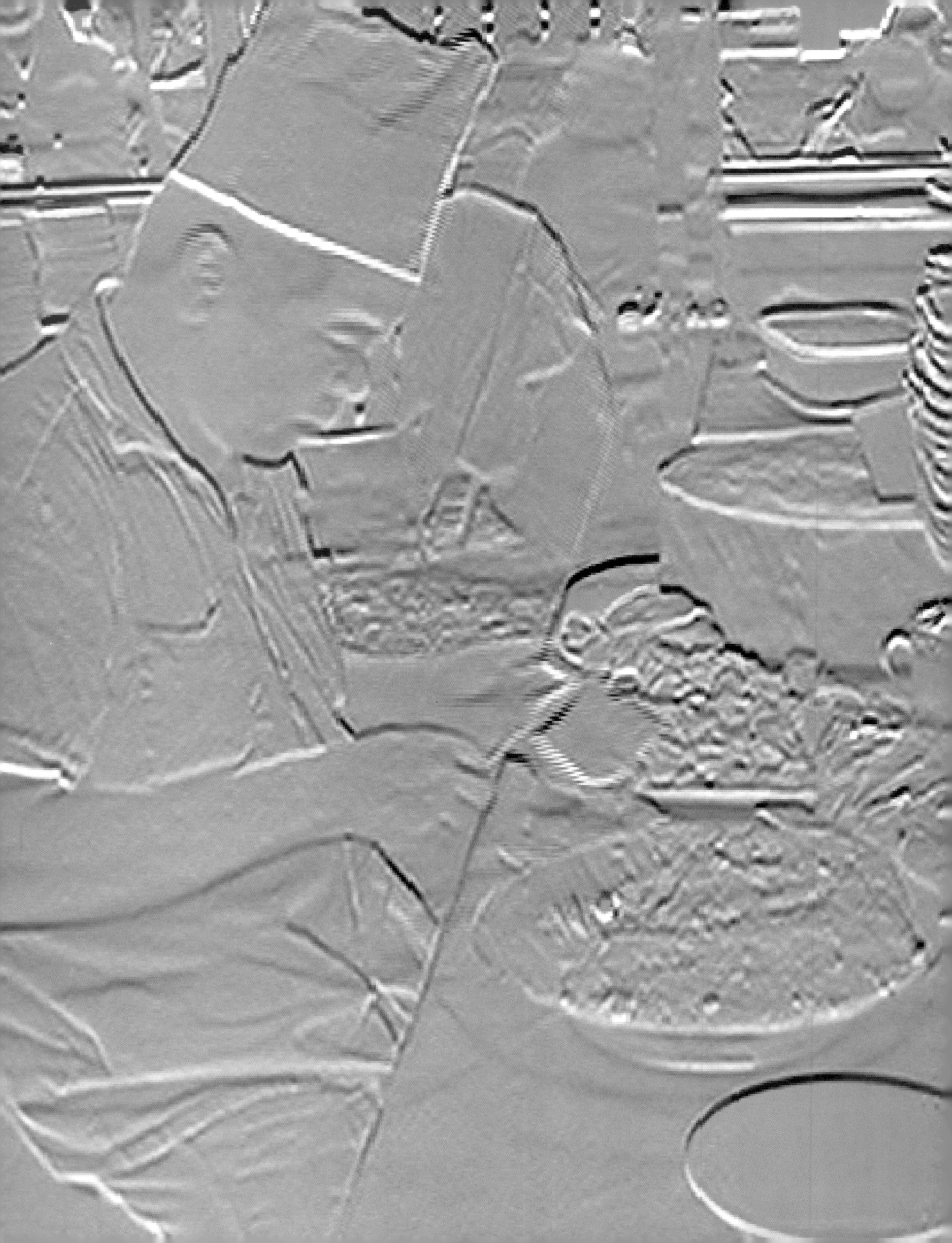

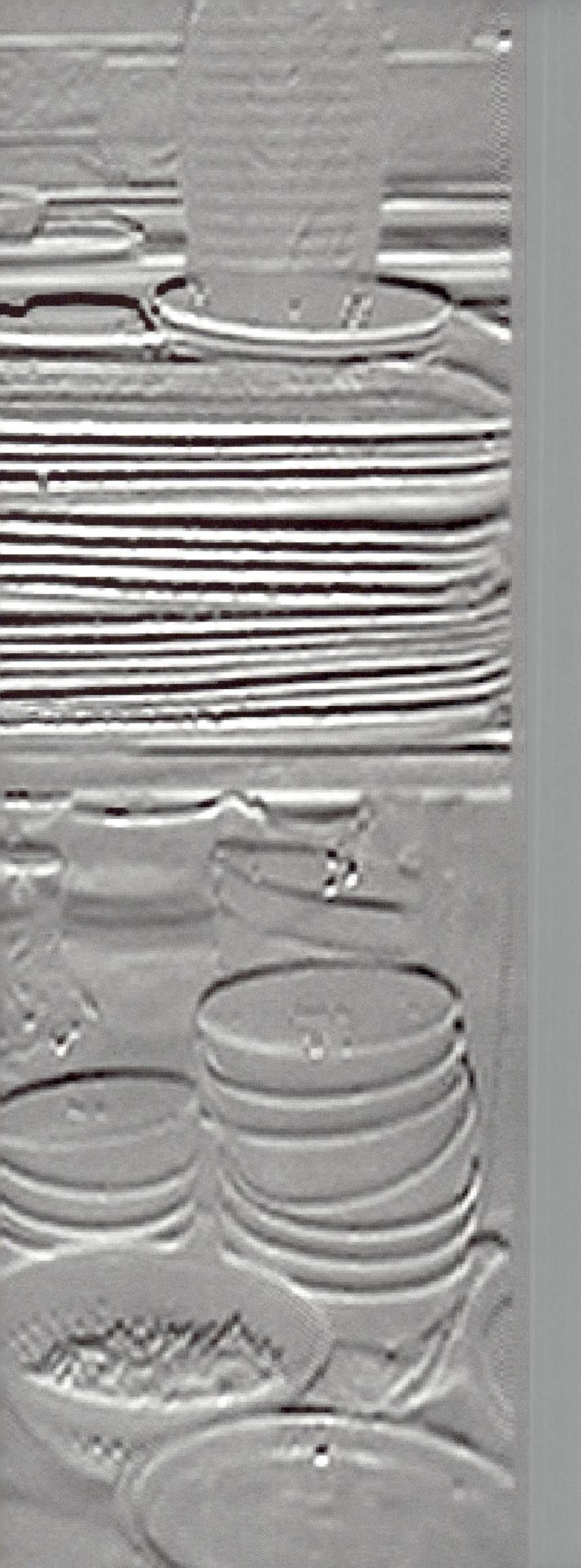

Won Ton

THE PENINSULA

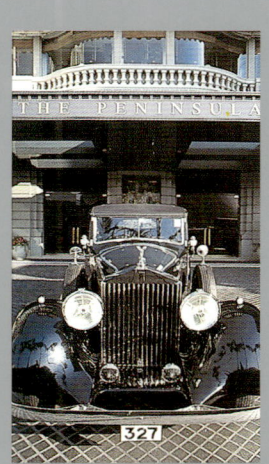

Gaddi's Restaurant

Gaddi's in the Peninsula Hotel is the opposite pole to the avant-garde Restaurant Felix: from top to toe a solid and tasteful first-class restaurant with blue and gold decor and seating for 80 guests. From the chandelier to the chairs to the cutlery, the hotel managers have shipped in only the finest of the fine from France's manufacturers. In keeping with such an ambience, the French cuisine is of the highest standard. The guarantor of this is Julien Bompard, six-foot-six including chef's hat, who has a loose overview of the entire kitchen staff. Barely 30 years old, he has an astonishing career behind him. Provençal blood flows in his veins, and he has learnt super-class Provençal cuisine under Louis Outhier at the famous "L'Oasis" on the Côte d'Azur near Cannes. Julien Bompard received his second formative influence in Burgundy with the three-star cook Jacques Lameloise. And it is just this mixture of the two great French regional cuisines that characterizes his cooking style and the charm of his creations: the rich, traditional style of Burgundy, where he received a sound basic training in "cuisine du terroir". And the "cuisine du soleil", the lighter, mediterranean cuisine of Provence with lots of vegetables, herbs and lighter sauces. Skilful combination of the best of the two styles results in a classical light cuisine, just as if it had been specially invented for the warm climate of Hong Kong.

Some of the convincing results of these exercises in style are the scallops with shrimps and a caviare-based beurre blanc; "agio boulido", namely blanched fresh vegetables of the season with truffles and extra virgin olive oil aromatized with garlic; or a sole, fried whole, with Provençal herbs and vegetables.

Gaddi's ist im Peninsula-Hotel der Gegenpol zum Avant-Garde-Restaurant Felix: ein vom Scheitel bis zur Sohle gediegenes und geschmackvolles First-Class-Restaurant im blaugoldenen Dekor mit Platz für 80 Gäste. Vom Kronleuchter übers Gestühl bis zum Besteck haben die Hotel-Manager nur das Feinste vom Feinen aus Frankreichs Manufakturen hierher schippern lassen. Dazu gibt es, dem Ambiente angemessen, eine französische Küche auf höchstem Niveau. Garant hierfür ist Julien Bompard, der mitsamt Kochmütze zwei Meter mißt und das gesamte Küchenpersonal locker überblickt. Für seine knapp 30 Lebensjahre hat er schon eine erstaunliche Karriere hinter sich. Provenzalisches Blut fließt in seinen Adern, provenzalische Küche der Extraklasse hat er bei Louis Outhier im berühmten „L'Oasis" an der Côte d'Azur bei Cannes gelernt. Den zweiten prägenden Einfluß bekam Julien Bompard im Burgund, beim Drei-Sterne-Koch Jacques Lameloise. Und genau der Mix aus diesen beiden großen französischen Regionalküchen macht auch seinen Kochstil und den Reiz seiner Kreationen aus: die reiche, traditionelle Küche des Burgund, wo er die solide Grundausbildung einer „cuisine du terroir" mitbekommen hat. Und die „cuisine du soleil", die leichtere, mediterrane Küche der Provence mit viel Gemüse, Kräutern und leichteren Saucen. Das Beste aus beiden Stilrichtungen gekonnt kombiniert ergibt eine klassische leichte Küche, gerade so, als ob sie für das warme Klima von Hong Kong erfunden worden wäre.

Überzeugende Ergebnisse dieser Stilübungen sind Saint-Jacques-Muscheln mit Crevetten und einer Beurre Blanc auf Kaviarbasis; „Agio Boulido", blanchierte frische Saisongemüse mit Trüffeln und einem mit Knoblauch aromatisierten Extra-Vergine-Olivenöl oder Seezunge, am Stück gebraten, mit provenzalischen Kräutern und Gemüsen.

SMOKED SALMON ROLLS WITH CAVIAR AND CHAMPAGNE VINEGAR

RÄUCHERLACHSRÖLLCHEN MIT KAVIAR UND CHAMPAGNERESSIG

For 4 persons:

300 g/10 oz smoked salmon, cut into fine slices

*120 ml/4 fl oz/¹/₂ cup cream,
1 tsp champagne vinegar, 1 sheet gelatin,
2 tbsp fresh chopped herbs
(e.g. parsley, dill, chives, chervil)*

*10 round thin slices of white bread without crust,
chives, whole stalks,
80 g/2²/₃ oz/¹/₃ cup Osietra caviar, 1 hard-boiled egg*

*To garnish:
herbs*

Flavor the cream with a little champagne vinegar and warm it so that the softened gelatin will dissolve in it. Allow to cool. Stir in the herbs and place the cream in the refrigerator until half-set.
Coat the slices of salmon with this mixture and roll up. Wrap in cling foil and allow to set in the refrigerator.
Remove the foil. Cut the rolls into pieces about 1 cm/²/₅ in thick.
To serve: Lay a slice of bread on each plate, cover the entire bread with the rolls. Scald the chives briefly with hot water, allow to cool and tie around the salmon rolls as one would with string. Decorate each with a tablespoonful of caviar.
Finely chop the egg yolk and egg white separately and sprinkle around the rim of the plate. Garnish with herbs.

Für 4 Personen:

300 g Räucherlachs in feine Scheiben geschnitten

*120 ml Sahne, 1 TL Champagneressig,
1 Blatt Gelatine,
2 EL frische gehackte Kräuter
(z. B. Petersilie, Dill, Schittlauch, Kerbel)*

*10 runde, dünne Weißbrotscheiben, ohne Rinde,
Schnittlauch,
80 g Osietra Kaviar, 1 hartgekochtes Ei*

*Garnitur:
Kräuter*

Die Sahne mit etwas Champagneressig würzen und soweit erwärmen, daß die eingeweichte Gelatine darin aufgelöst werden kann. Abkühlen lassen, die Kräuter unterrühren und die Sahne im Kühlschrank halbfest werden lassen.
Lachsscheiben mit dieser Masse bestreichen und einrollen. In Frischhaltefolie wickeln und im Kühlschrank fest werden lassen. Aus der Folie nehmen. Die Rollen in ca. 1 cm dicke Stücke schneiden.
Anrichten: Je eine Brotscheibe auf Teller legen. Die Röllchen daraufstellen, bis das ganze Brot bedeckt ist. Schnittlauch kurz mit heißem Wasser überbrühen, abkühlen lassen und die Lachsröllchen wie mit einem Bindfaden „zubinden". Mit je einem Löffel Kaviar dekorieren.
Eigelb und Eiweiß separat fein hacken und über den Tellerrand streuen. Mit Kräutern garnieren.

FRIED FILLET OF BEEF
ON A POTATO-TRUFFLE ROSETTE

For 4 persons:

4 slices of beef fillet of about 140 g/5 oz each

40 g/1 1/3 oz black truffle,
600 g/1 lb 5 oz small new potatoes,
3 tbsp olive oil, salt

600 g/1 lb 5 oz spinach, 2 tbsp truffle oil, salt

400 ml/13 fl oz/1 2/3 cups veal stock, 1 tbsp chopped truffle parings,
salt, pepper, 2 tbsp cold butter

1 tbsp olive oil, 1 tbsp butter
1 bunch of chives, finely chopped

Thinly slice the truffle. Likewise thinly slice the potatoes and fry in olive oil until done. Lightly season with salt. Blanch the spinach in salted water, drain through a sieve and sauté in truffle oil. Season with salt.
Heat the veal stock. Season with salt and pepper, add the chopped truffle and stir in the cold butter.
Salt and pepper the fillet steaks and fry as desired in a mixture of oil and butter.
To serve: Form a rosette of potato and truffle slices on each plate. In the middle, place a heap of spinach and lay the steaks on top. Pour over the sauce and sprinkle with chopped chives.

GEBRATENE RINDERLENDE
AUF EINER KARTOFFEL-TRÜFFELROSETTE

Für 4 Personen:

4 Rinderlendenscheiben von je ca. 140 g

40 g schwarzer Trüffel,
600 g kleine neue Kartoffeln,
3 EL Olivenöl, Salz

600 g Spinat, 2 EL Trüffelöl, Salz

400 ml Kalbsfond, 1 EL gehackte Trüffelabschnitte,
Salz, Pfeffer, 2 EL kalte Butter

1 EL Olivenöl, 1 EL Butter
1 Bund Schnittlauch, fein geschnitten

Trüffel in dünne Scheiben schneiden. Kartoffeln ebenfalls in dünne Scheiben schneiden und im Olivenöl braten bis sie gar sind. Leicht mit Salz würzen. Spinat in Salzwasser blanchieren, durch ein Sieb abgießen und im Trüffelöl dünsten. Mit Salz würzen.
Kalbsfond erhitzen. Mit Salz und Pfeffer würzen, gehackten Trüffel zugeben und die kalte Butter unterrühren. Lendensteaks salzen, pfeffern und in einem Öl-Buttergemisch nach Belieben braten.
Zum Servieren: Aus Kartoffel- und Trüffelscheiben eine Rosette auf die Teller legen. In die Mitte je eine Portion Spinat häufen und darauf die Lendensteaks legen. Mit der Sauce begießen und mit etwas Schnittlauch bestreuen.

CALVES' KIDNEYS
WITH SHERRY VINEGAR

For 4 persons:

600 g/1 lb 5 oz calves' kidneys,
2 tbsp oil

2 tbsp butter,
salt, pepper from the mill

2 shallots, finely chopped,
2 tbsp sherry vinegar,
200 ml/7 fl oz/⁴/₅ cup thickened, brown veal stock

1 tbsp cold butter,
2 tbsp parsley, chopped

KALBSNIERCHEN
AN SHERRYESSIG

Für 4 Personen:

600 g Kalbsnieren,
2 EL Öl

2 EL Butter,
Salz, Pfeffer aus der Mühle

2 Schalotten, fein geschnitten,
2 EL Sherryessig,
200 ml gebundener brauner Kalbsfond

1 EL kalte Butter,
2 EL Petersilie, gehackt

Halve the kidneys lengthwise, clean them inside and out, carefully removing membranes and veins. Cut into slices about 5 mm/ ¹/₅ in thick, and in a large skillet, briefly fry on all sides in hot oil, turning frequently. Drain through a sieve.

Return the skillet with the butter to the stove. Season the kidneys with salt and pepper and fry in the butter for one to two minutes. Remove with a slotted spoon and pour off the fat.

Finely chop the shallots and sauté them in the skillet. Quench with sherry vinegar, add the veal stock and reduce the sauce for a few minutes. Season and place the kidneys in the sauce.

Stir in the cold butter, sprinkle with parsley and serve. A suitable accompaniment would be mushroom risotto.

Nieren der Länge nach halbieren, innen und aussen sauber putzen, dabei sorgfältig von Häutchen und Adern befreien. In ca. 5 mm dicke Scheiben schneiden und in einer großen Pfanne im heißen Öl unter Wenden kurz rundum anbraten. Durch ein Sieb abgießen.

Pfanne mit der Butter zurück auf den Herd stellen. Nieren mit Salz und Pfeffer würzen und nun in der Butter ein bis zwei Minuten braten. Mit der Lochkelle herausnehmen und das Fett abgießen.

Schalotten fein schneiden und in der Pfanne anschwitzen. Mit Sherryessig ablöschen, Kalbsfond zugießen und die Sauce einige Minuten einreduzieren lassen. Abschmecken und die Nieren in die Sauce geben. Die kalte Butter einrühren, mit Petersilie bestreuen und servieren. Als Beilage paßt Champignonrisotto.

SOLE WITH BASIL
AND TOMATO SAUCE

For 4 persons:

4 soles of about 400 g/13 oz each

1 head of fennel,
8 sticks of green asparagus, 8 cherry tomatoes,
200 g/7 oz new potatoes

2 tbsp butter, 1 tbsp olive oil,
salt, pepper

250 ml/8 fl oz/1 cup tomato sauce, 3 tbsp basil oil,
8 black olives, pitted, 1 bunch basil

Wash, clean and skin the soles. Segment the fennel, halve the asparagus and the tomatoes, slice the potatoes. Boil the fennel and asparagus in salted water for five minutes, drain and set aside.
Heat the butter in a skillet and fry the potato slices until golden. Add the fennel, asparagus, tomatoes and olive oil and fry. Sprinkle with salt.
Fry the soles on the griddle on both sides. Season with salt and pepper. Warm the tomato sauce. Pluck off the basil leaves and fry in hot oil.
To serve: Distribute the tomato sauce on plates, lay one sole on each, surround with the vegetables and the potatoes and drizzle with basil oil. Serve garnished with the olives and the fried basil leaves.

SEEZUNGE MIT BASILIKUM
UND TOMATENSAUCE

Für 4 Personen:

4 Seezungen von je ca. 400 g

1 Fenchelknolle,
8 Stangen grüner Spargel, 8 Kirschtomaten,
200 g neue Kartoffeln

2 EL Butter, 1 EL Olivenöl,
Salz, Pfeffer

250 ml Tomatensauce, 1 Bund Basilikum,
3 EL Basilikumöl, 8 schwarze Oliven, entkernt

Seezungen waschen, ausnehmen und enthäuten. Fenchel in Spalten schneiden, Spargel und Tomaten halbieren, Kartoffeln in Scheiben schneiden. Fenchel und Spargel in Salzwasser fünf Minuten kochen, abgießen und beiseite stellen. Butter in einer Pfanne erhitzen und die Kartoffelscheiben goldbraun braten. Fenchel, Spargel, Tomaten und Olivenöl zugeben und mitbraten. Mit Salz bestreuen.
Seezungen auf dem Grill von beiden Seiten braten, mit Salz und Pfeffer würzen. Tomatensauce erwärmen. Basilikumblätter abzupfen und im heißen Öl fritieren.
Zum Servieren: Tomatensauce auf Teller verteilen, je eine Seezunge auflegen, mit dem Gemüse und den Kartoffeln umranden, mit Basilikumöl besprenkeln. Mit den Oliven und den fritierten Basilikumblättern garniert servieren.

Les Plats Traditionnels de Gaddi's

Caviar oscietre royal d'Iran
et ses gaufres de pommes de terre (50 gm)
Iranian oscietra caviar with waffle potatoes
630.00

Saumon fumé de Balik "Zar Nikolaj"
Finest smoked Balik salmon with caviar
380.00

Salade de homard tiède aux herbes
Warm lobster salad with herbs
380.00

Salade d'endives aux truffes noires
Endive salad with black truffles
285.00

Bisque de homard aux ravioles de crabe
Lobster bisque with crab ravioli
160.00

———❦———

Coquelet de Bresse rôti à l'ail doux et aux cèpes
Roast Bresse spring chicken with sweet garlic and cep mushrooms
330.00

Mignons de veau poêlés au foie gras et truffes noires
Panfried veal mignons with duck liver and black truffles
360.00

Côte de boeuf Américain Black Angus grillée, sauce béarnaise
pommes de terre rôties sur sa peau (pour deux)
*Grilled American Black Angus rib of beef with a béarnaise sauce
and roast potatoes (for two)*
350.00 par personne (each)

Carré d'agneau d'Écosse aux gousses d'ail et au thym
Roast Scottish rack of lamb with garlic and thyme
330.00

La Cuisine de Saison

Terrine de foie gras confit au céleri et vinaigre de balsamic
Duck liver terrine with a celery salad and balsamico vinegar
290.00

Suprêmes de volaille fumée en salade de mesclun
aux truffes noires et champignons des bois
Seasonal salad with smoked chicken breast, black truffles and wild mushrooms
270.00

Coquilles Saint-Jacques grillées au beurre blanc de caviar
Grilled bay scallops with a caviar beurre blanc
330.00

Véritable saumon d'Écosse fumé au bois d'aulne, blinis tièdes
Finest smoked Scottish salmon with warm blinis
280.00

———❦———

Consommé de boeuf aux légumes et ravioles
Double boiled beef consommé with vegetables and ravioli
160.00

Crème légère de champagne et d'asperges vertes, quenelles de volaille aux truffes
Light cream of champagne and asparagus soup with truffled chicken mousse dumplings
170.00

———❦———

Langoustines et asperges vertes poêlées, sauce à l'orange
Panfried langoustines and green asparagus with an orange sauce
330.00

Gnocchi de pommes de terre aux artichauts, sauce au vin rouge
Potato gnocchi with artichokes and a red wine sauce
240.00

Escargots poêlés en robe des champs au vin de Château Châlon
Panfried snails with parsley and Château Châlon wine in baby potatoes
255.00

Escalopes de foie gras sautées au miel de lavande et noix
Sautéed goose liver escalopes with lavender honey and walnuts
280.00

Loup de mer en croûte "Louis Outhier", sauce choron (pour deux)
Black sea bass from France baked in pastry with a choron sauce (for two)
380.00 par personne (each)

Filets de sole cuits au beurre de pistou et légumes vapeur en bouquetière
Roasted fillets of sole with a pesto sauce and steamed vegetables
340.00

Turbot de ligne cuit à l'arête en cocotte de cèpes
Braised turbot with a garnish of potatoes, asparagus and cep mushrooms
390.00

Tian de Saint-Pierre rôti entier en bouillabaisse, ravioles d'herbes
Whole roasted Mediterranean John Dory with bouillabaisse and herb ravioli
370.00

Nage de homard vapeur au vinaigre de cidre et jus de pommes douces
Steamed lobster with apples and a light cider sauce
430.00

———❦———

Canette de ferme et sa cuisse confite, lasagne de céleri et marrons
Panfried farmhouse duck breast with duck leg confit, celery and chestnut lasagne
310.00

Pigeon de Bresse rôti et sauce aux morilles et Cognac
Roast Bresse pigeon with a morel and cognac sauce
360.00

Gigot d'agneau de lait braisé au thym, fèves et gratin boulangère
Braised lamb gigot with fresh thyme, broad beans and potato gratin
290.00

Filet de boeuf poché au court bouillon de légumes et vin blanc, sauce béarnaise
Poached beef tenderloin in a white wine and vegetable broth with a béarnaise sauce
330.00

Demi faisan cuit en cocotte de truffes, façon Souvaroff
risotto aux champignons sauvages
Souvaroff-style baked half pheasant with truffles, goose liver and a wild mushroom risotto
420.00

Traditionnelle côte de veau de lait rôtie
polenta et jus de cuisson à l'ail confit (pour deux)
Traditional roast milk-fed veal chop, polenta and roasted jus with garlic confit (for two)
360.00 par personne (each)

———❦———

Les fromages frais et affinés par Maître Édouard Céneri
Selected French cheeses
160.00

White Bordeaux

Sauternes

CHATEAU D' YQUEM *1er Grand Cru Classé*	1976		7,980.00
CHATEAU D' YQUEM *1er Grand Cru Classé*	1959		8,800.00
CHATEAU D' YQUEM *1er Grand Cru Classé*	1955		8,500.00
CHATEAU GILETTE "Crême de Tête" *Preignac*	1961		2,680.00
CHATEAU GILETTE "Crême de Tête" *Preignac*	1959		4,680.00
CHATEAU GILETTE "Crême de Tête" *Preignac*	1955		3,280.00
CHATEAU GILETTE "Crême de Tête" *Preignac*	1953		3,800.00

Barsac

CHATEAU CLIMENS *1er Grand Cru Classé*	1976		2,800.00
CHATEAU CLIMENS *1er Grand Cru Classé*	1953		4,600.00
CHATEAU CLIMENS *1er Grand Cru Classé*	1947		5,200.00

Red Bordeaux

Saint-Estèphe

CHATEAU CALON-SEGUR *3e Cru Classé*	1959		4,800.00
CHATEAU CALON-SEGUR *3e Cru Classé*	1953	Magnum	8,800.00
CHATEAU COS D'ESTOURNEL *2e Cru Classé*	1970		3,200.00
CHATEAU MONTROSE *3e Cru Classé*	1966		4,800.00

Pauillac

CHATEAU BATAILLEY *5e Cru Classé*	1961		3,800.00
CHATEAU GRAND-PUY-LACOSTE *5e Cru Classé*	1970		2,200.00
CHATEAU LAFITE-ROTHSCHILD *1er Cru Classé*	1970		6,800.00
CHATEAU LAFITE-ROTHSCHILD *1er Cru Classé*	1966		8,800.00
CHATEAU LAFITE-ROTHSCHILD *1er Cru Classé*	1961		13,800.00
CHATEAU LAFITE-ROTHSCHILD *1er Cru Classé*	1961	1/2 bottle	6,300.00

CHATEAU MARGAUX *1er Cru Classé*	1966		6,800.00
CHATEAU MARGAUX *1er Cru Classé*	1961		12,800.00
CHATEAU MARGAUX *1er Cru Classé*	1959		11,800.00
CHATEAU MARGAUX *1er Cru Classé*	1955		9,800.00
CHATEAU PALMER *3e Cru Classé*	1970		4,500.00
CHATEAU PALMER *3e Cru Classé*	1966		6,800.00
CHATEAU RAUSAN-GASSIES *2e Cru Classé*	1928		7,800.00

Saint-Julien

CHATEAU BEYCHEVELLE *4e Cru Classé*	1970		3,500.00
CHATEAU BEYCHEVELLE *4e Cru Classé*	1966		3,800.00
CHATEAU BEYCHEVELLE *4e Cru Classé*	1953		4,800.00
CHATEAU BEYCHEVELLE *4e cru Classé*	1928		8,800.00
CHATEAU BRANAIRE-DUCRU *2e Cru Classé*	1966		3,800.00
CHATEAU DUCRU-BEAUCAILLOU *2e Cru Classé*	1966		3,600.00
CHATEAU GRUAUD-LAROSE *2e Cru Classé*	1961		5,800.00
CHATEAU LEOVILLE-BARTON *2e Cru Classé*	1961		3,803.00
CHATEAU LEOVILLE-POYFERRE *2e Cru Classé*	1961		2,800.00
CHATEAU TALBOT *4e Cru Classé*	1959		4,800.00

Graves

CHATEAU HAUT-BRION *1er Cru Classé*	1970		5,400.00
CHATEAU HAUT-BRION *1er Cru Classé*	1966		6,800.00
CHATEAU HAUT-BRION *1er Cru Classé*	1961		13,800.00
CHATEAU HAUT-BRION *1er Cru Classé*	1959		9,800.00
CHATEAU HAUT-BRION *1er Cru Classé*	1953		10,200.00

CHATEAU LAFITE-ROTHSCHILD *1er Cru Classé*	1955		8,800.00
CHATEAU LAFITE-ROTHSCHILD *1er Cru Classé*	1953		9,800.00
CHATEAU LAFITE-ROTHSCHILD *1er Cru Classé*	1949		10,800.00
CHATEAU LATOUR *1er Cru Classé*	1970		8,500.00
CHATEAU LATOUR *1er Cru Classé*	1971		4,800.00
CHATEAU LATOUR *1er Cru Classé*	1966		8,800.00
CHATEAU LATOUR *1er Cru Classé*	1959		12,800.00
CHATEAU LATOUR *1er Cru Classé*	1955		9,800.00
CHATEAU LATOUR *1er Cru Classé*	1953		10,800.00
CHATEAU LYNCH-BAGES *5e Cru Classé*	1970		4,800.00
CHATEAU LYNCH-BAGES *5e Cru Classé*	1966		4,200.00
CHATEAU LYNCH-BAGES *5e Cru Classé*	1961		6,500.00
CHATEAU MOUTON-ROTHSCHILD *2e Cru Classé*	1970		6,800.00
CHATEAU MOUTON-ROTHSCHILD *2e Cru Classé*	1961		13,800.00
CHATEAU MOUTON-ROTHSCHILD *2e Cru Classé*	1955		10,800.00
CHATEAU MOUTON-ROTHSCHILD *2e Cru Classé*	1953		12,800.00
CHATEAU PICHON-LALANDE *2e Cru Classé*	1970		4,600.00
CHATEAU PICHON-LALANDE *2e Cru Classé*	1966		4,800.00
CHATEAU PICHON-LALANDE *2e Cru Classé*	1928		11,800.00
CHATEAU PICHON-LONGUEVILLE *2e Cru Classé*	1953		5,100.00

Margaux

CHATEAU BRANE-CANTENAC *2e Cru Classé*	1970		2,100.00
CHATEAU GISCOURS *3e Cru Classé*	1961		3,800.00
CHATEAU MARGAUX *1er Cru Classé*	1970		4,500.00

CHATEAU HAUT-BRION *1er Cru Classé*	1949		11,800.00
CHATEAU HAUT-BRION *1er Cru Classé*	1928	1/2 bottle	6,800.00
CHATEAU PAPE-CLEMENT *Grand Cru Classé*	1961		4,500.00

Saint-Emilion

CHATEAU AUSONE *1er Grand Cru Classé A*	1953		6,800.00
CHATEAU CHEVAL-BLANC *1er Grand Cru Classé A*	1970		5,800.00
CHATEAU CHEVAL-BLANC *1er Grand Cru Classé A*	1955		7,200.00
CHATEAU CHEVAL-BLANC *1er Grand Cru Classé A*	1928		12,800.00

Pomerol

CHATEAU PETRUS *Cru Exceptionnel*	1982		16,800.00
CHATEAU PETRUS *Cru Exceptionnel*	1976		10,800.00
CHATEAU PETRUS *Cru Exceptionnel*	1975		15,800.00
CHATEAU PETRUS *Cru Exceptionnel*	1966		19,800.00
CHATEAU PETRUS *Cru Exceptionnel*	1961		58,000.00
CHATEAU PETRUS *Cru Exceptionnel*	1959		33,000.00
CHATEAU PETRUS *Cru Exceptionnel*	1953		28,000.00

Red Burgundies

Côte de Nuits

CHAMBERTIN *Leroy*	1989		4,800.00
ECHEZEAUX *Société Civile de la Romanée Conti*	1989		3,800.00
LA TACHE *Société Civile de la Romanée Conti*	1982		5,800.00
LA TACHE *Société Civile de la Romanée Conti*	1981		6,600.00
RICHEBOURG *Société Civile de la Romanée Conti*	1990		3,800.00
RICHEBOURG *Leroy*	1989		4,200.00
ROMANEE CONTI *Société Civile de la Romanée Conti*	1988		19,800.00

...mpagnes

Brut			680.00
Brut		1/2 bottle	350.00
Brut		Magnum	1,300.00
Brut Cuvée Spéciale			980.00
Brut Cuvée Spéciale		Jeroboam	4,500.00
EIDSIECK, Brut			920.00
de Blancs	1990		980.00
e Cuvée			2,680.00
e Cuvée		Magnum	5,800.00
	1982		3,800.00
	1979		4,200.00
u Mesnil	1983		5,200.00
tion	1969	Magnum	7,500.00
RRIER, Brut			780.00
RRIER, Cuvée Grand Siècle			1,800.00
ERER, Brut Premier			780.00
ERER, Brut	1990	1/2 bottle	580.00
ERER, Cristal Brut	1989		2,800.00
ERER, Cristal Brut	1985	Magnum	5,800.00
ANDON, Brut Impérial			880.00
ANDON, Brut Impérial		1/2 bottle	480.00
ANDON, Brut Impérial		Magnum	1,760.00
ANDON, Cuvée Dom Pérignon	1988		2,500.00
ANDON, Cuvée Dom Pérignon	1985	Magnum	5,000.00
on Rouge			750.00
ant de Cramant			1,150.00
e René Lalou	1985		1,380.00
ET, Belle Epoque	1988		2,380.00
ECK, Cuvée Brut			750.00
ECK, Brut Sauvage	1985		950.00
ECK "Rare"	1985		1,800.00
Brut	1988		950.00
Brut	1982	Jeroboam	4,000.00
Brut	1986	Salmanazar	12,000.00
rut	1988		980.00
, Réserve Brut			820.00
, Réserve Brut		1/2 bottles	420.00
, Réserve Brut		Magnum	1,680.00
, Comtes de Champagne	1988		1,980.00
Collection Masson	1983		2,000.00
QUOT, Brut Yellow Label			880.00
QUOT, La Grande Dame	1988		2,080.00
QUOT, Demi-Sec			860.00

Champagnes Rosés

CHARLES HEIDSIECK, Brut	1985		1,300.00
DEUTZ, Brut	1988		880.00
KRUG, Brut			4,880.00
LAURENT PERRIER, Cuvée Rosé Brut			980.00
LAURENT PERRIER, Cuvée Rosé Brut		Magnum	1,980.00
LOUIS ROEDERER, Cristal Brut	1985		4,500.00
MOET ET CHANDON, Cuvée Dom Pérignon	1985		4,580.00
PERRIER JOUET, Belle Epoque	1986		2,380.00
TAITTINGER, Comtes de Champagne	1986		2,080.00

Coteaux Champenois

LAURENT PERRIER, Blanc de Blancs de Chardonnay			480.00
LAURENT PERRIER, Bouzy Rouge			520.00

White Bordeaux

CHATEAU BLANC DE LYNCH-BAGES A.O.C.	1994		880.00
CHATEAU CARBONNIEUX A.O.C.	1992		680.00
CHATEAU HAUT BRION BLANC A.O.C.	1988		2,980.00
CHATEAU OLIVIER A.O.C.	1988		680.00
DOMAINE DE CHEVALIER Grand Cru Classé	1992		1,980.00
PAVILLON BLANC DU CHATEAU MARGAUX A.O.C.	1992		980.00

Sauternes and Barsac

CHATEAU CLIMENS 1er Cru Classé	1979		1,180.00
CHATEAU COUTET 1er Cru Classé	1986	1/2 bottle	480.00
CHATEAU COUTET 1er Cru Classé	1988		920.00
CHATEAU D'YQUEM 1er Grand Cru Classé	1988	1/2 bottle	3,500.00
CHATEAU D'YQUEM 1er Grand Cru Classé	1984		4,500.00
CHATEAU D'YQUEM 1er Grand Cru Classé	1985		5,500.00
CHATEAU FILHOT 2e Cru Classé	1989		980.00
CHATEAU FILHOT 2e Cru Classé	1990	1/2 bottle	480.00
CHATEAU SUDUIRAUT 1er Cru Classé	1985		1,280.00

Red Bordeaux

Médoc

CHATEAU FOURCAS-HOSTEN Cru Bourgeois, Listrac	1990		520.00
CHATEAU GRAND MOULIN Cru Bourgeois, Haut-Médoc	1992		420.00
CHATEAU LA LAGUNE 3e Cru Classé, Haut-Médoc	1975		1,500.00
CHATEAU LIVERSAN Cru Bourgeois, Haut-Médoc	1991		480.00
CHATEAU LIVERSAN Cru Bourgeois, Haut-Médoc	1991	Magnum	960.00
CHATEAU POTENSAC Cru Bourgeois	1990		550.00
CHATEAU VILLEGEORGE Cru Bourgeois, Haut-Médoc	1986		720.00

Saint- Estèphe

CHATEAU CALON-SEGUR 3e Cru Classé	1985		1,380.00
CHATEAU COS-D'ESTOURNEL 2e Cru Classé	1991		1,080.00
CHATEAU MONTROSE 2e Cru Classé	1992		980.00
CHATEAU MONTROSE 2e Cru Classé	1982		2,500.00

Pauillac

CHATEAU BATAILLEY 5e Cru Classé	1992	1/2 bottle	380.00
CHATEAU BATAILLEY 5e Cru Classé	1992		820.00
CHATEAU CROIZET-BAGES 5e Cru Classé	1992	1/2 bottle	450.00
CHATEAU HAUT-BAGES MONPELOU Cru Bourgeois	1992		480.00
CHATEAU LAFITE-ROTHSCHILD 1er Cru Classé	1986		4,800.00
CHATEAU LAFITE-ROTHSCHILD 1er Cru Classé	1985	1/2 bottle	2,100.00
CHATEAU LAFITE-ROTHSCHILD 1er Cru Classé	1985		4,200.00
CHATEAU LAFITE-ROTHSCHILD 1er Cru Classé	1983		4,280.00
CHATEAU LAFITE-ROTHSCHILD 1er Cru Classé	1983	Magnum	7,600.00
CHATEAU LAFITE-ROTHSCHILD 1er Cru Classé	1981		4,380.00
CARRUADES DE LAFITE-ROTHSCHILD A.O.C.	1990		950.00
CHATEAU LATOUR 1er Cru Classé	1985		4,380.00
CHATEAU LATOUR 1er Cru Classé	1983		3,600.00
CHATEAU LATOUR 1er Cru Classé	1982		8,800.00
CHATEAU LATOUR 1er Cru Classé	1978		4,980.00
CHATEAU LATOUR 1er Cru Classé	1975		5,800.00
LES FORTS DE LATOUR A.O.C.	1986		1,680.00
CHATEAU LYNCH-BAGES 5e Cru Classé	1991		980.00
CHATEAU LYNCH-BAGES 5e Cru Classé	1988		2,200.00
CHATEAU LYNCH-BAGES 5e Cru Classé	1988	Magnum	3,800.00
CHATEAU MOUTON-ROTHSCHILD 1er Cru Classé	1985		5,380.00
CHATEAU MOUTON-ROTHSCHILD 1er Cru Classé	1982		10,800.00
CHATEAU MOUTON-ROTHSCHILD 1er Cru Classé	1979		4,500.00
CHATEAU MOUTON-ROTHSCHILD 1er Cru Classé	1975		5,280.00
CHATEAU PICHON-LALANDE 2e Cru Classé	1988		2,280.00
CHATEAU PICHON-LALANDE 2e Cru Classé	1985		2,680.00
CHATEAU PICHON-LALANDE 2e Cru Classé	1982		5,500.00

Margaux

CHATEAU BRANE CANTENAC 2e Cru Classé	1982		1,680.00
CHATEAU CANTENAC-BROWN 3e Cru Classé	1993	1/2 bottle	420.00
CHATEAU LASCOMBES 2e Cru Classé	1993	1/2 bottle	420.00
CHATEAU LASCOMBES 2e Cru Classé	1993		750.00
CHATEAU LASCOMBES 2e Cru Classé	1989		980.00
CHATEAU MARGAUX 1er Cru Classé	1985		5,200.00
CHATEAU MARGAUX 1er Cru Classé	1982		9,800.00
CHATEAU MARGAUX 1er Cru Classé	1978		5,800.00
CHATEAU MARGAUX 1er Cru Classé	1976		3,800.00
CHATEAU PALMER 3e Cru Classé	1992		1,380.00
CHATEAU PALMER 3e Cru Classé	1982		3,200.00
CHATEAU PALMER 3e Cru Classé	1978		2,600.00
CHATEAU PALMER 3e Cru Classé	1975		2,500.00
CHATEAU RAUSAN-SEGLA 2e Cru Classé	1983		1,500.00
CHATEAU RAUSAN-SEGLA 2e Cru Classé	1989	Magnum	2,800.00
PAVILLON ROUGE DU CHATEAU MARGAUX A.O.C.	1989		1,380.00

Saint-Julien

CHATEAU BEYCHEVELLE 4e Cru Classé	1991		920.00
CHATEAU BEYCHEVELLE 4e Cru Classé	1985	1/2 bottle	880.00
CHATEAU BEYCHEVELLE 4e Cru Classé	1989		1,500.00
CHATEAU BEYCHEVELLE 4e Cru Classé	1983		1,380.00
CHATEAU BEYCHEVELLE 4e Cru Classé	1978		1,800.00
CHATEAU BRANAIRE-DUCRU 4e Cru Classé	1993	1/2 bottle	450.00

ANAIRE-DUCRU	1990		1,280.00
ANAIRE-DUCRU	1990	Magnum	2,500.00
VILLE BARTON	1989	1/2 bottle	680.00
CRU-BEAUCAILLOU	1983		1,580.00
VILLE-LAS CASES	1981		1,780.00
VILLE-LAS CASES	1976		2,000.00
BOT	1990		1,280.00
BOT	1982		3,280.00

RBONNIEUX ssé	1993		650.00
UT-BRION	1982		5,500.00
UT-BRION	1976		2,880.00
VIER ssé	1990		780.00
MISSION-HAUT-BRION ssé	1990		3,300.00
TH-HAUT-LAFITTE ssé	1993		720.00

n

SONE Classé A	1989		4,680.00
NON Classé B	1989		1,980.00
NTERANE	1989		680.00
EVAL-BLANC Classé A	1982		12,600.00
EVAL-BLANC Classé A	1989		4,280.00
EAC Classé B	1986	1/2 bottle	980.00
EAC Classé B	1986		2,200.00
UT-PONTET ssé	1990		820.00
GDELAINE Classé B	1986		1,680.00
GEORGES rges-Saint-Emilion	1990		560.00
TTEVIEILLE Classé B	1992		1,380.00

ICE	1990		680.00
MAINE DE L'EGLISE	1992		660.00
IN	1989		1,100.00
IN	1982		1,800.00
CONSEILLANTE	1991		2,200.00
LEUR-PETRUS	1990		2,680.00
RANGE	1982		1,800.00
T VILLAGE	1985		1,680.00
CHATEAU PETIT VILLAGE	1982		3,200.00
CHATEAU PETRUS Cru Exceptionnel	1980		6,200.00
CHATEAU PETRUS Cru Exceptionnel	1978		6,500.00
POMEROL JEAN-PIERRE MOUEIX A.O.C.	1993		430.00

White Burgundies

Chablis

CHABLIS Jean Herbet	1995		450.00
CHABLIS Henri Laroche	1995		450.00
CHABLIS 1er Cru Albert Pic et Fils	1992	1/2 bottle	350.00
CHABLIS "Pic 1er" Albert Pic et Fils	1990		1,080.00
CHABLIS 1er Cru "Montée de Tonnerre" Domaine François Raveneau	1993		680.00
CHABLIS 1er Cru "Vaillons" Domaine Long Depaquit	1995		580.00
CHABLIS Grand Cru "Bougros" William Fèvre	1989		820.00
CHABLIS Grand Cru "Clos des Hospices" J. Moreau et Fils	1993		1,200.00
CHABLIS Grand Cru "Vaudesir" Domaine Long Depaquit	1993		950.00
CHABLIS Grand Régnard Régnard	1993		580.00

Côte de Beaune

BATARD-MONTRACHET Louis Latour	1992		2,500.00
BEAUNE "Clos des Mouches" Joseph Drouhin	1994		1,180.00
CHASSAGNE-MONTRACHET "Marquis de Laguiche" Joseph Drouhin	1994		920.00
CHEVALIER-MONTRACHET, Grand Cru Domaine Jean Chartron	1993		2,980.00
CHATEAU DE MEURSAULT Domaine du Château de Meursault	1991		900.00
CORTON-CHARLEMAGNE Louis Latour	1992		1,680.00
CORTON-CHARLEMAGNE Michel Juillet	1991		2,980.00
CORTON-CHARLEMAGNE Michel Juillet	1991	Magnum	5,200.00
CLOS DU CHATEAU Domaine du Château de Meursault	1992		680.00
MEURSAULT CHARMES Leroy	1991		980.00
MEURSAULT Joseph Drouhin	1994		750.00
MEURSAULT Louis Latour	1993	1/2 bottle	350.00
MEURSAULT-Premier Cru Louis Latour	1994		780.00
MONTRACHET "Marquis de Laguiche" Joseph Drouhin	1991		4,200.00
PULIGNY-MONTRACHET "Clos du Cailleret" Domaine Jean Chartron	1993		1,080.00

Côte de Nuits

CLOS BLANC DE VOUGEOT 1er Cru Domaine l'Heritier Guyot	1988		680.00

Côte Mâconnaise

MACON-BLANC-VILLAGES Faiveley	1994		380.00
POUILLY-FUISSE Joseph Drouhin	1995	1/2 bottle	280.00
POUILLY-FUISSE "Château Fuissé" Domaine M. Vincent et Fils	1994		780.00
POUILLY-FUISSE Louis Latour	1994		490.00
ST.VERAN "Domaine de Cruis" Louis Jadot	1993		380.00

Red Burgundies

Côte de Beaune

ALOXE CORTON Louis Latour	1993		550.00
BEAUNE 1er Cru Louis Latour	1993		650.00
BEAUNE "Clos des Mouches" Joseph Drouhin	1991	1/2 bottle	510.00
BEAUNE "Clos des Mouches" Joseph Drouhin	1991		1,080.00
BEAUNE 1er Cru "Clos des Ursules" Louis Jadot	1991		980.00
CORTON RENARDES, Grand Cru Leroy	1989		1,580.00
POMMARD Faiveley	1989		980.00
SAINT AUBIN ROUGE Jean Herbet	1993		480.00
SANTENAY Louis Latour	1994		420.00
SAVIGNY-LES-BEAUNE Joseph Drouhin	1994		510.00
VOLNAY "Santenots" Louis Jadot	1989		1,150.00

Côte de Nuits

BONNES-MARES Domaine Comte Georges de Vogüé	1991		2,200.00
CHAMBERTIN "Clos de Bèze" Domaine Drouhin-Laroze	1991		1,680.00
CLOS DE TART Mommessin	1986		2,100.00
CLOS VOUGEOT Louis Jadot	1989		1,280.00
CLOS DE VOUGEOT Leroy	1989		1,980.00
CHAMBOLLE-MUSIGNY Faiveley	1992		720.00
GEVREY-CHAMBERTIN Domaine du CLos Frantin	1994		780.00
GEVREY-CHAMBERTIN Joseph Drouhin	1990		920.00
GEVREY-CHAMBERTIN Louis Latour	1994	1/2 bottle	420.00
LATRICIERES-CHAMBERTIN, Grand Cru Leroy	1992		2,680.00
MAZIS CHAMBERTIN, Grand Cru Faiveley	1982		1,780.00
MUSIGNY Domaine Comte Georges de Vogüé	1989		2,600.00
NUITS-SAINT-GEORGES Domaine du Clos Frantin	1993		820.00
NUITS-SAINT-GEORGES Joseph Drouhin	1989	1/2 bottle	460.00
VOSNE-ROMANEE, Premier Cru Domaine Méo-Camuzet	1992		1,280.00

Beaujolais

BROUILLY Jaffelin	1994		370.00
FLEURIE Cellier des Samson	1995		370.00
FLEURIE Georges Duboeuf	1994	1/2 bottle	190.00
MORGON Jaffelin	1994		370.00
MOULIN-A-VENT Louis Latour	1995		370.00
SAINT-AMOUR "Domaine de Paradis" Georges Duboeuf	1994		370.00

Rhône Valley

White

CHATEAUNEUF-DU-PAPE Château de Beaucastel	1991		1,080.00
HERMITAGE "Le Chevalier de Sterimberg" Paul Jaboulet Aîne	1987		550.00
CONDRIEU E. Guigal	1992		1,100.00
MUSCAT DE BEAUMES DE VENISE Domaine de Coyeux	1993		420.00

Rosé

TAVEL "L'Espiègle" Paul Jaboulet Aîne	1995		360.00

Red

CHATEAUNEUF-DU-PAPE "La Fiole du Pape" Père Anselme			450.00
CHATEAUNEUF-DU-PAPE "Les Cèdres" Paul Jaboulet Aîne	1993	1/2 bottle	260.00
CHATEAUNEUF-DU-PAPE Château de Beaucastel	1991		820.00
COTE-ROTIE "Brune et Blonde" E. Guigal	1991		980.00
HERMITAGE "La Chapelle" Paul Jaboulet Aîne	1987		680.00

Loire Valley

White

MUSCADET "Sèvre et Maine sur Lie" Madame Poiron	1992		350.00
POUILLY-FUME P.de Ladoucette	1994	1/2 bottle	300.00
POUILLY-FUME "Baron de L" P.de Ladoucette	1992		1,100.00
POUILLY-FUME "Baron de L" P.de Ladoucette	1989	Magnum	2,200.00
POUILLY-FUME "Les Griottes" Domaine Pascal Jolivet	1995		560.00
QUARTS DE CHAUME "Château de Bellerive" Domaine J. Lalanne	1986		650.00
SANCERRE "Comte Lafond" P.de Ladoucette	1994		550.00
SANCERRE "Comte Lafond" P.de Ladoucette	1994	1/2 bottle	280.00
SANCERRE "Clos du Roy" Domaine Pascal Jolivet	1995		550.00
VOUVRAY "Le Haut-Lieu" Domaine S.A.Huet	1992		480.00

France

Red

SANCERRE "Les Baronnes"	1994		450.00
Domaine Henri Bourgeois			
SAUMUR CHAMPIGNY "Vieilles Vignes"	1993		360.00
Domaine du Vieux Bourg			

Provence

Rosé

BANDOL	1994		400.00
Domaines Ott			

Red

BANDOL	1991		480.00
Domaines Ott			

Alsace

GEWURZTRAMINER	1991		380.00
Trimbach			
GEWURZTRAMINER	1993	1/2 bottle	200.00
Hugel et Fils			
GEWURZTRAMINER "Noble Grape"	1981		1,950.00
Hugel et Fils			
GEWURZTRAMINER "Vendange Tardive"	1990		1,200.00
Leon Beyer			
PINOT BLANC	1993		360.00
Hugel et Fils			
RIESLING	1991		620.00
Domaine Weinbach			
SYLVANER	1993		360.00
Hugel et Fils			

Germany

Mosel-Saar-Ruwer

MAXIMIN GRÜNHAUSER ABTSBERG	1993		580.00
Riesling Kabinett, QmP			
Carl von Schubert			
PIESPORTER MICHELSBERG	1994		360.00
Riesling, QbA			
Carl Graff			

Rheingau

FORSTER PECHSTEIN	1990		2,300.00
Riesling Beerenauslese, QmP			
Von Buhl			
SCHLOSS VOLLRADS BLAUSILBER	1992		450.00
Riesling Kabinett, QmP			
Graf Matuschka Greiffenclau			

Rheinhessen

FORSTER JESUITENGARTEN	1983		1,800.00
Riesling Eiswein, QmP			
Von Buhl			
NIERSTEINER GUTES DOMTAL	1993		320.00
Kabinett, QbA			
P.J.Valckenberg			

Franken

WÜRZBURGER STEIN	1992		420.00
Müller Thurgau Trocken, Kabinett, QmP			
Weingut Juliusspital			

Switzerland

Genève

White

CHARDONNAY "Le Bruant"	1994		420.00
Vitis			

Red

GAMAY DE DARDAGNY	1994		480.00
Claude Ramu			

Vaud

White

AIGLE "Le Grand Aire"	1995		550.00
Paul Tille			
DEZALEY "Medinette"	1994		690.00
L. Bovard			
EPESSES "La Braise d'Enfer"	1994		460.00
Dubois Frères			
ST. SAPHORIN "Roche Ronde"	1995		490.00
Jean & Pierre Testuz			
YVORNE "Domaine Maison Blanche"	1993		490.00
Domaine du Château de Maison Blanche			

Red

AIGLE "Le Grand Aire"	1994		550.00
Paul Tille			
DEZALEY ROUGE	1991		550.00
L. Bovard			
ST. SAPHORIN " Terra Mater "	1994		480.00
Jean & Pierre Testuz			
YVORNE PINOT NOIR "Feu d' Amour"	1994		550.00
Association Viticole d' Yvorne			

Valais

White

FENDANT "Brulefer"	1994		520.00
Charles Bonvin et Fils			
FENDANT "Brulefer"	1995	1/2 bottle	280.00
Charles Bonvin et Fils			

Red

DOLE "Clos du Château"	1994		550.00
Charles Bonvin et Fils			
DOLE "Clos du Château"	1994	1/2 bottle	320.00
Charles Bonvin et Fils			

Rosé

DOLE BLANCHE	1992		450.00
Gérald Clavien			

Lac de Bienne - Neuchâtel

White

NEUCHATEL BLANC	1994		400.00
Château d'Auvernier			
TWANNER "Rochaine"	1992		380.00
Mürset			

Red

NEUCHATEL PINOT NOIR	1993		550.00
Château d'Auvernier			
TWANNER PINOT NOIR	1992		420.00
Mürset			

Rosé

OEIL DE PERDRIX	1994		520.00
Château d'Auvernier			

Ticino

White

BIANCO DI MERLOT TICINESE	1994		550.00
"Terre Alte" Roberti Foc			

Red

MERLOT DEL TICINO "Giornico"	1993		520.00
Oro, Roberti Foc			

Italy

White

Piedmont

CHARDONNAY, Rossj-Bass	1994		720.00
Gaja			
GAVI DI GAVI "Ericetta Nera"	1995		750.00
La Scolca			

Friuli

COLLIO PINOT GRIGIO	1995		380.00
Collavini			

Veneto

SOAVE CLASSICO	1994		360.00
Pieropan			

Emilia-Romagna

RONCO DEL RE	1990		1,380.00
Baldi di Castelbuccio			

Umbria

CERVARO DELLA SALA	1993		520.00
Castello Della Sala, Antinori			
TORRE DI GIANO "Riserva Pino"	1991		380.00
Lungarotti			

Red

Piedmont

BARBARESCO	1991		1,680.00
Gaja			
BAROLO	1992		580.00
Prunotto			
BAROLO "Riserva"	1992		780.00
Pio Cesare			

Emilia-Romagna

RONCO DEI CILIEGI	1988		580.00
Baldi di Castelluccio			

Tuscany

BRUNELLO DI MONTALCINO	1988		680.00
Tenuta Col d'orcia			
CHIANTI CLASSICO RISERVA DUCALE	1991		450.00
I.L. Ruffino			
CHIANTI CLASSICO RISERVA	1990		520.00
DeVile			
GRIFI	1988		580.00
Avignonesi			
SASSICAIA	1992		1,200.00
Marchesi Della Rocchetta			
SOLAIA	1991		980.00
Cantine dei Marchesi Antinori			
TIGNANELLO	1993		720.00
Cantine dei Marchesi Antinori			
VINO NOBILE DI MONTEPULCIANO	1993		480.00
Avignonesi			

Spain

White

GRAN VINA SOLE "Green Label"	1991	
Miguel Torres		
VINO BLANCO "Crianza"	1990	
Marques de Cáceres		

Red

IMPERIAL "Grand Reserva"	1988	
C.V.N.E.		
VEGA SICILIA "Valbuena 5er Ano"	1990	
Bodegas Vega Sicilia		

China

DYNASTY		
TSING TAO RIESLING, Hua Dong	1992	
TSING TAO CHARDONNAY, Hua Dong	1993	

United States of America

Sparkling Wine

JORDAN "J"	1989	
SCHRAMSBERG, Blanc de Blancs	1988	

White

Napa Valley

CHARDONNAY "Private Reserve" Beringer	1994		
CHARDONNAY, Cuvaison	1994		
CHARDONNAY, Diamond Mountain Ranch, Sterling	1992		
CHARDONNAY, Farniente	1992		
CHARDONNAY, Heitz Wine Cellars	1994		
CHARDONNAY, Joseph Phelps	1992	1/2 bottle	
CHARDONNAY, Joseph Phelps	1990		
CHARDONNAY "Reserve" Merryvale Vineyard	1993		
CHARDONNAY "Reserve" Robert Mondavi	1993		
CHARDONNAY, Shafer	1994		
CHARDONNAY, Stag's Leap Wine Cellars	1994		
CHARDONNAY, Trefethen	1994		
DOLCE, Farniente	1989	1/2 bottle	
FUME BLANC "Reserve" Robert Mondavi	1993		
RIESLING, Trefethen	1992		
SAUVIGNON BLANC, Cakebread Cellars	1995		

Alexander Valley

CHARDONNAY, Jordan	1992	

Sonoma Valley

CHARDONNAY, Chalk Hill Winery	1993	
CHARDONNAY "Reserve" Simi	1992	
SAUVIGNON BLANC, Chalk Hill Winery	1993	

Red

Napa Valley

CABERNET SAUVIGNON "Private Reserve" Beringer	1991	
CABERNET SAUVIGNON, Farniente	1992	

CABERNET SAUVIGNON, Diamond Mountain Ranch, Sterling	1992		520.00
CABERNET SAUVIGNON "Martha's Vineyard" Heitz Wine Cellars	1987		1,880.00
CABERNET SAUVIGNON "Reserve" Robert Mondavi	1991		1,380.00
CABERNET SAUVIGNON, Robert Mondavi	1991	1/2 bottle	250.00
CABERNET SAUVIGNON, Stag's Leap Wine Cellars	1993		660.00
CABERNET SAUVIGNON, Trefethen	1992		480.00
MERLOT, Shafer	1993		720.00
PROFILE, MERRYVALE VINEYARD	1991		780.00
PINOT NOIR "Carneros" Clos du Val	1991		680.00

Alexander Valley

CABERNET SAUVIGNON, Jordan	1992		620.00

Sonoma Valley

CABERNET SAUVIGNON "Reserve" Simi	1991		720.00
MERLOT, Clos du Bois	1993		530.00

Australia

White

Victoria

CHARDONNAY, Windy Peak	1995		380.00
De Bortoli			
CHARDONNAY	1995		360.00
Salisbury Estate			
CHARDONNAY "Reserve"	1994		420.00
Mitchelton			

South Australia

CHARDONNAY	1994		560.00
Mount Adam Winery			
CHARDONNAY, "Padthaway Vineyard"	1994		450.00
Lindemans			
CHARDONNAY	1990		580.00
Geoff Merrill			
RIESLING, Clare Valley	1994		360.00
Petaluma			

Western Australia

CHARDONNAY, Margaret River	1993		880.00
Leeuwin Estate			
SAUVIGNON BLANC, Margaret River	1995		480.00
Leeuwin Estate			

Red

Victoria

CABERNET SAUVIGNON	1994		360.00
Salisbury Estate			
BLUE PYRENEES ESTATE	1993		380.00

South Australia

CABERNET MERLOT	1993		360.00
Mount Hurtle Winery			
CABERNET SAUVIGNON "St.George"	1992		880.00
Lindemans			
CABERNET SAUVIGNON "Rouge Homme"	1993		480.00
Lindemans			
CABERNET SAUVIGNON, Bin 407	1992		550.00
Penfolds			
CABERNET SAUVIGNON, Barossa Valley	1994		420.00
Wolf Blass			
SHIRAZ CABERNET	1995		360.00
Krondorf			

Western Australia

CABERNET SAUVIGNON, Margaret River	1991		550.00
Leeuwin Estate			
PINOT NOIR, Margaret River	1992		520.00
Leeuwin Estate			

New Zealand

White

CHARDONNAY, Hawkes Bay	1995		420.00
Esk Valley Estate			
CHARDONNAY, Cloudy Bay	1995		480.00
SAUVIGNON BLANC, Cloudy Bay	1996		450.00
SAUVIGNON BLANC, Villa Maria Estate	1995		360.00

Red

CABERNET SAUVIGNON, Stoneleight	1994		360.00
MERLOT-CABERNET SAUVIGNON, Kumeu River	1994		490.00
PINOT NOIR, Martinborough	1994		460.00

South Africa

White

CHARDONNAY, Hamilton Russel	1995		360.00
SAUVIGNON BLANC, Klein Constantia	1995		360.00

Red

PINOT NOIR, Hamilton Russel	1993		360.00
MARLBROOK, Klein Constantia	1990		360.00

Chile

White

CHARDONNAY, Los Vascos	1994		360.00
CHARDONNAY, Santa Rita	1994		360.00

Red

CABERNET SAUVIGNON, Los Vascos	1993		360.00
CABERNET SAUVIGNON "Gran Reserva"	1992		380.00
Portal del Alto			

Argentina

White

CHARDONNAY, Etchart	1995		360.00

Red

CABERNET SAUVIGNON, Etchart	1991		360.00

Felix Restaurant and Bar

No, the noodles on our plates have not been styled by Philippe Starck. They are long and of the same diameter from one end to the other, just as usual. Otherwise, however, up here on the 28th floor of the Peninsula Hotel there is hardly anything that the French grand master of design has not turned his hand to. An avant-garde collaboration, the hotel announces, not without pride.
The room itself is also a synthesis of the arts: the design of the walls, the wine bar, the American bar, the cloakroom, the tables, chairs, fitted carpets, lamps – everything bears his unmistakeable signature, recognizable at a glance. Plates, cutlery, bill of fare, cheese grater and corkscrew. Salt cellars and pepper mills of unusual dimensions are more like table decorations than utilitarian items.

The people, the staff, both male and female are in monk-like black dress, long and high-buttoned, below figures, above faces and hairstyles as if from another world, since all are – almost – immaculate.
And unapproachable. So much perfection is bound to create a certain detachment.
But in this case only for a short time.
A minute or two go by, and an unmistakeable sense of well-being settles in.
If it were not downright presumptuous in view of the provocative and extraordinary achievement of Philippe Starck: after a short acclimatization phase we would say, straight out: over the top, but basically quite cosy here.
It may well be – and this cannot be more than conjecture – the fitting proportions

"The Crazy Box" disco

Men's Room

everywhere and a characteristic, but ultimately not obtrusive, style throughout that trigger the secret feeling of wellbeing up here between earth and sky. And apropos of consistent design: Felix – named after Felix Bieger, manager of the Peninsula for many years – is the first and provisionally also the last restaurant during whose critical appreciation we (must) also make mention of the (gentlemen's) toilets: there never was a more spectacular urinal, nor a more beautiful washbasin.

The American Bar

But actually, we came here to eat. And one can eat here too, quite splendidly in fact. The dishes can hold their own beside and despite all the distractions round about. Bryan Nagao, born in 1959 in Los Angeles, is the chef, who spent his apprenticeship partly in Roy's Restaurant in Hawaii. His light-hearted, almost carefree way at the cooking range goes together with an astonishingly sure hand for bold seasoning and the skilfully kept balance, which makes more out of a Euro-Asian cooking concept than merely livening up a traditional, basic European recipe with oriental spices. Asiatic-Californian-Mediterranean is the line his cooking takes. Compositions are occasionally daring, but never nonsensical or thrown together just for show.

If you come here to eat, you are expected to show a little experimental courage. There is goose liver with figs marinated in ginger and sweet-and-sour Thai chili; macadamia nuts with shrimps, Thai cucumber salad and yellow curry-orange sauce, roast chicken with fresh water chestnuts, papaya and a mint-coriander leaf dressing, or a lobster cocktail with wild fennel and a pungent lemon-horseradish vinaigrette.

All this is based on fresh regional ingredients. Preparation is light and health-conscious, and the portions are larger than one might expect in such an establishment. This is without doubt a culinary trend with a future. And it matches up – we come full circle – quite loosely and congenially with Philippe Starck's characteristic design style.

Dining Room

Wine Room

The Balcony

Nein, die Nudeln auf unseren Tellern hat Philippe Starck nicht durchgestylt. Sie sind lang und vom einem Ende bis zum anderen von gleichbleibendem Durchmesser – wie gehabt. Sonst allerdings gibt es hier oben im 28. Stockwerk des Peninsula-Hotels kaum etwas, an das der französische Groß-meister des Designs nicht Hand angelegt hätte. Eine Avant-Garde-Collaboration, wie das Hotel nicht ohne Stolz vermeldet. Der Raum an sich ist denn auch ein Gesamt-kunstwerk: die Gestaltung der Wände, die Wein-Bar, die American Bar, die Garderobe, die Tische, die Stühle, der Teppichboden, die Lampen – alles trägt seine unverkennbare wie auch auf den ersten Blick wiedererkennbare Handschrift: Teller, Besteck, Speisekarte, Käsereibe und Korkenzieher, Salz- und Pfefferstreuer von ungewöhnlichen Ausmaßen und eher Tischdekoration als dem Gebrauch dienende Utensilien.

Der Mensch, das Personal, männlich wie weiblich: in mönchischem Schwarz, lang und hochgeschlossen, darunter Figuren, darüber Gesichter und Frisuren wie aus einer anderen Welt. Allesamt – fast – makellos und unnahbar. So viel Perfektion schafft fast zwangsläufig eine gewisse Distanz. Aber hier nur für eine kurze Zeit. Es vergeht eine Minute, vielleicht sind es zwei, und es stellt sich unverkennbar Wohlbehagen ein. Wäre es in Anbetracht der provozierenden und außergewöhnlichen Leistung von Philippe Starck nicht geradezu vermessen: wir würden nach kurzer Eingewöhnungsphase ohne Umschweife sagen: sehr abgehoben, aber im Grunde genommen doch ganz gemütlich hier. Es sind wohl – mehr als eine Vermutung kann es nicht sein – die überall stimmigen Proportionen und eine durchgängige, aber letztendlich doch nicht aufdringliche Handschrift, die das insgeheime Wohlbehagen hier oben zwischen Himmel und Erde auslösen. A propos durchgängiges Design: Felix – nach dem langjährigen Peninsula-Manager Felix Bieger benannt – ist das erste und vorläufig auch letzte Restaurant, bei dessen kritischer Würdigung wir auch die (Herren-)Toiletten mit einem Satz erwähnen (müssen): ein spektakuläreres Urinal gab's noch nie, ein schöneres Handwaschbecken auch nicht.

Aber wir sind ja eigentlich zum Essen gekommen. Und das kann man hier auch, und zwar ganz vorzüglich. Die Gerichte können neben und trotz der ganzen Ablenkung ringsum bestehen. Bryan Nagao, 1959 in Los Angeles geboren, heißt der

Küchenchef, der seine Lehrjahre unter anderem in Roy's Restaurant auf Hawaii verbracht hat. Seine unbeschwerte, fast unbekümmerte Art am Herd korrespondiert mit einem schon erstaunlich sicheren Händchen fürs beherzte Würzen und der gekonnt eingehaltenen Balance, die aus einem „Euro-Asian"-Konzept in der Küche mehr macht als lediglich das traditionelle europäische Grundrezept gerade mal mit fernöstlichen Gewürzen aufzupeppen. Asiatisch-kalifornisch-mediterran – so hat er seine Küche angelegt. Gelegentlich sind die Kompositionen zwar gewagt, nie jedoch unsinnig oder gar nur der Show wegen zusammengestellt. Wer hierher kommt zum Essen, dem darf ein bißchen Mut zum Experiment durchaus unterstellt werden. Da gibt es Gänseleber mit in Ingwer marinierten Feigen und süß-saurem Thai-Chili; Macadamia-Nüsse mit Shrimps, thailändischem Gurkensalat und gelber Curry-Orangen-Sauce; gebratenes Hühnchen mit frischen Wasserkastanien, Papaya und einem Minze-Cilantron-Dressing oder einen Hummer-Cocktail mit wildem Fenchel und einer scharfen Zitronen-Meerrettich-Vinaigrette. Das alles findet statt auf der Basis frischer regionaler Zutaten. Leicht und gesund ist die Zubereitung, die Portionen sind großzügiger, als man sie in einem solchen Lokal erwartet. Das ist ohne Zweifel ein Küchentrend, der Zukunft hat. Er passt – womit sich der Kreis schließt – ganz locker aber kongenial zu Philippe Starcks Design-Handschrift.

Bryan Nagao

GRILLED ANGUS BEEF TOURNEDOS
WITH FRIED PRAWNS AND TOMATO SAUCE

GEGRILLTE ANGUSLENDE
MIT GEBRATENEN GARNELEN UND TOMATENSAUCE

For 4 persons:

For the tomato sauce:
2 cloves garlic, 1 shallot, 40 g/1 1/3 oz root ginger,
50 g/1 2/3 oz dried tomatoes,
400 ml/13 fl oz/1 2/3 cups water,
100 g/3 1/2 oz long-grained rice, salt, pepper

150 g/5 oz prawns,
2 cloves garlic, finely chopped,
1 shallot, finely chopped,
90 g/3 fl oz shiitake mushrooms, sliced,
120 g/4 oz asparagus, cut into pieces,
400 g/13 oz peas, 50 g/1 2/3 oz/4 tbsp butter,
60 g/2 oz basil leaves, salt, pepper from the mill

4 Angus tournedos steaks of about 180 g/6 oz each,
1 tbsp oil, 1 tbsp butter,
crispy fried onions to garnish

For the tomato sauce: Coarsely chop the garlic, shallot, ginger, and tomatoes. Place in a pot, together with the rice and the water, and bring to the boil. Cover and simmer over a low heat for thirty minutes.

Purée in the blender. Pass the sauce through a sieve and season with salt and pepper.

Sauté the prawns in the butter with the garlic, shallot, mushrooms and vegetables until everything is slightly transparent. Add the basil leaves and fill up with the prepared tomato sauce. Season with salt and pepper. Bring to the boil. Remove from the stove and keep in a warm place.

Season the steaks with salt and pepper and fry in a skillet in the hot oil and butter mixture as desired.

To serve: Arrange the sauce and vegetables on plates, lay the steaks on top and sprinkle with crispy fried onions.

Für 4 Personen:

Für die Tomatensauce:
2 Knoblauchzehen, 1 Schalotte,
40 g Ingwerwurzel, 50 g getrocknete Tomaten,
400 ml Wasser,
100 g Langkornreis, Salz, Pfeffer

150 g Garnelen,
2 Knoblauchzehen, fein geschnitten,
1 Schalotte, fein geschnitten,
90 g Shiitakepilze, in Scheiben geschnitten,
120 g Spargel, in Stücke geschnitten,
400 g Erbsen, 50 g Butter, 60 g Basilikumblätter,
Salz, Pfeffer aus der Mühle

4 Angus-Lendensteaks von je ca. 180 g,
1 EL Öl, 1 EL Butter,
Röstzwiebeln zum Garnieren

Für die Tomatensauce: Knoblauch, Schalotte, Ingwer und Tomaten grob zerkleinern. Mit dem Reis und dem Wasser in einen Topf geben, zum Kochen bringen und dreißig Minuten zugedeckt bei kleiner Hitze köcheln lassen. Im Mixer pürieren. Die Sauce durch ein Sieb streichen, mit Salz und Pfeffer würzen.

Garnelen mit Knoblauch, Schalotte, Pilzen und Gemüse in der Butter anschwitzen, bis alles leicht glasig wird. Basilikumblätter zugeben und mit der vorbereiteten Tomatensauce auffüllen. Mit Salz und Pfeffer würzen, zum Kochen bringen, vom Herd nehmen und warmstellen. Die Steaks mit Salz und Pfeffer würzen und in einer Pfanne im heißen Öl-Buttergemisch nach Belieben braten.

Zum Servieren: Sauce mit Gemüse auf Teller verteilen. Steaks darüber legen und mit Röstzwiebeln bestreuen.

SWORDFISH ON FENNEL WITH TARO GNOCCHI

SCHWERTFISCH AUF FENCHEL MIT TARO GNOCCHI

For 4 persons:

800 g/1 lb 12 oz fennel, olive oil,
600 g/1 lb 5 oz potatoes, salt, pepper

For the gnocchi:
400 g/13 oz taro tubers (or sweet potatoes as a substitute),
100 g/3 1/2 oz potatoes, 400 g/13 1/2 oz/1 2/3 cups flour,
4 small eggs, 25 g/5/6 oz root ginger, grated

For the shiso sauce:
1 shallot, 1 garlic clove, 10 g/1/3 oz galanga root,
10 g/1/3 oz root ginger, 1 tbsp diced bacon,
40 g/1 1/3 oz lemon grass, 4 kaffir lime leaves,
2 tsp green Thai curry paste, 1 tbsp oil,
300 ml/10 fl oz/1 1/4 cups chicken broth,
400 ml/13 fl oz/1 2/3 cups mussel cooking liquid,
1 sprig thyme, 1 sprig basil, 50 g/1 2/3 oz spinach,
100 g/3 1/2 oz shiso leaves (Japanese red basil),
80 g/2 2/3 oz potatoes

60 g/2 oz/1/4 cup butter,
100 g/3 1/2 oz shiitake mushrooms, cut into quarters,
200 g/7 oz green beans, blanched,
4 swordfish fillets of about 160 g/5 1/2 oz each,
1 tomato, cut into cubes

Für 4 Personen:

800 g Fenchel, Olivenöl,
600 g Kartoffeln, Salz, Pfeffer

Für die Gnocchi:
400 g Taro-Knollen (ersatzweise Süßkartoffeln),
100 g Kartoffeln, 400 g Mehl,
4 kleine Eier, 25 g Ingwerwurzel, gerieben

Für die Shisosauce:
1 Schalotte, 1 Knoblauchzehe, 10 g Galangawurzel,
10 g Ingwerwurzel, 1 EL Speckwürfel,
40 g Zitronengras, 4 Kaffir Limonenblätter,
2 TL grüne Thai Currypaste, 1 EL Öl,
300 ml Hühnerbrühe,
400 ml Muschelsud,
1 Zweig Thymian, 1 Zweig Basilikum, 50 g Spinat,
100 g Shisoblätter (japanischer, roter Basilikum),
80 g Kartoffeln

60 g Butter,
100 g Shiitake Pilze, in Viertel geschnitten,
200 g grüne Bohnen, blanchiert,
4 Schwertfischfilets von je ca. 160 g,
1 Tomate, in Würfel geschnitten

Clean the heads of fennel, paint with olive oil, wrap in aluminum foil and roast for twenty minutes in the oven preheated to 180° C/360° F. Then purée in the blender. Peel the potatoes, cook through in salted water, drain, mash and pass through a sieve. Mix with the fennel purée and season with salt and pepper.

For the gnocchi: Cook the taro tubers and potatoes in their skins until done. Drain, dry, peel off the skins and squeeze through a potato press. Mix with the flour, the eggs and the ginger, season with salt and pepper, and rapidly knead to form a stiff dough. Shape finger-thick rolls of the dough and from these cut small gnocchi.

For the shiso sauce: Coarsely chop the shallot, garlic, galanga and ginger. Fry in oil together with the bacon, lemon grass and curry paste. Cover with broth and mussel cooking liquid. Boil down to half the volume. Cut the potatoes into small pieces and add, together with the herbs, the shiso leaves and the spinach. Boil until the potatoes are done. Purée in the blender and pass the sauce through a fine sieve.

Heat half of the butter in a skillet. Fry the gnocchi, shiitake mushrooms and green beans on a low heat until the beans are done but still crisp. Stir in four tablespoons of the shiso sauce and season with salt and pepper to taste. Spice the swordfish fillets and fry on both sides in the remaining butter.

To serve: Place the fennel-potato purée on plates, add the fish fillets, place the vegetables on top and surround with the sauce. Garnish with tomato cubes.

Fenchelknollen putzen, mit Olivenöl bestreichen und in Alufolie gewickelt im auf 180° C vorgeheizten Ofen zwanzig Minuten rösten. Anschließend im Mixer pürieren. Kartoffeln schälen, in Salzwasser gar kochen, abgießen, zerstampfen und durch ein Sieb pressen. Mit dem Fenchelpüree vermischen und mit Salz und Pfeffer würzen.

Für die Gnocchi: Taro-Knollen und Kartoffeln in der Haut gar kochen. Abgießen, trocknen lassen, aus der Schale pellen und durch eine Kartoffelpresse drücken. Mit Mehl, Eiern und Ingwer vermischen, mit Salz und Pfeffer würzen und schnell zu einem festen Teig kneten. Fingerdicke Rollen formen und davon kleine Gnocchi schneiden.

Für die Shisosauce: Schalotte, Knoblauch, Galanga und Ingwer grob zerkleinern. Mit Speck, Zitronengras und Currypaste im Öl anbraten. Mit Brühe und Muschelsud auffüllen. Auf die halbe Menge einkochen lassen. Kartoffeln kleinschneiden und mit Kräutern, Shisoblättern und Spinat kochen, bis die Kartoffeln gar sind. Im Mixer pürieren, die Sauce durch ein feines Sieb streichen. Die Hälfte der Butter in einer Pfanne erhitzen. Gnocchi, Shiitake Pilze und grüne Bohnen darin bei kleiner Hitze braten, bis die Bohnen knackig gar sind. Vier Eßlöffel Shisosauce unterrühren, mit Salz und Pfeffer abschmecken. Schwertfischfilets würzen und in der restlichen Butter von beiden Seiten braten.

Zum Servieren: Fenchel-Kartoffelpüree auf Teller geben, mit den Fischfilets belegen, Gemüse darübergeben und mit der Sauce umgießen. Mit Tomatenwürfeln garnieren.

GOOSE FOIE-GRAS WITH GINGER FIGS ON SWEET-AND-SOUR SAUCE
GÄNSESTOPFLEBER MIT INGWERFEIGEN AN SÜSS-SAURER SAUCE

For 4 persons:

For the figs:
80 g/2²/₃ oz/¹/₃ cup sugar, 80 ml/2²/₃ fl oz/¹/₃ cup water,
80 ml/2²/₃ fl oz/¹/₃ cup red-wine vinegar, 40 g/1¹/₃ oz root ginger,
10 g/¹/₃ oz kaffir lemon leaves, 8 fresh figs

For the sauce:
80 ml/2²/₃ fl oz/¹/₃ cup white-wine vinegar,
80 ml/2²/₃ fl oz/¹/₃ cup water,
60 g/2 oz/¹/₄ cup sugar, 1 tsp chili sauce,
20 g/²/₃ oz/2 tbsp root ginger, finely grated,
20 g/²/₃ oz/2 tbsp garlic, pressed,
1 tsp sesame oil, salt, pepper

4 slices of goose foie-gras of about 60 g/2 oz each,
80 g/2²/₃ oz/¹/₃ cup sugar, 1 tbsp butter

To garnish:
Kaiware sprouts (Japanese radish sprouts),
40 g/1¹/₃ oz preserved ginger

Für 4 Personen:

Für die Feigen:
80 g Zucker, 80 ml Wasser,
80 ml Rotweinessig, 40 g Ingwerwurzel,
10 g Kaffir Zitronenblätter, 8 frische Feigen

Für die Sauce:
80 ml Weißweinessig,
80 ml Wasser,
60 g Zucker, 1 TL Chilisauce,
20 g Ingwerwurzel, fein gerieben,
20 g Knoblauch, durchgedrückt,
1 TL Sesamöl, Salz, Pfeffer

4 Scheiben Gänsestopfleber von je ca. 60 g,
80 g Zucker, 1 EL Butter

Garnitur:
Kaiware Sprossen (japanische Rettichsprossen),
40 g eingemachter Ingwer

In a pot, bring to the boil the sugar, red-wine vinegar, water, lemon leaves and ginger. Boil down to half the quantity, then add the whole figs, allow to cool and marinate for two days in the refrigerator.

For the sauce: Bring to the boil the white-wine vinegar with water, sugar, chili sauce, ginger and garlic. Add the sesame oil and season with salt and pepper. Remove the pot from the stove and keep in a warm place.

Sprinkle the foie gras with sugar and fry on both sides in the hot butter.

To serve: Cut the marinated figs into quarters and arrange on the plates. Place the fried liver on top and pour over the hot sauce. Garnish with sprouts and preserved ginger.

Zucker mit Rotweinessig, Wasser, Zitronenblättern und Ingwer in einem Topf zum Kochen bringen. Auf die halbe Menge einkochen lassen, dann die ganzen Feigen zugeben, erkalten lassen und zwei Tage im Kühlschrank marinieren.

Für die Sauce: Weißweinessig mit Wasser, Zucker, Chilisauce, Ingwer und Knoblauch zum Kochen bringen. Sesamöl zufügen und mit Salz und Pfeffer würzen. Topf vom Herd nehmen und warmstellen.

Stopfleber mit Zucker bestreuen und in der heißen Butter auf beiden Seiten anbraten.

Zum Servieren: Die marinierten Feigen in Viertel schneiden und auf Teller verteilen. Die gebratene Leber darüber legen, mit der heißen Sauce begießen. Mit Sprossen und eingemachtem Ingwer garnieren.

LOBSTER COCKTAIL WITH SPICY LEMON-HORSERADISH VINAIGRETTE

HUMMERCOCKTAIL AN WÜRZIGER ZITRONEN-MEERRETTICH VINAIGRETTE

For 4 persons:

2 lobsters (Boston) of 750 g/1 lb 7 oz each,
olive oil

For the vinaigrette:
1 egg yolk, juice of 1/2 lemon,
10 g/1/3 oz horseradish, 10 g/1/3 oz shallots,
10 g/1/3 oz root ginger,
120 ml/4 fl oz/1/2 cup olive oil, salt, pepper

1 small head of fennel,
1 red bell pepper, 1 yellow bell pepper,
1 red onion

Für 4 Personen:

2 Hummer (Boston) von je 750 g,
Olivenöl

Für die Vinaigrette:
1 Eigelb, Saft einer halben Zitrone,
10 g Meerrettich, 10 g Schalotte,
10 g Ingwerwurzel,
120 ml Olivenöl, Salz, Pfeffer

1 kleine Fenchelknolle,
1 rote Paprika, 1 gelbe Paprika,
1 rote Zwiebel

Boil the lobster in fast boiling water for one to two minutes, remove and drain. Break out the flesh from the claws and cook it in court-bouillon for two minutes.

Split the lobster tails in half, paint with olive oil, and roast on the griddle on all sides.

For the vinaigrette: Purée the egg yolk with lemon juice, horseradish, shallot and ginger in the blender. Stir in the olive oil and season with salt and pepper. Cut the vegetables into strips, mix with a little vinaigrette and arrange on plates. Lay the boiled lobster claws and grilled lobster tails on top and drizzle with the remaining vinaigrette. Serve lukewarm.

Hummer in sprudelnd kochendem Wasser ein bis zwei Minuten kochen, herausnehmen und abtropfen lassen. Das Fleisch aus den Scheren brechen und in Courtbouillon zwei Minuten kochen. Die Hummerschwänze halbieren, mit Olivenöl bestreichen und auf dem Grill rundum rösten.

Für die Vinaigrette: Eigelb mit Zitronensaft, Meerrettich, Schalotte und Ingwer im Mixer pürieren. Olivenöl einrühren und mit Salz und Pfeffer würzen. Die Gemüse in Streifen schneiden, mit etwas Vinaigrette vermischen und auf Teller anrichten. Gekochte Hummerscheren und gegrillte Hummerschwänze darüber legen und mit der restlichen Vinaigrette beträufeln. Lauwarm servieren.

That Lauda Air is one of those airlines that are cloaked in an aura of quite special exclusivity is due not only to its world-famous president with the red baseball cap crowning his striking features. A little of the aura is also due to the baseball cap turning up again in duplicate, namely on the heads of young ladies who are considered to be the most attractive, friendliest and most helpful flight attendants anywhere in the world. For us gourmets and trenchermen, Lauda Air fortunately has far above average renown for a different reason: better food high above the clouds is hard to find. A menu in Amadeus Class reads like an excerpt from the bill of fare of a top restaurant. This begins quite harmlessly with a champagne cocktail, then soars away practically from the start to the culinary heights of Irish lobster with ruccola salad and olive oil-herb vinaigrette. The next course remains at this gourmet altitude, a cep consommÈ without problems, only to pull away to even greater heights with grilled turbot on leaf spinach, asparagus and chervil potatoes. This is followed by lamb chop with fresh thyme in Dijon mustard sauce. With cheese from the trolley and a final Viennese chocolate pancake, a clean and confident culinary landing is executed.

Such menus may sound mouth-watering, but if the preparation is not in order it has all been in vain. And this is where the Lauda crew deserve a special compliment: how in the cramped conditions of an aircraft and with limited kitchen apparatus they manage to cook the lobster au point, serve the turbot perfectly and keep the lamb tender and pink inside, other airlines can only tear a big, informative page out of their book.

Daß Lauda-Air zu jenen Fluglinien gehört, die der Hauch ganz besonderer Exklusivität umweht, liegt nicht nur an ihrem weltweit bekannten Präsidenten mit dem roten Käppi auf dem markanten Kopf. Es hat auch ein bisschen damit zu tun, daß diese roten Käppi im Flugzeug vermehrt wieder auftauchen, und zwar auf den Köpfen von jungen Damen, die als die attraktivsten, freundlichsten und zuvorkommendsten Stewardessen weltweit gelten. Für uns Feinschmecker und Schlemmer hat Lauda-Air glücklicherweise noch aus einem anderen Grund ein weit über dem Durchschnitt liegendes Renommee: Besseres Essen hoch über den Wolken findet man sonst kaum. Ein Menü in der Amadeus-Class liest sich wie ein Auszug aus der Speisekarte eines Top-Restaurants. Das beginnt noch ganz brav mit einem Champagner-Cockail, schwingt sich dann aber praktisch vom Start weg hinauf auf die kulinarischen Höhen eines irischen Hummers mit Ruccola-Salat und Olivenöl-Kräutervinaigrette. Auf dieser Schlemmer-Flughöhe hält sich der nächste Gang, eine Steinpilz-Consommé, ohne Probleme, um dann mit gegrilltem Steinbutt auf Blattspinat, Spargel und Kerbelkartoffeln nochmals deutlich nach oben zu ziehen. Lammkotelett mit frischem Thymian an Dijon-Senfsauce folgt. Mit Käse vom Wagen und einem abschließenden Wiener Schokoladenpalatschinken, gefüllt mit Marillenkonfitüre, wird eine saubere und souveräne kulinarische Landung hingelegt.

Nun lesen sich derartige Menüs lecker, wenn jedoch die Zubereitung nicht stimmt, war alles vergebens. Und hier nun muß man der Lauda-Mannschaft ein besonderes Kompliment machen: Wie sie in der Enge eines Flugzeuges und mit den dort zwangsläufig beschränkten Küchenmitteln den Hummer auf den Punkt gegart hinbekommen, den Steinbutt tadellos serviert und das Lamm butterzart und innen noch rosa ist, davon können sich die meisten anderen Fluglinien wirklich eine ebenso dicke wie leckere Scheibe abschneiden.

Menu

Champagne-cocktail

* * *

Prawns on salade Nicoise

* * *

Tom Ka Gai

and/or

Gardenfresh seasonal salads with Italian dressing

* * *

Plakapong & tuna brochette
on spaghetti with calamari and olive oil from Tuscany

* * *

Roasted duck breast in thyme jus
Potato-cellery puree, sautéed haricots verts & buttered carrots

* * *

Assorted cheese & exotic fruits from our trolley

* * *

Desserts:

Eclairs with moccacream

and/or

Fried pineapple and apple slices
with cinnamon sugar

and/or

Coconut parfait

Fresh brewed coffee or tea

Digestifs from our trolley

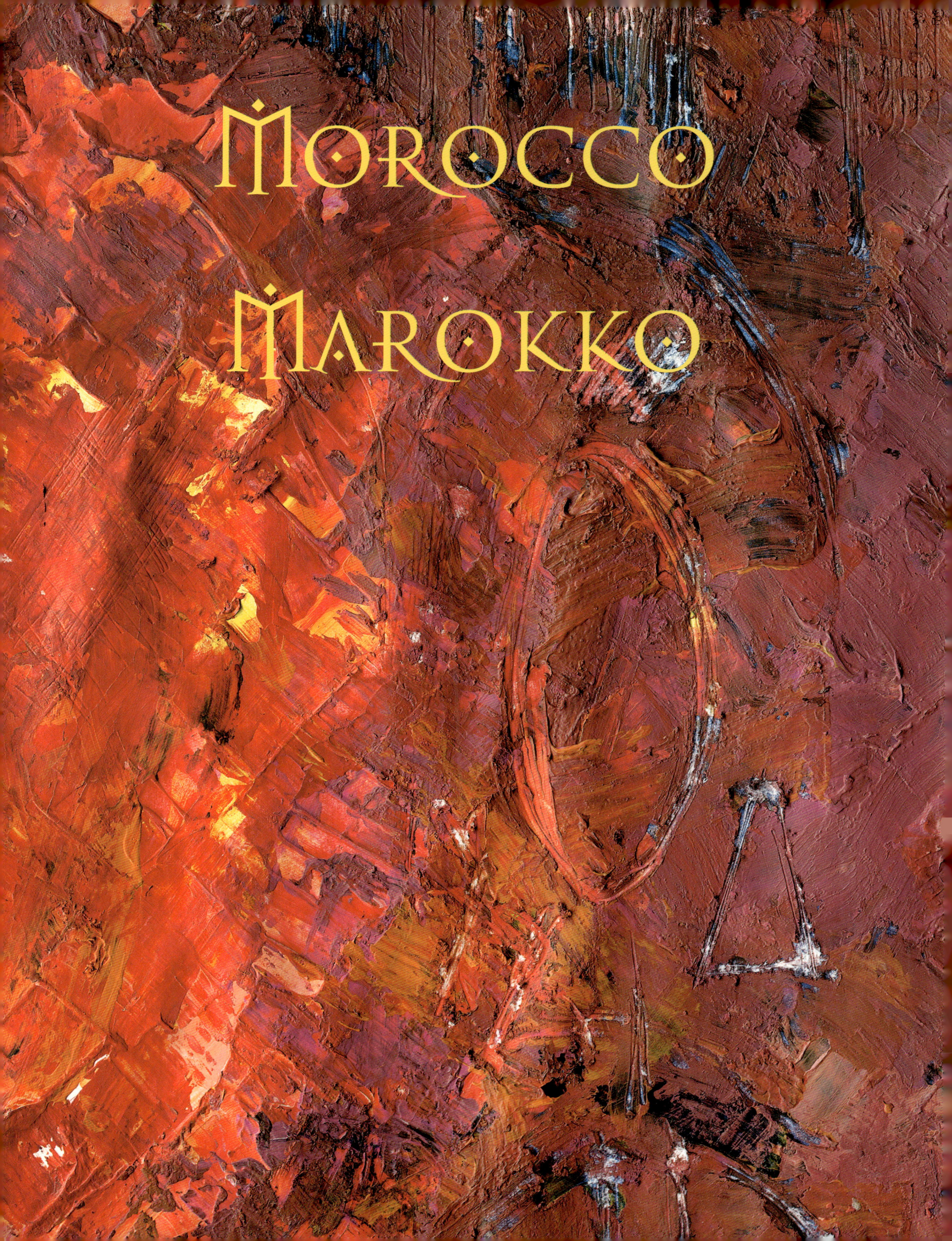

Morocco

Marokko

Morocco – light and shade, proud, dark-skinned people in flowing white robes, sometimes cloaked in earth-colored brown djellabas, from the darkness of which a glint of white flashes only from the corner of an eye or from a bashful smile.

Morocco – harsh islands of light amid the dusty semi-darkness of the souks, fairy-tale colors of spices and products that glow all the more exuberantly against the drab tones of the robes and walls.

Morocco – an ordered confusion of lines and light, mosaics and filigree carvings, the ordered clutter of light and dark, of people, colors and smells – an Arabian yin and yang.

The wealth of impressions that the country leaves on the visitor are reflected by the Moroccan cuisine. A densely woven fabric, rooted in the soil, yet permeated by fine aromas, foreign influences, the cuisine of Morocco reads like a culinary picture-book of the history of this country, of its variety, its legends.

The Berbers were the original inhabitants of the Maghreb, a wide strip of land along the north African coast to the Mediterranean, the land of the Phoenicians and Carthaginians. They contributed to the bill of fare the many stew dishes, which originated due to a dearth of fuel for fires. With deliberation and care, the ingredients are cooked in an unglazed earthenware pot over a moderate fire.

Harira is a thick soup of dried pulses and eggs that is eaten as the first evening dish to recover strength during the fasting month of Ramadan.

Harira

Couscous is made from the ground grain of various cereals. Layered upon the meat, bones and vegetables, as it slowly cooks it draws in the wealth of flavors of the ingredients. Today, couscous is still the traditional fare on the Muslim holy day, Friday.

Couscous

Tajines are the great specialty of Moroccan cuisine. These simple looking dishes, vegetables and pieces of meat braised with saffron in a lot of oil, accentuate the individual flavors of the ingredients in an inexhaustible variety of ways – simple yet at the same time of intricate refinement.

Tajine

Saffron became known in Spain only via the Moors; just as for sugar cane, the Moroccan rulers in Spain kept large areas under cultivation for the prized threads of spice. Today, the stigmas of "Crocus sativus" are only known by their Arabic name "sahafaran", saffron. The end of Moorish rule in Spain had far-reaching consequences for the southern part of Europe. Morocco too became darker, and its face changed upon having to withdraw upon itself, having lost its Spanish possessions – in the same year as Europe set about discovering America, with a rattling of sabers in its eagerness to bestow its attentions and greed upon the rest of the world. Lying even closer than Spain to America's doorstep – the final port of call before the great crossing was at the Canary Islands off the coast of Morocco – very soon the new fruits, potatoes, tomatoes, peppers, pumpkins and cayenne were thriving in the vegetable gardens of Morocco beside the indigenous carrots and the aubergines, an earlier import by the Arabs from India.

In the heyday of the Almoravide ascendancy, the borders of Morocco reached from the Ebro to Senegal, from the Atlantic to today's Algiers. A trade route ran across Moroccan territory from Spain to the goldfields of Galam-Bambuk in the north of Mali. More than any other north African country, Morocco was always historically also a "European" country. The Arab rule in Spain was for a long time Moroccan rule, and brought a cultural blessing to the country. Toward the end of the first millennium, Morocco was a cosmopolitan country, brighter and more interested than the dull, monastic central Europe of the middle ages. Many of the ingredients of Moroccan cuisine originate from the time of the Moorish occupation of Spain. Almond, lemon and orange trees, which the Arabs made endemic on their Spanish possessions, were retained on their way across northern Africa; with their fruits and with the use of olives and olive oil, the sources on which Moroccan cuisine could draw were enriched. To this were added the spices that the Arabs imported from the spice islands of the Moluccas, long before Europeans ever came to enjoy such flavors permanently: nutmeg, cloves and cinnamon, turmeric, ginger and saffron.

Up to the time of the great overseas plantations, Morocco remained a rich cultivation region – and one of Europe's main suppliers of sugar. Today still, sugar remains an important ingredient in Moroccan cuisine. The first tea arrived in the country only two hundred years ago, but strong green tea has become the most popular drink. A "whisky marocain" is part of every meal and rounds off the meal as a digestif, also for the wine-drinking European. Flavored with many fresh mint leaves and very sweet, it is drunk from small, richly ornamented glasses.

From the east and
the south, goods and dealers
continuously came to Morocco via salt
routes and caravan trails, nomadic Bedouins
with friendly or warlike intentions. They soon
integrated with the natives and brought with them the
ingredients of their fare. Hence many ingredients of
Moroccan cuisine are heirlooms of endless journeys, the
eternal bounce and sway of camel saddles across the sands of
the Sahara. Dates, dried vegetables, dried meat, as well as corn
and dried pastries would result in unanticipated delicacies on
long migrations across the solitude of the desert. The many
varieties of bread, which is present at every Moroccan meal,
were a useful means of circumventing the sensitivity of loose
flour. Long before Marco Polo's introduction of noodles to
northern Italy, dried pasta, similar to lasagne cut into strips,
was enriching dishes such as trid marrakshia, the legendary
favorite food of the Prophet Mohammed. The caravans have
gone, the variety of pastry products has remained: simple sour
dough bread and thin sheets of pastry, w'harka and b'stilla,
that can contain a variety of delicious fillings, with pigeon
and cinnamon, with seafood or with almonds and sweet milk.
Then as now, Morocco, a cold land with hot sun, through the
diversity of its soils and its climate, brings forth a multiplicity
of aromas in its kitchen herbs and fruits that sometimes casts
doubt upon their botanical kinship. The locally varying
ingredients are likewise a reason for the new fragrances of
each new region. Argan seeds, used in the south for producing oil, have a spicy, nutty flavor that creates different taste
impressions than would arise, for example when preparing a
tajine stew with smen, a pungent-tasting butter fat. The same
applies to the dishes: "poulet au citron", chicken with lemon,
served in Fès tastes completely different to that served in
Marrakech, even though both bear the same name.

With the decay of the mighty north African empires, the Europeans came to the country, but were able to capture only individual bastions. The Spaniards occupied Ceuta, the Portuguese established themselves on the Atlantic coast. Until the 20th century, Morocco remained an independent state. As proud and unconquered as those that produce them, the dishes of Morocco's cuisine have been preserved with less falsification than those of other Maghreb cuisines. The self-assuredness of the people, the clarity seen in the filigree lines of the ornamentation, the same fairy-tale harmony of the colored mosaics is reflected in the dishes.

T

he diversity of tastes, ripe, fresh fruits and the variety of spices make Moroccan cooking a feast for the palate, in which the piquancy of the individual aromas is woven into a dense oriental carpet of tastes, without letting any individual component lose any of its significance. The wide repertoire of intense spices is conducive to curiosity, to experimentation, and tempts committed chefs all over the world to use this luxuriant "palette" to create new taste variations, rich in nuances. The first symposium with top cooks from all over the world and one of the Grands Maîtres of Moroccan cuisine, chef Boujemaa Mars of the Hotel Mamounia, took place last year in Marrakech – with fabulous results, one hears.

Marokko, das ist Licht und Schatten, das sind stolze, dunkelhäutige Menschen in weiten weißen Gewändern, manchmal auch in erdfarbene braune Djellabas gehüllt, aus deren Dunkel ein Weiß nur aus einem Augenwinkel oder in einem verschämten Lachen hervorblitzt.

Marokko, das sind grelle Lichtinseln im staubigen Halbdunkel der Souks mit einer märchenhaften Farbigkeit von Gewürzen und Produkten, die vor dem Ton in Ton der Menschen und Mauern nur umso übermütiger leuchten.

Marokko, das ist ein geordnetes Gewirr von Linien und Licht, Mosaiken und filigranem Schnitzwerk, das geordnete Durcheinander von Hell und Dunkel, von Menschen, Farben und Gerüchen, – ein arabisches Yin und Yang.

Ein Ebenbild der reichen Eindrücke, die das Land beim Besucher hinterläßt, bietet die marokkanische Küche. Dicht gewebt, bodenständig und zugleich von feinen Düften, von fremdländischen Einflüssen durchzogen, liest sich die Küche Marokkos wie ein kulinarisches Bilderbuch der Geschichte dieses Landes, seiner Vielfalt, seiner Märchen.

Die Berber waren die ursprüngliche Bevölkerung des Maghreb, eines breiten Streifens entlang der Küste Nordafrikas zum Mittelmeer, dem Land der Phönizier und Karthager. Sie steuern dem Speisenplan die vielen Eintopfgerichte bei, die aus einem Mangel an Feuerungsmaterial entstanden. Bedächtig und behutsam werden die Zutaten in einem unglasierten Tontopf über mäßigem Feuer gegart.

Harira ist eine dicke Suppe aus trockenen Hülsenfrüchten und Eiern, die während des Fastenmonats Ramadan zur Stärkung als erstes Gericht am Abend gereicht wird.

Couscous wird aus dem Grieß verschiedener Getreide gemacht. Es gart langsam über Fleisch, Knochen und Gemüse und nimmt dabei die Aromenfülle der Zutaten in sich auf. Noch heute ist Couscous das traditionelle Gericht am „heiligen" Tag der Muslims, dem Freitag.

Tagines sind die besondere Spezialität der marokkanischen Küche. Diese scheinbar einfachen Gerichte, mit Safran in viel Öl geschmorte Gemüse und Fleischstücke, heben den Eigengeschmack der Zutaten in einer unerschöpflichen Vielfalt von Variationen hervor, – zugleich schlicht und doch von einer feinziselierten Raffinesse.

Vom Ebro bis zum Senegal, vom Atlantik bis zum heutigen Algier reichten in der Blütezeit der Almoraviden-Herrschaft die Grenzen Marokkos. Eine Handelsstraße führte auf marokkanischem Gebiet von Spanien bis in die Goldgebiete von Galam-Bambuk im Norden Malis. Mehr als ein anderes Land in Nordafrika war Marokko seiner Geschichte nach daher auch ein „europäisches" Land.

Die arabische Herrschaft in Spanien war lange Zeit eine marokkanische Herrschaft und bedeutete für das Land einen kulturellen Segen. Marokko war gegen Ende des ersten Jahrtausends ein weltoffenes Land, heller und interessierter als das dumpfe klösterliche Zentraleuropa des Mittelalters.

Aus der Zeit der maurischen Herrschaft in
Spanien stammen viele Ingredienzien der
marokkanischen Küche. Mandel-, Zitronen- und
Orangenbäumchen, die die Araber in ihren
Besitzungen in Spanien heimisch machten,
blieben auf ihrem Weg durch das nördliche Afrika
in Marokko erhalten. Mit ihren Früchten und der
Verwendung von Oliven und Olivenöl bereicherte
sich der Fundus, aus dem die marokkanische Küche
schöpfen konnte. Dazu kamen die Gewürze,
die die Araber von den Inseln der Molukken
einführten, lange bevor die Europäer in den
dauernden Genuß solcher Würze kamen: Muskat,
Safran und Zimt, Kurkuma, Ingwer und Nelken.

Safran wurde erst durch die Mauren in Spanien
bekannt. Wie für das Zuckerrohr unterhielten die
marokkanischen Herrscher in Spanien große Anbau-
flächen für die begehrten Gewürzfäden.
Heute sind uns die Blütennarben des „Crocus
sativus" nur noch unter ihrem arabischen Namen
„Sahafaran", „zafran" bekannt.

Das Ende der maurischen Herrschaft in
Spanien hatte schwerwiegende Folgen für den süd-
lichen Teil Europas. Auch Marokko wurde düsterer
und veränderte sein Gesicht, als es sich durch den
Verlust der spanischen Besitzungen auf sich zurückziehen mußte, – im selben Jahr, in dem sich Europa
mit der Entdeckung Amerikas anschickte, waffen-
klirrend die restliche Welt mit seiner Aufmerksamkeit und Habgier zu beglücken.

Näher noch als Spanien an der Schwelle zu
Amerika gelegen, – der letzte Halt vor der großen
Überfahrt wurde auf den vor Marokko gelegenen
Kanarischen Inseln gemacht – wuchsen schon bald
die neuen Früchte, Kartoffeln, Tomaten, Paprika,
Kürbis und Cayenne in den Gemüsegärten
Marokkos neben den heimischen Karotten
und den Auberginen, einem früheren Mitbringsel
der Araber aus Indien.

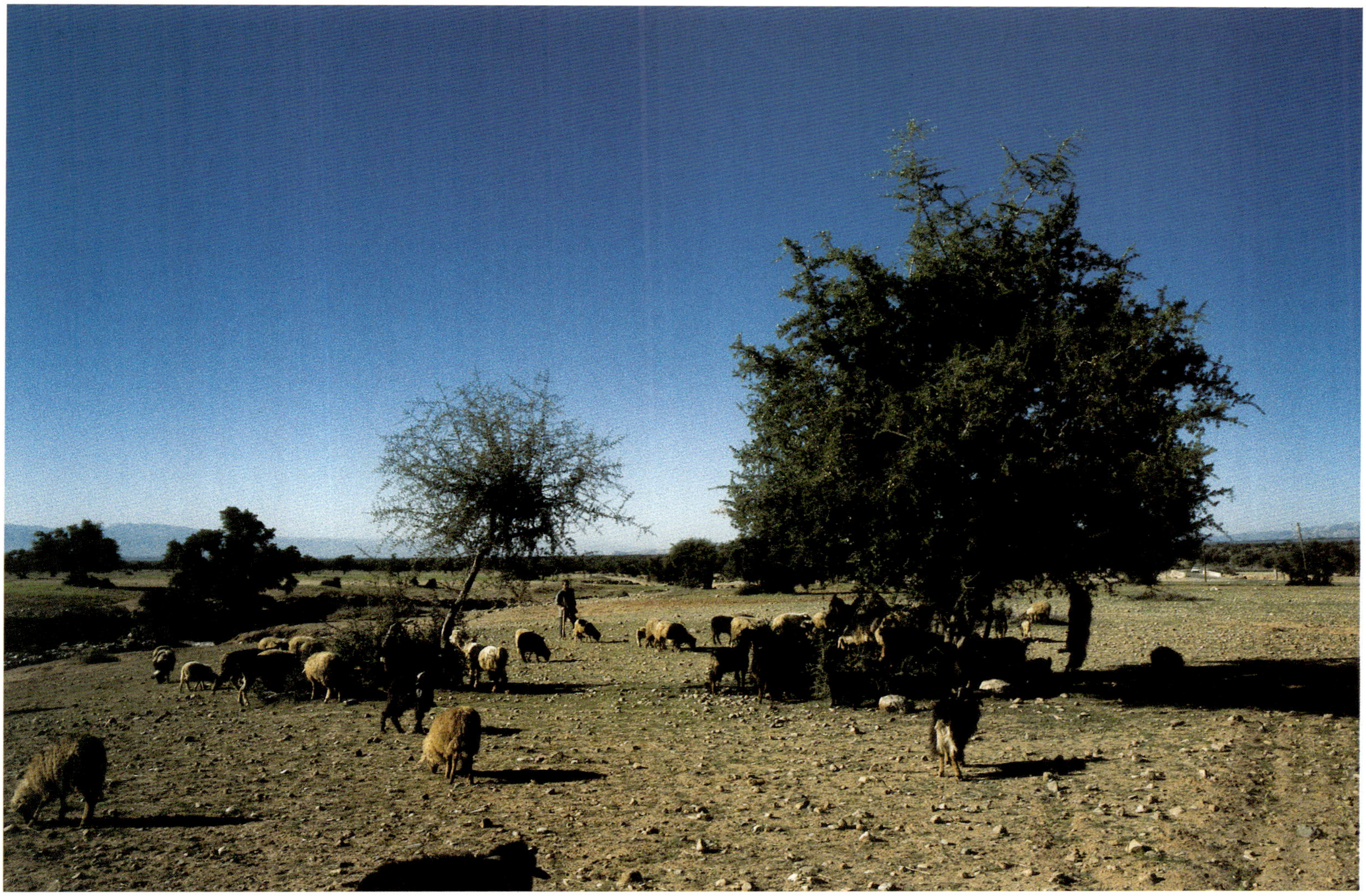

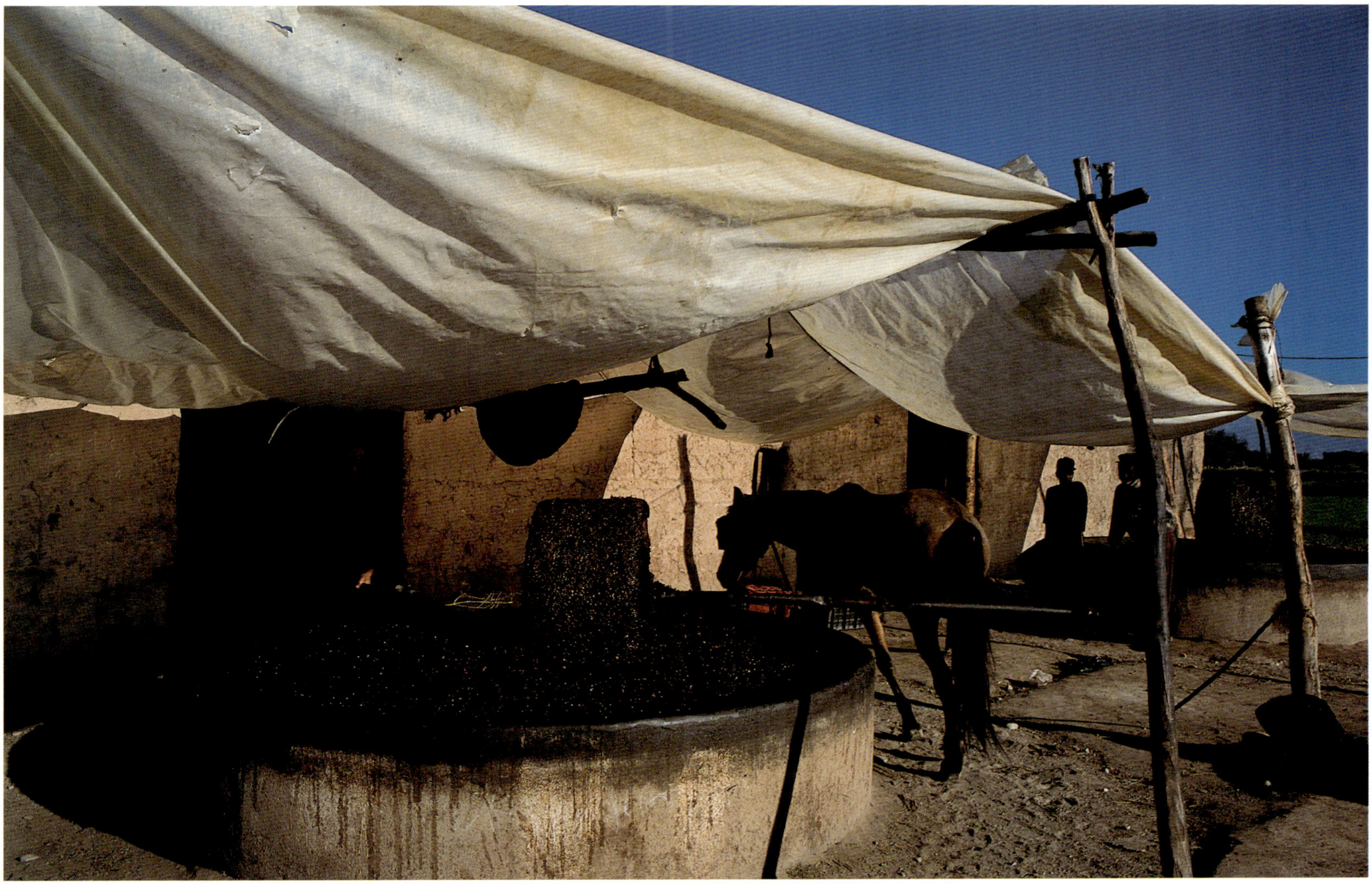

Bis zur Zeit der großen Plantagen in Übersee blieb Marokko eine einträgliche Anbauregion, – und einer der wichtigen Zuckerlieferanten Europas. Bis heute ist Zucker eine wichtige Zutat zu vielen Gerichten der marokkanischen Küche geblieben. Der erste Tee kam zwar erst vor zweihundert Jahren ins Land, starker grüner Tee ist aber das beliebteste Nationalgetränk geworden. Ein „Whisky marocain" gehört zu jedem Essen und rundet auch für den weintrinkenden Europäer als Digestiv das Essen ab. Mit vielen frischen Minzeblättern aromatisiert wird er sehr süß aus kleinen reichverzierten Gläsern getrunken.

Aus dem Osten wie dem Süden kamen über Salzstraßen und Karawanenwege kontinuierlich Waren und Händler nach Marokko; nomadische Beduinen in freundschaftlicher oder in kriegerischer Absicht. Sie vermischten sich bald mit den Einheimischen und brachten die Ingredienzen ihrer Verpflegung mit. So sind viele der kulinarischen Zutaten der marokkanischen Küche Erbstücke endloser Reisen im ewigen Auf und Ab der Kamelsättel durch die Wüsten der Sahara. Datteln, Trockengemüse, Trockenfleisch, daneben Korn und getrocknete Teigwaren konnten bei langen Wanderungen durch die Einsamkeit zu unverhofften Leckereien beitragen.
Die vielen Varianten von Brot, das bei keinem marokkanischen Essen fehlen darf, waren nützliche Mittel, die Empfindlichkeit des losen Mehls zu umgehen.
Lange schon vor Marco Polos Einführung der Nudel im nördlichen Italien bereicherten getrocknete Teigwaren, wie Bandnudeln in Streifen geschnitten, Gerichte wie die Trid Marrakshia, die legendäre Lieblingsspeise Mohammeds, des Propheten.

Die Karawanen sind verschwunden, die Vielfalt der Teigwaren ist geblieben; einfaches Sauerteigbrot und dünne Teigblätter, W'harka und B'stilla, die mit vielerlei Leckereien gefüllt werden können, – mit Tauben und Zimt, mit Meeresfrüchten oder mit Mandeln und süßer Milch. Damals wie heute bringt Marokko, ein kaltes Landes mit heißer Sonne, durch die Verschiedenartigkeit seiner Böden und seines Klimas in den heimischen Gewürzkräutern und Früchten eine Aromenfülle hervor, die manches Mal an der botanischen Verwandtschaft zweifeln läßt. Die lokal unterschiedlichen Zutaten tragen ebenfalls dazu bei, daß sich in jeder Region ein neuer Duft zeigt. Arganien, die im Süden zur Ölbereitung verwendet werden, schaffen mit ihrem rassigen, nußartigen Aroma andere Geschmackseindrücke als sie bei der Zubereitung beispielsweise einer Tajine mit Smen, dem streng schmeckenden Butterschmalz, entstehen.
Das gleiche gilt auch für die Speisen: „Poulet au citron", Zitronenhuhn, schmeckt in Fez gegessen völlig anders als dasselbe Gericht in Marrakesch, selbst wenn beide den gleichen Namen tragen.

Mit dem Zerfall der mächtigen nord-
afrikanischen Reiche kamen die Europäer ins
Land, konnten in Marokko aber nur einzelne
Bastionen erobern. Die Spanier besetzten
Ceuta, die Portugiesen setzten sich an der
Atlantikküste fest. Bis ins 20. Jahrhundert
blieb Marokko ein selbständiger Staat.

Stolz und unbesiegt wie ihre Pro-
duzenten, haben sich in der Küche Marokkos
die Speisen unverfälschter erhalten als in den
anderen Küchen des Maghreb.
Die Selbstbewußtheit der Menschen, die Klarheit, die sich in dem filigranen Linienwerk
der Ornamente findet, der gleiche märchen-
artige Zusammenklang der farbigen Mosaike
wiederspiegelt in den Gerichten.

Die Verschiedenartigkeit der
Geschmacksstoffe, reife, frische Früchte, und
die Vielfalt der Gewürze machen die marokkanische Küche zu einem Gaumenschmaus, in
dem sich die Prägnanz der einzelnen Aromen
zu einem dichten orientalischen Geschmacks-
teppich verflicht, ohne die einzelnen Komponenten an Deutlichkeit verlieren zu lassen.
Das vielfältige Repertoire intensiver Gewürze
lädt zur Neugier ein, zum Experimentieren
und verführt überall in der Welt engagierte
Küchenchefs dazu, mit dieser üppigen
kulinarischen „Farbpalette" neue, nuancenreiche Geschmacksvariationen zu erfinden.

Das erste Symposion mit Spitzenköchen
aus aller Welt und einem der Grands Maîtres
der marokkanischen Küche, Küchenchef
Boujemaa Mars vom Hotel La Mamounia, hat
letztes Jahr bereits in Marrakesch stattgefunden,
– wie man hört mit märchenhaften Resultaten.

LA GAZELLE D'OR TAROUDANT

un paradis
un ange —
tu me voits

ma gazelle
avec des ailes
et m'ensorcelle

il reviendras, toujours
privilégiés qui te visite.

A la detente et à l'amour,
à bras ouvert tu l'invite

à faire un tour,
dans tes jardins Magnifiques

au Milieu des fleurs,
des vendanges féeriques

Amalien

"Golden Gazelle"

The French Colonel Pellenc created himself an oasis when, together with his American wife, he laid out a park in the vicinity of Taroudannt where, surrounded by tangerine trees, ten small guest houses were to provide accommodation for friends from all over the world. They called their property "Golden Gazelle" which lies at the foot of the Atlas amid 100 hectares of orange groves.

To this day La Gazelle d'Or has remained a gem, an oasis of peace and seclusion. The new lady owner has retained the style of the house and the widow of Baron Pellenc remains one of the many faithful guests of this country seat.

Like a taste of paradise, the Gazelle d'Or offers its guests, for the duration of their stay, every conceivable luxury, yet, at the same time, inclusion in a family atmosphere, where the ban on mobile telephones is such a matter of course that one would suspect a secret agreement has been made. Quiet, stylish, well-mannered intercourse with one's fellows is expected and the staff provide the best example of this, here in this tangible heaven on earth.

The peaceful atmosphere begins already at breakfast. A friendly Moroccan in white robes, like an angel with a white fez, brings a richly laden tray to the terrace of your chalet. Without any stage or audience, anyone, even the most popular star, can start the day quite undisturbed, gaze across the expanse of parkland and take delight in the luscious bitter-orange marmalade, and all the other delicacies that are offered.
Thus refreshed, the day can now commence; each guest has lots of space for himself, so much time to relax that he has difficulty in tearing himself away and plunging into the turbulence of the nearby souks of Taroudannt, of little Marrakech. Nor is there any other reason to step outside the Gazelle d'Or than curiosity, the desire for sudden bustle which makes the subsequent peace all the more relaxing. For also inside the Gazelle d'Or there are many possibilities: strolls through the tangerine and orange groves, there are horses to ride, and a small golf course, pool, hammam.

Gastronomic delights are available: at mid-day an opulent buffet invites the gourmet, with fresh salads from the vegetable garden, various tajines, meat and fish. In the evening, a menu carefully assembled by chef Frédéric Nef from Moroccan and international cuisine offers enjoyment that can only be enhanced by the attentive yet discreet personal service of the staff.

This service to the guest, which is not affected friendliness for the job's sake, but which radiates cordial and genuine amiability, is evidenced by no-one better than Amahou, the long serving maître d'hôtel himself, who modestly replies in response to praise: "La clientèle, c'est mon miroir." The guest is my mirror. For this spacious house the word "hotel" can only express the class, not the style of the establishment.
For the departing guest "La Gazelle d'Or" means more than just the name of a first-class hotel.
As the Moroccans say, when a particularly enchanting person, a child or a beautiful woman, passes by, flatteringly and appreciatively: "Ah, la gazelle!"

Eine Oase schuf sich der französische Colonel Pellenc, als er mit seiner amerikanischen Gattin in der Nähe von Taroudannt einen Park anlegen ließ, in dem, umgeben von Mandarinenbäumchen, zehn kleine Gästehäuser Platz bieten sollten für die Freunde aus aller Welt. „Goldene Gazelle" nannten sie ihr Anwesen, das am Fuß des Atlas inmitten von 100 ha Orangenplantagen liegt.

Bis heute ist La Gazelle d'Or ein Kleinod geblieben, eine Oase der Ruhe und der Abgeschiedenheit. Die neue Besitzerin hat den Stil des Hauses erhalten, und die Witwe des Barons Pellenc gehört noch immer zu den vielen treuen Gästen des Landsitzes. Wie ein Paradies auf Zeit bietet das Gazelle d'Or seinen Gästen für die Dauer ihres Aufenthalts allen denkbaren Luxus, zugleich aber die Einbezogenheit in eine familiäre Atmosphäre, in der das Verbot von Handies so selbstverständlich ist wie nach einer geheimen Übereinkunft. Ein ruhiger, stilvoller Umgang miteinander ist als Einverständnis vorausgesetzt, und das Personal gibt das beste Beispiel für diesen greifbaren Himmel auf Erden.

Friedlich stimmt schon am Morgen das Frühstück. Ein freundlicher Marokkaner, weißgekleidet wie ein Engel mit weißem Fez, bringt ein reichhaltiges Tablett auf die Terrasse des Häuschens. Ganz ohne Bühne, ohne Publikum, kann jeder, auch ein sonst heftig umworbener Star, ganz für sich den Tag beginnen, auf den weiten Park blicken und sich an einer traumhaften Bitterorangen-Marmelade erfreuen und was an Leckereien sonst geboten wird.

Es fällt nicht schwer, so gestärkt den Tag zu verbringen, denn immer bleibt für jeden Gast viel Raum für sich, viel Gelassenheit, die es ihm fast schwer macht, sich davon loszureißen und sich in das Gewühl der nahen Souks von Taroudannt, dem kleinen Marrakesch, zu stürzen. Es gibt auch keinen anderen Grund, sich aus dem Gazelle d'Or wegzubewegen als die Neugier, den Wunsch nach plötzlicher Betriebsamkeit, der die Ruhe danach umso erholsamer macht. Denn auch innerhalb des „Gazelle d'Or" finden sich vielfältige Möglichkeiten: Streifzüge durch die Mandarinen- und Orangenhaine, Reitpferde und ein kleiner Golfplatz, Pool, Hammam.

Für die Gaumenfreuden ist gesorgt: mittags lädt ein opulentes Buffet zum Schlemmen ein, mit frischen Salaten aus dem eigenen Gemüsegarten, verschiedenen Tagines, Fleisch und Fisch. Am Abend bietet ein von Küchenchef Frédéric Nef sorgsam aus marokkanischer und internationaler Küche zusammen-gestelltes Menü einen Genuß, der nur durch den aufmerksamen und zugleich so diskreten wie persönlichen Service noch gesteigert werden kann.

Diesen Dienst am Gast, der keine dienstbare Freundlichkeit ist, sondern eine herzlich empfundene Freundschaftlichkeit ausstrahlt, kann keiner besser kennzeichnen als Amahou, der langjährige Maître d'hôtel selbst, der auf ein Lob bescheiden antwortet: La clientèle, c'est mon mirroir – der Gast ist mein Spiegel.

Für dieses weitläufige Gäste Domizil kann das Wort Hotel nur die Klasse, nicht den prägenden Stil aus-sagen. „La Gazelle d'Or" bedeutet dem Abschied nehmenden Gast mehr als nur der Name eines First Class Hotels. Wie sagen doch die Marokkaner, wenn an ihnen ein besonders bezauberndes Wesen, ein Kind oder eine wunderschöne Frau vorübergeht, schmeichelnd und voll Anerkennung: „Ah, la gazelle!"

Brined lemons

Brining the lemons removes most of the acidity and gives them a special taste which goes especially well with braised dishes.

Recipe:
Untreated lemons, preferably thin-skinned,
coarse salt, 1 - 2 tsp per lemon,
freshly pressed lemon juice, 1 - 2 tsp per lemon

Make lengthwise cuts in the lemons on both sides, leaving the ends intact. Press a little salt into the cuts, rinse out a large preserving jar with boiling water. Place the lemons in the jar, sprinkling each one with a little salt. Pour over the lemon juice, sprinkle again with salt, then fill up with boiling water until the lemons are covered. Immediately seal the jar closely. Allow the brined lemons to stand in the sun for three to four weeks.

Eingelegte Zitronen

Das Einlegen in Salz entzieht den Zitronen weitgehend die Säure und verleiht ihnen einen speziellen Geschmack, der besonders bei Schmorgerichten gut zur Geltung kommt.

Rezept:
Unbehandelte Zitronen, möglichst mit dünner Schale,
grobes Salz, 1 - 2 TL pro Zitrone,
frischgepreßter Zitronensaft, 1 - 2 TL pro Zitrone

Zitronen der Länge nach von zwei Seiten tief einschneiden; sie sollen an den Enden noch zusammenhalten. In die Schnitte etwas Salz drücken. Ein großes Einmachglas mit kochendem Wasser ausspülen. Zitronen in das Glas füllen, dabei jeweils mit etwas Salz bestreuen. Zitronensaft darübergießen, nochmal mit Salz bestreuen und dann mit kochendheißem Wasser auffüllen, bis die Zitronen bedeckt sind. Glas sofort fest verschließen. In der Sonne die eingelegten Zitronen drei bis vier Wochen ziehen lassen.

MIXED SALAD WITH COUSCOUS

BUNTER SALAT MIT COUSCOUS

For 4 - 6 persons:

400 g/14 oz couscous,
¹/₂ liter/1 pint/2 cups boiling water

3 tomatoes, skinned and seeded,
3 yellow bell peppers, grilled and skinned,
1 piece of cucumber, peeled,
2 scallions

6 tbsp olive oil, 6 tbsp lemon juice,
salt, black pepper from the mill,
1 bunch mint, chopped,
1 bunch parsil, chopped

Place the couscous in a bowl and pour over the boiling water, mash with a fork until all the grains are moistened, cover, and allow to swell for half an hour. Then steam the couscous in a sieve insert.
Cut all the vegetables into small cubes and mix with the couscous. Stir the olive oil with the lemon juice, salt, pepper and herbs and mix into the salad. Allow to stand in the refrigerator for one hour. To serve: Garnish with mint and slices of lemon.

Taboulet

Für 4 - 6 Personen:

400 g Couscous,
¹/₂ Liter kochendes Wasser

3 Tomaten, enthäutet und entkernt,
1 gelbe Paprika, gegrillt und enthäutet,
1 Stück Salatgurke, geschält,
2 Frühlingszwiebeln

6 EL Olivenöl, 6 EL Zitronensaft,
Salz, schwarzer Pfeffer aus der Mühle,
1 Bund Minze, gehackt,
1 Bund Petersilie, gehackt

Den Couscous in einer Schüssel mit dem heißem Wasser übergießen, mit einer Gabel zerdrücken, bis alle Körnchen befeuchtet sind und zugedeckt eine halbe Stunde quellen lassen. Anschließend den Couscous in einem Siebeinsatz über Wasserdampf garen.
Alle Gemüse in kleine Würfel schneiden und mit dem Couscous vermengen. Das Olivenöl mit Zitronensaft, Salz, Pfeffer und den Kräutern verrühren und unter den Salat mischen. Eine Stunde im Kühlschrank ziehen lassen. Zum Servieren mit Minze und Zitronenscheiben garnieren.

STEWED WHITE BEANS

GESCHMORTE WEISSE BOHNEN

For 4 persons:

*300 g/10 oz white beans,
steeped in water overnight*

*2 onions, cut into fine strips,
2 garlic cloves, finely chopped,
4 tomatoes, skinned,
seeded and cut into strips,
1 small red chili, ¹/₂ tsp ground ginger,
¹/₂ tsp ground cumin, ¹/₂ tsp allspice,
1 knife-tip saffron,
salt, pepper, 4 tbsp olive oil,
450 ml/15 fl oz vegetable broth*

*1 bunch coriander leaves, chopped,
juice of 1 lemon*

Drain the beans through a sieve. Fry the vegetables and spices in the olive oil, add the beans, pour in the broth, cover, and cook for 1¹/₂ - 2 hours.
Stir occasionally, adding a little water, if necessary.
Finally, mix in the coriander leaves and lemon juice to taste.

Für 4 Personen:

*300 g weiße Bohnen,
über Nacht in Wasser eingeweicht*

*2 Gemüsezwiebeln,
in feine Streifen geschnitten,
2 Knoblauchzehen, fein geschnitten,
4 Tomaten, enthäutet,
entkernt und in Streifen geschnitten,
1 kleine, rote Chilischote,
¹/₂ TL Ingwerpulver,
¹/₂ TL Kreuzkümmelpulver,
¹/₂ TL Piment, 1 Msp Safran,
Salz, Pfeffer, 4 EL Olivenöl,
450 ml Gemüsebrühe*

*1 Bund Koriandergrün, gehackt,
Saft einer Zitrone*

Bohnen durch ein Sieb abgießen. Gemüse und Gewürze im Olivenöl andünsten, Bohnen zugeben, mit Brühe augießen und zugedeckt eineinhalb bis zwei Stunden schmoren lassen. Von Zeit zu Zeit umrühren, bei Bedarf etwas Wassser zufügen. Zum Schluß das Koriandergrün unterheben und mit Zitronensaft abschmecken.

For 4 persons:

600 g/1 lb 5 oz shin beef, 4 tbsp olive oil,
1 onion, finely chopped,
2 garlic cloves, crushed,
$^1/_2$ liter/1 pint/2 cups beef broth

1 bunch parsley, chopped, 1 tsp paprika,
$^1/_2$ tsp turmeric,
$^1/_2$ tsp ground coriander, salt, pepper

8 artichoke hearts,
rubbed with lemon juice
200 g/7 oz garden peas

Fry the beef in hot oil on all sides. Add the onion and garlic and sauté briefly, then quench with the broth. Stir in the parsley and season with paprika, turmeric, salt and pepper.
Cover and braise the meat on a low heat for 1$^1/_2$ - 2 hours.
For the last half hour add the artichoke hearts and peas and allow them to cook in the meat sauce.

KNUCKLE OF BEEF WITH ARTICHOKES AND PEAS

RINDERHAXEN MIT ARTISCHOCKEN UND ERBSEN

Für 4 Personen:

600 g Rindfleisch aus der Wade,
4 EL Olivenöl,
1 Gemüsezwiebel, fein geschnitten,
2 Knoblauchzehen, zerdrückt,
$^1/_2$ Liter Rinderbrühe

1 Bund Petersilie, gehackt,
1 TL Paprika, $^1/_2$ TL Kurkuma,
$^1/_2$ TL Korianderpulver, Salz, Pfeffer

8 Artischockenböden,
mit Zitronensaft eingerieben,
200 g Gartenerbsen

Das Rindfleisch im heißen Öl rundum anbraten. Die Zwiebel und den Knoblauch kurz mitdünsten, dann mit der Brühe ablöschen. Die Petersilie unterrühren, mit Paprika, Kurkuma, Salz und Pfeffer würzen.
Zugedeckt bei kleiner Hitze das Fleisch eineinhalb bis zwei Stunden schmoren.
Die Artischockenböden und Erbsen während der letzten halben Stunde zugeben und in der Fleischsauce mitkochen lassen.

LAMB TAJINE WITH ONIONS

LAMM-TAGINE MIT ZWIEBELN

For 4 - 6 persons:

600 g/1 lb 5 oz shoulder of lamb, boned,
3 tbsp olive oil,
1 onion, cut into fine strips,
1 garlic clove, finely chopped,
1 bunch parsley, chopped,
¹/₂ tsp ground ginger,
¹/₂ tsp cumin,
1 knife-tip saffron,
1 tsp white pepper,
1 tsp salt

1 kg small onions,
1 tsp ground ginger, 1 tbsp ground cinnamon,
1 tbsp sugar,
1 tsp salt, ¹/₂ tsp white pepper,
4 tbsp olive oil

Cut the lamb into cubes. Heat the oil in a braising pan, briefly sear the meat on all sides, add the onion and garlic, and fry. Add the parsley and spices, pour over about two cups water, cover and braise for one hour.
Peel the onions and lay them on a greased baking tray. Mix the spices with the oil and paint over the onions.
Bake the onions in the oven at 150° C/300° F for about one hour until they are soft, brown and glazed, drizzling occasionally with the spiced oil. Add the onions to the lamb and cook for half an hour more. Adjust the seasoning of the sauce.
To serve: Transfer the tajine to a deep earthenware bowl.

Für 4 - 6 Personen:

600 g Lammfleisch aus der Schulter,
3 EL Olivenöl,
1 Zwiebel, in feine Streifen geschnitten,
1 Knoblauchzehe, fein geschnitten,
1 Bund Petersilie, gehackt,
¹/₂ TL Ingwerpulver,
¹/₂ TL Kreuzkümmel,
1 Msp Safran,
1 TL weißer Pfeffer,
1 TL Salz

1 kg kleine Gemüsezwiebeln,
1 TL Ingwerpulver, 1 EL Zimtpulver,
1 EL Zucker,
1 TL Salz, ¹/₂ TL weißer Pfeffer,
4 EL Olivenöl

Lammfleisch in Würfel schneiden. In einem Schmortopf das Öl erhitzen, das Fleisch rundum kurz anbraten, die Zwiebel und Knoblauch hinzufügen und mitbraten. Petersilie und Gewürze zugeben, mit ungefähr zwei Tassen Wasser aufgießen und zugedeckt eine Stunde schmoren lassen.
Zwiebeln schälen und auf ein gefettetes Backblech legen. Gewürze mit dem Öl verrühren und darüber verteilen. Im Ofen bei 150° C ca. eine Stunde backen, bis sie weich und braun glasiert sind, dabei die Zwiebeln von Zeit zu Zeit mit dem Gewürzöl beträufeln. Die Zwiebeln zum Lamm dazugeben und eine weitere halbe Stunde garen. Sauce abschmecken. Zum Servieren die Tagine in eine tiefe Tonschüssel füllen.

TUNA TAJINE
WITH BRINED LEMONS

THUNFISCH-TAGINE
MIT EINGEMACHTEN ZITRONEN

For 4 persons:

800 g/1 lb 12 oz fillet of tuna

For the marinade:
150 ml/5 fl oz olive oil, 2 garlic cloves, crushed,
2 tbsp vinegar, 1 tbsp sweet paprika,
2 tsp ground cumin, 1/2 tsp turmeric,
1/4 tsp cayenne pepper,
1 bunch coriander leaves, chopped

4 tomatoes,
1 brined lemon (see p. 230),
150 g/5 oz pink-brown olives,
plumped up in boiling water,
juice of 1 lemon

Cut the fillet of tuna into 8 slices. Stir all the ingredients for the marinade in a fireproof (preferably earthenware) dish. Place the slices of fish in the marinade, cover, and allow to stand in the refrigerator for two to three hours. Spread the slices of fish flat in the dish and top each with a half tomato and a small wedge of lemon. Drizzle with the marinade and cook in the preheated oven for thirty minutes. For the last ten minutes add the olives. Before serving, add lemon juice to the sauce to taste. The best accompaniment to this spicy dish is rice.

Für 4 Personen:

800 g Thunfischfilet

Für die Marinade:
150 ml Olivenöl, 2 Knoblauchzehen, zerdrückt,
2 EL Essig, 1 EL süsses Paprikapulver,
2 TL Kreuzkümmelpulver, 1/2 TL Kurkuma,
1/4 TL Cayennepfeffer,
1 Bund Koriandergrün, gehackt

4 Tomaten,
1 eingelegte Zitrone (siehe Seite 230),
150 braun-rosa Oliven, in Wasser aufgekocht,
Saft einer Zitrone

Thunfischfilet in acht Scheiben schneiden. Alle Zutaten für die Marinade in einer feuerfesten (möglichst irdenen) Form verrühren. Die Fischscheiben einlegen und im Kühlschrank zugedeckt zwei bis drei Stunden in der Marinade ziehen lassen.
Die Fischscheiben in der Form flach ausbreiten und mit je einer halben Tomate und einer kleinen Zitronenspalte belegen. Mit der Marinade beträufeln und das Ganze im vorgeheizten Ofen eine halbe Stunde schmoren lassen. Während der letzten zehn Minuten die Oliven zugeben. Vor dem Servieren die Sauce mit Zitronensaft abschmecken. Als Beilage zu diesem würzigen Gericht paßt am besten Reis.

TURKEY TAJINE
WITH COUSCOUS AND ALMONDS

TRUTHAHN-TAGINE
MIT COUSCOUS UND MANDELN

For 4 persons:

*4 small turkey legs, 3 tbsp peanut oil,
1 onion, finely chopped, 1 garlic clove, crushed,
400 ml/13 fl oz/1²/₃ cups chicken broth,
100 g/3¹/₂ oz almonds, scalded, peeled and chopped,
1 bunch coriander leaves, chopped,
¹/₂ stick cinnamon, ¹/₂ tsp turmeric,
¹/₂ tsp ground ginger, salt, white pepper*

For the couscous:
*200 g/7 oz couscous, 300 ml/10 fl oz/1 ¹/₄ cups hot water,
100 g/3¹/₂ oz almonds, scalded, peeled and chopped,
2 tbsp soft butter, 1 tbsp cinnamon,
salt, sugar*

Fry the turkey legs in hot oil. Add the onion and garlic and fry briefly. Quench with broth, stir in the almonds, coriander and spices, cover and braise for about forty minutes.
For the couscous: Place the couscous in a bowl and pour over the hot water. Mix well with a fork, cover and allow to swell for thirty minutes. Then mix the couscous with the almonds, butter, cinnamon and a little salt and sugar. Place in a sieve insert and steam over fast boiling water until cooked. Occasionally loosen the couscous with a fork. Adjust the seasoning of the sauce of the turkey legs and, if necessary, reduce a little.
To serve: Transfer the turkey meat with the sauce to a deep earthenware dish. Heap the couscous in the middle of the dish, dust with cinnamon and serve hot.

Für 4 Personen:

*4 kleine Putenkeulen, 3 EL Erdnußöl,
1 Gemüsezwiebel, fein geschnitten,
1 Knoblauchzehe, zerdrückt, 400 ml Hühnerbrühe,
100 g Mandeln, überbrüht, abgezogen und gehackt,
1 Bund Koriandergrün, gehackt,
¹/₂ Zimtstange, ¹/₂ TL Kurkuma
¹/₂ TL Ingwerpulver, Salz, weißer Pfeffer*

Für den Couscous:
*200 g Couscous, 300 ml heißes Wasser,
100 g Mandeln, überbrüht, abgezogen und gehackt,
2 EL weiche Butter, 1 EL Zimt,
Salz, Zucker*

Putenkeulen im heißen Öl anbraten. Zwiebel und Knoblauch kurz mitbraten. Mit Brühe ablöschen, Mandeln, Koriander und Gewürze unterrühren und zugedeckt ca. vierzig Minuten schmoren lassen.
Für den Couscous: Couscous in eine Schüssel geben und mit dem heißen Wasser übergießen. Mit einer Gabel gut vermischen, zudecken und dreißig Minuten quellen lassen. Dann mit den Mandeln, der Butter, dem Zimt, etwas Salz und Zucker vermischen und in einem Siebeinsatz über sprudelnd kochendem Wasser dämpfen, bis er gar ist. Von Zeit zu Zeit den Couscous mit einer Gabel auflockern. Die Sauce von den Putenkeulen abschmecken, wenn nötig etwas einkochen lassen. Zum Servieren: Putenfleisch mit der Sauce in eine tiefe Tonschale füllen. Couscous in die Mitte der Schale häufen, mit Zimt bestreuen und heiß servieren.

For 4 persons:

4 slices veal suckle,
250 g/8 oz small brown lentils,
steeped in water overnight,
4 tbsp olive oil,
1 onion, finely chopped,
2 garlic cloves, crushed,
2 sticks celery, finely chopped,
1 carrot, cut into fine cubes,
2 tomatoes, skinned, seeded, finely chopped,
2 tbsp tomato purée, 1 bunch parsley, chopped,
1/4 stick cinnamon, 1 tsp ground coriander,
1/2 tsp turmeric, 1/4 tsp harissa (optional),
salt, pepper
300 ml/10 fl oz/1 1/4 cups beef broth,
2 tbsp lemon juice

LENTIL STEW

LINSENEINTOPF

Drain the lentils through a sieve. Heat the olive oil in a braising pan. Place the meat and the lentils in the pan together with the onion, garlic, vegetables, tomato purée and spices and fry briefly.
Pour in the broth, cover, and cook the lentils for one and a half hours. Stir occasionally, adding a little water if necessary.
Finally, add lemon juice to taste and serve in a shallow earthenware dish.

Für 4 Personen:

4 Scheiben Kalbshaxe,
250 g kleine braune Linsen,
über Nacht in Wasser eingeweicht,
4 EL Olivenöl,
1 Gemüsezwiebel, fein geschnitten,
2 Knoblauchzehen, durchgedrückt,
2 Stangen Sellerie, fein geschnitten,
1 Karotte, in feine Würfel geschnitten,
2 Tomaten, enthäutet, entkernt, fein geschnitten,
2 EL Tomatenmark, 1 Bund Petersilie, gehackt,
1/4 Zimtstange, 1 TL Korianderpulver,
1/2 TL Kurkuma, 1/4 TL Harissa (nach Belieben),
Salz, Pfeffer,
300 ml Rinderbrühe,
2 EL Zitronensaft

Linsen durch ein Sieb abgießen. Olivenöl in einem Schmortopf erhitzen. Das Fleisch und die Linsen mit der Zwiebel, Knoblauch, Gemüse, Tomatenmark und den Gewürzen andünsten. Mit der Brühe aufgießen und zugedeckt die Linsen eineinhalb Stunden schmoren lassen. Von Zeit zu Zeit umrühren, wenn nötig etwas Wasser zufügen.
Zum Schluß das Gericht mit Zitronensaft abschmecken und in einer flachen Tonschüssel servieren.

STUFFED SEA BREAM, FES STYLE

GEFÜLLTE GOLDBRASSE NACH ART VON FES

For 4 persons:

*1 sea bream of about 1.5 kg/3^1/$_3$ lb,
cleaned and scaled*

For the sauce:
*100 ml/3^1/$_2$ fl oz/^{2}/$_5$ cup olive oil,
2 garlic cloves, crushed, 2 tbsp tomato purée,
1 tsp ground cumin, 2 tsp paprika, 1 tsp salt,
^{1}/$_2$ tsp pepper, 1 tbsp vinegar, 3 tbsp lemon juice,
100 ml/3^1/$_2$ fl oz/^{2}/$_5$ cup water,
1 bunch coriander leaves, 1 bunch parsley*

*150 g/5 oz/^{3}/$_5$ cup rice,
2 green bell peppers,
3 tomatoes, sliced,
1 brined lemon (see p. 230), thinly sliced,
200 g/7 oz pink-brown olives,
plumped up in boiling water*

Wash the sea bream under running cold water and dry.

For the sauce: Heat the olive oil in a small pan. Sauté the garlic over a low heat. Then stir in the tomato purée, spices, vinegar, lemon juice, water and herbs, and remove from the stove.

Cook the rice in salted water until al dente and season with a little sauce, mixing well. Stuff the fish with the rice. On a greased baking dish, first spread out the halved and seeded bell peppers. Then lay the fish on top and cover with the slices of tomato and lemon.

Pour over the remaining sauce, sprinkle with salt and pepper and bake in a preheated oven at 170° C/340° F for forty minutes.

To serve: Place the hot olives on a serving platter. Lay the fish and the pepper halves on top and pour over the cooking liquid.

Für 4 Personen:

*1 Goldbrasse von ca. 1,5 kg,
ausgenommen und geschuppt*

Für die Sauce:
*100 ml Olivenöl, 2 Knoblauchzehen,
durchgedrückt, 2 EL Tomatenmark,
1 TL Kreuzkümmelpulver, 2 TL Paprikapulver,
1 TL Salz, ^{1}/$_2$ TL Pfeffer, 1 EL Essig,
3 EL Zitronensaft, 100 ml Wasser,
1 Bund Koriandergrün, 1 Bund Petersilie*

*150 g Reis, 2 grüne Paprika,
3 Tomaten, in Scheiben geschnitten,
1 eingelegte Zitrone (siehe Seite 230),
in dünne Scheiben geschnitten,
200 g rosa-braune Oliven,
in Wasser aufgekocht*

Goldbrasse unter fließendem, kaltem Wasser waschen und abtrocknen.

Für die Sauce: Olivenöl in einem kleinen Topf erhitzen. Knoblauch bei schwacher Hitze dünsten. Dann Tomatenmark, Gewürze, Essig, Zitronensaft, Wasser und Kräuter unterrühren, vom Herd nehmen. Den Reis mit Salzwasser al dente kochen und mit etwas Sauce würzen, gut vermengen. Den Fisch mit dem Reis füllen. Auf ein gefettetes Backblech zuerst die halbierten, entkernten Paprika ausbreiten. Dann den Fisch darüber legen und mit den Tomaten- und Zitronenscheiben bedecken. Mit der restlichen Sauce begießen, mit Salz und Pfeffer bestreuen und im vorgeheizten Ofen bei 170° C vierzig Minuten garen. Zum Servieren: Die heißen Oliven auf eine Servierplatte geben. Den Fisch und die Paprikahälften darüberlegen und mit der Garflüssigkeit begießen.

PASTILLA WITH SEAFOOD

PASTILLA MIT MEERESFRÜCHTEN

For 4 persons:

200 g/7 oz sea bass,
200 g/7 oz John Dory,
200 g/7 oz shrimps, peeled

For the marinade:
1 garlic clove, crushed,
2 sprigs coriander leaves, chopped,
2 sprigs parsley, chopped,
2 tbsp lemon juice, 1 tbsp vinegar,
¹/₂ tsp cayenne pepper, 1 tsp paprika,
1 tsp cumin, 1 knife-tip saffron,
¹/₂ tsp white pepper, 1 tsp salt

2 tbsp olive oil, 2 tbsp butter,
1 onion, finely chopped,
2 tomatoes, skinned,
seeded and cut into small cubes

400 g/13 oz puff pastry,
olive oil,
1 egg yolk

Cut the fish fillets into small cubes. Stir together the ingredients for a marinade, add the fish and the shrimps and allow to stand in the refrigerator for one hour. Then drain through a sieve.

Heat the oil and the butter in a pan. Add the onion and sauté until transparent.

Then add the fish with the shrimps and the residue of the marinade together with the tomato cubes and braise until the fish is done. Adjust seasoning as desired.

Roll out the puff pastry very thinly. Cut out several large rounds. Layer half of these on a baking tray, painting a little olive oil between each layer. Now ladle on the fish-shrimp mixture, leaving an edge of about 2 cm/⁴/₅ in free.

Cover with the remaining pastry rounds, likewise painted with oil. Paint the edge with egg yolk and seal well.

Preheat the oven to 180° C/360° F and bake for about half an hour until golden.

Für 4 Personen:

200 g Wolfsbarschfilet,
200 g Sankt Petersfischfilet,
200 g Crevetten, geschält

Für die Marinade:
1 Knoblauchzehe, zerdrückt,
2 Zweige Koriandergrün, gehackt,
2 Zweige Petersilie, gehackt,
2 EL Zitronensaft, 1 EL Essig,
¹/₂ TL Cayennepfeffer, 1 TL Paprikapulver,
1 TL Kreuzkümmelpulver, 1 Msp Safran,
¹/₂ TL weißer Pfeffer, 1 TL Salz

2 EL Olivenöl, 2 EL Butter,
1 Gemüsezwiebel, fein geschnitten,
2 Tomaten, enthäutet, entkernt
und in kleine Würfel geschnitten

400 g Blätterteig,
Olivenöl,
1 Eigelb

Fischfilets in kleine Würfel schneiden. Zutaten für die Marinade verrühren, den Fisch und die Crevetten einlegen und im Kühlschrank eine Stunde ziehen lassen. Anschließend in einem Sieb abtropfen lassen.

Das Öl und die Butter in einem Topf erhitzen. Die Zwiebel zugeben und glasig dünsten. Dann den Fisch mit den Crevetten und den Marinadenrückständen sowie die Tomatenwürfel zugeben und dünsten, bis der Fisch gar ist. Nach Belieben nachwürzen.

Den Blätterteig sehr dünn ausrollen. Mehrere grosse Kreise ausschneiden. Die Hälfte davon auf ein Backblech schichten, zwischen jede Lage etwas Olivenöl pinseln. Nun die Fisch-Crevettenmasse daraufschöpfen, dabei einen Rand von ca. 2 cm freilassen. Mit den restlichen, ebenfalls mit Öl bepinselten Teigrondellen zudecken. Den Rand mit Eigelb bepinseln und gut verschließen.

Im vorgeheizten Ofen bei 180° C ungefähr eine halbe Stunde goldgelb backen.

MEATBALLS "KEFTA" WITH EGGS

HACKFLEISCHBÄLLCHEN „KEFTA" MIT EIERN

For 4 persons:

*500 g/1 lb 2 oz ground meat
(beef or lamb as desired),
2 garlic cloves, crushed,
$^1/_2$ tsp ground cumin,
$^1/_2$ tsp ground coriander,
1 tbsp cayenne pepper,
salt,
2 sprigs coriander leaves, finely chopped*

*3 tbsp peanut oil,
1 onion, finely chopped,
1 garlic clove, crushed,
2 tbsp tomato purée,
1 tsp paprika,
$^1/_2$ tsp ground cumin,
salt,
pepper,
harissa as desired
(north African chili sauce)*

4 eggs

Mix the ground meat well with the spices and coriander, then shape small balls from this mixture. Heat the oil in a fire-proof pot (preferably earthenware). Fry the meatballs on all sides until golden. Remove from the pot and keep in a warm place.

Sauté the onion and garlic in the oil until transparent. Add the tomato purée and spices, then the meatballs and pour in enough water to barely cover the meat. Cover the pot and simmer on a low heat for about twenty minutes, stirring occasionally.

Adjust the seasoning of the sauce. Preheat the oven to 200° C/390° F.

Crack an egg into a cup and slip it whole into the hot sauce. Add the other eggs in the same manner.

Place the pot without the lid in the hot oven and bake for ten minutes.

Für 4 Personen:

*500 g Hackfleisch
(Rind oder Lamm, nach Belieben),
2 Knoblauchzehen, durchgedrückt,
$^1/_2$ TL Kreuzkümmelpulver,
$^1/_2$ TL Korianderpulver,
1 TL Cayennepfeffer,
Salz,
2 Zweige Koriandergrün, fein gehackt*

*3 EL Erdnußöl,
1 Gemüsezwiebel, fein geschnitten,
1 Knoblauchzehe, durchgedrückt,
2 EL Tomatenmark,
1 TL Paprikapulver,
$^1/_2$ TL Kreuzkümmelpulver,
Salz,
Pfeffer,
Harissa, nach Belieben
(nordafrikanische Chilisauce)*

4 Eier

Hackfleisch mit Gewürzen und Koriandergrün gut vermengen. Aus der Masse kleine Kugeln formen. In einem feuerfesten Topf (nach Möglichkeit aus Ton) das Öl erhitzen. Fleischbällchen darin rundum goldbraun anbraten. Aus dem Topf nehmen und warm stellen.

Zwiebel und Knoblauch im Öl glasig dünsten. Tomatenmark und Gewürze zugeben, Fleischbällchen hinzufügen und soviel Wasser zugießen, bis das Fleisch knapp bedeckt ist. Bei kleiner Hitze ohne Deckel ungefähr zwanzig Minuten köcheln lassen, von Zeit zu Zeit umrühren.

Die Sauce abschmecken, den Ofen auf 200° C vorheizen.

Ein Ei in eine Tasse schlagen und in einem Rutsch in die heiße Sauce gleiten lassen. Die restlichen Eier auf die gleiche Weise hinzufügen. Den Topf abgedeckt in den heißen Ofen geben und zehn Minuten überbacken.

STUFFED PASTRY ENVELOPES (BREWATTES)

GEFÜLLTE TEIGTASCHEN (BREWATTES)

For 4 - 6 persons:

400 g/13 oz sheets of brik pastry (north African puff pastry, or filo as a substitute), peanut oil for frying, 1 white of egg

For the meat filling:
200 g/7 oz ground lamb, 2 tbsp olive oil,
1/2 bunch parsley,
1 small onion, finely chopped,
1/2 tsp ground ginger, 1 knife-tip saffron,
salt, black pepper, 1 egg

For the pigeon filling:
200 g/7 oz cooked pigeon meat (offcuts, remnants),
finely chopped,
1 small onion, cut into strips, 2 tbsp butter,
1/2 bunch coriander leaves, chopped,
2 tbsp almond slivers, 1 knife-tip saffron,
1/2 tsp ground cinnamon,
salt, black pepper, 1 egg

For the spinach filling:
200 g/7 oz spinach, blanched, 2 tbsp butter,
1 garlic clove, crushed, salt, pepper,
1 tbsp sesame, 1 egg

Für 4 - 6 Personen:

400 g Brikteigblätter
(nordafrikanischer Blätterteig, ersatzweise Philoteig),
Erdnußöl zum Ausbacken, 1 Eiweiß

Für die Fleischfüllung:
200 g Lammhackfleisch, 2 EL Olivenöl,
1/2 Bund Petersilie,
1 kleine Gemüsezwiebel, fein geschnitten,
1/2 TL Ingwerpulver, 1 Msp Safran,
Salz, schwarzer Pfeffer, 1 Ei

Für die Taubenfüllung:
200 g gekochtes Taubenfleisch
(Abschnitte, Reste), fein geschnitten,
1 kleine Gemüsezwiebel, in Streifen geschnitten,
2 EL Butter, 1/2 Bund Koriandergrün, gehackt,
2 EL Mandelblättchen, 1 Msp Safran,
1/2 TL Zimtpulver,
Salz, schwarzer Pfeffer, 1 Ei

Für die Spinatfüllung:
200 g Blattspinat, blanchiert , 2 EL Butter,
1 Knoblauchzehe, zerdrückt, Salz, Pfeffer,
1 EL Sesam, 1 Ei

For the ground meat filling: Heat the olive oil in a pan and fry the meat briefly.
Add and fry the onion, spices, and parsley, then stir in the beaten egg. Remove from the stove and allow to cool.
For the pigeon filling: Heat the butter in a pan and sauté the onion until transparent.
Add the pigeon meat, coriander and spices. Allow to get hot and mix in the beaten egg. Allow to cool.
For the spinach filling: Press out the spinach well in the sieve.
Heat the butter, sauté the garlic, add the spinach, season, stir in the sesame and pour over the beaten egg. Mix well and allow to cool.
To finish: Cut the brik pastry sheets to shape, as desired, stuff with the filling, paint the edges with white of egg and seal to form triangles, rectangles, or rolls. Fry the pastry envelopes in hot oil on both sides. Serve hot garnished with wedges of lemon.

Für die Hackfleischfüllung: Olivenöl in einem Topf erhitzen und das Fleisch darin anbraten. Zwiebel mitbraten, Gewürze und Petersilie zufügen und dann das verquirlte Ei unterrühren. Vom Herd nehmen und auskühlen lassen.
Für die Taubenfüllung: Butter in einem Topf erhitzen und die Zwiebel darin glasig dünsten. Taubenfleisch, Koriander und Gewürze zugeben, heiß werden lassen und mit dem verquirlten Ei vermischen. Auskühlen lassen.
Für die Spinatfüllung: Spinat im Sieb gut ausdrücken. Butter erhitzen, Knoblauch dünsten, Spinat zugeben, würzen, Sesam untermischen und das verquirlte Ei darübergeben. Gut vermengen, auskühlen lassen.
Fertigstellung: Brikteigblätter nach Belieben zuschneiden, mit der Füllung füllen, Ränder mit Eiweiß bepinseln und fest zu Dreiecken, Vierecken oder Rollen verschließen. Teigtaschen im heißen Öl von beiden Seiten goldbraun ausbacken. Mit Zitronenspalten garniert heiß servieren.

GAZELLE HORNS

Filling:
250 g/8 ¹/₂ oz/1 cup almonds, peeled and grated,
175 g/6 oz/³/₄ cup confectioners' sugar,
3 tbsp orange-blosson water, 1 tsp ground cinnamon

Pastry:
250 g/8 ¹/₂ oz/1 cup flour, 50 g/1 ²/₃ oz/¹/₅ cup butter,
1 pinch salt, 1 egg, 1 tbsp orange-blossom water

For the filling: Knead all the ingredients by hand to a stiff consistency.

For the pastry: Sift the flour into a bowl. Add all other ingredients. Stir a little at first and then knead on the work surface into a smooth dough. Add a little more water, if necessary. Cover the dough with a damp cloth and allow to stand in the refrigerator for one hour.

Roll out the pastry thinly on the floured work surface. Cut out rectangles of about 10 x 5 cm/4 x 2 in. For each rectangle take one tablespoon of the almond mixture and roll it by hand into a thin sausage, place it on the piece of dough, paint the edges with water, and shape into a curved croissant. Place on a greased and floured baking tray and bake in the preheated oven at 170° C/340° F for about twenty minutes until golden. Allow to cool and, before serving, dredge thickly with confectioners' sugar.

GAZELLENHÖRNCHEN

Füllung:
250 g Mandeln, geschält und gerieben,
175 g Puderzucker, 3 EL Orangenblütenwasser,
¹/₂ TL Zimtpulver

Teig:
250 g Mehl, 50 g Butter, 1 Prise Salz, 1 Ei,
1 EL Orangenblütenwasser

Für die Füllung: Alle Zutaten von Hand zu einer festen Masse kneten.

Für den Teig: Das Mehl in eine Schüssel sieben. Alle anderen Zutaten zugeben, zuerst etwas verrühren und dann auf der Arbeitsplatte zu einem glatten Teig kneten. Bei Bedarf noch etwas Wasser zugeben. Den Teig mit einem feuchte Tuch bedecken und im Kühlschrank eine Stunde ruhen lassen.

Teig auf der bemehlten Arbeitsfläche dünn ausrollen. Rechtecke von ca. 10 x 5 cm ausschneiden. Jeweils einen Esslöffel von der Mandelmasse von Hand zu dünnen Würsten rollen, auf das Teigstück legen, die Ränder mit Wasser bestreichen, verschliessen und zu gebogenen Hörnchen formen.

Auf ein gefettetes und bemehltes Backblech setzen und im auf 170° C vorgeheizten Ofen ca. zwanzig Minuten goldgelb backen. Auskühlen lassen und vor dem Auftragen dick mit Puderzucker bestäuben.

SESAME AND HONEY PASTRIES

200 g/7 oz sheets of filo pastry,
100 g/3 ¹/₂ oz/²/₅ cup honey, 2 tbsp rose water,
sesame for sprinkling, peanut oil for frying

For the filling:
150 g/5 oz almonds, roasted, peeled and grated,
2 tbsp sesame,
4 tbsp confectioners' sugar, 1 tsp cinnamon,
1 tbsp liquid butter, 1 tsp rose water

For the filling: Knead the ingredients to form a paste. Warm the honey with rose water until runny. Cut the filo sheets into triangles of about 10 cm/4 in, place a little filling in the center of each, paint the edges with oil and seal into triangular parcels.
Deep-fry in hot oil until light-brown. Remove with a slotted spoon, drain, dip in the hot honey and sprinkle with sesame. Allow to cool before serving.

SESAM-HONIGGEBÄCK

200 g Philoteigblätter,
100 g Honig, 2 EL Rosenwasser,
Sesam zum Bestreuen,
Erdnußöl zum Ausbacken

Für die Füllung:
150 g Mandeln, geröstet, geschält und gerieben,
2 EL Sesam, 4 EL Puderzucker,
1 TL Zimt, 1 EL flüssige Butter,
1 EL Rosenwasser

Für die Füllung: Zutaten zusammen zu einer Paste verarbeiten. Den Honig mit dem Rosenwasser erwärmen, bis er dünnflüssig wird. Die Philoteigblätter in ca. 10 cm große Dreiecke schneiden, jeweils etwas Füllung in die Mitte geben, Ränder mit Öl bestreichen und zu dreieckigen Päckchen verschließen.
Im heißen Öl hellbraun fritieren. Mit der Schaumkelle herausnehmen, gut abtropfen lassen, in den heißen Honig tauchen und anschließend mit Sesam bestreuen. Ausgekühlt servieren.

Das Atlasgebirge, auf dem Weg von Taroudannt über Tizi-n-Test und Asni nach Marrakesch.
Zahlreiche winzige Dörfer, die meisten ohne Strom- und Telefonanschluß, schmiegen sich an die sanften Hänge. Die Täler des Atlasgebirges sind sehr fruchtbar. Auf den Terrassenfeldern gedeihen neben Obst und Getreide hauptsächlich Mandel- und Walnußbäume.

The Atlas mountains on the way from Taroudannt via Tizi-n-test and Asni to Marrakech.
Numerous tiny villages, mostly without electricity or telephones, cling to the gentle slopes.
The valleys of the Atlas are very fertile. The terraced fields bear fruit and grain, but chiefly almonds and walnuts.

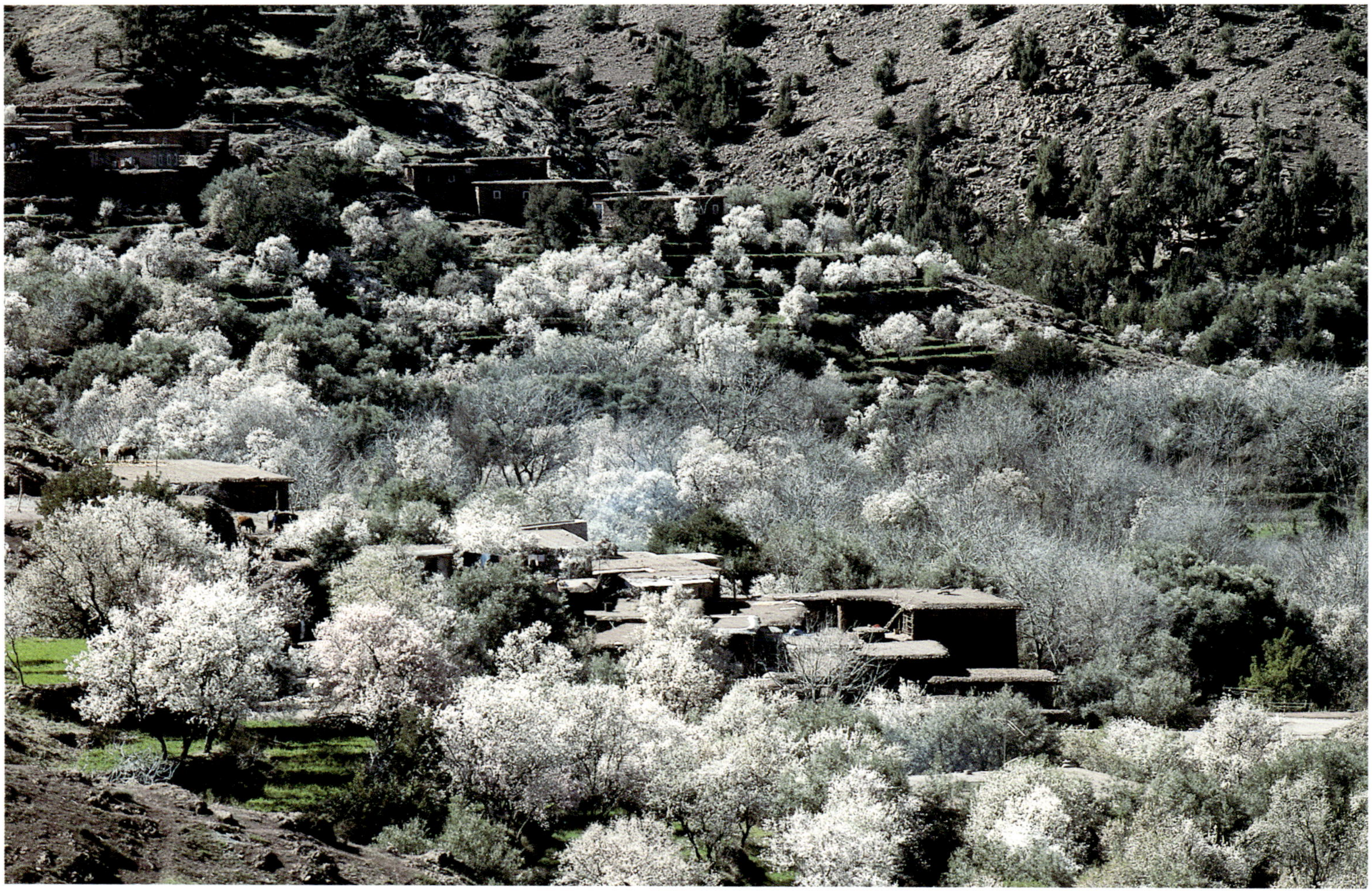

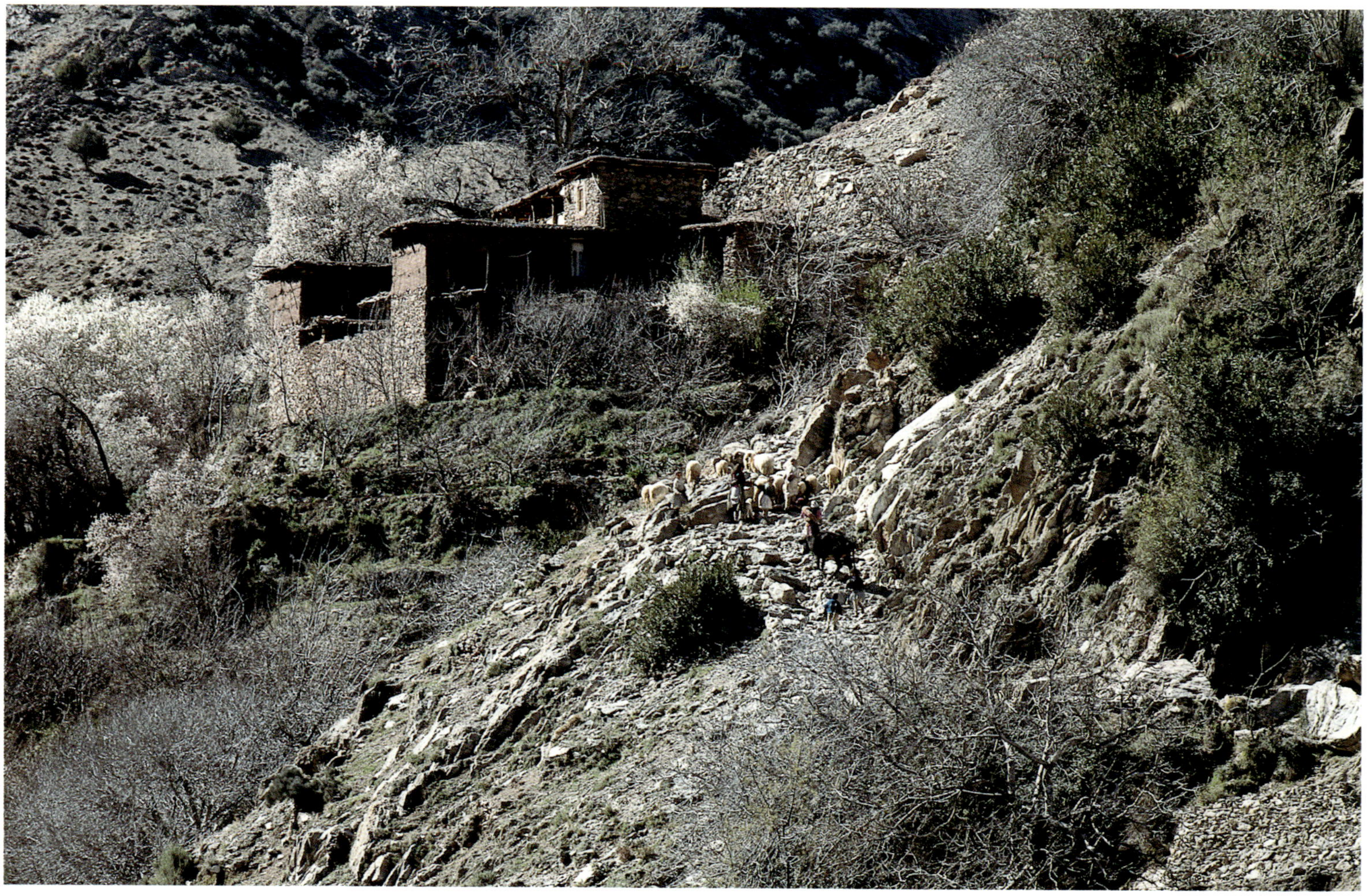

La Roseraie

Out of a small staging post, on the old road from Marrakech to Agadir, "La Roseraie" has gradually become a hidden dream destination. Here enjoyment of nature can be harmoniously combined with a wish for personal luxury.

A living symbol of this is the pair of storks that, just a few feet above the brightly lit terrace of the restaurant, suddenly break the silence with their joyous rattle of bills. The stork and his wife stretch their necks into the fragrant mountain air and let the wind ruffle their feathers. This is just a brief episode in the otherwise peaceful and unhurried mid-day meal of the guests, people from all over the world seeking tranquility and recreation in the mountains of the Atlas.

This old coaching inn is luxurious yet modest. Out of a resting place at which a snowbound traveller could seek help and accommodation there has developed a stylish hotel – and it has remained a place of solace. Small inviting chalets lie widely scattered over 5 hectares of terrain full of rose beds, which have given the establishment its name, "La Roseraie" – the rose garden. Orchards surround the hotel, sheep and cattle graze nearby and in many little garden beds the strong aromatic spices are grown that are used in the restaurant kitchen.

In the daytime, the exquisite cuisine of Fatima and her helpers attracts many day-trippers but in the evening it is the exclusive preserve of the hotel guests, so that returning tired from long walks, from riding, hunting, or fishing, they may look forward to a tranquil close of the day. Perhaps they have spent a day in the beauty farm, where the spaciously appointed, bright halls are reminiscent of the feudal pump-rooms of spas in bygone times. In the quiet, carefully equipped rooms mainly natural essences are used that are made here using the home-grown herbs from the garden.

The peaceful seclusion and the agreeable mountain climate are very inviting. Especially in summer, when the hot sun burns down mercilessly on Marrakech, the climate in the foothills of the Atlas is a pleasant relief. It is significantly milder, and a gentle constant breeze from the mountains brings additional refreshment.

When Monsieur Fentiro gave up his post as director of the Grand Hotel La Mamounia in Marrakech, in 1971, and devoted his whole passion to the Roseraie in the Val d'Ouirgane his friends still mocked him. Today they envy him his self-made paradise in the mountains.

Aus einem kleinen Gasthaus an der alten Straße von Marrakesch nach Agadir ist nach und nach ein verstecktes Traumziel geworden – „La Roseraie". Hier lassen sich die Freude an der Natur und der Wunsch nach persönlichem Luxus in eine harmonische Einheit bringen. Ein lebendiges Sinnbild dafür ist das Storchenpaar, das nur wenige Meter über der lichtdurchfluteten Terrasse des Restaurants plötzlich die Stille mit seinem fröhlichen Geklapper durchbricht. Storch und Störchin recken ihre Hälse in die würzige Bergluft und lassen sich vom Wind das Gefieder zausen. Es ist nur ein kurzes Schaustück in dem eher ruhig und beschaulich ablaufenden Mittagsmahl der anwesenden Gäste, Menschen aus aller Welt, die in der Bergwelt des Atlas Ruhe und Erholung suchen.

Gleichzeitig luxuriös und bescheiden ist dieses Relais. Aus einer Raststätte, in der im Schnee steckengebliebene vorüberziehende Reisende Hilfe und Unterkunft finden sollten, ist ein stilvolles Hotel gewachsen, – ein wohltuender Ort ist es geblieben. Kleine einladende Häuschen liegen weitläufig verstreut in einem fünf Hektar großen Gelände voller Rosenbeete, die dem Anwesen seinen Namen gaben, „La Roseraie" - der Rosengarten. Obstgärten umgeben das Hotel, Schafe und Kühe weiden in der Nähe, und in vielen kleinen Beeten werden starke, aromatische Gewürze gezogen, die bei der Zubereitung der Gerichte im Restaurant Verwendung finden.

Tagsüber ist das Restaurant,
in dem die feine Küche von Fatima und
ihren Helferinnen serviert wird, ein
beliebtes Ausflugsziel, am Abend ist es
ausschließlich den Hotelgästen
vorbehalten, damit diese, von Spazier-
gängen müde zurückgekehrt, nach
einem Reitausflug, der Pirsch oder dem
Fischfang in aller Ruhe den Tag
ausklingen lassen können.
Vielleicht haben sie auch einen Tag in der
Beauty Farm genossen; die großzügig
angelegten, hellen Hallen erinnern an die
feudalen Wandelhallen vergangener
Badezeiten. In den stillen, sorgfältig aus-
gestatteten Räumen werden überwiegend
natürliche Essenzen verwendet,
die aus den selbstgezogenen Kräutern
im Haus hergestellt werden.
Die ruhige Abgeschiedenheit und das
angenehme Bergklima laden zum
Verweilen ein. Besonders im Sommer,
wenn die heiße Sonne gnadenlos auf
Marrakesch herunterbrennt,
erweist sich das Klima in den Ausläufern
des Atlas als wohltuend. Es ist deutlich
milder, und ein leichter, ständig von
den Bergen wehender Wind sorgt für
zusätzliche Erfrischung.

Als Monsieur Fentiro 1971 seine
Tätigkeit als Direktor des Grand Hotel
„La Mamounia" in Marrakesch aufgab
und sich ganz seiner Leidenschaft für
das Roseraie im Val d'Ouirgane hingab,
belachten ihn seine Freunde noch.
Heute beneiden sie ihn um sein selbst-
geschaffenes Paradies in den Bergen.

OVEN-BRAISED SEA BREAM "M'CHERMEL"

DORADE IM OFEN GESCHMORT „M'CHERMEL"

For 4 persons:

1 sea bream (daurade) of about 1.5 kg/3 lb 5 oz

1 bunch coriander leaves, chopped,
2 garlic cloves, crushed,
2 tbsp cumin, ground,
¹/₂ tsp cayenne pepper, 1 tsp salt,
60 ml/2 fl oz/¹/₄ cup olive oil,
120 ml/4 fl oz/¹/₂ cup water

800 g/1 lb 12 oz potatoes, peeled,
and thinly sliced,
1 kg/2 lb 3 oz tomatoes, seeded, sliced,
1 green and 1 yellow bell pepper,
seeded, grilled, and skinned, cut into strips,
2 chilis, cut into strips,
60 ml/2 fl oz/¹/₄ cup olive oil,
salt, pepper

1 bunch parsley, chopped,
1 brined lemon (see p. 230),
cut into segments

Scale and clean the fish and wash thoroughly under running cold water.

Slash the skin on both sides so that the marinade can soak in.

For the marinade: Stir the coriander, garlic, cumin, cayenne pepper and salt with the oil and the water. Lay the fish in this mixture and allow to stand for three to four hours, turning the fish occasionally.

In a fireproof deep dish place a layer of potato slices.

Lay the fish on top and cover with the tomatoes. Add a layer of bell pepper and chili strips and pour over the remaining marinade, a glass of water, and the oil. Season with salt and pepper, then cook the fish in the oven at 180° C/360° F for about forty minutes. Occasionally baste with the cooking liquid.

When the bream is done pour the jus into a pan. Boil down on the stove until the jus thickens slightly, then season with salt and pepper.

To serve: Sprinkle the fish with parsley and garnish with lemon segments.

Serve the sauce separately.

Für 4 Personen:

1 Dorade (Goldbrasse) von ca. 1,5 kg

1 Bund Koriandergrün, gehackt,
2 Knoblauchzehen, durchgedrückt,
2 EL Kreuzkümmel, gemahlen,
¹/₂ TL Cayennepfeffer, 1 TL Salz,
60 ml Olivenöl,
120 ml Wasser

800 g Kartoffeln, geschält,
in dünne Scheiben geschnitten,
1 kg Tomaten, in Scheiben geschnitten, Kerne entfernt,
1 grüne und 1 gelbe Paprika, entkernt, gegrillt und
geschält, in Streifen geschnitten,
2 Chilischoten, in Streifen geschnitten,
60 ml Olivenöl,
Salz, Pfeffer,

1 Bund Petersilie, gehackt,
1 eingelegte Zitrone (siehe Seite 230),
in Schnitze geschnitten

Die Dorade schuppen, ausnehmen und unter fließendem kalten Wasser gründlich waschen. Die Haut auf beiden Seiten leicht einschneiden, damit die Marinade besser einziehen kann.

Für die Marinade: Koriander, Knoblauch, Kümmel, Cayennepfeffer und Salz mit dem Öl und dem Wasser anrühren. Die Dorade einlegen und drei bis vier Stunden darin ziehen lassen. Von Zeit zu Zeit den Fisch wenden.

In einer ofenfesten, tiefen Form die Kartoffelscheiben flach auslegen. Den Fisch darauflegen und das Ganze mit den Tomaten bedecken. Paprika- und Chilistreifen darübergeben und das Gericht mit der verbliebenen Marinade, einem Glas Wasser und dem Öl begießen. Salzen, pfeffern, dann den Fisch im Ofen bei 180° C ungefähr vierzig Minuten garen. Von Zeit zu Zeit mit der Garflüssigkeit begießen. Wenn die Dorade gar ist, die Jus in einen Topf abgießen. Einkochen lassen, bis sie leicht eindickt, mit Salz und Pfeffer abschmecken.

Zum Servieren: Den Fisch mit Petersilie bestreuen, mit Zitronenschnitzen garnieren.

Sauce separat dazu reichen.

TAJINE WITH LAMB AND OLIVES

For 4 - 6 persons:

1 kg/2 lb 3 oz lean lamb, salt, pepper,
120 ml/4 fl oz/¹/₂ cup olive oil,
1 tsp ground ginger, 3 garlic cloves, crushed, 1 knife-tip saffron,
500 g/1 lb 2 oz green olives, pitted,
1 brined lemon (see p. 230), cut into segments,
1 tbsp sweet paprika, 1 tsp ground cumin,
1 bunch parsley, chopped

Cut the lamb into large portions, season with salt and pepper. Heat the oil in a braising pan and fry the meat over a high heat on all sides. Add the ginger and garlic and fry briefly. Add the saffron and pour in half a liter of water. Cover and braise over a medium heat for one and a half hours. Stir occasionally and add a little water, if necessary.

In the meantime, place the olives in water in a pan and bring to the boil, drain through a sieve, then repeat this process twice. Finally, press the olives firmly in the sieve with a ladle.

When the meat is well done remove and keep in a warm place. Stir the lemon segments, paprika, and cumin into the sauce and boil without a lid until the sauce thickens slightly. Add the olives and cook for two minutes more. Season with salt and pepper.

To serve: Transfer the meat to a warmed, deep earthenware dish and pour over the sauce, sprinkle with parsley and serve.

TAJINE WITH VEGETABLES AND OLIVES

For 4 - 6 persons:

60 ml/2 fl oz/¹/₄ cup olive oil,
4 carrots, peeled and quartered lengthwise,
2 red bell peppers, seeded, quartered lengthwise,
2 onions, peeled and sliced, 2 garlic cloves, thinly sliced,
2 zucchinis, halved and quartered lengthwise,
4 potatoes, peeled, cut into wedges, 4 tomatoes, cubed,
250 g/8 oz chickpeas, pre-cooked, 1 tbsp cumin, 1 tsp ground coriander, salt, ¹/₂ liter/17 fl oz/2 cups vegetable broth,
250 g/8 oz green olives, pitted, juice of 1 lemon,
1 bunch parsley, finely chopped

Heat the oil in a braising pan. Sweat the carrots, bell peppers, onions and garlic. Add the zucchini and potatoes and cook briefly, stirring. Add the chickpeas, tomato cubes and spices. Pour over the broth and season with salt.

Cover and braise over a low heat for about fourty minutes. Cook the olives in plenty of water for three minutes, then drain through a sieve.

Before serving, stir in the lemon juice and the chopped parsley. Scatter the olives over the tajine and serve hot.

TAGINE MIT LAMMFLEISCH UND OLIVEN

Für 4 - 6 Personen:

1 kg mageres Lammfleisch, Salz, Pfeffer,
120 ml Olivenöl, 1 TL Ingwerpulver,
3 Knoblauchzehen, durchgedrückt, 1 Msp Safran,
500 g grüne Oliven, entkernt,
1 eingelegte Zitrone (siehe Seite 230), in Schnitze geschnitten,
1 EL süßes Paprikapulver, 1 TL Kreuzkümmelpulver,
1 Bund Petersilie, gehackt

Lammfleisch in große Portionsstücke schneiden, mit Salz und Pfeffer würzen. In einem Schmortopf das Öl erhitzen. Fleisch rundum heiß anbraten. Ingwer und Knoblauch kurz mitbraten. Safran zugeben, mit einem halben Liter Wasser aufgießen. Bei mittlerer Hitze zugedeckt eineinhalb Stunden schmoren lassen. Von Zeit zu Zeit umrühren, bei Bedarf etwas Wasser zugießen. Unterdessen die Oliven mit Wasser in einem Topf zum Kochen bringen, durch ein Sieb abgießen und diesen Vorgang anschließend zweimal wiederholen. Zum Schluß die Oliven mit einer Kelle im Sieb sehr gut ausdrücken. Wenn das Fleisch sehr gar ist, herausnehmen und warmstellen. Zitronenschnitze, Paprika und Kreuzkümmel in die Sauce rühren und ohne Deckel kochen lassen, bis die Sauce leicht bindet. Oliven zugeben und zwei Minuten mitkochen lassen. Mit Salz und Pfeffer abschmecken.

Zum Servieren: Das Fleisch in eine vorgewärmte, tiefe Tonschale füllen. Mit der Sauce übergießen, mit Petersilie bestreut servieren.

TAGINE MIT GEMÜSE UND OLIVEN

Für 4 - 6 Personen:

60 ml Olivenöl, 4 Karotten, geschält, längs in Viertel geschnitten,
2 rote Paprika, entkernt, längs in Viertel geschnitten,
2 Gemüsezwiebeln und 2 Knoblauchzehen, in dünne Scheiben geschnitten, 2 Zucchini, halbiert, längs in Viertel geschnitten,
4 Kartoffeln, geschält, in Spalten geschnitten,
4 Tomaten, in Würfel geschnitten, 250 g Kichererbsen, vorgekocht,
1 EL Kreuzkümmel, 1 TL Korianderpulver, Salz,
¹/₂ Liter Gemüsebrühe, 250 g grüne Oliven, entsteint,
Saft einer Zitrone,
1 Bund Petersilie, fein gehackt

Öl in einem Schmortopf erhitzen. Karotten, Paprika, Zwiebeln und Knoblauch anschwitzen. Zucchini und Kartoffeln zugeben und unter Rühren kurz mitdünsten. Kichererbsen, Tomatenwürfel und Gewürze beifügen, mit der Brühe aufgießen und mit Salz abschmecken. Zugedeckt bei kleiner Hitze ca. vierzig Minuten schmoren lassen. Oliven in viel Wasser drei Minuten kochen, dann durch ein Sieb abgießen. Vor dem Servieren den Zitronensaft und die gehackte Petersilie unterrühren, die Oliven darüberstreuen und heiß servieren.

The Atlantic along Morocco's coastline has rich fishing grounds. Of the many species of fish and other seafoods brought ashore here, the sardine is the most important. Morocco is the world's second-largest producer of canned sardines.

Der Atlantik entlang der Küste Marokkos birgt ertragreiche Fischgründe. Neben der Artenvielfalt von Fischen und Meeresfrüchten, die hier eingebracht werden, ist die Sardine die wichtigste. Marokko ist weltweit der zweitgößte Produzent von Sardinenkonserven.

The fishing port of Agadir is one of the most important in the country. The fishermen sell the major part of their haul at the early-morning auction. Some customers stand by as the boats are unloaded and seek out the pick of the catch before practising the Arab's special skills of bargaining and haggling.

Der Fischereihafen von Agadir zählt zu den wichtigsten des Landes. Den Hauptteil ihres Fanges verkaufen die Fischer bei der am frühen Morgen stattfindenden Auktion. Manche Käufer stehen bereits beim Entladen der Boote bereit und suchen sich hier die frischeste Ware aus, bevor sie mit der hohen arabischen Kunst des Handelns und Feilschens beginnen.

Restaurant Marocain

Hotel Tivoli

Agadir

FISH BROCHETTES

For 4 persons:

800 g/1 lb 12 oz fillet of monkfish

For the marinade:
4 tbsp olive oil, ¹/₂ tsp turmeric, ¹/₂ tsp ground coriander,
¹/₂ tsp ground ginger, 1 garlic clove, crushed,
salt, white pepper, 1 bunch coriander leaves, chopped
1 brined lemon (see page 230), finely sliced

Cut the fillets of monkfish into cubes of about
3 cm/1 ¹/₅ in. Mix the ingredients for the marinade
well and soak the fish in this for two hours.
Fill wooden skewers alternately with fish cubes and
lemon slices. Fry the brochettes in a skillet on all
sides over medium heat. Serve with saffron rice.

FISCHSPIESSCHEN

Für 4 Personen:

800 g Lottefilets

Für die Marinade:
4 EL Olivenöl, ¹/₂ TL Kurkuma,
¹/₂ TL Korianderpulver, ¹/₂ TL Ingwerpulver,
1 Knoblauchzehe, zerdrückt, Salz, weißer Pfeffer,
1 Bund Koriandergrün, gehackt
1 eingelegte Zitrone (siehe Seite 230), in dünne
Scheiben geschnitten

Lottefilets in ca. 3 cm große Würfel schneiden. Die
Zutaten für die Marinade gut verrühren, Lotte-
würfel darin zwei Stunden ziehen lassen. Holzspieße
abwechslungsweise mit Fischwürfeln und Zitronenscheiben bestecken. In einer Bratpfanne die Spieße
von allen Seiten bei mittlerer Hitze braten. Als Beilage paßt Safranreis.

VEGETABLE SOUP "CHORBA"

For 4 persons:

1 carrot, 1 white turnip, 1 zucchini,
200 g/7 oz green beans, 1 onion,
1 garlic clove, crushed, 1 tomato, skinned and seeded,
3 tbsp olive oil, ¹/₂ tsp cayenne pepper, meat broth

1 large potato, 120 g/4 oz vermicelli, salt, lemon juice,
1 tbsp chopped fresh mint

Cut all the vegetables into small cubes. Sauté in
olive oil, add cayenne pepper and pour over the
broth. Bring to the boil and simmer over a low heat
for half an hour. Likewise, cut the potato into small
cubes. Add to the soup, together with the noodles.
Cook for twenty minutes more, then finally season
with salt and a dash of lemon juice. Before serving,
sprinkle with mint.

GEMÜSESUPPE „CHORBA"

Für 4 Personen:

1 Karotte, 1 weiße Rübe, 1 Zucchini,
200 g grüne Bohnen, 1 Gemüsezwiebel,
1 Knoblauchzehe, zerdrückt,
1 Tomate, enthäutet und entkernt, 3 EL Olivenöl
¹/₂ TL Cayennepfeffer, Fleischbrühe

1 große Kartoffel, 120 g Fadennudeln,
Salz, Zitronensaft,
1 EL gehackte frische Minze

Alle Gemüse in feine Würfel schneiden. Im Olivenöl andünsten, Cayennepfeffer zugeben und mit der
Brühe aufgießen. Zum Kochen bringen und auf
kleiner Hitze eine halbe Stunde köcheln lassen. Kartoffel ebenfalls in feine Würfel schneiden und mit
den Nudeln in die Suppe geben. Weitere zwanzig
Minuten kochen lassen, zum Schluß mit Salz und
einem Schuß Zitronensaft die Suppe abschmecken.
Vor dem Servieren mit Minze bestreuen.

CHICKEN WITH ALMONDS "M'QALLI"

For 4 persons:

1 corn-fed chicken, kitchen-ready, 3 tbsp sunflower oil,
2 onions, finely chopped,
100 g/3 $^1/_2$ oz almonds, scalded and skinned,
1 tsp ground ginger, $^1/_2$ tsp turmeric,
$^1/_4$ tsp white pepper, 1 tsp salt,
1 bunch coriander leaves, chopped,
1 bunch parsley, chopped,
2 tbsp almond slivers, lightly roasted,
2 hard-boiled eggs, in quarters

Heat the oil in a braising pan. Segment the chicken and fry in the hot oil on all sides. Add the onions and fry briefly. Pour in two cups water, add the almonds, spices and herbs, cover, and cook over a low heat for one hour. Adjust the seasoning of the sauce. To serve: Transfer the chicken with the sauce to a shallow earthenware dish, decorate with roasted almond slivers and egg quarters. The best side-serving is rice or couscous.

PASTILLA WITH RICE PUDDING

For 4 persons:

200 g/7 oz puff pastry or filo, peanut oil

$^1/_2$ liter/16 fl oz/2 cups milk, 60 g/2 oz/$^1/_4$ cup sugar,
125 g/4 oz/$^1/_2$ cup short-grain rice,
60 g/2 oz/$^1/_4$ cup butter,
2 tbsp orange-blossom water,
2 tbsp roasted almond slivers, cinnamon

Roll out the pastry thinly. Cut into a round shape and fry in a large skillet in peanut oil on both sides until light brown. If such a large skillet is not available make several small layers. For the filling: Heat the milk with the sugar in a pan. Stir in the rice and cook on a very low heat for about half an hour, stirring occasionally. Finally, stir in the butter and the orange-blossom water.
To serve: Lay the puff pastry base on a serving platter, coat with the rice and sprinkle with the almond slivers. Dust with cinnamon as desired.

HUHN MIT MANDELN „M'QALLI"

Für 4 Personen:

1 Maishähnchen, küchenfertig, 3 EL Sonnenblumenöl,
2 Gemüsezwiebeln, fein geschnitten,
100 g Mandeln, überbrüht und geschält,
1 TL Ingwerpulver, $^1/_2$ TL Kurkuma,
$^1/_4$ TL weißer Pfeffer, 1 TL Salz,
Je 1 Bund Koriandergrün und Petersilie, gehackt,
2 EL Mandelblättchen, leicht geröstet,
2 hartgekochte Eier, in Viertel geschnitten

Öl in einem Schmortopf erhitzen. Huhn in Stücke zerteilen und im heißen Öl von allen Seiten anbraten. Zwiebeln zugeben und kurz anbraten. Mit zwei Tassen Wasser auffüllen, Mandeln, Gewürze und Kräuter zugeben und zugedeckt bei schwacher Hitze eine Stunde garen. Sauce abschmecken.
Zum Servieren: Das Huhn mit der Sauce in eine flache Tonschale füllen, mit gerösteten Mandelblättchen und Eivierteln dekorieren. Dazu paßt am besten Reis oder Couscous.

PASTILLA MIT MILCHREIS

Für 4 Personen:

200 g Blätterteig oder Philoteig, Erdnußöl

$^1/_2$ Liter Milch, 60 g Zucker,
125 g Rundkornreis, 60 g Butter,
2 EL Orangenblütenwasser,
2 EL geröstete Mandelblätter, Zimt

Teig dünn ausrollen, rund ausschneiden und in einer großen Pfanne in Erdnußöl von beiden Seiten hellbraun backen. Wenn keine so große Pfanne vorhanden ist, mehrere kleine Schichten herstellen. Für die Füllung: Milch mit Zucker in einem Topf erhitzen. Reis einrühren und unter gelegentlichem Rühren auf sehr kleiner Hitze etwa eine halbe Stunde garen. Zum Schluß die Butter und das Orangenblütenwasser einrühren. Anrichten: Blätterteigboden auf eine Servierplatte legen, mit dem Reis bestreichen und mit den Mandelblättern bestreuen. Nach Belieben mit Zimt bestreuen.

COUSCOUS WITH LAMB AND VEGETABLES
COUSCOUS MIT LAMM UND GEMÜSE

For 4 persons:

For the stew:
600 g/1 lb 5 oz lamb shank,
boned and cut into large pieces,
2 tbsp olive oil, 1 tbsp clarified butter,
400 ml/13 fl oz/1²/₃ cups beef broth,
200 g/7 oz chickpeas, steeped overnight,
2 tomatoes, skinned and cubed,
1 bunch parsley, 1 bunch coriander leaves,
¹/₄ tsp allspice, ¹/₂ tsp cumin,
1 tsp paprika, ¹/₂ tsp cayenne pepper, salt,
2 carrots, 1 white turnip, 1 zucchini,
1 piece of pumpkin, 1 piece of white cabbage

For the couscous:
*400 g/13 oz/1²/₃ cups couscous (special durum wheat
semolina), 1 tsp salt, 500 ml/16 fl oz/2 cups hot water*

*harissa as desired
(north African chili paste, very hot)*

Place the couscous and salt in a bowl and pour in
half of the hot water. Mix well with a fork so that
all the semolina is moistened. Cover and allow to
swell for fifteen minutes. Then add the remaining
water with the oil. Mix, cover, and allow to swell
for fifteen minutes more.
Fry the lamb in olive oil and butter on all sides.
Add the onion and garlic and fry. Pour in the
broth, add the chickpeas, tomatoes and herbs and
season with allspice, cumin, paprika, cayenne
pepper and salt. Cover and simmer on a low heat
for one and half hours.
After forty minutes, add the coarsely chopped
vegetables to the lamb.
Spread the couscous on a fine sieve insert, cover
with a heavy lid and steam over the lamb stew for
the last twenty minutes.
To serve: Mix a ladle full of the sauce, as desired,
with harissa and transfer to a sauce boat. Place the
couscous in a deep serving dish. Make a depression
in the middle and pour in the stew.

Für 4 Personen:

Für den Eintopf:
600 g Lammfleisch aus der Haxe,
in grobe Stücke geschnitten,
2 EL Olivenöl, 1 EL geklärte Butter,
400 ml Rinderbrühe,
200 g Kichererbsen, über Nacht eingeweicht,
2 Tomaten, enthäutet und in Würfel geschnitten,
1 Bund Petersilie, 1 Bund Koriandergrün,
¹/₄ TL Piment, ¹/₂ TL Kreuzkümmel,
1 TL Paprikapulver, ¹/₂ TL Cayennepfeffer, Salz,
2 Karotten, 1 weiße Rübe, 1 Zucchini,
1 Stück Kürbis, 1 Stück Weißkohl

Für den Couscous:
*400 g Couscous (spezieller Hartweizengrieß),
1 TL Salz, 500 ml heißes Wasser*

*Harissa nach Belieben
(nordafrikanische Chilisauce, sehr scharf)*

Couscous und Salz in eine Schüssel geben und mit
der Hälfte des heißen Wassers übergießen. Mit einer
Gabel gut vermischen, so daß der ganze Grieß ange-
feuchtet wird. Zudecken und eine Viertelstunde
quellen lassen. Dann das restliche Wasser mit dem
Öl zugießen, vermengen und erneut eine Viertelstunde zugedeckt quellen lassen.
Das Lammfleisch im Olivenöl und der Butter von
allen Seiten anbraten. Zwiebel und Knoblauch zugeben und mitbraten. Mit der Brühe aufgießen,
Kichererbsen, Tomaten und Kräuter zugeben, mit
Piment, Kreuzkümmel, Paprika, Cayennepfeffer und
Salz würzen. Das Ganze zugedeckt eineinhalb Stunden bei kleiner Hitze köcheln lassen. Nach vierzig
Minuten Kochzeit die grob geschnittenen Gemüse
zum Lamm geben und mitkochen. Den Couscous
auf einen feinen Siebeinsatz streichen, mit einem
schweren Deckel fest verschließen und über dem
Eintopf die letzten zwanzig Minuten dämpfen.
Zum Servieren: Von der Sauce nach Belieben einen
Schöpflöffel voll mit Harissa anrühren und in eine
Sauciere geben. Den Couscous in eine tiefe Servier-
schale füllen. In die Mitte eine Mulde drücken und
den Eintopf einfüllen.

Villa Maroc

Amid vast fields of argan, Essaouira lies on the shore of the Atlantic like a forgotten bastion, left behind by the Portuguese.

The pennants fluttering at the mast-heads in the harbor of Essaouira are as multicolored as the mixture of peoples who have passed through or remained here: Moors, Portuguese, Spaniards, Jews and Bedouins. Together they created a blue and white township of peace, of wandering through tranquil, cool alleyways, markets with spices, carpets, jewelry and all the riches that Morocco has to offer.

Is it its unspoilt appearance, the long history of the town, the cool wind that wafts over the town from the sea, that makes Essaouira breathe more peacefully and gives it a less Arabian, oriental aura? The colors are varied – but with a touch of pastel, never do they look hard or harsh. The traders appear calm and composed, waiting patiently for their customers rather than trying to drag them into their stores.

At the edge of town lies the Villa Maroc, a hotel that conveys the same composure as a blue lagoon in the gentle sea breeze. Essaouira and its markets were for a long time in the hands of Europeans, and the Villa Maroc is today still run by a Swiss lady. But what would she be without her staff who, like a family in the house, show homely loyalty, a touching personal concern that is the pleasant mark of hospitality in all the large houses here in Morocco. The cuisine too accentuates a family feeling, a sense of belonging to the region without having to fear comparison with any other. Each evening, on the patio, in the lounge or on the terrace, an exquisite menu of "souiri" specialties is served. The wines are Moroccan, no great growths perhaps, but they are a pleasant accompaniment at table. The building itself is constructed as if around a core of light. Facing onto the bright atrium there are many rooms and suites on several storeys. The sky is reflected in the blue of their doors and windows; luxuriant climbing plants in many pots add their greenery, and birdcages a gentle breath of sound. The effect is simultaneously that of an opera set and of welcoming hospitality. As if in a dream the elements meld together and appear scarcely separable from each other. It gives the expression of being exaggeratedly lush and colorful, yet is subdued and not overdone. The rooms are bright and pleasantly cool; the pictures and calligraphy drawn in fine lines on animal hides adorn them without appearing to be mere decor. From the rooftop, in the two little penthouse suites, the guest simply must feel lightness and freedom, can let his gaze drift over the town, the roofs, the minarets, until far beyond the harbor wall it is lost between the horizon and the waves.

Auch die Küche betont die „familiäre", regionale Zugehörigkeit, ohne daß sie einen Vergleich scheuen müßte. Jeden Abend wird im Patio, in der Lounge oder auf der Terrasse ein erlesenes Menü mit „Souiri"-Spezialitäten gereicht. Die Weine sind aus Marokko, vielleicht keine großen Gewächse, aber sie sind angenehme Tischbegleiter.

Das Gebäude selbst ist wie um eine Seele aus Licht herumgebaut. Dem hellen Innenhof zu öffnen sich in mehreren Stockwerken viele Zimmer und Suiten. Im Blau ihrer Türen und Fenster findet sich der Himmel nachgezeichnet wieder. Ein aus vielen Töpfen üppig gedeihendes Pflanzengerank fügt sein Grün dazu, Vogelkäfige einen leisen Hauch von Klang. Es ist eine Wirkung von opernhafter Kulisse und willkommener Gastlichkeit zugleich. Wie in einem Traum sind die Elemente ineinander verwischt und erscheinen kritisch betrachtet voneinander kaum zu trennen. Es wirkt übertrieben üppig, farbig und gleichzeitig gebändigt und nicht überladen. Die Zimmer sind hell und behaglich kühl. Die mit feinen Strichen auf Tierhaut gezeichneten Bilder und Kalligraphien schmücken sie, ohne daß sie dekoriert wirken.

Vom Dach aus – in den zwei kleinen Dachsuiten muß der Gast einfach Licht und Freiheit fühlen – kann der Blick über die Stadt schweifen, die Dächer, die Minarette, ehe er sich weit hinter der Hafenmauer am Horizont in den Wellen verliert.

*I*nmitten von weiten Arganienfeldern liegt Essaouira an der Küste des Atlantiks wie eine vergessene Bastion, von den Portugiesen zurückgelassen. Bunt flattern die Wimpel im Hafen von Essaouira, wie das Durcheinander der Völker, die hier querten oder blieben: Mauren, Portugiesen, Spanier, Juden und Beduinen. Sie alle schufen ein weißblaues Städtchen der Ruhe, des Wandelns durch beschauliche, kühle Gassen, Märkte mit Gewürzen, Teppichen, Schmuck und allem Reichtum, den das Land Marokko zu bieten hat. Ist es die Unberührtheit, die lange Geschichte des Ortes, der kühle Wind, der vom Meer über die Stadt streift, die Essaouira einen anderen, einen ruhigeren Atem ausströmen, ein weniger arabisches, orientalisches Flair verspüren lassen? Die Farben sind bunt, – aber mit einem Hauch von Pastell, niemals erscheinen sie hart oder grell. Die Händler wirken gelassen, sie warten eher geduldig auf ihre Kundschaft, als daß sie diese in ihre Geschäfte ziehen wollten.

Am Rand dieser Stadt liegt mit der Villa Maroc ein Hotel, das dieselbe Gelassenheit ausstrahlt wie eine blaue Lagune im leichten Wind des Meeres. Essaouira und seine Märkte waren lange in der Hand von Europäern, die Villa Maroc wird noch heute von einer Schweizerin geführt. Doch was wäre sie ohne ihre Bediensteten, die wie eine Familie im Haus eine heimatliche Loyalität verspüren lassen, eine rührende, persönliche Besorgtheit zeigen – ein angenehmes Merkmal der Gastfreundschaft, das in allen großen Häusern Marokkos anzutreffen ist.

MARRAKECH

The grand hotel "La Mamounia" in Marrakech is the epitome of a mundane hotel, a palace, an absolute temple for politicians, artists and stars from all over the world. Here Eric von Stroheim made the film "Alerte au Sud", Alfred Hitchcock "The Man Who Knew Too Much", and Josef von Sternberg "Morocco" with Marlene Dietrich. For Sir Winston Churchill, a faithful regular guest, "La Mamounia" was one of the most beautiful places on earth. Inspired by the sunset, which bathed the peaks of the Atlas range in rosy light, he sat on the terrace of the Mamounia and began to paint.

The surrounding fragrant gardens, called "Arset El Mamoun" gave their name to this grand hotel in the center of royal Marrakech. These gardens were so extraordinary that, as legend has it, they were given by the Sultan Sidi Mohamed Ben Abdellah to his son Prince Moulay Mamoun as a wedding present. And there, the story goes, the prince gave glittering parties. To this day the gardens have lost none of their original splendor. In accordance with Moroccan tradition, the garden exhibits a wide variety of flowers and trees and a simply endless wealth of scents and birdsong. An overabundance of lemons, oranges and bananas hand from the trees. Palms, yuccas and bamboo grow to the sky, the carefully tended paths are lined with roses and mimosas. The radiant blossoms of bougainvillaea and hibiscus that proliferate up the garden walls create carpets of color amid the lush greenery.

GRAND HOTEL

In 1922 the first hotel arose on this wonderful site, which soon became legendary. La Mamounia unified traditional Moroccan architecture with the technical elegance of the 1930's bourgeoisie. With the same exquisiteness in which the architect Prost equipped ocean liners, the restaurants, suites and rooms of La Mamounia were appointed. To this day the first-class restaurant "Marrakech l'Impériale" is reminiscent of the stylish atmosphere of a luxury liner. Original furnishings in the "Orient Express" suite create for the nostalgic guest an imaginary stay in the salon car of the legendary train.

But in the other rooms too, the aura of art deco is retained in modern elegance. One feels transported onto a movie set when entering a spacious foyer with pillars, arcades, pools and chandeliers. This splendid reception area opens onto an atrium, light and cool, simultaneously dainty and intricately carved in the Moorish-Spanish style. Beyond, almost hidden, lies the temple of Moroccan epicurean delights, the "Restaurant Marocain".

The Moroccan haute cuisine of Boujemaa Mars and the light-flooded, richly decorated interior of the restaurant bring alive the magnificence of the golden age of Moroccan gastronomic culture. Who could convey the niceties and quintessence of Moroccan cuisine better than Boujemaa Mars, a committed chef de cuisine with international experience, whose profound knowledge of the history and peculiarities of the regional cuisines of Morocco speaks out from each individual dish.

MARRAKECH

Das Grand Hotel „La Mamounia" in Marrakesch ist der Inbegriff eines mondänen Hotels; ein Palast, ein Tempel schlechthin für Politiker, Künstler und Stars aus aller Welt. Hier drehte Eric von Strohheim den Film „Alerte au Sud", Alfred Hitchcock „Der Mann, der zuviel wußte" und Josef von Sternberg „Marokko, Herz in Flammen" mit Marlene Dietrich. Für Winston Churchill, den treuen Stammgast, war das „La Mamounia" einer der schönsten Plätze auf Erden. Inspiriert von dem Sonnenuntergang, der die Gipfel des Atlas in rotes Licht taucht, setzte er sich auf die Terrasse des Mamounia und begann zu malen.

Die umliegenden, duftenden Gärten, genannt „Arset El Mamoun", waren namengebend für das Grand Hotel im Herzen des königlichen Marrakesch. Diese Gartenanlage war so außergewöhnlich, daß sie, wie die Legende erzählt, der Sultan Sidi Mohamed Ben Abdellah seinem Sohn Prinz Moulay Mamoun als Hochzeitsgeschenk vermachte. Und dort, so erzählt man sich, gab der Prinz rauschende Feste. Bis heute hat die Gartenanlage nichts von ihrer ursprünglichen Pracht verloren. Der marokkanischen Tradition entsprechend, bietet der Garten eine Vielfalt von Blumen und Bäumen, eine schier unerschöpfliche Fülle von Gerüchen und Vogelstimmen. Überreich hängen Zitronen, Orangen und Bananen an den Bäumen. Dem Himmel zu wachsen Palmen, Yuccas und Bambus, entlang der gepflegten Wege Rosen und Mimosen. Die leuchtenden Blüten der Bougainvilla und des Hibiskus, die die Gartenmauern emporwuchern, schaffen bunte Farbteppiche in üppigem Grün.

1922 entstand an diesem wunderbaren Ort das erste Hotel, das bald zu einer Legende wurde. La Mamounia vereinigte die traditionelle marokkanische Architektur mit der technischen Eleganz des Bürgertums der dreißiger Jahre. Mit der gleichen Erlesenheit, in der der Architekt Prost Ozeanriesen gestaltete, wurden auch die Restaurants, die Suiten und Zimmer des La Mamounia ausgestattet. Noch heute läßt das First-Class-Restaurant „Marrakech l'Impériale" die stilvolle Atmosphäre eines Luxusdampfers nachvollziehen. Originales Mobilar entführt den nostalgischen Gast in der Suite „Orient-Express" zu einem imaginären Aufenthalt im Salonwagen des legendären Zuges. Aber auch in den anderen Zimmern hat sich der Flair des Art Deco in moderner Eleganz erhalten. Wie in eine Filmwelt entrückt findet man sich beim Betreten in einer weitläufigen Eingangshalle mit Säulen, Arkaden, Wasserbecken und Lüstern wieder. Dieser prachtvolle Empfang öffnet sich zu einem Innenhof, hell und kühl, gleichzeitig verspielt und ziseliert, in maurisch-spanischen Stil. Dahinter, fast versteckt, findet sich als Tempel marokkanischer Gaumenfreuden das „Restaurant Marocain".

Die marokkanische Haute Cuisine von Boujemaa Mars und das lichtdurchflutete, reich verzierte Internieur des Restaurants rufen den Glanz der Hochzeit marokkanischer Eßkultur wieder wach. Wer auch könnte die Feinheit und die Quintessenz der marokkanischen Küche besser vermitteln als Boujemaa Mars, ein engagierter Küchenchef mit internationaler Erfahrung, dessen tiefe Kenntnis der Geschichte und Eigenart der regionalen Küchen Marokkos aus jedem einzelnen Gericht spricht.

SHOULDER OF LAMB "MÉCHOUI"

LAMMSCHULTER „MÉCHOUI"

For 4 persons:

1 shoulder of lamb with bone, about 1.5 kg/3 lb 5 oz,
2 garlic cloves, cut into fine strips,
1 tsp cumin, 1 tsp paprika, salt, pepper, olive oil,
1 bunch fresh mint

Wash and dry the meat and rub in the spices. Lay in a fireproof dish and pour in the olive oil. Preheat the oven to 250° C/485° F and roast the meat for ten to fifteen minutes until it begins to change color, turning once or twice. Then turn down the oven to 80° C/175° F and slowly braise the meat for two hours.
To serve: Arrange the shoulder of lamb on a bed of fresh mint.

Für 4 Personen:

1 Lammschulter mit Knochen, ca. 1,5 kg,
2 Knoblauchzehen, in feine Streifen geschnitten,
1 TL Kreuzkümmel,
1 TL Paprikapulver, Salz, Pfeffer,
1 Bund frische Minze

Fleisch waschen, trocknen und mit den Gewürzen einreiben. In eine feuerfeste Form legen; das Olivenöl zugießen. Ofen auf 250° C vorheizen und das Fleisch zehn bis fünfzehn Minuten braten, bis es anfängt Farbe anzunehmen, dabei ein- zweimal wenden. Dann den Ofen auf 80° C zurückschalten und das Fleisch zwei Stunden langsam schmoren lassen. Zum Servieren die Lammschulter auf einem Bett von frischer Minze anrichten.

BRAISED LAMB MARRAKECH STYLE

For 6 persons:

6 portions of leg of lamb (with bone),
about 300 g/10 oz each, 1 garlic clove, finely chopped,
1 small onion, finely chopped, 1 tsp ground cumin,
4 saffron threads, 1 knife-tip nutmeg, grated,
¹/₂ tsp ground ginger,
1 brined lemon (see p. 230), cut into pieces, ¹/₂ tsp salt,
1 tsp white pepper, 120 ml/4 fl oz/¹/₂ cup olive oil,
120 ml/4 fl oz/¹/₂ cup water

Wash and dry the leg of lamb and place in a glazed, fireproof earthenware vessel. Mix the garlic, onion, cumin, saffron, nutmeg, ginger, lemons, salt and pepper with the olive oil and water.
Pour over the meat. Close the pot with a lid and braise in the preheated oven at 170° C/340° F for about two hours. Season the sauce before serving.

The "tangia" is a fireproof earthenware pot in which this dish is traditionally prepared. With a sealed lid, it is placed for about six hours in hot embers so that it is also covered from above. In this way, the tender meat braises slowly and remains juicy. The hot ashes are often a by-product of heating the hammam, the Moroccan steam bath.

Die „Tangia", in dem dieses Gericht traditionell zubereitet wird, ist ein feuerfester Tonkrug. Er wird verschloßen und während ungefähr sechs Stunden in heiße Asche gestellt, so daß er oben auch bedeckt ist. Das zarte Fleisch schmort langsam vor sich hin und bleibt saftig. Die heiße Asche ensteht unter anderem beim Einheizen des Hammam, des marokkanischen Dampfbades.

GESCHMORTES LAMM NACH ART VON MARRAKESCH

Für 6 Personen:

6 Portionen von der Lammkeule (mit Knochen),
je ca. 300 g,
1 Knoblauchzehe, fein geschnitten,
1 kleine Zwiebel, fein geschnitten,
1 TL Kreuzkümmelpulver, 4 Safranfäden,
1 Msp Muskat, gerieben, ¹/₂ TL Ingwerpulver,
1 eingelegte Zitrone (siehe Seite 230),
in Stücke geschnitten, ¹/₂ TL Salz, 1 TL weißer Pfeffer,
120 ml Olivenöl, 120 ml Wasser

Die Lammfleischstücke waschen, trocknen und in ein glasiertes, feuerfestes Tongefäß füllen. Den Knoblauch, die Zwiebel, den Kreuzkümmel, Safran, Muskat, Ingwer, die Zitronenstücke, Salz und Pfeffer mit dem Olivenöl und Wasser verrühren.
Über das Fleisch geben, den Topf mit einem Deckel verschließen und im vorgeheizten Ofen bei 170° C ungefähr zwei Stunden schmoren.
Vor dem Servieren die Sauce abschmecken.

SEA BASS WITH DATES, TAFILALET STYLE

For 4 persons:

1 sea bass of about 1.5 kg/3 lb 5 oz,
200 g/7 oz/⁴/₅ cup rice,
500 g/1 lb 3 oz fine fresh dates, pitted,
3 tbsp raisins, 3 tbsp walnuts, preferably unripe, crushed,
3 tbsp peeled almonds,
1 onion, finely chopped, ¹/₂ tsp saffron threads,
1 tsp salt, 2 sticks cinnamon, 1 tbsp chopped parsley,
1 glass water, 120 ml/4 fl oz/¹/₂ cup peanut oil,
salt, white pepper

Scale and clean the sea bass and wash thoroughly under running cold water. Cook the rice in water for ten minutes. Finely chop half of the dates and mix into the rice, together with the raisins, walnuts and almonds. Simmer for ten minutes more until the rice is done. Season with salt. Stuff the fish with this mixture and lay in an ovenproof dish. Sprinkle with onions, add the spices and parsley, finally drizzle with water and oil. Preheat the oven to 160° C/320° F and cook for thirty to forty minutes. Baste occasionally with the juice. After cooking, pour the jus into a small pan, add the remaining dates and boil down a little. Season with salt and pepper. To serve: Pour the jus over the fish and garnish with the dates.

WOLFSBARSCH MIT DATTELN NACH ART VON TAFILALET

Für 4 Personen:

1 Wolfsbarsch von ca. 1,5 kg,
200 Reis,
500 g schöne, frische Datteln, entkernt,
3 EL Rosinen,
3 EL Walnüße, nach Möglichkeit noch unreif, zerdrückt,
3 EL geschälte Mandeln,
1 Gemüsezwiebel, fein gehackt,
¹/₂ TL Safranfäden, 1 TL Salz,
2 Zimtstangen, 1 EL gehackte Petersilie,
1 Glas Wasser, 120 ml Erdnußöl,
Salz, weißer Pfeffer

Den Wolfsbarsch schuppen, ausnehmen und unter fließendem kalten Wasser gründlich waschen. Den Reis mit Wasser zehn Minuten kochen. Die Hälfte der Datteln fein schneiden und mit den Rosinen und den Nüssen unter den Reis mischen. Weitere zehn Minuten köcheln lassen, bis der Reis gar ist. Mit Salz würzen. Den Fisch mit dieser Masse füllen und in eine ofenfeste Form legen. Mit den Zwiebeln bestreuen, Gewürze und Petersilie zugeben, zum Schluß mit Wasser und Öl begießen. Im vorgeheizten Ofen bei 160° C dreißig bis vierzig Minuten garen. Von Zeit zu Zeit mit dem Saft begießen. Die Jus am Schluß in einen kleinen Topf gießen, restliche Datteln zugeben und etwas einkochen lassen. Mit Salz und Pfeffer abschmecken. Zum Servieren den Fisch mit der Jus begießen, mit den Datteln garnieren.

MOROCCAN LAYERED PASTRY WITH CHICKEN "BELDI"

For 4 - 6 persons:

1 corn-fed chicken of about 1.4 kg/3 lb 2 oz,
coarse salt, 120 ml/4 fl oz/¹/₂ cup peanut oil,
3 onions, peeled and finely chopped,
2 tbsp semolina,
1 bunch coriander leaves, chopped,
1 tsp ground coriander,
¹/₂ tsp ground white pepper,
¹/₂ tsp ground ginger,
1 knife-tip saffron threads,
¹/₂ tsp ground cinnamon,
1 stick cinnamon,
2 tsp sugar, 2 tbsp butter,
¹/₄ tsp gum arabic

Dough (or puff pastry as a substitute):
500 g/17 oz/2 cups flour, 2 tsp salt,
peanut oil
3 tbsp confectioners' sugar mixed with cinnamon

Segment the chicken and rub with the coarse salt. Heat the oil lightly in a braising pan and add the chicken pieces with onions, semolina, coriander, spices, butter and gum arabic. Pour in half a liter water and cook the chicken over a low heat for about one and a quarter hours. Add a little water if necessary.

Remove the chicken from the sauce, pick the meat off the bones and chop into small pieces. Reduce the sauce to thicken, if necessary, and season.

For the dough: Mix the flour with salt. Gradually add water and knead to obtain a soft dough. Cover with a damp cloth and allow to stand in the refrigerator for half an hour. Form the dough into small balls. On a floured surface, carefully roll them out as thinly as possible. Heat a little oil in a large, shallow skillet and fry the sheets of dough over a high heat until the dough begins to blister. Flip the dough-cake over and fry for a few seconds on the other side. Keep in a warm place.

To serve: On a serving platter, form a base of thin dough-cakes. Lay a little chicken mixture on top, pour over some sauce, cover with a dough-cake, and repeat the process twice. Finally, dust with confectioners' sugar and cinnamon and serve hot.

MAROKKANISCHE PASTETE MIT HUHN „BELDI"

Für 4 bis 6 Personen:

1 Maishähnchen von ca. 1,4 kg,
grobes Salz, 120 ml Erdnußöl,
3 Gemüsezwiebeln, geschält und fein geschnitten,
2 EL Grieß,
1 Bund Koriandergrün, gehackt,
1 TL Korianderpulver,
¹/₂ TL weißer Pfeffer, gemahlen,
¹/₂ TL Ingwerpulver,
1 Msp Safranfäden,
¹/₂ TL Zimtpulver,
1 Stück Zimtstange,
2 TL Zucker, 2 EL Butter,
¹/₄ TL Gummi arabicum

Teig: (ersatzweise geht auch Blätterteig)
500 g Mehl, 2 TL Salz,
Erdnußöl
3 EL Puderzucker, mit Zimt gemischt

Das Huhn in Stücke zerteilen und mit dem groben Salz abreiben. In einem Schmortopf das Öl leicht erhitzen. Die Hühnerstücke mit Zwiebeln, Grieß, Koriander, Gewürzen sowie die Butter und das Gummi arabicum zugeben. Mit einem halben Liter Wasser aufgießen und das Huhn bei kleiner Hitze ca. eineinviertel Stunden garen. Nach Bedarf etwas Wasser zufügen. Huhn aus der Sauce nehmen, das Fleisch herauslösen und kleinschneiden. Die Sauce wenn nötig dick einkochen lassen, abschmecken.

Für den Teig: Mehl mit Salz vermischen. Nach und nach soviel Wasser zugießen und kneten, bis ein weicher Teig entsteht. Mit feuchtem Tuch bedecken und eine halbe Stunde in den Kühlschrank stellen. Aus dem Teig kleine Kugeln formen. Diese auf genügend Mehl sorgfältig so dünn wie möglich ausrollen. In einer großen, flachen Pfanne etwas Öl erhitzen. Teigblätter sehr heiß backen, bis der Teig anfängt, Blasen zu werfen. Umdrehen und den Teig auf der anderen Seite einige Sekunden backen. Warmstellen. Zum Servieren: Auf eine Servierplatte einen Boden aus dünnen Teigfladen legen. Etwas Hühnerfleisch darübergeben, mit etwas Sauce begießen, mit Fladen zudecken und den Vorgang zweimal wiederholen. Zum Schluß mit Puderzucker und Zimt bestäuben und heiß servieren.

CINNAMON PIGEON WITH NOODLES

For 4 persons:

4 pigeons, kitchen-ready, segmented,
4 tbsp butter,
1 onion, chopped,
1 bunch coriander leaves and parsley mixed, chopped,
1 stick cinnamon, 1 tsp ground cinnamon,
6 threads of saffron,
$^1/_2$ tsp gum arabic,
1 tsp salt,
$^1/_2$ tsp white pepper,
4 tbsp peanut oil,
200 ml/7 fl oz/$^4/_5$ cup water,
120 ml/4 fl oz/$^1/_2$ cup orange-blossom water

200 g/7 oz almonds, peeled,
2 tbsp sugar, 1 egg,
200 g/7 oz vermicelli, cooked in salted water,
ground cinnamon

Heat the butter in a braising pan and sweat the pigeons and onions briefly. Add the herbs, cinnamon, saffron, gum arabic, salt, pepper, oil, water and orange-blossom water and braise everything over a low heat for one hour.
Lightly roast the almonds in the skillet and then grind finely with the sugar in the mortar.
When the meat is done remove the bones and skin and cut into large pieces. Take out the cinnamon sticks and thicken the sauce with the almond paste and the egg. Season and stir in the meat. Transfer to a serving dish, cover with the boiled vermicelli, dust with cinnamon, and serve.

ZIMT-TAUBE MIT NUDELN

Für 4 Personen:

4 Tauben, küchenfertig, in Stücke zerteilt,
4 EL Butter,
1 Zwiebel, gehackt,
1 Bund Koriander und Petersilie gemischt, gehackt,
1 Zimtstange, 1 TL Zimtpulver,
6 Safranfäden,
$^1/_2$ TL Gummi arabicum, 1 TL Salz,
$^1/_2$ TL weißer Pfeffer,
4 EL Erdnußöl,
200 ml Wasser,
120 ml Orangenblütenwasser

200 g Mandeln, geschält,
2 EL Zucker, 1 Ei,
200 g Fadennudeln, in Salzwasser gekocht,
Zimtpulver

In einem Schmortopf die Butter erhitzen, Tauben und Zwiebeln anschwitzen. Kräuter, Zimt, Safran, Gummi arabicum, Salz, Pfeffer, Öl, Wasser und Orangenblütenwasser zugeben und das Ganze zugedeckt bei kleiner Hitze eine Stunde schmoren lassen.
Mandeln in der Pfanne leicht anrösten und dann mit dem Zucker im Mörser fein zerstossen.
Wenn das Fleisch gar ist, von Knochen und Haut befreien und größere Stücke kleinschneiden. Zimtstangen entfernen; die Sauce mit der Mandelpaste und dem Ei andicken. Abschmecken und das Fleisch unterrühren.
In eine Servierschüssel füllen, mit den gekochten Fadennudeln bedecken, mit Zimt bestäuben und servieren.

PASTILLA WITH MILK

For 6 persons:

500 g/17 oz puff pastry,
300 g/10 oz chopped almonds,
4 tbsp sugar,
200 g/7 oz melted butter

200 ml/7 oz milk,
2 tbsp honey,
1 tsp gum arabic,
2 tbsp orange-blossom water,
ground cinnamon

Roll out the puff pastry very thinly. Mix the almonds with the sugar. Paint a baking tray with butter. Cut out rounds of pastry about twenty centimeters across. Paint with butter, sprinkle with almonds. Cover with another sheet of pastry and repeat the process until all ingredients are used up.
Preheat the oven to 170° C/340° F and bake for thirty minutes until golden.
For the milk: Warm the milk with honey and gum arabic until everything has dissolved. Add the orange-blossom water and pour this mixture, shortly before serving, over the hot pastilla. Finally, dust with a little cinnamon.

PASTILLA MIT MILCH

Für 6 Personen:

500 g Blätterteig,
300 g gehackte Mandeln,
4 EL Zucker,
200 g zerlassene Butter

200 ml Milch,
2 EL Honig,
1 TL Gummi arabicum,
2 EL Orangenblütenwasser,
Zimtpulver

Blätterteig sehr dünn ausrollen. Mandeln mit Zucker vermischen. Ein Backblech mit Butter bepinseln. Aus dem Teig Kreise von ungefähr zwanzig Zentimeter ausschneiden. Mit Butter bestreichen, Mandeln darüber streuen, mit Teigblatt zudecken und den Vorgang wiederholen, bis alle Zutaten aufgebraucht sind. Im vorgeheizten Backofen bei 170° C dreißig Minuten goldgelb backen.
Für die Milch: Milch mit Honig und Gummi arabicum erwärmen, bis sich alles aufgelöst hat. Orangenblütenwasser zufügen und diese Mischung kurz vor dem Servieren über die noch heiße Pastille gießen. Zum Schluß mit etwas Zimt bestäuben.

In the souk, traditionally located in the medina (old part of town), many handicraft workshops are hidden in the multitude of shops along the maze of alleyways. The quarter is divided up into the different trades, so there are for example the souks of leatherwork, jewelry, metalworking, tailoring, pottery, spice merchants, wool dyers and carpenters. The visitor can watch wooden furniture being turned on the lathe, brass lamps being artistically beaten into shape, leather handbags being hand-sewn, or in the huge carpet stores have someone explain the Berber patterns and natural dyes of the colorful rugs. The narrow alleys are filled with the sounds and sights of hammering, welding, weaving, dyeing, woodworking; people extol their wares, bargain and haggle, drink tea and ultimately make sales.

The alleys are sheltered from the blazing sun by straw mats, making it pleasant to take a morning stroll around the shops. In this twilight chiaroscuro the air is heavy with different fragrances: here oriental spices, there tanned leather or freshly brewed mint tea. Donkey carts laden with sweet delicacies push through the crowd, and the shoe salesman tries in vain to interest a customer in bargaining. The souk is an important part of oriental life. For the visitor it is a colorful, impressive experience – and an opportunity to purchase high-quality, handcrafted products direct from the maker.

Im Souk, traditionell in der Medina (Altstadt) gelegen, verbergen sich in den vielen Geschäften entlang der verwinkelten Gassen zahlreiche Handwerksbetriebe. Das Viertel ist nach verschiedenen Berufszweigen aufgeteilt, so gibt es u.a. den Leder-, den Schmuck-, den Schmiede-, den Schneider-, den Töpfer-, den Gewürz-, den Wollfärber- und den Tischlersouk.
Der Besucher kann der Entstehung von gedrechselten Holzmöbeln, kunstvoll geschmiedeten Messinglampen, handgenähten Ledertaschen beiwohnen, oder sich im riesigen Teppichladen die Berbermuster und Naturfarben der bunten Teppiche erklären lassen.
In den schmalen Gassen wird gehämmert, geschweißt, gewebt, gefärbt, getischlert, es wird angepriesen, verhandelt, gefeilscht, Tee getrunken und schließlich verkauft.

U K

Strohmatten überdachen die Gassen und gestalten den morgendlichen Einkaufsbummel trotz gleißender Sonne angenehm. In dem Zwielicht aus Licht und Schatten duftet es hier nach orientalischen Gewürzen, da nach gegerbtem Leder, dort nach frisch-gebrühtem Minzetee. Eselskarren mit süßen Köstlichkeiten schieben sich durch das Gedränge und der Schuhverkäufer versucht vergeblich, einen Kunden für ein Verkaufsgespräch zu begeistern. Der Souk ist wichtiger Bestandteil orientalischen Lebens.
Für den Besucher ist es ein farben-prächtiges, eindrückliches Erlebnis – und die Möglichkeit, handwerklich hochwertige Produkte direkt beim Hersteller einzukaufen.

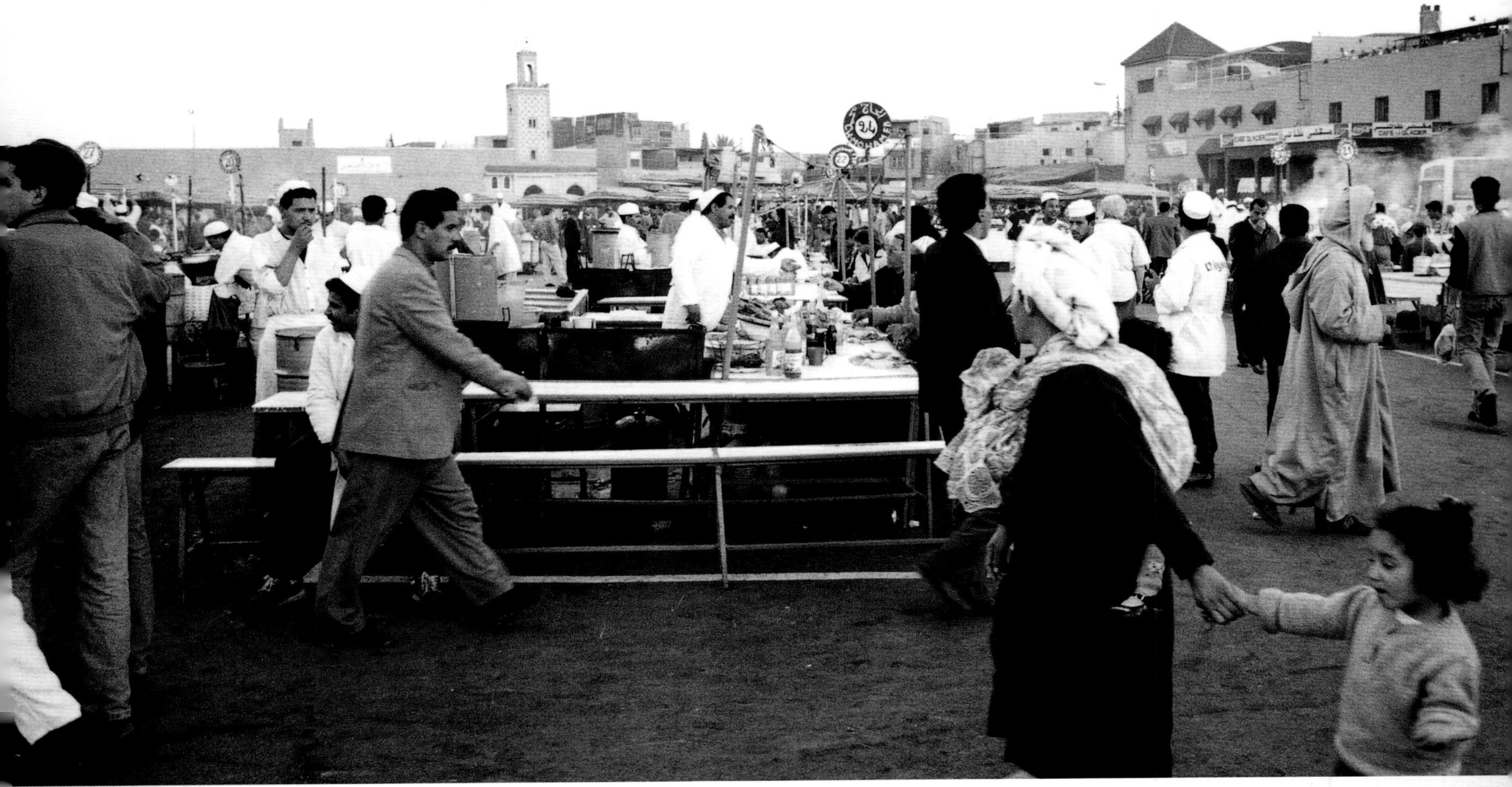

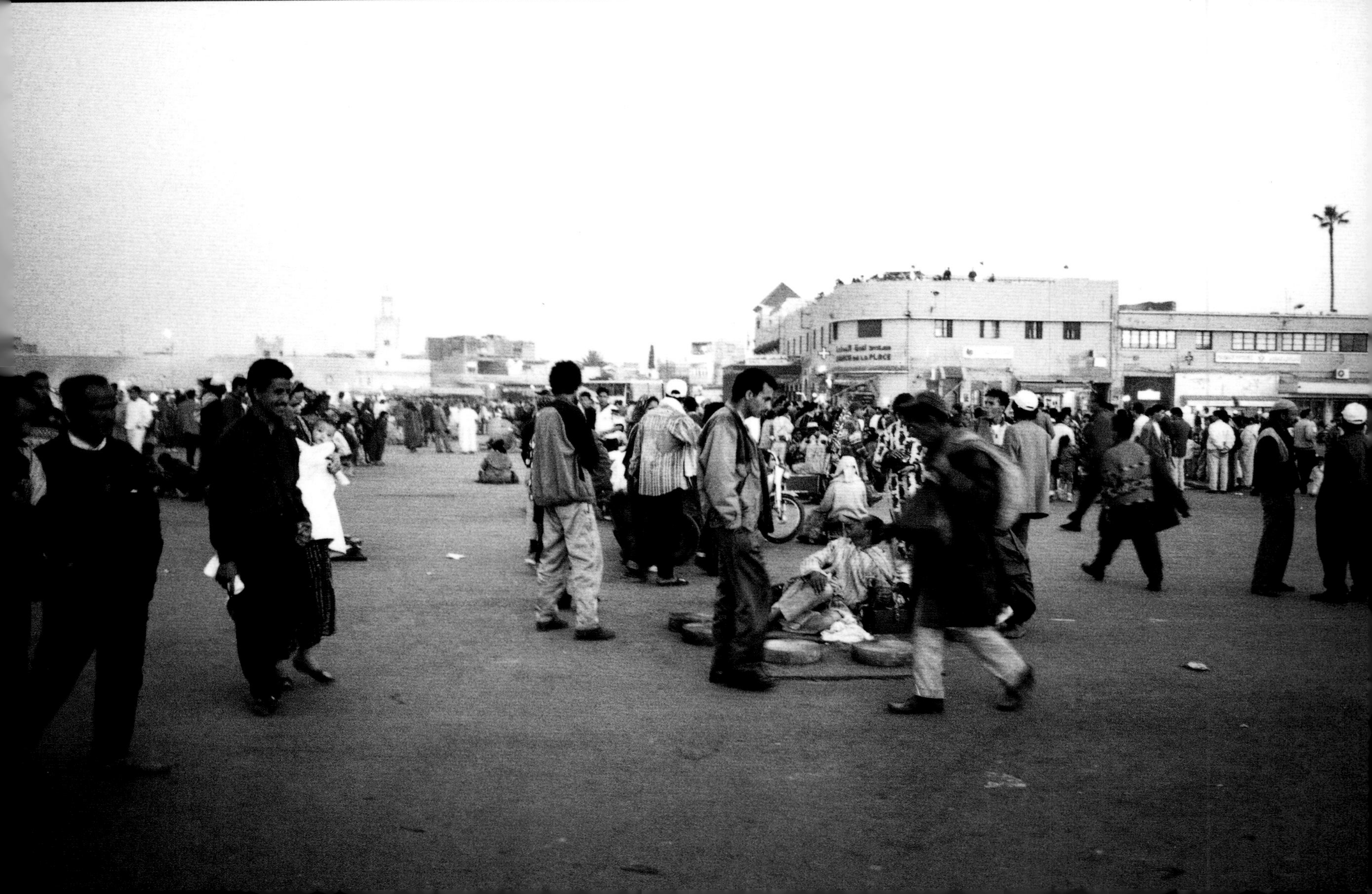

EL
YACOUT

The orient has enchanted men not only since the Tales of the Arabian Nights. One place where the dreams of the foreigner have combined the knowledge of the native is the small restaurant El Yacout in Marrakech.

El Yacout, which means the blue diamond, is a real jewel. An old city palace from the 17th century was transformed in the hands of the American interior designer Bill Willies and the proprietor Zkiri into a place of exquisite hospitality. Here old objets d'art and furnishings, delicacies and Moroccan hospitality blend into a paradise of the senses.

A Fairy-tale

Arabian Restaurant

On stepping out of the hurly-burly of the medina into the restaurant "El Yacout", one is enveloped by the tranquility of the house. The only link with the outside world is the sky above the large patio with its pool of water, lit at night by numerous lanterns. From the roof terrace one can scarcely take in the maze of houses and slender minarets, bathed in the red lights of Marrakech, bounded only on the horizon by the shining snow-covered peaks of the Atlas Mountains. Through the orange-blue glass of the windows the light falls on the old mosaic floor of the dining room and fills the room with an enchanting light. Petals float in a little fountain. Gentle music murmurs like a spring in a room of many nooks and corners, where in the evenings a large candelabra brings light into the mysterious semi-darkness.

detail that shows in the design of the interior is also found in the preparation and serving of dishes. To dine in the El Yacout is to celebrate food. In the twilight of the candles the dishes acquire a fairy-tale appearance, wine is poured from precious carafes, various hors-d'oeuvres, couscous, chicken with lemon, tajine with peas and artichokes, b'stilla with almonds and milk arrive in succession, masterfully prepared and served. It seems like sorcery when with acrobatic skill the waiter, an artist at his trade, carves the chicken with a supple movement while simultaneously holding a knife and a fork in each hand.

Just as elsewhere in Morocco the finely harmonized use of the various spices and the careful combination of ingredients creates an individual taste that is unmistakable for the El Yacout. The female kitchen crew under Fatima, the chef, produce first-class cuisine, rich in nuances, with a never-ending variety of aromas and tastes. El Yacout – this is a jewel, this is harmony. El Yacout is the place at which the westerner's dreamy concept of the orient has become reality.

Nicht erst seit den Märchen von Tausendundeiner Nacht hat der Orient die Menschen verzaubert. Ein Ort, an dem sich die Träume des Fremden mit dem Wissen des Einheimischen verbunden haben, ist das kleine Restaurant El Yacout in Marrakesch.

El Yacout, übersetzt der blaue Diamant, ist ein wahres Kleinod. Ein altes Stadtpalais aus dem 17. Jahrhundert verwandelte sich unter den Händen des amerikanischen Innenarchitekten Bill Willies und des

Inhabers Zkiri zu einem Ort erlesener Gastlichkeit. Hier fügen sich alte Kunstgegenstände und Möbel, Köstlichkeiten und marokkanische Gastfreundschaft zu einem sinnlichen Paradies.

FASTING SOUP "HARIRA"

For 4 persons:

400 g/13 oz lamb, cut into small cubes,
2 onions, finely chopped, 4 tbsp olive oil,
1 tsp white pepper, 1 knife-tip saffron,
1/2 tsp cinnamon, 1/2 tsp ground ginger,
150 g/5 oz/3/5 cup chickpeas, steeped overnight

150 g/5 oz/3/5 cup small lentils, steeped,
60 g/2 oz/1/4 cup rice,
2 sticks celery, cut into small cubes,
1 bunch coriander leaves, 1 bunch parsley, chopped,
3 tomatoes, skinned, seeded and chopped,
1 tbsp tomato purée, salt

2 tbsp flour, mixed into a roux
with 2 tbsp butter, 2 eggs
accompaniment (as desired): dates and honey-cake

Fry the lamb and onions in the oil until they begin to change color. Pour in one and a half liters water. Add the spices and chickpeas. Bring to the boil, and simmer the soup for half an hour.
Add the lentils, rice, celery, herbs, tomatoes, and tomato purée, salt and simmer for thirty minutes more.
Finally, thicken the soup with the flour roux and the eggs. Serve hot with dates and honey-cake on the side.
This rich soup is traditionally eaten as the first course during the fasting month of Ramadan, after sunset.

FASTENSUPPE HARIRA

Für 4 Personen:

400 g Lammfleisch, in feine Würfel geschnitten,
2 Gemüsezwiebeln, fein geschnitten, 4 EL Olivenöl,
1 TL weißer Pfeffer, 1 Msp Safran,
1/2 TL Zimt, 1/2 TL Ingwerpulver,
150 g Kichererbsen, über Nacht eingeweicht

150 g kleine Linsen, eingeweicht,
60 g Reis,
2 Stangen Sellerie, in feine Würfel geschnitten,
je 1 Bund Koriandergrün und Petersilie, gehackt,
3 Tomaten, enthäutet, entkernt und gehackt,
1 EL Tomatenmark, Salz,

2 EL Mehl, im Topf mit 2 EL Butter
zu einer Roux verrührt, 2 Eier
Beilage (nach Belieben): Datteln und Honigkuchen

Lammfleisch und Zwiebeln im Öl andünsten, bis sie anfangen Farbe anzunehmen. Mit eineinhalb Litern Wasser auffüllen. Gewürze und Kichererbsen hinzufügen. Zum Kochen bringen, und die Suppe eine halbe Stunde köcheln lassen. Die Linsen, den Reis, den Sellerie, die Kräuter, die Tomaten und das Tomatenmark dazugeben, salzen, dann weitere dreißig Minuten köcheln lassen. Zum Schluß mit der Roux und den Eiern die Suppe binden. Heiß servieren, mit Datteln und Honigkuchen als Beilage.
Diese kräftige Suppe wird traditionell während des Fastenmonats Ramadan nach Sonnenuntergang als erste Speise gegessen.

Tritt man aus dem bunten Treiben der Medina in das Restaurant „El Yacout", so wird man von der Stille des Hauses umfangen. Die einzige Verbindung mit der Außenwelt ist der Himmel über dem großen Patio mit seinem Wasserbecken, das nachts von zahlreichen Laternen erleuchtet wird. Von der Dachterrasse aus überblickt man kaum das Gewirr der Häuser und der schlanken Minarette, eingetaucht in das rote Licht von Marrakesch, das erst am Horizont von den glänzenden, schneebedeckten Gipfeln des Atlas begrenzt wird.

EIN MÄRCHEN
AUS 1001 NACHT

Durch das orange-blaue
Glas der Fenster fällt das
Licht auf den alten
Mosaikboden des
Speisesaals und taucht den
Raum in ein
verzauberndes Licht.
Blütenblätter treiben in
einem kleinen Brunnen,
leise Musik murmelt wie
eine Quelle in einem
verwinkelten Raum, dem
ein großer, kerzen-
bestückter Leuchter
abends Licht in das
geheimnisvolle Halb-
dunkel trägt. Die Liebe
zum Detail, die sich in der
Gestaltung des Interieurs
erspüren läßt, findet
sich auch in der Bereitung
und Darbietung der
Speisen wieder.

Im El Yacout zu speisen, heißt
Essen zu zelebrieren. Das Dämmerlicht
der Kerzen verleiht den Speisen
ein märchenhaftes Aussehen, der Wein
wird aus edlen Karaffen gereicht.
Verschiedene Vorspeisen, Couscous,
Zitronenhuhn, Tagine mit Erbsen und
Artischocken, B'stilla mit Mandeln und
Milch folgen aufeinander, meisterlich
zubereitet und serviert. Es grenzt
an Zauberei, mit welch akrobatischem
Geschick der Service, ein Künstler
seines Faches, in einer geschmeidigen
Bewegung das Poulet zerteilt, zugleich
in jeder Hand je ein Messer und eine
Gabel führend. Wie auch anderswo in
Marokko, schafft der fein aufeinander
abgestimmte Einsatz der verschiedenen
Gewürze und die sorgfältige Zusammen-
stellung der Zutaten einen eigenen,
für das El Yacout unverwechselbaren
Geschmack. Die weibliche Küchencrew um Fatima, die Küchenchefin,
gestaltet eine nuancenreiche Küche
auf höchster Ebene, mit einer nicht
enden wollenden Vielfalt an Gerüchen
und Geschmacksnoten.

El Yacout, das ist ein Juwel, ist
Harmonie. El Yacout ist der Ort,
an dem der Traum des Westens vom
Orient zur Wirklichkeit geworden ist.

BRAISED CHICKEN
WITH LEMON AND OLIVES

For 4 persons:

1 free-range chicken, about 1.5 kg/3 lb 5 oz

For the marinade:
1 onion, finely chopped,
1 garlic clove, crushed, 4 tbsp olive oil,
1 tsp ground ginger, $^1/_2$ tsp turmeric,
$^1/_2$ tsp ground cinnamon,
$^1/_2$ tsp ground coriander, salt, pepper,
500 ml/17 fl oz/2 cups vegetable broth

1 brined lemon (see p. 230), segmented,
200 g/7 oz pink-brown olives,
lemon juice,
1 tbsp chopped coriander leaves

For the marinade: Sweat the onion and garlic in the oil. Add the spices and continue to sauté, stirring, until everything is well mixed. Allow to cool a little and spread this paste on the chicken inside and out. Cover and allow to stand in the refrigerator for two to three hours.
Place the chicken in a braising pan and pour in the broth. Bring to the boil, then cover and braise over a low heat for at least an hour.
Scald the olives in a sieve with boiling water and add to the jus together with the lemon segments. Simmer for twenty minutes more, then remove the chicken and keep in a warm place.
Reduce the sauce and season with a dash of lemon juice and salt.
To serve: Lay the chicken on a serving platter, surround with olives and lemon segments. Sprinkle a little chopped coriander over the sauce and serve separately.

GESCHMORTES ZITRONENHUHN
MIT OLIVEN

Für 4 Personen:

1 Huhn aus Freilandhaltung, ca. 1,5 kg

Für die Marinade:
1 Gemüsezwiebel, fein geschnitten,
1 Knoblauchzehe, durchgedrückt, 4 EL Olivenöl,
1 TL Ingwerpulver, $^1/_2$ TL Kurkuma,
$^1/_2$ TL Zimtpulver,
$^1/_2$ TL Korianderpulver, Salz, Pfeffer,
500 ml Gemüsebrühe

1 eingelegte Zitrone (siehe Seite 230),
in Schnitze geschnitten,
200 g rosa-braune Oliven, Zitronensaft,
1 EL gehacktes Koriandergrün

Für die Marinade: Zwiebel und Knoblauch im Öl anschwitzen. Gewürze zugeben und unter Rühren weiterdünsten, bis sich alles gut vermischt hat. Das Huhn innen und aussen mit dieser Paste einstreichen. Zwei bis drei Stunden zugedeckt in den Kühlschrank stellen. Das Huhn in einen Schmortopf geben; die Brühe zugießen. Zum Kochen bringen und dann zugedeckt bei kleiner Hitze eine gute Stunde schmoren lassen.
Oliven in einem Sieb mit kochendem Wasser überbrühen und mit den Zitronenschnitzen in die Jus geben. Weitere zwanzig Minuten köcheln lassen, dann das Huhn herausnehmen und warmstellen.
Die Sauce einreduzieren lassen; mit einem Spritzer Zitronensaft und Salz abschmecken.
Zum Servieren: Das Huhn auf eine Servierplatte anrichten; mit Oliven und Zitronenschnitzen umlegen. Die Sauce mit etwas Koriandergrün bestreuen und separat servieren.

PIGEONS
WITH ALMONDS AND RAISINS

For 4 persons:

4 pigeons, kitchen-ready,
4 tbsp peanut oil,
salt, pepper,
1 onion, cut into fine strips,
250 ml/8 fl oz/2 cups water,
1 tsp turmeric,
1 tsp ground ginger,
¹/₂ tsp ground coriander,
1 bunch parsley

150 g/5 oz peeled almonds,
4 tbsp raisins

Heat the oil in a braising pan. Salt and pepper the pigeons and fry on all sides until they begin to change color. Add the onion and fry. Quench with water, then add the spices and herbs, cover and cook over a low heat for forty minutes.
For the last ten minutes add the peeled almonds and the raisins. Remove the parsley and adjust the seasoning of the sauce.

TAUBEN
MIT MANDELN UND ROSINEN

Für 4 Personen:

4 Tauben, küchenfertig,
4 EL Erdnußöl,
Salz, Pfeffer,
1 Zwiebel, in feine Streifen geschnitten,
250 ml Wasser,
1 TL Kurkuma,
1 TL Ingwerpulver,
¹/₂ TL Korianderpulver,
1 Bund Petersilie

150 g geschälte Mandeln,
4 EL Rosinen

Öl in einem Schmortopf erhitzen. Tauben salzen, pfeffern, dann rundum anbraten, bis sie anfangen, Farbe anzunehmen. Zwiebel zugeben und mitbraten. Mit Wasser ablöschen, die Gewürze und Kräuter zugeben, zugedeckt bei kleiner Hitze vierzig Minuten garen lassen. Die letzten zehn Minuten die Mandeln und die Rosinen zugeben und mitkochen. Petersilie entfernen und die Sauce abschmecken.

LAMB TAJINE
WITH ARTICHOKES AND PEAS

For 4 persons:

600 g/1 lb 5 oz lean shoulder of lamb,
boned and cut into 4 portions,
4 tbsp olive oil,
2 onions, chopped,
2 garlic cloves, crushed,
300 ml/10 fl oz/1 1/4 cups water,
1 knife-tip saffron,
1/2 tsp ground cinnamon,
1/2 tsp ground cumin,
1 tsp pepper, salt

8 artichoke hearts,
300 g/10 oz garden peas

Heat the oil in a braising pan and fry the lamb on all sides. Add the onions and garlic and sweat briefly. Quench with water and add the spices. Cover and braise over a low heat for one and a half to two hours.
Then add the artichokes and the peas and simmer for twenty minutes more.
When the meat is done, add lemon juice to the sauce to taste.

LAMM-TAGINE
MIT ARTISCHOCKEN UND ERBSEN

Für 4 Personen:

600 g mageres Lammfleisch aus der Schulter,
in 4 Portionsstücke geschnitten,
4 EL Olivenöl,
2 Zwiebeln, gehackt,
2 Knoblauchzehen, zerdrückt,
300 ml Wasser,
1 Msp Safran,
1/2 TL Zimtpulver,
1/2 TL Kreuzkümmelpulver,
1 TL Pfeffer, Salz

8 Artischockenherzen,
300 g Gartenerbsen

In einem Schmortopf das Öl erhitzen, dann das Lammfleisch von allen Seiten anbraten. Zwiebeln und Knoblauch hinzufügen und anschwitzen. Mit Wasser ablöschen und Gewürze zugeben.
Zugedeckt bei kleiner Hitze eineinhalb bis zwei Stunden schmoren. Artischocken und Erbsen dazugeben und weitere zwanzig Minuten köcheln lassen. Wenn das Fleisch gar ist, die Sauce mit Zitronensaft abschmecken.

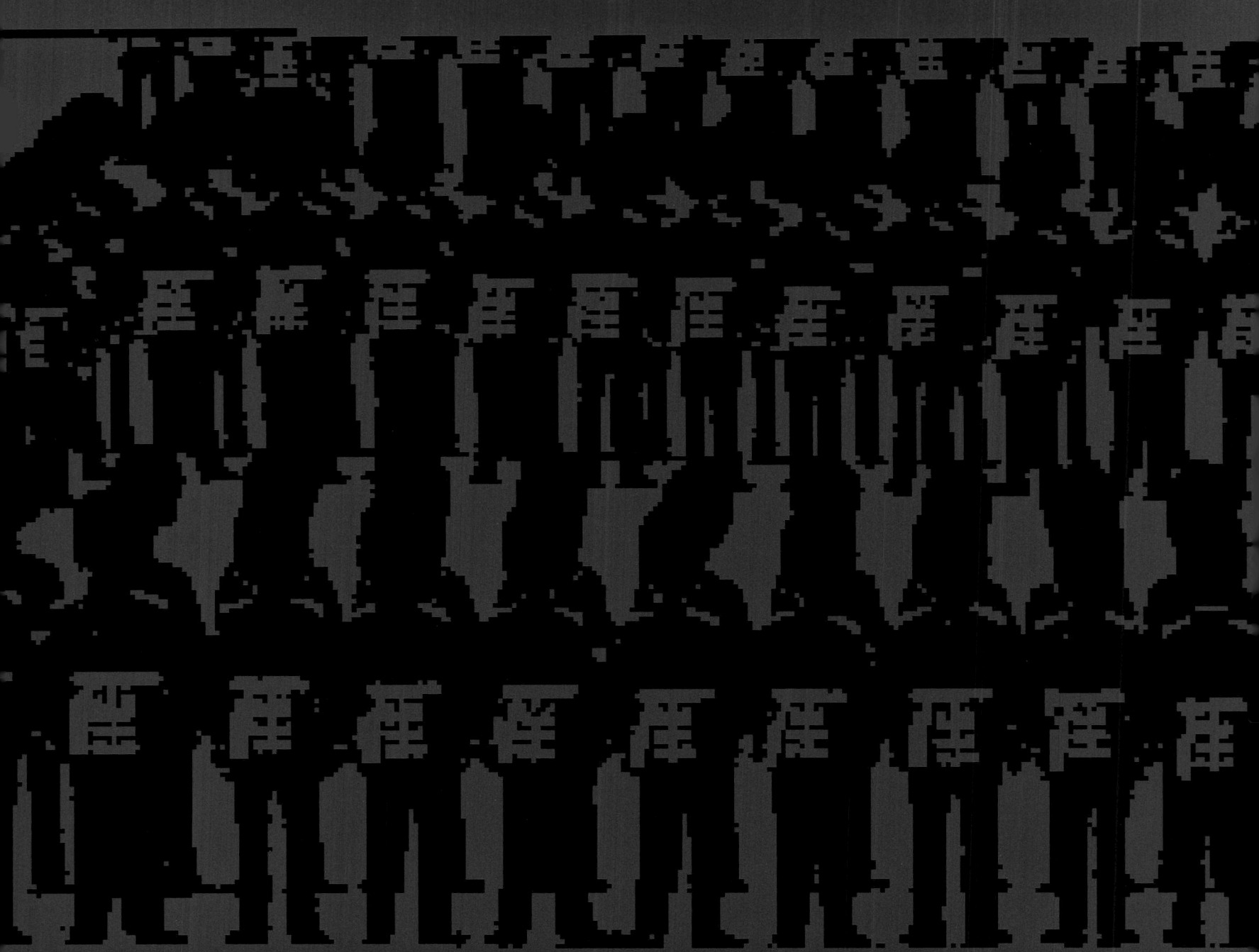

LONDON

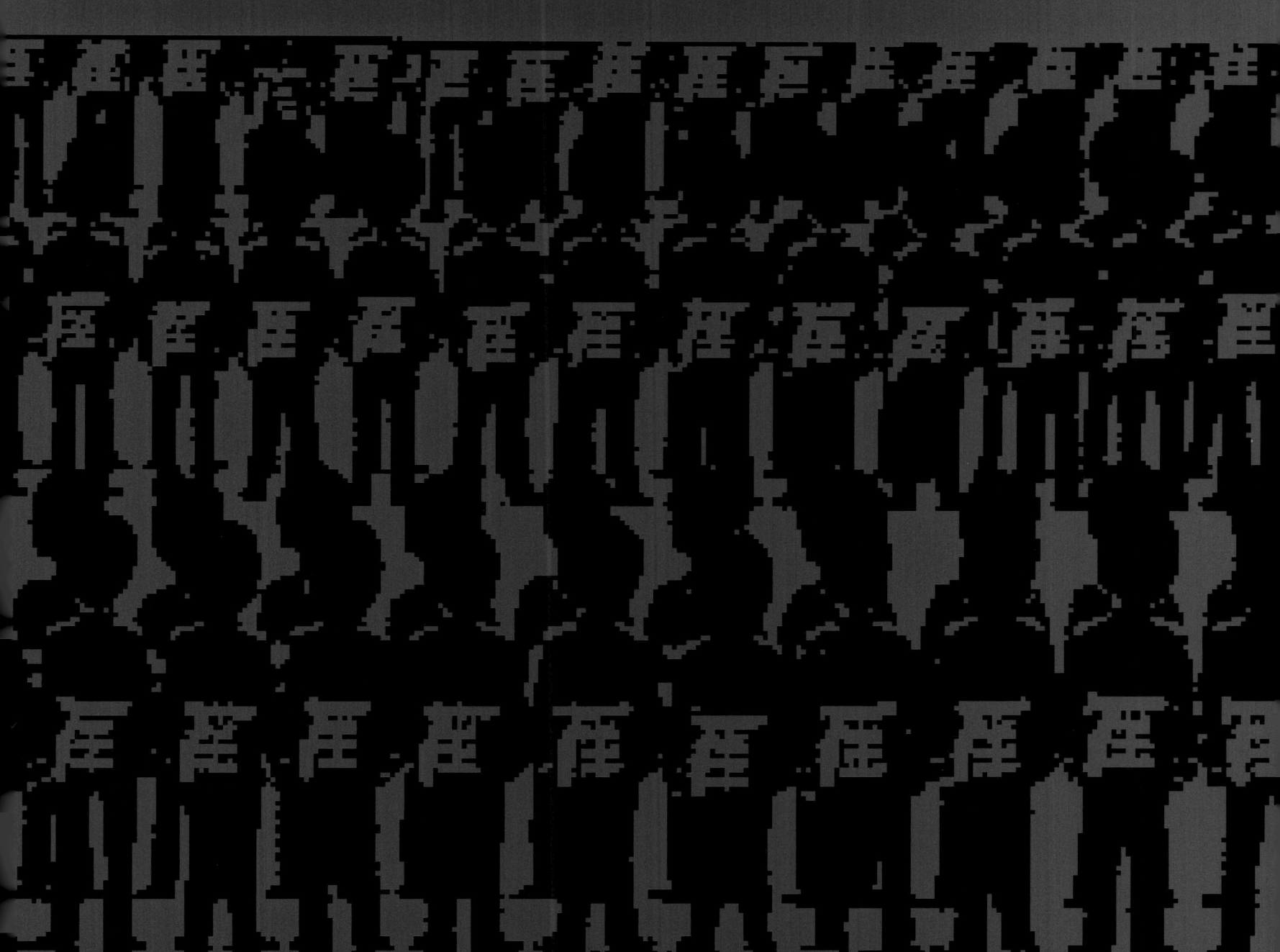

London is stepping on the gas like never before. No, not the cab drivers. They trundle their ancient, black, diesel taxis through the city rush hour just as stoically as ever, giving the stressed-out continental passenger an incomparable impression, which needs some getting used to, that it does not matter in the slightest whether the gas pedal is pressed to the floorboards or only half way. The liveried doormen of the hotels too seem to stand way above the hectic pace of everyday life. No trace of hurry, just like the heavy revolving doors behind them, which calmly propel one guest into the distinguished and expensive house while propelling another out.

No – they are turning on the gas like never before one storey deeper, in the basement. Here, usually reachable only by narrow, steep staircases, where the heat sometimes reaches the pain threshold, where the light of day, if at all, penetrates only diffusely, where, apart from those who work here, practically no-one ever comes. Down here we are in the restaurant kitchens, in the belly of the top-class catering establishments. They conceal culinary workshops and studios of experimentation; here stand the cooking ranges and ovens at which taste fanatics and creative geniuses motivate and tirelessly drive on their staff teams; here they conjure up their works of art. Works of art that moments later will be delighting the gourmets upstairs, and that have brought to London's cuisine the reputation of being the most creative, innovative and simply the best to be found far and wide.

What has happened? The British Isles in general, and London in particular, have suddenly become the culinary center of the (old) world? How can this be, in view of the globally known negative image of British cooking? Quite simple: the British have discovered good food. Food markets with opulent, fantastic assortments in department stores such as Harrods or Harvey Nichols give evidence of this, just as do the small but finest of the fine specialty shops that cater to every epicurean need: cheese from Paxton & Whitfield, chocolate from Rococo Chocolates, Mediterranean products from Le Pont de la Tour, tea from Fortnum & Mason and wine without end from Berry Bros. & Rudd. Secondly, the British are prepared to spend money, a lot of money, on good food. For the economic crisis that still weighs heavily upon the French and Germans and is causing suffering to top-class gastronomy is here largely a thing of the past. Thirdly: because Britain has no superb gastronomic tradition of its own, it can all the more freely access the top cuisines of elsewhere, such as the French, Italian or Asian cuisines. To be enthusiastic in London about a top restaurant with French cuisine is not an act of treason, such as a Frenchman would be accused of if he praised an Italian restaurant and turned his back on the traditional bistro. Fourthly, and last but not least: such an explosion of creativity together with perfectly learned mastery of the culinary craft (for only this combination can lead to the top) that London is currently experiencing does not, of course, just appear from nowhere. It needs a solid basis, the soil on which it can develop over a period of years and then come into blossom. For London this means: there is a little bit of Anton Mosimann's influence almost everywhere. For almost all the expert and creative youngsters on today's London food scene have at one time, directly or indirectly, tasted their way into the haute école and hence the cuisine of this doyen of all successful culinary art and culture in Great Britain. And youngsters most of them are. Some of them are in their mid- to late twenties and have already won one or even two Michelin stars by their cooking.

They are all chefs who have their finger on the pulse of the culinary times: no minimalist frivolity on the plate, but a mouthful of aromas and taste; sophisticated, sometime risky compositions that however harmonize, proving the mastery of the cook; and always preferably a spoonful more than one too little on the plate. A paradise, in fact, for the trencherman.

In London wird Gas gegeben wie nie zuvor. Nicht von den Taxifahrern, nein. Die drehen in ihren schwarzen Uralt-Dieseln ihre Rush-Hour-Runden durch die City so stoisch wie eh und je und vermitteln dem gestreßten Fahrgast vom Kontinent das so unvergleichliche wie gewöhnungsbedürftige Gefühl, daß es doch völlig wurscht ist, ob das Gaspedal ganz oder nur halb durchgedrückt ist. Auch die Livrierten vor den Hotels scheinen weit über der Hektik des Alltags zu stehen. Von Beschleunigung keine Spur, so wenig wie bei den schweren Drehtüren hinter ihnen, die gelassen den einen Gast hineinschaufeln ins vornehme und teure Haus und den anderen wieder hinaus.

Nein, Gas gegeben wie nie zuvor wird eine Etage tiefer, im Souterrain. Dort, wo meist nur steile und enge Treppen hinunterführen, wo die Hitze schon mal die Schmerzgrenze erreicht, wo das Tageslicht, wenn überhaupt, nur noch diffus hineinscheint, wo außer denen, die dort arbeiten, sonst kaum einer hinkommt. Hier unten sind wir in den Küchen der Restaurants, im Bauch der Top-Gastronomie. Hier verstecken sich kulinarische Werkstätten und Experimentierstudios, hier stehen jene Herde, an denen Geschmacksfanatiker und Kreativbolzen ihre Teams motivieren und rastlos antreiben, hier zaubern sie ihre Kunstwerke. Kunstwerke, die Minuten später die Feinschmecker eine Etage höher entzücken und die der Küche Londons den Ruf eingebracht haben, die kreativste, die innovativste, ganz einfach die beste weit und breit zu sein.

Was ist passiert? Die Britische Insel im allgemeinen und London im besonderen soll plötzlich der kulinarische Nabel der (alten) Welt sein? Wie kann das angehen beim doch weltweit bekannten Minus-Image britischer Kochkunst? Ganz einfach. Erstens: Die Engländer haben für sich das gute Essen entdeckt. Opulente und traumhaft sortierte Food-Märkte in Kaufhäusern wie Harrods oder Harvey Nichols sind hierfür ebenso Beleg wie kleine und allerfeinste Spezialitätengeschäfte, die keinen Feinschmeckerwunsch offen lassen: Käse bei Paxton & Whitfield, Schokolade bei Rococo Chocolates, mediterrane Produkte bei Le Pont de la Tour, Tee bei Fortnum & Mason und Wein ohne Ende bei Berry Bros. & Rudd. Zweitens: Die Engländer sind bereit, für gutes Essen Geld, auch viel Geld, auszugeben, denn die Wirtschaftskrise, unter der Franzosen und Deutsche zur Zeit heftig und sehr zu Lasten den Spitzengastronomie leiden, hat man hier schon weitgehend hinter sich. Drittens: Weil man keine tolle und überragende eigene gastronomische Kultur hat, kann man sich hier umso unbefangener anderen Hochküchen, also den Küchen Frankreichs, Italiens und Asiens, zuwenden. Wer in London von einem französisch kochenden Top-Restaurant schwärmt, begeht keinen Landesverrat, so wie dies einem Franzosen schon mal vorgehalten werden kann, wenn er in Paris einen Italiener hochlobt und dem klassischen Bistro die kalte Schulter zeigt. Viertens und last but not least: Eine solche Explosion an kreativer und gleichzeitig handwerklich perfekt beherrschter Kochkunst (nur diese Kombination führt an die Spitze), wie sie London derzeit erlebt, kommt natürlich nicht aus dem Nichts. Sie braucht eine solide Grundlage, braucht den Humus, auf dem sie wachsen kann. Für London bedeutet dies: ein bißchen Mosimann ist hier fast überall mit dabei. Denn in die hohe Schule und mithin in die Küche des Dojens aller arrivierten Kochkunst und Kochkultur in Großbritannien hat hier fast jeder schon einmal hineingeschmeckt, der heute zu den jungen Könnern und Kreativen der Londoner Koch-Szene zählt. Und jung sind die meisten. Manche gerade mal Mitte/Ende zwanzig und haben sich doch schon einen oder gar zwei Michelin-Sterne erkocht.

Es sind allesamt Küchenchefs, die den Nerv der kulinarischen Zeit treffen: keine minimalistischen Spielereien auf den Tellern, sonden ein Mund voll Aromen und Geschmack; raffinierte, oft gewagte Kompositionen, die aber stimmen und so den Meister am Herd beweisen; und immer lieber einen Löffel zuviel als einen zu wenig auf dem Teller. Schlemmers Paradies eben.

Mosimann's London

*O*ne can take an intellectual approach to Anton Mosimann. He then comes alive via the principles that he has prescribed himself. First of all: "Satisfying the customer is a race without a finish". Or his creed of the light cuisine: "Everything simple is beautiful, everything beautiful is simple". Or a good dash of joie de vivre: "Never let yesterday spoil today". And: "You never get a second chance to make a first impression". You can philosophize with him splendidly on these and many other things over a glass of champagne. For example, on the irony of fate that he, of all people, a Swiss, should have revolutionized the boring and monotonous British cuisine and set it on the path toward haute cuisine. He can see the typically Swiss mixture of precision, refinement and imagination that stands behind this success. And that he was never just a chef, but always someone who has cared for taste in the broadest sense, namely also the ambience, arrangements, in fact everything that is part of the lifestyle, enjoyment and style of dining.

Well then: since with Anton Mosimann we are bound to always come around to the subject of food, or to be more exact, food culture, let us take the second possible approach to get to know him. This leads direct to the mouth and stomach, without excluding an intellectual remainder, however. For in order to dine well – and this

means for him perfectly – there is always more to matters than merely first-class cooking. The framework and cultural background must be right, aspects such as healthy nourishment must not be forgotten, and it is also important that his immense professional experience be passed on to the next generation of professional cooks – or quite simply also to keen amateur cooks. But more of this later.

Let us first stay with the food: following his unparalleled career as chef de cuisine at the Dorchester Hotel between 1975 and 1988, where his cooking brought two Michelin stars to the first hotel kitchen outside of France, he made himself independent with his private club, the former Belfry Club. This was a crossroads, a decision that gourmets had to accept with a tear in at least one eye. For without club membership or at least as the guest of a member, there is barely any opportunity to taste Mosimann's fantastic mushroom risotto, his marvelous salad creations, the chicken with an Asiatic touch, or the melt-in-the-mouth lamb subtly refined with herbs. If you are however fortunate enough to dine here in the club, you can at the same time enjoy the incomparable ambience of a secularized and rebuilt former Presbyterian church with glass-enclosed wine cellar and rooms for small private functions, which not for nothing bear the names Fabergé, Wedgwood, Gucci, Veuve Clicquot and Bulthaup.

But Mosimann would not be Mosimann were he to withdraw behind the club walls or stay in hiding. The opposite is the case, and partly for this reason about a year ago he founded a new basis of activity, his cookery school, 20 minutes by car

away from the club, in a beautiful old brick-built house. Here, not only professionals can profit from his expertise and knowledge, acquired at stages in his career all over the world. Here he keeps also his private collection of cookery books with over 6000 volumes, for historical and scientific research. For example, British Airways sends its first-class staff here for training. Here too, any private amateur cook can take advanced courses or train his palate at wine tastings. And if you absolutely wish, Mosimann can also demonstrate how to tie a bow-tie properly – his ever correctly fitting trademark. He has a permanent choice of 126 of them at his fingertips. Only his collection of wine and cookery books is larger!

Man kann sich Anton Mosimann über den Kopf nähern. Dann wird er lebendig mit den Grundsätzen, die er sich selbst verordnet hat. Zu allererst: „Den Gast zufriedenzustellen ist eine Aufgabe, mit der man nie fertig ist". Oder sein Credo auf die leichte Küche: „Alles Einfache ist wunderbar, alles Wunderbare ist einfach". Oder ein guter Schuß Lebenslust: „Laß dir niemals den heutigen Tag durch den gestrigen verderben", und: „Du hast niemals eine zweite Chance, um einen ersten Eindruck zu bekommen". Hierüber und über vieles mehr läßt sich mit ihm bei einem Glas Champagner trefflich philosophieren. Etwa über die Ironie des Schicksals, daß ausgerechnet er, ein Schweizer, die langweilige und eintönige britische Küche revolutioniert und auf den Weg zur Haute Cuisine gebracht hat. Er sieht die typische schweizerische Mischung aus Präzision, Verfeinerung und Phantasie, die hinter diesem Erfolg steht und daß er nie nur Küchenchef war, sondern immer auch einer, der sich um Geschmack im weitesten Sinne, also auch ums Ambiente, ums Arrangement gekümmert hat, eben um alles, was zum Lebens-, Genuß- und Eßstil dazugehört.

Also: Da man bei Anton Mosimann zwangsläufig und sowieso beim Thema Essen, genauer: beim Thema Eßkultur landet, nehmen wir den zweiten möglichen Weg, um sich ihm zu nähern. Der führt direkt in Mund und Bauch, ohne jedoch den Rest vom Kopf auszuschalten. Denn um gut – und das heißt bei ihm: perfekt – zu speisen, gehört immer mehr dazu, als nur ein top gekochtes Menü. Da müssen der Rahmen und der kulturelle Hintergrund stimmen, da dürfen Themen wie gesunde Ernährung nicht fehlen, und da geht es auch um die Weitergabe seiner immensen beruflichen Erfahrung an die nächste Generation von Profiköchen – oder ganz einfach auch an engagierte Hobbyköche. Doch davon später. Bleiben wir zunächst beim Essen: Nach seiner beispiellosen Karriere als Küchenchef des Dorchester-Hotels in den Jahren 1975 bis 1988, wo er als erster einer Hotelküche außerhalb Frankreichs zwei Michelin-Sterne herbeikochte, machte er sich mit seinem Privatclub, dem ehemaligen Belfry-Club, selbständig. Das war eine Weichenstellung, eine Entscheidung, die Feinschmecker mit mindestens einem weinenden Auge zur Kenntnis nehmen mußten. Denn ohne Clubmitgliedschaft oder wenigstens als Clubgast hat man nun kaum noch Chancen, Mosimanns traumhaftes Pilz-Risotto, seine wunderbaren Salatkreationen, das asiatisch angehauchte Hühnchen oder das mit Kräutern subtil verfeinerte, butterzarte Lamm zu kosten. Wer allerdings das Glück hat, hier im Club zu speisen, der kommt gleichzeitig in den Genuß des unvergleichlichen Ambientes einer säkularisierten und umgebauten ehemaligen Presbyterianer-Kirche mit verglastem Weinkeller und Räumen für kleine private Feiern, die nicht von ungefähr Fabergé, Wedgwood, Gucci, Veuve Clicquot und Bulthaup heißen.

Nun wäre Mosimann nicht Mosimann, würde er sich hinter Clubmauern zurückziehen oder gar verstecken. Das Gegenteil ist der Fall, und unter anderem deshalb hat er vor rund einem Jahr eine neue Wirkungsstätte, seine Kochschule, gegründet, 20 Autominuten vom Club entfernt, in einem wunderschönen alten Backsteinhaus gelegen.

Hier können nicht nur angehende Profis von seinem Können und Wissen, das er sich auf Stationen rund um den Globus erarbeitet hat, profitieren. Hier steht auch seine private Kochbuchsammlung mit über 6000 Bänden für historische und wissenschaftliche Forschungen zur Verfügung. Hier läßt auch, nur zum Beispiel, British Airways sein First-Class-Personal ausbilden. Hier kann sich auch jeder private Hobbykoch in einem Kochkurs fortbilden oder bei Weinverkostungen die Zunge schulen. Wer unbedingt will, dem zeigt Mosimann auch, wie man eine Fliege – sein immer korrekt sitzendes Markenzeichen – richtig bindet. 126 Stück davon hat er ständig zur Auswahl. Nur seine Wein- und Kochbuchsammlung ist größer!

ANTON'S CAESAR SALAD

ANTONS CÄSARSALAT

For 4 persons:

2 heads of cos lettuce,
2 slices white bread, without crust,
cut into small cubes,
2 tbsp olive oil,
1 tbsp butter,
1 small garlic clove crushed,
60 g/2 oz freshly grated Parmesan cheese

Finely cut chives

For the dressing:
$^1/_2$ garlic clove,
1 egg yolk,
1 fillet of anchovy,
50 ml/1$^2/_3$ fl oz/$^1/_5$ cup sherry vinegar,
2 tbsp finely grated Parmesan cheese,
100 ml/3$^1/_2$ fl oz/$^2/_5$ cup olive oil,
50 ml/1$^2/_3$ fl oz/$^1/_5$ cup vegetable stock,
Worcestershire sauce,
salt, freshly ground pepper

Für 4 Personen:

2 Köpfe Römersalat,
2 Scheiben Weißbrot, ohne Rinde,
in kleine Würfel geschnitten,
2 EL Olivenöl,
1 EL Butter,
1 kleine Knoblauchzehe, zerdrückt,
60 g frisch geriebener Parmesan

Schnittlauch, fein geschnitten

Für die Sauce:
$^1/_2$ Knoblauchzehe,
1 Eigelb,
1 Sardellenfilet,
50 ml Sherryessig,
2 EL feingeriebener Parmesan,
100 ml Olivenöl,
50 ml Gemüsebrühe,
Worcestershiresauce,
Salz, Pfeffer aus der Mühle

Wash the lettuce and remove the outer leaves. Heat the olive oil with the butter and sauté the garlic until transparent. Remove the garlic and fry the white bread cubes until golden brown. Drain the croûtons on kitchen paper and place back in a clean pan. Toss in about one third of the Parmesan cheese and allow to melt. Heat the pan again, if necessary, to melt the cheese.

For the dressing: Place the garlic with the egg yolk, anchovy fillet, vinegar and cheese in the blender and blend until smooth. Add the olive oil to the dressing in a slow, steady stream and thin with the stock. Season with a dash of Worcestershire sauce, salt and pepper.

To serve: Lay the lettuce leaves on plates, drizzling each layer with a little dressing and sprinkle over the remaining cheese. Finally, garnish with the croûtons and chives.

Den Salat waschen, die äußeren Blätter entfernen. Das Olivenöl mit Butter erhitzen und den Knoblauch darin glasig dünsten, entfernen und die Weißbrotwürfel goldbraun braten. Die Croûtons auf einem Küchenpapier entfetten, dann zurück in eine saubere Pfanne geben. Etwa ein Drittel des Parmesankäses darüberstreuen und schmelzen lassen. Wenn nötig, die Pfanne nochmals erhitzen, um den Käse schmelzen zu lassen.

Für die Sauce: Knoblauch mit Eigelb, Sardellenfilet, Essig und Käse im Mixer fein pürieren. Nach und nach das Öl zugießen, dann mit der Brühe verdünnen. Mit einem Spritzer Worcestershiresauce, Salz und Pfeffer würzen.

Zum Servieren: Salatblätter auf Teller auslegen, dabei jede Lage mit etwas Sauce beträufeln und mit dem restlichen Käse bestreuen. Zum Schluß den Salat mit den Croûtons und Schnittlauch bestreuen.

LEEK TERRINE WITH HORN OF PLENTY MUSHROOMS

LAUCHTERRINE MIT HERBSTTROMPETEN

For 8 - 10 persons:

1 kg/2 lb 3 oz baby leeks or thin leeks, cleaned,
200 g/7 oz horn of plenty mushrooms, cleaned,
3 tbsp olive oil,
salt, freshly ground pepper

For the tomato vinaigrette:
2 tomatoes, skinned, seeded
and cut into small cubes,
50 ml/1²/₃ fl oz/¹/₅ cup red-wine vinegar,
100 ml/3¹/₂ fl oz/²/₅ cup olive oil,
1 tbsp finely chopped chives

Line a terrine (about 26 cm/10 in long) with cling film. Cut the leeks to the length of the terrine and cook until tender in salted water; then refresh in ice-cold water and drain well.

Heat the olive oil and sauté the mushrooms. Season with salt and pepper and allow to go cold.

Place about one third of the mushrooms in the terrine and press them flat. Now place a close layer of leeks on top, the green and white ends alternating with each other. Cover with a further layer of mushrooms, and continue in this manner until all the mushrooms and leeks are used up. Fold the foil together over the filled terrine.

Weight down well and keep in a cold place for at least six hours.

For the tomato vinaigrette: Mix together all the ingredients and season with salt and pepper.

To serve: Turn out the terrine onto a cutting board and slice with a sharp knife. Arrange on plates, then remove the cling film. Circle with the tomato vinaigrette and serve.

Für 8 - 10 Personen:

1 kg Minilauch oder dünne Lauchstangen, geputzt,
200 g Herbsttrompeten, geputzt,
3 EL Olivenöl,
Salz, schwarzer Pfeffer aus der Mühle

Für die Tomaten-Vinaigrette:
2 Tomaten, enthäutet, entkernt
und in kleine Würfel geschnittten,
50 ml Rotweinessig,
100 ml Olivenöl,
1 EL feingeschnittener Schnittlauch

Eine Terrine (ca. 26 cm lang) mit Frischhaltefolie auskleiden. Die Lauchstangen auf Terrinenlänge zurechtschneiden und in Salzwasser weichkochen; anschließend in eiskaltem Wasser abschrecken und abtropfen lassen. Das Olivenöl erhitzen und darin die Pilze dünsten. Mit Salz und Pfeffer würzen und erkalten lassen.

Etwa ein Drittel der Pilze in die Terrinenform legen und flachdrücken. Darauf eine Lage Lauchstangen dicht einlegen, dabei mit den grünen und den weißen Enden abwechseln. Mit einer weiteren Schicht Pilze bedecken und fortfahren, bis Pilze und Lauchstangen aufgebraucht sind. Die Folie über der gefüllten Terrine zusammenschlagen, gut beschweren und mindestens sechs Stunden kaltstellen.

Für die Tomatenvinaigrette: Alle Zutaten verrühren und mit Salz und Pfeffer würzen. Zum Servieren: Die Terrine auf ein Schneidebrett stürzen und mit einem scharfen Messer in Scheiben schneiden. Auf Teller anrichten, dann die Folie entfernen. Mit der Tomatenvinaigrette umgießen und servieren.

RISOTTO WITH WILD MUSHROOMS

RISOTTO MIT WALDPILZEN

For 4 persons:

1 tbsp butter
1 shallot, finely chopped,
160 g/5 oz/²/₃ cup arborio rice, washed,
160 ml/5 fl oz/²/₃ cup strong chicken stock

For the mushroom sauce:
1 tbsp butter,
1 shallot, finely chopped,
350 g/12 oz mixed wild mushrooms, sliced,
1 tsp flour,
2 tbsp Madeira,
2 tbsp white wine,
150 ml/5 fl oz/³/₅ cup brown veal stock,
100 ml/3¹/₂ fl oz/²/₅ cup double cream,
¹/₂ tsp lemon juice,
salt, freshly ground pepper

80 ml/2²/₃ fl oz/¹/₃ cup chicken stock,
4 tbsp freshly grated Parmesan,
2 tbsp whipped cream,
40 g/1¹/₃ oz/¹/₆ cup horn of plenty mushrooms,
2 tbsp champagne,
finely chopped chives

Melt the butter in a saucepan with a heavy base. Sauté the shallot until transparent without changing colour. Add the rice and sauté, stirring until it becomes slightly transparent.

Pour in the stock and simmer the rice for ten minutes on a low heat, stirring frequently. Remove from the stove.

For the mushrooms: Heat the butter in a saucepan and sauté the shallot over a low heat until transparent. Add the mushrooms and cook until softened. Dust with the flour and stir well. Add the white wine and Madeira and reduce a little. Then add the veal stock and reduce again. Stir in the double cream and reduce to half the quantity. Add the lemon juice and season with salt and freshly ground pepper.

Gradually stir the remaining stock, mushroom sauce, cheese, whipped cream and horn of plenty mushrooms into the pre-cooked risotto and simmer again for ten minutes on a low heat. Stir frequently with a wooden spoon.

Finally fold in the champagne and the chives. If necessary adjust the seasoning with salt and pepper, then serve immediately.

Für 4 Personen:

1 EL Butter,
1 Schalotte, fein gehackt,
160 g Arborio-Reis, gewaschen,
160 ml kräftige Hühnerbrühe

Für die Pilzsauce:
1 EL Butter,
1 Schalotte, fein gehackt,
350 g gemischte Waldpilze, in Scheiben geschnitten,
1 TL Mehl,
2 EL Madeira,
2 EL Weißwein,
150 ml brauner Kalbsfond,
100 ml Doppelrahm,
¹/₂ TL Zitronensaft,
Salz, Pfeffer aus der Mühle

80 ml Hühnerbrühe,
4 EL frisch geriebener Parmesan,
2 EL geschlagene Sahne,
40 g Herbsttrompeten,
2 EL Champagner,
Schnittlauch, fein geschnitten

Butter in einem Topf mit dickem Boden schmelzen lassen. Schalotte darin glasig dünsten, ohne daß sie Farbe nimmt. Reis zufügen und unter Rühren dünsten, bis er leicht durchsichtig wird. Die Brühe eingießen und den Reis zehn Minuten bei kleiner Hitze köcheln lassen, dabei immer wieder umrühren. Vom Herd nehmen.

Für die Pilze: Butter in einem Topf erhitzen und die Schalotte bei kleiner Hitze glasig dünsten. Pilze zugeben und weichdünsten. Mit Mehl bestäuben und gut umrühren. Den Weißwein und Madeira zugeben, etwas einkochen lassen. Dann den Kalbsfond dazu gießen, erneut einkochen lassen. Den Doppelrahm einrühren und auf die halbe Menge reduzieren. Mit Zitronensaft würzen, mit Salz und Pfeffer abschmecken.

Restliche Brühe, Pilzsauce, Käse, Schlagsahne und Herbsttrompeten nach und nach unter das vorgekochte Risotto rühren und bei kleiner Hitze insgesamt nochmal zehn Minuten köcheln lassen. Dabei oft mit einem Holzlöffel umrühren.

Zum Schluß den Champagner und den Schnittlauch unterrühren. Risotto wenn nötig mit Salz und Pfeffer abschmecken, dann sofort servieren.

SALMON AND HALIBUT SASHIMI
WITH SPRING ONION AND TOASTED SESAME

SASHIMI VON LACHS UND HEILBUTT
MIT FRÜHLINGSZWIEBELN UND SESAM

For 4 persons:

250 g/9 oz extremely fresh salmon fillet,
finely sliced,
200 g/7 oz extremely fresh halibut fillet,
finely sliced

For the sashimi dressing:
2 tbsp sake,
3 tbsp mirin (sweet rice wine),
1 piece kombu (dried kelp)
of about 2 cm/⁴/₅ in, soaked,
1 tbsp tamari sauce
(made from fermented soy beans),
225 ml/7¹/₂ fl oz/⁴/₅ cup dark soy sauce,
2 tsp dried bonito flakes

2 tbsp finely sliced spring onions,
2 tsp lightly toasted sesame seeds,
a few coriander leaves

Für 4 Personen:

250 g sehr frisches Lachsfilet,
in dünne Scheiben geschnitten,
200 g sehr frisches Heilbuttfilet,
in dünne Scheiben geschnitten

Für die Sashimisauce:
2 EL Sake,
3 EL Mirin (süßer Reiswein),
1 ca. 2 cm großese Stück Kombu
(getrockneter Seetang), gewässert,
1 EL Tamari-Sauce (wird aus
gegärten Sojabohnen hergestellt),
225 ml dunkle Sojasauce,
2 TL getrocknete Thunfischflocken

2 EL in feine Scheiben geschnittene Frühlingszwiebeln,
2 TL leicht geröstete Sesamsamen,
etwas Koriandergrün

For the sashimi dressing: Lightly warm the sake and mirin in a saucepan and ignite with a match to burn off the alcohol.

Add the remaining ingredients and simmer for five minutes. Allow to go cold and stand the dressing in the refrigerator for five to six hours.

Paint a spoon of sashimi dressing on each plate and sprinkle lightly with salt and pepper. Lay the halibut and salmon slices on the plates. Paint the fish liberally with sashimi dressing. Sprinkle with spring onions and sesame and decorate with coriander leaves.

Für die Sashimisauce: Sake und Mirin in einem Topf leicht erwärmen und dann mit einem Streichholz anzünden, damit sich der Alkohol verflüchtigt. Die restlichen Zutaten zugeben und fünf Minuten köcheln lassen. Erkalten lassen und die Sauce im Kühlschrank fünf bis sechs Stunden ziehen lassen. Die Teller mit je einem Löffel Sashimisauce auspinseln und leicht mit Salz und Pfeffer bestreuen. Heilbutt- und Lachsscheiben auf den Tellern auslegen. Das Fischfleisch großzügig mit Sashimisauce bepinseln. Mit Frühlingszwiebeln und Sesam bestreuen, mit Korianderblättchen dekorieren.

LAMB NOISETTES WITH A MUSTARD AND HERB CRUST

LAMMNÜSSCHEN MIT SENF- UND KRÄUTERKRUSTE

For 4 persons:

4 lamb noisettes, 150 g/5 oz each, cut from the loin,
trimmed and all fat removed,
a sprig of thyme and rosemary,
2 tbsp olive oil,
salt, freshly ground pepper,
2 tsp Dijon mustard,
2 tsp grain mustard,
4 tbsp finely chopped herbs:
chives, parsley, basil, and tarragon,
200 ml/7 fl oz/⁴/₅ cup brown lamb stock,
1 tsp grain mustard

300 g/10 oz cut vegetables (carrots, red onions,
baby leeks, red and yellow bell pepper),
1 tbsp olive oil

Place the oil with the sprigs of herbs in a plate, turn the lamb in it until it is evenly coated with oil, then marinate for two hours.

Remove the meat from the marinade and dab off the oil with kitchen paper. Sprinkle with salt and pepper and grill the lamb noisettes on both sides for two to three minutes; they should remain pink inside.

Mix together the two kinds of mustard and coat the lamb noisettes with mustard on one side. Press the mustard side into the herbs, brown briefly under the grill, then keep the meat in a warm place.

For the sauce: Reduce the lamb stock to half the volume, then stir in the mustard.

Stir-fry the vegetables in the oil for a few minutes, leaving them slightly crisp. Season with salt and pepper and arrange on warmed plates.

Pour over a little sauce, then lay the lamb on top and serve.

Für 4 Personen:

4 Lammnüßchen von je 150 g, aus der Lende
geschnitten, pariert und von jeglichem Fett befreit,
je ein Zweig Thymian und Rosmarin,
2 EL Olivenöl,
Salz, Pfeffer aus der Mühle,
2 TL Dijon Senf,
2 TL grobkörniger Senf,
4 EL feingeschnittene Kräuter:
Schnittlauch, Petersilie, Basilikum und Estragon,
200 ml brauner Lammfond,
1 TL grobkörniger Senf

300 g geputztes, zugeschnittenes Gemüse (Karotten,
rote Zwiebeln, Minilauch, rote und gelbe Paprika),
1 EL Olivenöl

Das Öl mit den Kräuterzweigen in einen Teller geben, das Lammfleisch darin wenden, bis es gleichmäßig mit Öl überzogen ist, dann zwei Stunden marinieren lassen. Das Fleisch aus der Marinade nehmen und mit Küchenpapier das Öl abtupfen. Mit Salz und Pfeffer bestreuen und die Lammnüßchen auf beiden Seiten zwei bis drei Minuten grillieren; innen sollen sie noch rosa bleiben. Die zwei Senfsorten vermischen und die Lammnüßchen auf einer Seite damit bestreichen. Die Senfseite in die Kräuter drücken, kurz unter dem Grill bräunen, das Fleisch anschließend warmhalten.

Für die Sauce: Den Lammfond auf die halbe Menge einkochen, dann mit dem Senf verrühren.

Die Gemüse im Öl einige Minuten unter Rühren knackig-weich dünsten. Mit Salz und Pfeffer würzen und auf vorgewärmte Teller verteilen. Mit etwas Sauce übergießen, dann das Lammfleisch obendrauf legen und servieren.

BREAD AND BUTTER PUDDING

BROT- UND BUTTERPUDDING

For 4 persons:

250 ml/8 fl oz/1 cup milk,
250 ml/8 fl oz/1 cup double cream,
a pinch of salt,
1 vanilla pod, split,
3 eggs,
125 g/4 oz/1/2 cup sugar,
3 white bread rolls,
2 tbsp butter,
1 tbsp sultanas, soaked in water,
2 tbsp apricot jam,
icing sugar to dust

Place the milk, double cream, salt and vanilla in a saucepan and bring to the boil.

Stir the eggs with the sugar in a bowl until pale. Remove the vanilla pod and gradually pour the hot milk into the egg mixture, stirring vigorously. Strain through a sieve. Slice the rolls, removing most of the crust. Butter an ovenproof porcelain dish. Spread the remaining butter on the slices of bread and arrange them in the base of the dish.

Drain the sultanas in a sieve and sprinkle over the bread slices. Then pour on the hot milk and egg mixture. The bread will now float to the top.

For the bain-marie lay a folded newspaper in an ovenproof vessel that is larger than the pudding dish. Place the pudding dish on the newspaper and half-fill the vessel with boiling water.

Bake in the preheated oven at 160° C/320° F for forty-five to fifty minutes.

When the pudding is ready it should wobble very slightly in the middle. Remove from the oven and cool a little.

Gently heat the apricot jam, thinning with a little water if necessary. Lightly brush the top of the pudding with the glaze. Dust with icing sugar and serve slightly warm.

Für 4 Personen:

250 ml Milch,
250 ml Doppelrahm,
eine Prise Salz,
1 Vanillestengel, aufgeschnitten,
3 Eier,
125 g Zucker,
3 weiße Brötchen,
2 EL Butter,
1 EL Sultaninen, in Wasser eingeweicht,
2 EL Aprikosenmarmelade,
Puderzucker zum Bestäuben

Milch mit Doppelrahm, Salz und Vanille in einem Topf zum Kochen bringen. Eier und dem Zucker in einer Schüssel verrühren, bis die Masse hellgelb ist. Vanillestengel herausnehmen und die heiße Milch unter kräftigem Rühren nach und nach in die Eiermasse gießen, durch ein Sieb passieren.

Brötchen in Scheiben schneiden, dabei die Kruste größtenteils entfernen. Eine feuerfeste Porzellanform mit Butter bepinseln. Die Brotscheiben mit der restlichen Butter betreichen und flach in der Form auslegen. Gut abgetropfte Sultaninen über die Brotscheiben streuen, dann die heiße Milch-Eiermasse darübergießen. Das Brot wird jetzt obenauf schwimmen. Für das Wasserbad in ein feuerfestes Gefäß, das größer ist als die Puddingform, eine gefaltete Zeitung legen. Die Form hineinstellen und das Wasserbad bis auf halbe Höhe des Gefäßes mit kochendem Wasser aufgießen. Das Ganze im auf 160° C vorgeheizten Ofen 45 - 50 Minuten backen. Der Pudding ist fertig, wenn er nur in der Mitte noch leicht wabbelig ist. Aus dem Ofen nehmen und etwas abkühlen lassen. Die Marmelade leicht erhitzen, wenn nötig mit etwas Wasser verdünnen. Mit einem Pinsel die Puddingkruste damit bestreichen. Mit Puderzucker bestäubt lauwarm servieren.

SUMMER PUDDING

SOMMERPUDDING

For 4 persons:

2 gelatine leaves, soaked in cold water,
3 tbsp water,
juice of $^1/_2$ lemon,
100 g/3 $^1/_2$ oz/$^2/_5$ cup each of ripe strawberries,
raspberries, and blackberries (or blueberries)

4 large, thin slices of bread, without crust

Coulis:
200 g/7 oz/$^4/_5$ cup ripe raspberries,
2 tbsp icing sugar,
1 tbsp freshly pressed lemon juice

To garnish:
strawberries, raspberries, and blackberries,
4 small sprigs of mint,
icing sugar

Für 4 Personen:

2 Blätter Gelatine, in kaltem Wasser eingeweicht,
3 EL Wasser,
Saft einer halben Zitrone,
je 100 g reife Erdbeeren, Himbeeren und Brombeeren
(oder Blaubeeren)

4 große, dünn geschnittene Brotscheiben, ohne Kruste

Coulis:
200 g reife Himbeeren,
2 EL Puderzucker,
1 EL frischgepreßter Zitronensaft

Zum Garnieren:
Erdbeeren, Himbeeren und Brombeeren,
4 kleine Zweigchen Minze,
Puderzucker

Squeeze the gelatine dry, then warm gently with the water and lemon juice until dissolved. Divide this liquid into three small pans.

Slowly heat the berries separately in the pans until the juices just start to run but the fruits still hold their shape (do not boil). Allow to cool. Cut the bread slices into triangles.

Lightly oil four dariole moulds (preferably round and without sharp edges), and line as completely as possible with about half of the bread.

Place alternate layers of individual fruits and some of the remaining bread in the moulds, pour over the remaining fruit juice, and top with a layer of bread. Cover each mould with a saucer, and weight down so that the pudding is lightly pressed. Stand in the refrigerator overnight so that the juices can soak through the bread.

For the coulis: Press the raspberries through a non-metal sieve and mix the pulp with the icing sugar and lemon juice.

To serve: Unmould the puddings onto plates and cover evenly with the coulis.

Decorate with the mixed berries and sprigs of mint, and dust as desired with icing sugar.

Gelatine ausdrücken und mit dem Wasser und dem Zitronensaft leicht erwärmen, bis sie sich auflöst. Die Mischung in drei kleine Töpfe verteilen.

Die Beeren einzeln in den Töpfchen langsam erwärmen, bis der Saft heraustritt, die Früchte aber größtenteils noch intakt sind (nicht kochen). Abkühlen lassen. Brotscheiben in Dreiecke schneiden.

Vier Puddingförmchen (vorzugsweise rund und ohne Kanten) leicht mit Öl bestreichen und mit ca. der Häfte des Brotes möglichst vollständig auskleiden. Die drei Beerensorten abwechselnd mit dem restlichen Brot einfüllen, mit dem verbleibenden Beerensaft begießen und zum Schluß mit einer Lage Brot belegen. Jedes Förmchen mit einer Untertasse bedecken, diese beschweren, so daß der Pudding leicht gepreßt wird. Im Kühlschrank über Nacht stehen lassen, damit das Brot den Beerensaft voll aufnehmen kann. Für den Coulis: Himbeeren durch ein nicht metallenes Sieb streichen und das Fruchtmark mit dem Puderzucker und dem Zitronensaft verrühren. Zum Servieren: Die Puddings einzeln auf Teller stürzen und gleichmäßig mit dem Coulis überziehen. Mit gemischten Beeren und Minze dekorieren, nach Belieben mit Puderzucker bestäuben.

THE DORCHESTER

*T*he Dorchester, by Hyde Park, is a legend of an hotel that goes back 65 years. Legends can grow dusty and then exist actually only as a memory. But they can also be kept fresh and made fit for the next 65 years. This has happened, and this house now sets the standard on these islands as concerns luxury hotels. For this purpose – of necessity – a lot of money was needed, and was forthcoming after the Sultan of Brunei had chosen the Dorchester as the nucleus of his exclusive Audley Group. Money that was

also invested to let a quite special Dorchester tradition live on: namely the ambition to prove that hotel cuisine can be first-class. That this is posssible has been demonstrated by another Dorchester tradition: Anton Mosimann, from 1977 to 1988 master of all the Dorchester cooking pots, cooked up two Michelin stars for the first time in any hotel kitchen outside of France. Today Willi Elsener, a fellow Swiss, and his right-hand man, the Swabian Henry Brosi, direct the 150-member kitchen team of the Dorchester restaurant with cool authority.

The Dorchester Grill is the London address where proof is to be had that traditional British fare can also be outstanding. The cook must only want to prove it! This commences with an incomparable Scotch wild salmon with capers, continues with butter-tender pink roast Angus beef with Yorkshire pudding from the trolley with the impressive silver dome. Then comes a perfect shepherd's pie, lamb topped with a layer of mashed potato and baked. To finish, there is a stupendous selection of English cheeses and desserts.

In the Oriental, Hong Kong-born Simon Yung, regarded as one of the best east-Asian chefs in Europe, shows what Chinese cuisine means at Michelin star level. Stepping from the hotel promenade through the door into the Oriental is like stepping into another world. Oriental works of art and silk wall hangings welcome the guest. Three private dining rooms are appointed with valuable Thai, Chinese and Indian objects.

Star at the wok Yung composes Cantonese cuisine here, known to be one of China's best: ravishing dim sum, dishes of chicken with such deliciously exotic spicing as one has never tasted before. And of course such Asian classics as shark's fin soup or abalone clams. But Simon Yung likes best of all to discuss the sequence of dishes with a guest and then match the guest's special preferences with his own creativity.

The bar of the Dorchester offers light Italian pasta dishes as well as an opulent antipasti buffet for anyone hungry between meals. Whether traditionally British, Chinese or Italian: above all there stands Willi Elsener's culinary philosophy, which sounds so simple, but which must be newly applied and worked at each day afresh: "Physical health and spiritual wellbeing depend not least on what we eat. We are what we eat!"

*D*as Dorchester am Hyde Park ist eine Hotel-Legende mit nunmehr über 65 Jahren Geschichte. Legenden können verstauben, und dann existieren sie wirklich nur noch in der Erinnerung. Man kann sie aber auch frisch halten und fit machen für die nächsten 65 Jahre. Das ist hier geschehen, und das Haus setzt nunmehr die Maßstäbe auf der Insel in Sachen Hotel. Hierzu war – notwendigerweise – viel Geld nötig, das da war, nachdem der Sultan von Brunei das Dorchester als Keimzelle seiner exklusiven Audley Group auserwählt hatte. Geld, das auch eingesetzt wurde, um eine besondere

Dorchester-Tradition
weiterleben zu lassen:
den Ehrgeiz nämlich,
zu beweisen, daß Hotel-
küche erstklassig sein
kann. Daß dies möglich
ist, hat eine andere
Dorchester-Legende
vorgemacht: Anton
Mosimann, von 1975 bis
1988 Herrscher über alle
Dorchester-Kochtöpfe,
hat hier erstmals einer
Hotelküche außerhalb
Frankreichs zwei
Michelin-Sterne herbei-
gekocht. Heute dirigieren
Willi Elsener, ein
Schweizer wie Mosimann,
und dessen rechte Hand,
der Schwabe Henry Brosi,
mit souveräner Gelassen-
heit das 150-köpfige
Küchenteam der
Dorchester-Restaurants.

Willi Elsener

Der Dorchester-Grill-Room ist jene Adresse in London, wo bewiesen wird, daß auch traditionelle englische Küche ihre Höhepunkte haben kann. Man muß als Koch nur wollen! Das beginnt etwa mit einem unvergleichlichen schottischen Wildlachs mit Kapern, geht weiter mit einem butterzarten, rosa gebratenen Angus-Beef mit Yorkshire-Pudding vom Trolley mit der beeindruckenden Silberhaube. Das setzt sich fort mit einem perfekten Shepherd's Pie, dem mit Kartoffelpüree überbackenem Lammfleisch und hört bei einer stupenden Auswahl englischer Käse und Süßspeisen noch lange nicht auf.

Im Oriental zeigt Simon Yung, der in Hong Kong geboren ist und als einer der besten östlichen Küchenchefs in Europa gilt, was chinesische Küche auf Sterne-Niveau heißt. Der Schritt von der Hotel-Promenade durch die Türe ins Oriental ist ein Schritt in eine andere Welt. Fernöstliche Kunstwerke und Seidentapeten empfangen den Gast. Drei private Speiseräume sind mit thailändischen, chinesischen beziehungsweise indischen Pretiosen ausgestattet. Wok-Star Yung komponiert hier kantonesische Küche, ohnehin eine der besten Chinas: hinreißende Dim Sum. Gerichte mit Hühnerfleisch, so lecker exotisch gewürzt, wie man es zuvor nicht erlebt hat. Und natürlich die asiatischen Klassiker wie Haifisch-flossensuppe oder Abalone-Muscheln. Am liebsten aber ist es Simon Yung, wenn er mit einem Gast das Menü vorbesprechen und dann dessen spezielle Vorstellungen mit seiner eigenen Kreativität paaren kann.

Die Bar im Dorchester bietet leichte italienische Pasta-Gerichte nebst einem opulenten Antipasti-Buffet für den Hunger zwischendurch. Ob klassisch englisch, chinesisch oder italienisch: über allem steht Willi Elseners Küchenphilosophie, die so einfach klingt, die aber jeden Tag neu durchgesetzt und erarbeitet werden muß: „Körperliche Gesundheit und geistiges Wohlbefinden hängen nicht zuletzt von dem was wir essen ab. Wir sind, was wir essen!"

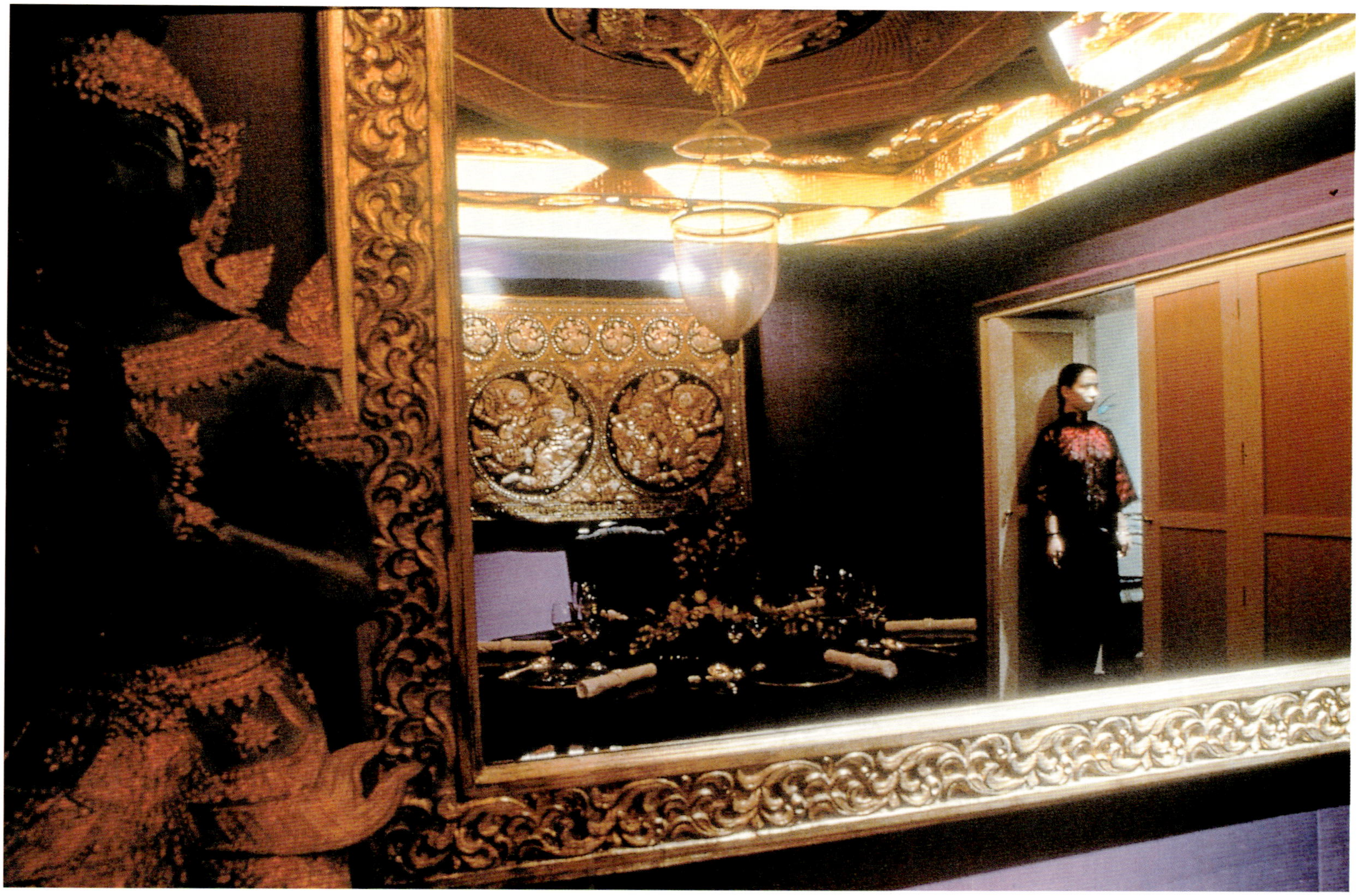

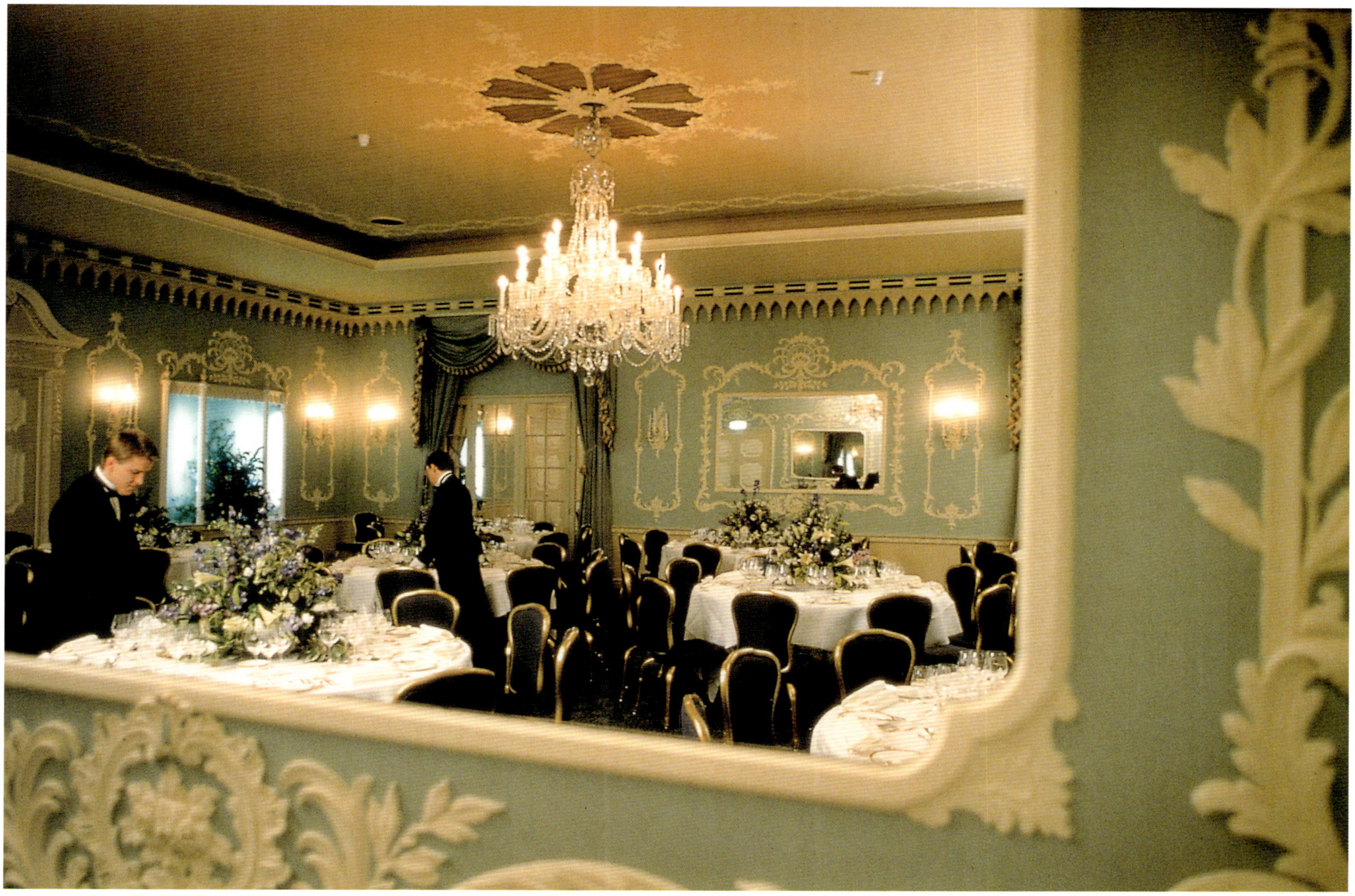

THE DORCHESTER CLUB

DAILY MENU

Starters

Salad of warm, pan-fried south coast scallops in lime and kumquat dressing
£19.50

Chicken livers and bacon served on young spinach leaves and marinated mushrooms
£13.00

Pan-fried foie gras served on a toasted brioche
£27.50

Club Caesar salad
£11.00

Scottish smoked salmon
£16.00

Cornish dressed crab
£17.00

Half Scottish lobster served with a mango salad
£28.00

Tomato and mozzarella salad with balsamic vinaigrette
£12.00

Scottish wild salmon and char-grilled vegetable terrine served with spicy red radish cream
£13.00

Soups

Chicken broth with vegetables
£8.50

Lobster bisque
£9.50

Gazpacho with condiments
£9.00

Pastas

Fusilli with traditional pesto and parmesan shavings
£12.00

Classic risotto with pan-fried goose liver
£17.50

Pennette with wild mushrooms and gorgonzola sauce
£14.00

Tagliolini with spicy scampi and tomatoes
£16.00

Seafood

Grilled prawns with a hint of lemon and garlic
£25.00

Pan-fried fillet of sea bass on spicy aubergine purée with light curry sauce
£26.50

Breaded goujons of sole, sauce tartare
£21.00

Grilled red snapper served with stir-fried vegetables
£17.00

Seafood mixed grill with warm lemon and oil dressing
£23.00

Grilled Dover sole
£25.00

Whole Lobster Thermidor
£48.00

Oven-roasted escalope of brill with cracked wheat, tomato and herb crust
£18.00

Meat

Grilled chicken breast with salad and roasted peppers
£17.50

Peppered sirloin steak
£25.00

Grilled veal cutlet with wild mushrooms
£26.00

Club-beefburger served with French fries
£16.50

Roast duck breast and sausage with orange and coriander gravy
£21.00

Chateaubriand (for two)
£50.00

Rack of lamb with a herb and shallot crust
£27.00

Desserts

Selection of sorbets
£7.50

Apple and banana cake
£7.50

White and dark chocolate mousse
£7.50

Exotic fruit salad
£8.00

Passion fruit brulée
£7.50

Club Breakfast is served from 1.00am to 2.30am

Dining Room Manager: Claudio Micci   Service & Tax included   Executive Chef: Willi Elsener

THE GRILL ROOM

APPETIZERS

Scottish wild salmon and char-grilled vegetable terrine served with spicy red radish	£12.00
Warm Stilton and leek tart	£11.00
Morecambe Bay potted shrimps	£9.50
Chicken livers served on young spinach leaves with marinated wild mushrooms	£13.50
Cornish dressed crab	£17.00
Layered goose liver and lentils with fig and onion chutney	£20.50
Salad of warm, pan-fried south coast scallops in lime and kumquat dressing	£19.50
Pan-fried goat's cheese 'piccata' with asparagus and mixed leaf salad with grape seed oil dressing	£11.00
Smoked Scottish salmon carved at the trolley	£16.00
B Ginger crab cakes	£18.00

SOUPS AND BROTHS

Cock-a-leekie soup	£8.50
Cream of lobster soup	£9.50
Brown onion soup with crusty cheese bread	£8.50

FISH AND SHELLFISH

Pan-fried fillet of seabass on aubergine puree with a light curry sauce	£24.50
Oven-roasted escalope of brill with cracked wheat, tomato and herb crust	£21.00
Glazed ragout of Finnan haddock and asparagus with a poached egg	£19.50
Pan-fried Dover sole stuffed with prawns and wild mushrooms	£28.00
B Pan-seared seabass with celery root ravioli	£24.50

GRILL ROOM FAVOURITES

Roast Angus beef with Yorkshire pudding and roast potatoes	£21.00
Classic shepherd's pie	£17.50
Rosette of beef with wild mushrooms and artichokes flavoured with horseradish	£28.50
Rack of lamb with a herb and shallot crust and East Anglian mustard	£27.50
Traditional steak and kidney pie	£18.50
Hereford duck breast and sausage with orange and coriander gravy	£22.00
Roast loin of lamb wrapped in Cumberland ham with crepe mushrooms on a rice galette	£28.00
B Corn-crusted chicken breast with horseradish	£19.50

GRILLS

Dover sole (300g)	£28.00	Liver and bacon	£23.00
Turbot steak (250g)	£27.50	Dorchester mixed grill	£27.00
Salmon (250g)	£21.00	Scottish sirloin steak (200g)	£26.00
Whole Scottish lobster	£48.00	T-bone steak (200g)	£28.00
		Fillet steak (200g)	£27.50

B Signature dishes from The Dorchester's sister hotel, The Beverly Hills Hotel in California
All Main Course dishes are served with potatoes and vegetables of the day.
A selection of vegetarian dishes is available.

4.97

THE DORCHESTER

PENTHOUSE & PAVILION

SPECIAL MENU SELECTION
PRICES

Lunch or Dinner

PPA	£45.00	*Lunch only*
PPB	£45.00	*Lunch only*
PPC	£50.00	
PPD	£52.00	
PPE	£52.00	
PPF	£55.00	
PPG	£57.00	
PPH	£60.00	
PPI	£60.00	
PPJ	£62.00	
PPK	£65.00	
PPL	£67.50	

Cocktail Party

CPAA	£21.00
CPBB	£22.00
CPCC	£24.00
CPDD	£26.00

Prices include both hot and cold canapes

ALL PRICES INCLUDE SERVICE AND VALUE ADDED TAX

4/96

THE DORCHESTER

M E N U

PENTHOUSE & PAVILION

Special Selection

Lunch Only

TERRINE DE TROIS POIVRONS ACCOMPAGNÉ DE SUPRÊME DE CANARD FUMÉ
Three Pepper Terrine accompanied by Smoked Breast of Duck

ESCALOPE DE SAUMON SOUFFLÉ
SAUCE À L'OSEILLE
Escalope of Salmon with a Salmon Mousse
Sorrel Sauce

RIZ SAUVAGE À LA BRUNOISE DE POIREAUX
Wild Rice with diced Leek

FLEUR DE BROCOLI ET PETIT MAÏS
Florets of Broccoli and Baby Corn

GATEAU DE POMMES ET GINGEMBRE, GLACE À LA CANNELLE
Warm Apple and Ginger Cake served with a Cinnamon Ice Cream

CAFÉ
Délices des Dames

PPB

THE DORCHESTER

BANQUETING

MENU SELECTION
PRICES

Cocktail Party

CPAA	£21.00
CPBB	£22.00
CPCC	£24.00
CPDD	£26.00

ALL PRICES INCLUDE SERVICE AND VALUE ADDED TAX

4/96

THE DORCHESTER

MENU

Cocktails

HORS-D'OEUVRE FROIDS
A selection of cold canapes to include:

ROSETTE DE SAUMON FUME
Scotch smoked salmon

BARQUETTE AU FOIE DE VOLAILLE
Chicken liver parfait

TARTELETTE AUX POIVRONS DOUX
Tartlets of roasted red peppers and pesto

PIZZA AUX OLIVES ET MOZZARELLA
Olive and mozzarella pizza

RILLETTE DE CANARD SUR TOAST ET COMPOTE DE REINETTES
Rilettes of duck on toasted French bread with apple chutney

HORS-D'OEUVRE CHAUDS
A selection of hot canapes to include:

PALMIERS DE CHAMPIGNONS ET PARMESAN
Puff pastry with mushrooms and Parmesan cheese

GOUJONS DE SUPREME DE VOLAILLE, SAUCE AIGRE-DOUX
Strips of chicken with sweet and sour sauce

PETITES QUENELLES DE SAUMON
Mini salmon fish cakes

QUICHE AU JAMBON ET CONFIT D'ECHALOTES
Mini ham and shallot quiche

CPAA

THE DORCHESTER

M E N U

Cocktails

HORS-D'OEUVRE FROIDS
A selection of cold canapes to include:

CARPACCIO DE BOEUF ET TOMATE AU PARMESAN
*Carpaccio of beef on crusty French bread with sun-dried tomatoes
and shaved parmesan*

SALPICON DE POULET ET MANGUE
Ragout of chicken and mango

SAUMON FUME ET MOUSSE DE TRUITE
Smoked salmon and trout mousse

MEDAILLONS DE HOMARD ET CONFIT D'ASPERGES ET TOMATES
Lobster medallions with asparagus and tomato relish

PROFITEROLES A LA MOUSSE D'AVOCAT ET TRUITE
Choux pastry filled with avocado and trout mousse

HORS-D'OEUVRE CHAUDS
A selection of hot canapes to include:

KOFTA KEBAB
Lamb kofta kebab with coriander

QUICHE AUX ASPERGES ET CHAMPIGNONS SAUVAGES
Mini asparagus and wild mushroom tartlets

CREVETTES ET OKRA FRITES
Deep-fried king prawns and lady fingers

PETIT FEUILLETE AU CHOU-FLEUR
Puff pastry case with cauliflower cheese

CPBB

THE DORCHESTER

M E N U

Cocktails

HORS-D'OEUVRE FROIDS
A selection of cold canapes to include:

SAUMON FUME SUR PAIN D'ITALIE, CREME FRAICHE
Smoked salmon pizza with sour cream and chives

CONFIT DE CANARD ET OIGNONS SUR BAGUETTE
Toasted French bread topped with a confit of onion and duck

JAMBON DE PARME ET RAISINS
Parma ham with grapes

RAGOUT DE POISSONS DE MER AU CAVIAR
Flaked fish bound with cocktail sauce and topped with caviar

BOULES DE STILTON AUX PERLES DE SESAME
Creamed Stilton cheese coated with sesame seeds

HORS-D'OEUVRE CHAUDS
A selection of hot canapes to include:

PETIT HAMBURGER AU CORIANDRE
Meatballs in tomato sauce with coriander

ROULADES DE PRINTEMPS, SAUCE AIGRE-DOUX
Spring rolls with sweet and sour dip

CREVETTES GEANTES FRITES
Deep-fried king prawns with tartare sauce

RISSOLES AUX CHAMPIGNONS SAUVAGES
Small pork and chicken patties filled with wild mushrooms and herbs

CPCC

CHICKEN BREAST WRAPPED IN PARMA HAM ON ASPARAGUS SALAD

HÜHNERBRUST IN PARMASCHINKEN AUF SPARGELSALAT

For 2 persons:

2 chicken breasts,
2 basil leaves,
2 slices Parma ham,
2 tbsp sunflower oil,

3 sticks of white asparagus,
3 sticks of green asparagus,
mixed salad leaves, ruccola, frisée,
mâche (lamb's lettuce),
2 small plum tomatoes, sliced

For the dressing:
1 tbsp balsamic vinegar,
1 tbsp white-wine vinegar,
1 tbsp sesame oil,
3 tbsp sunflower oil,
salt, freshly ground pepper

Lay a basil leaf on each chicken breast and carefully wrap each one with a slice of Parma ham. Peel the asparagus, cut off 2 cm/ $^4/_5$ in from the dry ends and boil for ten minutes in salted water until cooked but still crisp. Refresh in cold water. Then cut into 3 cm/ 1 $^1/_5$ in pieces, retaining the cooking liquid.
For the dressing: Stir all the ingredients together with two spoons of the asparagus cooking liquid. Mix the asparagus pieces with the dressing and set aside.
Heat the sunflower oil in a non-stick ovenproof frying pan. Fry the chicken breasts on both sides until golden, then bake through in the oven preheated to 180° C/360° F for eight to ten minutes, depending on thickness.
To serve: Lay the tomato slices in a circle on the plates. Pile the leaf salads in the middle and arrange the asparagus pieces on top. Drizzle the salad with the remaining dressing. Lay the fried chicken on top and serve.

Für 2 Personen:

2 Hühnerbrüste,
2 Basilikumblätter,
2 Scheiben Parmaschinken,
2 EL Sonnenblumenöl

3 weiße Spargelstangen,
3 grüne Spargelstangen,
gemischte Blattsalate: Ruccola, Frisée,
Feldsalat,
2 kleine Flaschentomaten, in Scheiben geschnitten

Für das Dressing:
1 EL Balsamico Essig,
1 EL Weißweinessig,
1 EL Sesamöl,
3 EL Sonnenblumenöl,
Salz, Pfeffer aus der Mühle

Jede Hühnerbrust mit einem Basilikumblatt belegen, dann mit je einer Scheibe Parmaschinken vorsichtig umwickeln.
Spargel schälen, von den untere Enden 2 cm wegschneiden und in Salzwasser ca. 10 Minuten knackig-gar kochen. Kalt abschrecken, dann in 3 cm lange Stücke schneiden, Spargelsud aufheben.
Für das Dressing: Alle Zutaten zusammen mit zwei Eßlöffel Spargelsud verrühren. Spargelstücke mit dem Dressing vermischen, beiseite stellen.
Das Sonnenblumenöl in einer beschichteten, ofenfesten Pfanne erhitzen. Hühnerbrüste von beiden Seiten goldbraun anbraten, dann im auf 180° C vorgeheizten Ofen je nach Dicke acht bis zehn Minuten fertig garen.
Zum Servieren: Tomatenscheiben kreisförmig auf den Tellern auslegen. Blattsalate in die Mitte häufen und die Spargelstücke darüber verteilen. Verbleibendes Dressing über den Salat träufeln. Die gebratenen Hühnerbrüste darüber legen und servieren.

PAN-FRIED SCALLOPS ON TOMATO CONFIT

GEBRATENE JAKOBSMUSCHELN AUF TOMATENCONFIT

For 2 persons:

10 scallops, cleaned, no roe,
salt, freshly ground pepper,
2 tbsp sunflower oil

For the confit:
150 g/5 oz ripe cherry tomatoes, cut in half,
100 ml/3 ¹/₂ fl oz/²/₅ cup olive oil,
25 ml/2 tbsp white-wine vinegar,
20 g/²/₃ oz white caster sugar,
50 ml/1²/₃ fl oz/¹/₅ cup tomato juice,
¹/₂ clove garlic, finely chopped,
1 small shallot, finely chopped,
¹/₄ tsp each of rosemary and thyme, finely chopped,
¹/₂ tsp each of coriander and basil, finely chopped

Garnish:
2 gaufrette potato baskets filled with
mixed leaf salads (e.g. lollo rosso, oakleaf,
curly endive, mâche)

Für 2 Personen:

10 Jakobsmuscheln, ausgelöst, ohne Korail,
Salz, Pfeffer aus der Mühle,
2 EL Sonnenblumenöl

Für das Confit:
150 g vollreife Kirschtomaten, halbiert,
100 ml Olivenöl,
25 ml Weißweinessig,
20 g Grießzucker,
50 ml Tomatensaft,
¹/₂ Knoblauchzehe, feingehackt,
1 kleine Schalotte, feingehackt,
je ¹/₄ TL Rosmarin und Thymian, fein gehackt,
je ¹/₂ TL Koriandergrün und Basilikum, fein gehackt

Dekoration:
2 Körbchen aus Waffelkartoffeln, gefüllt mit
gemischten Blattsalaten (z.B. Lollo rosso, Eichblatt,
Krause Endivie, Feldsalat)

For the confit: Mix together in a small saucepan the olive oil, vinegar, sugar, tomato juice, garlic and shallots.
Add the tomatoes and heat through gently without boiling. Season with salt and pepper, stir in the chopped herbs, and keep warm.
Season the scallops with salt and pepper. Put them in the pan and fry on both sides in hot sunflower oil until light brown. Reduce the heat and cook the scallops through in about two minutes.
To serve: Distribute the tomato confit onto plates, place the filled potato baskets in the centre of the plate, and arrange the scallops around the baskets. Serve immediately.

Für das Confit: In einem kleinen Topf das Olivenöl mit dem Essig, dem Zucker, dem Tomatensaft, dem Knoblauch und der Schalotte vermischen. Tomaten zugeben und langsam erhitzen, ohne zu kochen. Mit Salz und Pfeffer würzen, die gehackten Kräuter unterrühren, warmhalten.
Jakobsmuscheln mit Salz und Pfeffer würzen, dann in einer Pfanne im heißen Sonnenblumenöl von beiden Seiten hellbraun anbraten. Hitze reduzieren, und ca. 2 Minuten fertiggaren.
Zum Servieren: Das Tomatenconfit auf Teller verteilen, die gefüllten Kartoffelkörbchen darauf setzen und die Jakobsmuscheln darum herum legen. Sofort servieren.

BAKED SALMON ON POTATO GNOCCHI WITH LIME AND BASIL

LACHS AUF KARTOFFELGNOCCHI MIT LIMONE UND BASILIKUM

For 2 persons:

*2 escalopes of salmon, each about 150 g/5 oz,
salt, freshly ground black pepper,
2 tbsp sunflower oil,
2 small sticks of lemon grass*

*Pesto:
1 tbsp pine kernels, finely crushed,
¹/₂ clove garlic, crushed,
2 tbsp olive oil,
1 tsp finely chopped parsley,
1 tsp finely chopped basil*

*Sauce:
150 ml/5 fl oz/³/₅ cup fish stock,
3 tbsp cream,
1 pinch grated lime zest*

*2 tbsp sunflower oil,
¹/₂ clove garlic, crushed,
¹/₂ a red and ¹/₂ green bell pepper, halved lengthways
and finely sliced,
4 button mushrooms, washed and cut into quarters,
160 g/5 oz potato gnocchi, cooked,
¹/₂ spring onion, finely sliced*

Für 2 Personen:

*2 Lachssteaks von je ca. 150 g,
Salz, schwarzer Pfeffer aus der Mühle,
2 EL Sonnenblumenöl,
2 kleine Stengel Zitronengras*

*Pesto:
1 EL Pinienkerne, fein zerstossen,
¹/₂ Knoblauchzehe, durchgedrückt,
2 EL Olivenöl,
1 TL feingehackte Petersilie,
1 TL feingehackter Basilikum*

*Sauce:
150 ml Fischfond,
3 EL Sahne,
1 Prise geriebene Zitronenschale*

*2 EL Sonnenblumenöl,
¹/₂ Knoblauchzehe, durchgedrückt,
je ¹/₂ rote und grüne Paprika, der Länge nach halbiert
und in dünne Streifen geschnitten,
4 Champignons, geputzt und in Viertel geschnitten,
160 g Kartoffelgnocchi, gekocht,
¹/₂ Frühlingszwiebel, in dünne Scheiben geschnitten*

Mix well all the ingredients for the pesto. For the sauce: Bring the fish stock to the boil in a saucepan over medium heat. Stir in the cream, simmer for three minutes, then stir in the pesto, flavour with the lime zest and season with salt and pepper. Set the saucepan aside.

Season the salmon steaks with salt and freshly ground pepper.

Heat the oil in a non-stick frying pan and fry the salmon on both sides until brown. Push the lemon grass sticks crosswise through the salmon and transfer the fish to an ovenproof dish. Heat the oven to 180° C/360° F and, depending on thickness, bake for six to eight minutes until done.

For the vegetables: Heat the oil with the garlic in a non-stick frying pan, then stir-fry the bell pepper and button mushrooms for one minute. Remove the vegetables and brown the gnocchi in the same frying pan. Add the spring onion and vegetables and season with salt and pepper.

To serve: Arrange the vegetables and gnocchi on plates and lay a salmon steak on top. Dribble a little hot sauce over the gnocchi and serve the remaining sauce separately.

Alle Zutaten für den Pesto gut verrühren. Für die Sauce: Den Fischfond in einem Topf bei mittlerer Hitze zum Kochen bringen. Sahne einrühren, drei Minuten köcheln lassen, dann den Pesto einrühren, mit der Zitronenschale würzen und mit Salz und Pfeffer abschmecken. Den Topf beiseite stellen.

Die Lachssteaks mit Salz und frisch gemahlenem Pfeffer würzen. Das Öl in einer beschichteten Pfanne erhitzen, dann den Lachs von beiden Seiten braun anbraten. Die Zitronengrasstengel quer durch die Filets stecken und den Fisch in ein feuerfestes Geschirr umfüllen. Im auf 180° C vorgeheizten Ofen je nach Dicke sechs bis acht Minuten fertiggaren.

Für die Gemüse: Das Öl mit dem Knoblauch in einer beschichteten Pfanne erhitzen, dann die Paprika und die Champignons darin eine Minute unter Rühren braten. Gemüse herausnehmen, dann die Gnocchi in der gleichen Pfanne bräunen. Frühlingszwiebel und Gemüse zugeben, mit Salz und Pfeffer würzen.

Zum Servieren: Die Gemüse und Gnocchi auf Teller anrichten, je ein Lachssteak darüber legen. Etwas heiße Sauce über die Gnocchi träufeln, die restliche Sauce separat dazu reichen.

FILLET OF SEA BASS WITH CHINESE GREENS
WOLFSBARSCHFILET MIT CHINAGEMÜSE

<table>
<tr><td>

For 2 persons:

For the sauce:
1 shallot, peeled and finely sliced,
100 ml/3 1/2 fl oz/ 2/5 cup red wine, 2 tbsp port wine,
100 ml/3 1/2 fl oz/ 2/5 cup fish stock, 2 tbsp double cream,
3 tbsp cold butter, cut into cubes,
salt and freshly ground pepper

2 thick sea bass fillets, each about 150 g/5 oz,
4 tsp sesame oil, 1/2 tsp chopped, fresh coriander,
1 pinch finely grated lemon zest,
6 new potatoes, peeled and cooked not quite through,
6 silverskin onions, peeled and cooked,
6 medium-sized shiitake mushrooms, cut in half,
6 heads of Chinese flowering cabbage, thick stalks only, cooked,
6 slices of carrot, cooked,
6 baby corn cobs, cooked,
salt, freshly ground pepper,

2 bayleaves, fried in hot oil

</td><td>

Für 2 Personen:

Für die Sauce:
1 Schalotte, geschält und in feine Scheiben geschnitten,
100 ml Rotwein, 2 EL Portwein,
100 ml Fischfond, 2 EL Doppelrahm,
3 EL kalte Butter, in Würfel geschnitten,
Salz, Pfeffer aus der Mühle

2 dicke Scheiben Wolfsbarschfilet, je ca. 150 g,
4 TL Sesamöl, 1/2 TL gehacktes Koriandergrün,
1 Prise feingeriebene Zitronenschale,
6 neue Kartoffeln, geschält und knapp gar gekocht,
6 Silberzwiebeln, geschält und gekocht,
6 mittelgroße Shiitakepilze, halbiert,
6 Chinakohl, nur den mittleren dicken Stengel, gekocht,
6 Karottenscheiben, gekocht,
6 Minimaiskolben, gekocht,
Salz, Pfeffer aus der Mühle

2 Lorbeerblätter, in heißem Öl fritiert

</td></tr>
</table>

For the sauce: Place the shallot, red wine, port wine and fish stock in a saucepan, bring to the boil and simmer till only three spoons of liquid remain. Add the double cream. Return to the boil, then pass through a sieve into a smaller saucepan, pressing out all the liquid with a spoon. Return to the boil, then remove from the heat and stir in the butter. Season with salt and pepper and keep the sauce warm.

Slash the skin of the fish steaks twice. Lay flat with the skin down and cut a pocket from one side to beyond the centre. Stir a tsp of the sesame oil with the coriander and the lemon zest and stuff into the fish.

Heat a non-stick ovenproof frying pan with the remaining sesame oil. Season the fish steaks with salt and freshly ground pepper, then lay in the hot oil skin-side down and fry until the skin is brown and crispy. Turn the fish steaks over and place the pan in the oven preheated to 180° C/360° F. Bake for about eight minutes.

Remove the fish from the pan and keep warm. Then place the potatoes and the onions in the pan and roast in the oven for four minutes.

Add the mushrooms, stir, and roast for five minutes more. Then place the frying pan on the stove and heat the Chinese cabbage, carrots, and baby corn. Season with salt and pepper.

To serve: Place the fish steaks in the middle of the plate, surround with the vegetables and stick one fried bayleaf into each piece of fish. Serve the sauce separately.

Für die Sauce: Schalotte mit Wein, Portwein und Fischfond in einem Topf zum Kochen bringen und bis auf drei Eßlöffel einkochen lassen. Doppelrahm hinzufügen, zum Kochen bringen, dann durch ein Sieb in ein Saucenpfännchen passieren, dabei mit einem Löffel alle Flüssigkeit durchpressen. Nochmals erhitzen, dann vom Herd nehmen und die Butter einrühren; mit Salz und Pfeffer abschmecken, warmstellen. Die Haut der Fischsteaks je zweimal einschneiden. Mit der Haut nach unten flach hinlegen und von einer Seite bis über die Mitte eine Tasche einschneiden. Einen Teelöffel von dem Sesamöl mit dem Koriander und der Zitronenschale verrühren und in den Fisch füllen.

Eine beschichtete, ofenfeste Pfanne mit dem restlichen Sesamöl erhitzen. Fischsteaks mit Salz und frischgemahlenem Pfeffer würzen, dann mit der Hautseite nach unten in das heiße Fett legen, braten, bis die Haut knusprig braun ist. Fischsteaks umdrehen und die Pfanne in den auf 180° C vorgeheizten Ofen schieben. Ungefähr acht Minuten backen. Fisch aus der Pfanne nehmen, warmhalten. Dann die Kartoffeln und die Zwiebeln in die Pfanne geben und im Ofen vier Minuten braten. Pilze zugeben, umrühren und weitere fünf Minuten braten. Die Pfanne auf den Herd stellen und den Chinakohl, die Karotten und den Minimais darin heiß werden lassen. Mit Salz und Pfeffer würzen.

Zum Servieren: Die Fischsteaks in die Mitte der Teller geben, mit dem Gemüse umlegen und zum Schluß je ein fritiertes Lorbeerblatt in den Fisch stecken. Sauce separat dazu reichen.

LOIN OF LAMB WRAPPED IN NOODLE PASTE FLAVOURED WITH CORIANDER

LAMMLENDCHEN IM NUDELTEIG MIT KORIANDER

For 4 persons:

For the mousse:
120 g/4 oz lean, boneless lamb (leg or shoulder), chilled,
2 egg whites, 75 ml/2¹/₂ fl oz/¹/₃ cup double cream,
1 tbsp sunflower oil, 2 tbsp finely chopped shallots,
¹/₂ tbsp finely chopped parsley, 1 tbsp finely chopped fresh coriander,
4 tbsp cubes of white bread, crusts removed, fried in oil until golden,
salt, freshly ground black pepper,
4 loins of lamb, about 200 g/7 oz each, 1 bone left on,
trimmed and without fat, 100 g/3¹/₂ oz noodle paste,
100 g/3¹/₂ oz pork caul, thoroughly rinsed, cut into 4 intact pieces,
3 tbsp sunflower oil

For the sauce:
1 tbsp sunflower oil, 1 shallot, finely chopped,
2 fresh coriander stalks, 50 ml/1²/₃ fl oz/¹/₅ cup red wine,
2 tbsp port wine, 300 ml/10 fl oz/1¹/₄ cups brown lamb stock,
2 tbsp cornflour, mixed with 1 tbsp water,
1 tbsp cold butter, ¹/₂ tsp finely chopped, fresh coriander

Garnish:
16 silverskin onions, peeled and cooked, snap peas, cooked,
yellow courgettes, cooked, 4 sprigs thyme, 4 small sprigs rosemary,
risotto dumplings, fried in a little oil, inoki mushrooms

For the mousse: Place the chilled lamb meat in a blender, add the egg whites, and blend until smooth. Use a scraper to pass the mixture through a fine sieve into a bowl, set into a larger bowl, filled with ice. Chill again, gradually stir in the cream and place in the refrigerator. Heat the oil in a small frying pan and sauté the shallots until soft, then allow to cool. Thoroughly mix the puréed lamb with the parsley, coriander, sautéed shallots and croûtons, and season with salt and pepper.

Roll out the noodle paste about 2 mm/¹/₁₀ in thick, and cut into four rectangular shapes the same size as the lamb pieces, cook al dente in salted water, drain, dab dry. Lay flat, coat with the mousse, and wrap each of the loins of lamb in a sheet. Then wrap each piece of meat tightly in a piece of caul so that all the meat is enclosed in the mousse. Allow to stand in the refrigerator for half an hour.

Heat the oil in a frying pan. Fry the lamb parcels on all sides until well browned, then place the pan in the oven preheated to 180° C/360° F. Bake for eight to ten minutes. Remove and allow to rest for five minutes. Fry the prepared vegetables in the remaining oil until they begin to change colour. Drain off the fat and lightly season the vegetables with salt and pepper.

For the sauce: Heat the oil in a small frying pan. Sauté the shallot and coriander, then add the wine and the port wine, and reduce to half the quantity. Pour in the lamb stock, simmer for four minutes, bind with the cornflour, season with salt and pepper. Pass the sauce through a sieve. Stir in the cold butter and the coriander.

To serve: Cut the lamb parcels in half and arrange on plates. Garnish with vegetables, risotto dumplings and inoki mushrooms and pour around a little sauce. Decorate with sprigs of herbs and serve.

Für 4 Personen:

Für die Farce:
120 g mageres Lammfleisch aus der Schulter oder der Keule, gut gekühlt, 2 Eiweiß, 75 ml Doppelrahm, 1 EL Sonnenblumenöl,
2 EL feingehackte Schalotten, ¹/₂ EL feingehackte Petersilie,
1 EL feingehacktes Koriandergrün,
4 EL Weißbrotwürfel ohne Kruste, in Öl goldbraun gebraten,
Salz, schwarzer Pfeffer aus der Mühle,
4 Stück vom Lammkarree, je ca. 200 g, mit je einem Knochen belassen, pariert und ohne Fett, 100 g Nudelteig,
100 g Schweinenetz, sorgfältig gewaschen, in 4 intakte Stücke geschnitten, 3 EL Sonnenblumenöl

Für die Sauce:
1 EL Sonnenblumenöl, 1 Schalotte, feingehackt,
2 frische Korianderstengel, 50 ml Rotwein, 2 EL Portwein,
300 ml brauner Lammfond,
2 TL Maisstärke, mit 1 EL Wasser angerührt,
1 EL kalte Butter, ¹/₂ TL feingehacktes Koriandergrün

Garnitur:
16 Silberzwiebelchen, geschält und gekocht, Zuckerschoten, gekocht,
gelbe Zucchini, gekocht, 4 Thymianzweige, 4 kleine Rosmarinzweige,
Risottobällchen, in wenig Öl gebraten, Inoki-Pilze

Für die Farce: Gekühltes Lammfleisch im Mixer mit Eiweiß fein pürieren. Mit einer Kelle durch ein feines Sieb in eine auf Eis liegende Schüssel drücken. Erneut durchkühlen lassen, nach und nach die Sahne einrühren, kühlstellen. Öl in einer kleinen Pfanne erhitzen und die Schalotten darin weich dünsten, erkalten lassen. Lammpüree mit Petersilie, Koriander, gedünsteten Schalotten und Croûtons sorgfältig vermischen, mit Salz und Pfeffer würzen.

Den Nudelteig ca. 2 mm dick ausrollen und in vier rechteckige Stücke von der Größe der Lammfleischstücke schneiden, in Salzwasser al dente kochen, abgießen, trockentupfen. Flach ausbreiten, mit der Farce bestreichen und die Lammkarrees einzeln damit umwickeln. Danach jedes Fleischstück dicht in Schweinenetz wickeln, so daß das gesamte Fleisch mit der Mousse umhüllt ist. Eine halbe Stunde in den Kühlschrank stellen. Öl in einer Pfanne erhitzen. Die Lammpaketchen darin von allen Seiten heiß anbraten. In ein feuerfestes Gefäß umfüllen und im auf 180° C vorgeheizten Ofen acht bis zehn Minuten fertig garen. Herausnehmen und fünf Minuten ruhen lassen. Die vorbereiteten Gemüse im verbliebenen Öl anbraten, bis sie anfangen Farbe anzunehmen. Fett abgießen, die Gemüse mit Salz und Pfeffer leicht würzen.

Für die Sauce: Öl in einer kleinen Pfanne erhitzen. Schalotte und Koriander darin andünsten, dann den Wein und den Portwein zugeben, auf die halbe Menge einkochen lassen. Den Lammfond zugießen, vier Minuten köcheln lassen, mit der Stärke binden, mit Salz und Pfeffer würzen. Sauce durch ein Sieb passieren. Die kalte Butter und den Koriander einrühren. Zum Servieren: Die Lammpaketchen halbieren und auf Teller anrichten. Mit Gemüsen, Risottoklößen und Inokipilzen garnieren, mit etwas Sauce umgießen. Mit Kräuterzweiglein dekoriert servieren.

CHOCOLATE TEARS WITH CARAMELISED BANANA AND PISTACHIO ICE-CREAM

SCHOKOLADENTRÄNEN MIT KARAMELISIERTER BANANE UND PISTAZIENEIS

For 10 persons:

Chocolate tear:
200 g/7 oz white couverture, 200 g/7 oz dark couverture
10 strips plastic foil, 4 x 35 cm/1 3/5 x 14 inches

Cream for the pastry fans:
100 ml/3 1/2 fl oz/2/5 cup milk, 1 egg yolk, 5 tsp sugar,
1 tsp cornflour, 1 tsp cake flour, 1/4 vanilla pod, slit open

Filling:
5 bananas, sliced,
200 g/7 oz/4/5 cup sugar, 50 ml/1 2/3 fl oz/1/5 cup water

Chocolate mousse:
250 g/8 oz dark chocolate, 3 egg yolks, 50 g/1 2/3 oz/1/5 cup soft butter,
3 egg whites, 40 g/1 1/3 oz/1/6 cup sugar,
250 g/8 oz semi-whipped cream

Garnish:
Chopped pistachios, icing sugar, a little mocha, vanilla, and chocolate
sauce, mint leaves, raspberries, pistachio ice-cream

Für 10 Personen:

Schokoladenträne:
200 g weiße Kuvertüre, 200 g dunkle Kuvertüre
10 Streifen Plastikfolie von 4 x 35 cm

Creme für die Fächer:
100 ml Milch, 1 Eigelb, 5 TL Zucker, 1 TL Maisstärke,
1 TL Mehl, 1/4 Vanillestange, aufgeschnitten

Einlage:
5 Bananen, in Scheiben geschnitten,
200 g Zucker, 50 ml Wasser

Schokoladenmousse:
250 g dunkle Schokolade, 3 Eigelb, 50 g weiche Butter
3 Eiweiß, 40 g Zucker
250 g halbfest geschlagene Sahne

Garnitur:
gehackte Pistazien, Puderzucker, etwas Mokka-, Vanille- und
Schokoladesauce, Minzeblättchen, Himbeeren, Pistazieneis

For the chocolate tears: Separately soften the two sorts of chocolate. With a pallet knife spread the dark chocolate on the plastic strip. Using a plastic comb scraper, score straight lines through the chocolate. Allow to set, then spread on the white chocolate. Allow to set a little, then pick up both ends and press together, and place the tears in the refrigerator. When the chocolate is hard pull off the plastic foil and cut off the ends cleanly with a hot knife.

For the cream: Bring the milk to the boil with the vanilla. Whip the egg yolk with the sugar. Mix the cornflour with the cake flour and stir into the egg yolk. Stirring vigorously, pour in the hot milk, return the mixture to the pan and bring to the boil, stirring constantly. Pour into a container and allow to go cold. Spread the cream thinly in the shape of 10 x 6 cm/4 x 2 2/5 in rectangles on a non-stick baking tray. Preheat the oven to 180° C/360° F and bake the cream until golden brown. Remove from the oven, then press together the two lower corners of each piece, thus forming little fans. Allow to cool.

Filling: Caramelise the sugar in a saucepan. Quench with the water and boil until the caramel has dissolved. Allow to cool and use to marinate the slices of banana.

Chocolate mousse: Melt the chocolate and stir in the egg yolk and butter. Beat the egg white until stiff and gradually work in the sugar. Fold in the whipped cream, then fold this white mixture in two steps into the chocolate. Using a piping bag, fill the tears halfway with the mousse, then add a little caramelised banana, and fill up with the remaining mousse to make a pretty pattern. Place the tears in the refrigerator.

To serve: Sprinkle a few chopped pistachios on dessert plates and dust with icing sugar. Carefully lay the tears on the plates. Decorate as desired with dessert sauces of different colours. Stick a fan in the mousse and garnish with mint leaves and raspberries. Place a bowl of pistachio ice-cream on each plate and serve immediately.

Für die Tränen: Beide Schokoladensorten separat weich werden lassen. Mit einem Messerrücken die dunkle Schokolade auf die Plastikstreifen streichen. Mit einem gezackten Teigschaber möglichst gerade Furchen durch die Schokolade ziehen. Festwerden lassen, dann die weiße Schokolade aufstreichen. Ebenfalls etwas setzen lassen, dann die beiden Enden zusammenfassen und die Tränen in die Kühle stellen. Wenn die Schokolade fest ist, die Plastikstreifen abziehen und die Enden mit einem warmen Messer sauber abschneiden. Für die Creme: Milch mit der Vanille zum Kochen bringen. Eigelb mit dem Zucker schaumig schlagen. Stärke mit Mehl vermischen und unter das Eigelb rühren. Die heiße Milch unter kräftigem Rühren zugießen, die Masse zurück in den Topf geben und unter ständigem Rühren aufkochen lassen. Umfüllen und erkalten lassen. Die Creme dünn, in Form von ca. 10 x 6 cm großen Rechtecken, auf ein beschichtetes Blech streichen. Im auf 180° C vorgeheizten Ofen goldbraun werden lassen. Aus dem Ofen nehmen, dann jeweils die zwei unteren Ecken zusammendrücken und so kleine Fächer formen. Erkalten lassen.

Einlage: Den Zucker in einem Topf karamelisieren. Mit dem Wasser ablöschen und kochen, bis sich der Karamel aufgelöst hat. Erkalten lassen und die Bananenscheiben damit marinieren.

Schokoladenmousse: Schokolade schmelzen, dann die Eigelb und die Butter unterrühren. Eiweiß steif schlagen, nach und nach den Zucker einarbeiten. Die Sahne unterziehen, dann diese weiße Masse in zwei Schritten unter die Schokolade ziehen. Mit einem Spritzsack die Tränen halb hoch mit der Mousse füllen. Etwas karamelisierte Banane einlegen und mit der restlichen Mousse in einem hübschen Muster zuspritzen. Die Tränen kühlstellen. Zum Servieren: Dessertteller mit gehackten Pistazien bestreuen und mit Puderzucker überstäuben. Die Tränen vorsichtig auf die Teller legen. Nach Belieben mit verschiedenfarbigen Dessertsaucen dekorieren. Je einen Fächer in die Mousse stecken und mit Minzeblatt und Himbeere garnieren. Mit einer Kugel Pistazieneis sofort servieren.

*F*ortunately there is no need to decide which "Stafford" to fall in love with. The cosy, originally private house on the edge of St. James's Park renovated by Terry Holmes and converted into a most luxurious town hotel. Or the "Stafford Cellars" where, in the 350-year old vaults, sommelier Gino Nardella guards a treasure of about 35,000 bottles, chiefly claret and Burgundy. Or the "American Bar", where the legendary Charles mixes the dryest martini far and wide. Or in the creations of chef Chris Oakes, who skillfully combines traditional British fare with elements of modern culinary art. We are fortunate and can enjoy all four in turn and at leisure.

Whether lunch or dinner – Chris Oakes takes a line comprising on the one hand British tradition and on the other the repertoire of contemporary kitchen craft: for example classical English apple pie combined with sorbet; traditional summer blancmange with a very light sauce of dark fruits; fillet of beef with paper-thin, crisp-baked Parma ham; goose liver with a dressing of blackcurrants and lamb's lettuce. And to go with this the inexhaustible choice from the cellars.

If you like, you can go down and sit among the bottles, for a vaulted cellar is available for private functions. There is seating for up to 42 guests at the nine-meter long festive table.
But just as a twosome it is also enjoyable to sit here, even though this may lead to communication problems. As in the case of the British gentleman who invited his beloved to dine here, sat her at the head of the table and himself at the other end, then after an extensive dinner asked "Will you marry me?"
To which she replied with a brusque "No" and departed.
It cannot have been due to the quality of the food and wine.

There is never a "No" in the American Bar, for Charles' selection of drinks is limitless. This is esteemed evidently not only by the American tourists who frequent the place in droves. Also prominent figures, crowned and uncrowned heads, are found in the guest book. And if ever a member of the royal family, or a genuine lady prime minister take a drink here, the glass does not go into the dishwasher but is preserved unwashed in a glass cabinet with a little label. There they stand like votive objects. And so today we can say with absolute assurance that e.g. on February 11, 1988 the Queen Mother drank a glass here, and on July 24, 1988 a certain Mrs. Margaret Thatcher. Chemists could surely still analyse today what lipstick they were wearing. Very British, one can only say as a central European.

Zum Glück muß man sich nicht entscheiden, in welches „Stafford" man sich denn nun verlieben soll. Ins familiäre, ursprünglich als Privathaus erbaute und unter Terry Holmes hochkomfortabel renovierte Stadthotel am Rande des St. James's Parks, in die „Stafford Cellars", wo Sommelier Gino Nardella in den 350 Jahre alten Gewölben einen Schatz von rund 35'000 Flaschen, vornehmlich Bordeaux und Burgunder, hütet, in die „American-Bar", wo der legendäre Charles den trockensten Martini weit und breit mixt oder in die Kreationen von Küchenchef Chris Oakes, der englische Klassiker gekonnt mit den Elementen moderner Kochkunst verbindet. Wir haben es gut und genießen alle vier in Ruhe und der Reihe nach.

Ob Lunch oder Dinner – Chris Oakes verfolgt eine Linie, die zur einen Hälfte aus englischer Tradition besteht und zur anderen aus dem Repertoire zeitgemäßen Küchenhandwerks resultiert: Etwa klassischer englischer Apfelkuchen mit Sorbet kombiniert; traditioneller Sommerpudding mit einer ganz leichten Sauce aus dunklen Früchten; Rinderfilet mit hauchdünnem, knusprig gebackenem Parma-Schinken; Gänseleber mit einem Dressing aus schwarzen Johannisbeeren und Feldsalat. Dazu die unerschöpfliche Auswahl aus den Cellars. Wer will, kann sich auch gleich zu den Weinflaschen hinuntersetzen, denn für private Festlichkeiten steht einer der Gewölbekeller zur Verfügung. Bis zu 42 Gäste finden hier an der neun Meter langen Festtafel Platz. Aber auch nur zu zweit kann man sich hier vergnügen, was allerdings zu Kommunikationsproblemen führen kann. So wie bei jenem britischen Gentleman, der seine Angebetete hierher zum Abendessen lud, sie an das eine Kopfende des langen Tisches bat, er sich ans andere Ende setzte, um sie nach einem ausgedehnten Dinner dann zu fragen: „Will you marry me?" Worauf sie knapp mit „No" antwortete und entschwand. An der Qualität des Essens und der Weine kann es nicht gelegen haben.

Niemals „No" gibt es in der American Bar, denn Charles' Auswahl an Drinks kennt keine Grenzen. Dies schätzen offenbar nicht nur Touristen aus Amerika, diesen Platz hier kräftig frequentieren. Auch prominente Häupter, gekrönte und ungekrönte, stehen in der Gästeliste. Und wenn gar ein Mitglied der königlichen Familie oder eine veritable Regierungschefin hier ihren Drink nehmen, dann kommen die Gläser anschließend nicht in die Spülmaschine, sondern ungeputzt in eine Glasvitrine mit kleinen Zettelchen dran. So können wir noch heute mit absoluter Gewissheit sagen, daß z. B. am 11. Februar 1988 die Queen Mother hier ein Gläschen genommen hat und am 24. Juli 1988 eine gewisse Mrs Margaret Thatcher. Very British, kann man da als Zentraleuropäer nur sagen.

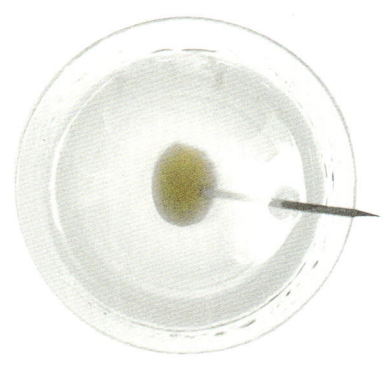

No.	Wine	Bottle	Half	Vintage
1.	Pol Roger, White Foil (House champagne)	39.00	21.00	NV
5.	Bollinger, Spécial Cuvée	49.00		NV
7.	Veuve Clicquot-Ponsardin Yellow Label, Brut	47.00		NV
10.	Charles Heidsieck, Brut Réserve	44.00		NV
11.	Taittinger, Brut Réserve	49.00		NV
14.	Moët et Chandon, Première Cuvée	46.00		NV
16.	Louis Roederer, Brut Premier	49.00		NV
18.	Lanson, Black Label	45.00		NV
34.	Krug, Grande Cuvée	99.00		NV
30.	Perrier Jouet, Brut	57.00		1988
32.	Cuvée Dom Perignon	105.00		1988
35.	Krug, Brut	120.00		1985
36.	Perrier Jouet, Belle Epoque	94.50		1989
12.	Taittinger, Comtes de Champagne	100.00		1988
24.	Louis Roederer, Cristal Brut	115.00		1988
33.	Bollinger RD ,Extra Brut	98.00		1982

Service and VAT are included

BORDEAUX
Red Wine
Cru Bourgeois and Petits Châteaux

No.	Wine	Bottle	Half	Vintage
100.	Stafford Claret Appellation Bordeaux Contrôlée	15.50	8.50	NV
149.	Domaine Du Galet Bordeaux A.O.C	17.00		1995
104.	Château Bel Air Bordeaux Superieur AOC	17.50		1993
106.	Les Brulières de Beychevelle Haut Médoc	26.50		1993
109	Château Lafleur Cailleau Canon Fronsac	36.50		1990
123.	Château Loudenne Cru Bourgeois Haut Médoc	29.50		1990
124.	Château Beaumont Cru Bourgeois Haut Médoc	32.50		1990
122.	Château Meyney Cru Bourgeois St. Estèphe	39.50		1989
133.	Château Cissac Cru Bourgeois Médoc	33.00		1989
166.	Château Beau Site Cru Bourgeois St. Estèphe	34.00		1982
223.	Château Meyney Cru Bourgeois St. Estèphe	168.00 (Double - Magnum)		1985

SWEET WINE

No.	Wine	Bottle	Half	Vintage
62.	Recioto Di Soave "I Capitelli" Domaine Anselmi Italy		25.00	1994
66.	Muscat de Beaumes de Venise Vignerons De Beaumes deVenise France		19.50	NV
73.	Château Guiraud 1er Grand Cru Sauternes France	65.00		1983
70.	Château Coutet 1er Cru Barsac France		28.50	1985
71.	Château Coutet 1er Cru Barsac France	60.00		1986
68.	Tokaji "Aszu" 5 Puttonyos Hungary		33.00	1981
64.	Liqueur Muscat Carlyle Estate Australia		16.50	NV

BORDEAUX
Red Wine
Cru Classés

No.	Wine	Bottle	Half	Vintage
127.	Château Montrose 2ème Cru St. Estephe	105.50		1989
182.	Château Mouton Rothschild 1er Cru Classé	94.00		1987
118.	Château Mouton Baronne-Philippe 5ème Cru Pauillac	42.50		1983
120.	Château Pontet Canet 5ème Cru Pauillac	48.50		1990
158.	Château Beychevelle 4ème Cru St. Julien	82.50		1989
135.	Château Batailley 5eme cru Pauillac		28.50	1982
111	Chateau La Tour Martillac Grand Cru Classé Pessac-Leognan,Graves	42.50		1990
102	Château Siran Grand Cru Exceptionnel Margaux	38.50		1990
139	Château Latour 1er Cru Pauillac	137.00		1985

BORDEAUX
Red Wine
Cru Classés

No.	Wine	Bottle	Half	Vintage
130.	Château Cos d'Estournel 2ème Cru St. Estèphe	125.00		1982
146.	Château Gruaud-Larose 2ème Cru St. Julien	74.00		1981
154.	Château Palmer 3eme cru margaux	91.00		1978
150.	Château Branaire-Ducru 4ème Cru St. Julien	55.50		1978
144.	Château Cos Labory 5ème Cru St. Estèphe	44.50		1985
175.	Château Lafite Rothschild 1er Cru Pauillac		73.00	1976
172.	Château Léoville-Las-Cases 2ème Cru St. Julien		31.50	1976
180.	Château Durfort-Vivens 2ème Cru Margaux	66.50	31.50	1970

BURGUNDY
Red Wine
Côte de Nuits

		Bottle	Half	Vintage
433	Morey St Denis 1er Cru "Clos des Ormes" Domaine Faiveley	51.00		1989
406	Echezeaux, Grand Cru Domaine Dujac		39.00	1989
415	Echezeaux Domaine A.F Gros	80.00		1989
413	Grands Echezeaux Domaine René Engel	92.00		1989
423	Nuits St. Georges, 1er Cru "Les Charmois" Domaine Grivot	45.00		1990
435	Nuits St.Georges 1er Cru "Les Terres Blanches" Hospices De Nuits	44.00		1990
401	Nuits St.Georges Domaine Jean Chauvenet	44.00		1990
438	Nuits St. Georges 1er Cru "Clos de la Marechale" Domaine Faiveley	52.00		1989
439	Nuits St.Georges 1er Cru "Les Porets St George" Domaine Faiveley	49.00		1989

BURGUNDY
Red Wine
Côte de Nuits

		Bottle	Half	Vintage
421	Gevrey -Chambertin "Les Evocelles" Domaine Lucien Boillot	44.50		1993
434	Charmes Chambertin Grand Cru Domaine André Séguin	55.50		1985
416	Morey St. Denis "En la Rue de Vargy" Domaine H. Perrot Minot	45.50		1985
419	Morey St. Denis Domaine Dujac		23.50	1991
425	Chambolle-Musigny Domaine H. Perrot Minot	39.50		1990
411	Chambolle-Musigny "Les Combes d'Orveau" Domaine H. Perrot Minot	48.50		1990
427	Vosne-Romanée Domaine Grivot	46.00		1990
426	Vosne-Romanée, "Aux Reas" Domaine A. F. Gros	52.00		1990
430	Romanée St Vivant Domaine de la Romanée Conti	161.50		1978
428	Clos Vougeot "Château de la Tour"	58.50		1985

BURGUNDY
Red Wine
Côte de Beaune, Chalonnais, Beaujolais

		Bottle	Half	Vintage
420	Pommard 1er Cru "Clos des Epenots" Domaine du Château de Meursault	49.00		1990
436	Corton Grand Cru "Cuvée Charlotte Dumay" Hospices De Beaune	72.00		1990
437	Corton Grand Cru "Cuvée Docteur Peste" Hospices De Beaune	72.00		1988
407	Volnay 1er Cru "Les Caillerets" "Clos des 60 Ouvreés" Domaine de la Pousse D'Or		27.50	1990
410	Volnay 1er Cru "Caillerets" Domaine Yves Clerge	49.50		1989
429	Volnay Domaine Jean Marc Boillot	47.00		1989
440	Pommard "Croix Blanche" Domaine Parent		23.50	1992

BURGUNDY
Red Wine
Côte de Beaune, Chalonnais, Beaujolais

		Bottle	Half	Vintage
424	Aloxe-Corton 1er Cru "Les Chaillots" Domaine Louis Latour	40.50		1991
412	Corton Grand Cru "Clos de la Vigne au Saint" Domaine Louis Latour	48.00		1990
408	Savigny -Les -Beaune Maison Louis Latour	28.50		1994
414	Beaune 1er Cru "Vignes Franches" Maison Louis Latour	36.50		1993
418	Mercurey "Clos L'Evêque" Domaine de Suremain	38.50		1994
400	Côte de Brouilly Domaine de la Feuillée	23.50		1994
402	Morgon Domaine Vatoux	23.50		1995
404	Fleurie "La Madonne" Domaine Georges Duboeuf	26.00		1995
404	Fleurie "La Madonne" Domaine Georges Duboeuf		14.00	1996

BURGUNDY
White Wine

		Bottle	Half	Vintage
304	Chablis "Saint Martin" Domaine Laroche	27.50		1995
303	Mercurey 1er Cru "Les Champs Martins" Domaine Michel Juillot	39.50		1994
310	Macon-Lugny "La Fontaine" Maison Louis Jadot	23.00		1994
315	Saint-Véran "Château de Fuissé" Domaine Vincent	23.50		1995
313	Pouilly-Fuissé "Château de Fuissé" Domaine Vincent	39.00		1994

		Bottle	Half	Vintage
302	Chablis Domaine Laroche		14.50	1995
320	Chablis 1er Cru "Mont de Millieu" Domaine J. Billaud-Simon	38.00		1993
308	Montagny 1 er Cru " La Grande Roche" Maison Louis Latour	27.00		1995
309	Montagny 1er Cru "Les Cloux" Domaine Olivier Leflaive		13.50	1994
306	Bourgogne Chardonnay Domaine Henri Clerc	25.50		1993
316	Saint-Aubin 1er Cru "En Remilly" Domaine Olivier Leflaive	33.50		1994

Service and VAT are included

BORDEAUX
Red Wine
St Emilion, Pomerol, Lalande de Pomerol

		Bottle	Half	Vintage
129	Chateau Mazeyres Pomerol	38.50		1990
103	Château Beausejour Duffau-Lagarosse 1er Grand Cru Classe St.Emilion	44.50		1985
121	Chateau La Croix St.Georges Pomerol	84.00 (Magnum)		1992
140	Château St.Georges St.Georges St.Emilion	84.00 (Magnum)		1990
141	Château St.Georges St.Georges St.Emilion	38.50		1990
151.	Château La Croix Pomerol	36.50		1992
116.	Château Vieux Sarpe Grand Cru St. Emilion	42.50		1990
107.	Château Graviers Plagnolles St. Emilion	25.50		1994
112.	Chateau Des Annereaux Lalande de Pomerol	29.50		1993
137.	Château Lafleur Petrus Pomerol	92.50		1986
138.	Château La Conseillante Pomerol	120.00		1982
165.	Château La Conseillante Pomerol		43.00	1982

BORDEAUX
Fine and Rare Wines

		Bottle	Half	Vintage
152.	Château Margaux 1er Cru Margaux	148.00		1985
162.	Château Cheval Blanc 1er Grand Cru St. Emilion	165.00		1985
156.	Château Mouton Rothschild 1er Cru Pauillac	148.00		1978
174.	Château Lafite Rothschild 1er Cru Pauillac	143.00		1976
183.	Château Haut-Brion 1er Cru Graves	163.50		1970
270	Château Margaux 1er Cru Classé	185.00		1970
272	Château Lafite 1er Cru Classé Pauillac	250.00		1970
274	Château Cos d'Estournel 2ème Cru St Estephe	110.00		1970
276	Château Margaux 1er Cru Classé Margaux	230.00		1966
278	Château Mouton Rothschild 1er Cru Classé Pauillac	360.00		1966
280	Château Lafite 1er Cru Classé Pauillac	255.00		1966
281	Château Ducru Beaucaillou 2 ème Cru Classé St Julien	145.00		1966

BORDEAUX
Fine and Rare Wines

		Bottle	Half	Vintage
283	Château Pavie 1er Grand Cru St Emilion	110.00		1966
187.	Château Haut-Brion 1er Cru Graves	105.00		1964
284	Château Haut Brion 1er Cru Classé Graves	175.00		1962
188.	Château Talbot 4ème Cru St. Julien	152.50		1961
189.	Château Mouton Baron-Philippe 5ème Cru Pauillac	141.50		1961
191.	Château Lafite 1er Cru Pauillac	620.00		1947
190.	Château Talbot 4ème Cru St. Julien	280.50		1945

COTES DU RHONE
White Wine

		Bottle	Half	Vintage
500.	Châteauneuf-du-Pape Domaine de Nalys	33.00		1994

Red Wine

		Bottle	Half	Vintage
506.	Côtes du Rhone Domaine Sainte Anne	20.50		1989
507.	Châteauneuf-du-Pape Domaine E Guigal	34.50		1991
509.	Côte Rôtie "Côtes Brune et Blonde" Maison E Guigal	47.00		1985
510.	Hermitage Maison Chapoutier	38.50		1991

BORDEAUX
White Wine

		Bottle	Half	Vintage
80.	Château Haut Grelot 1er Côtes de Blaye	18.50		1996
84.	Château Cabannieux Cru Exceptionnel Graves	26.00		1993
88.	Château La Tour Martillac Grand Cru Classé Graves	46.50		1991
81.	Domaine du Chevalier Grand Cru Classé Graves	80.50		1964
86.	Château Fieuzal Grand Cru Classé Graves	60.00		1983

ALSACE
White Wine

		Bottle	Half	Vintage
540.	Pinot Blanc "Les Tilleuls" Domaine L. Albrecht	19.00		1992
542.	Gewürztraminer "Cuvée Tradition" Maison Hugel	29.50	15.00	1994
543.	Gewürtztraminer "Vendages Tardives" Cave Vinicole de Turckheim		20.00	1989
545.	Riesling Kitterle "Grand Cru" Domaine Schlumberger	45.00		1988

Red Wine

		Bottle	Half	Vintage
548.	Pinot Noir "Princes Abbes" Domaine Schlumberger	25.00		1994

LOIRE
White Wine

		Bottle	Half	Vintage
520.	Muscadet "La Roche Renard" Domaine Philippe Denis	17.00		1996
522.	Sancerre "Clos de la Croix au Garde" Domaine Henry Pellé	28.00	14.00	1996
525.	Pouilly-Fumé "Domaine des Berthiers" Domaine Serge Dagueneau	27.50		1995
526.	Menetou-Salon "Morogues" Domaine Henry Pellé	26.00		1996
527.	Vouvray "Domaine des Barguins" Maison Mallein	70.00		1964
529.	Reuilly Domaine H. Beurdin	24.00		1995

Red Wine

		Bottle	Half	Vintage
532.	Sancerre "Domaine du Grand Moulin" Domaine Pierre Girault	27.50		1995
533.	Chinon "Domaine De La Perrière" Domaine Michel Page	26.00		1995

Rosé

		Bottle	Half	Vintage
535.	Sancerre, "Domaine Du Grand Moulin" Domaine Pierre Girault	28.50		1995

CHILE
White Wine

		Bottle	Half	Vintage
611.	Santa Rita "Medalla Real" Sauvignon Blanc Rapel Valley	17.00		1995
613.	Cunepa Reserva Chardonnay Rancagua Valley	19.00		1995

Red wine

		Bottle	Half	Vintage
614	Los Vascos Cachagua	19.50		1994

BURGUNDY
White Wine

		Bottle	Half	Vintage
317.	Meursault Domaine Michelot	47.50		1993
328.	Puligny Montrachet Domaine Henri Clerc	59.50		1994
324.	Clos du Château de Meursault Domaine du Château de Meursault	38.00	19.00	1993
314	Meursault Domaine du Château de Meursault	59.50		1992
336.	Corton Charlemagne Domaine Bonneau du Martray	108.50		1992
333.	Chassagne Montrachet 1er Cru "Vide Bourse" Domaine F & L Pillot	62.50		1991
335	Bartard Montrachet Domaine Leflaive	130.00		1990
338.	Corton Charlemagne Domaine Bonneau du Martray	108.50		1990
339.	Chevalier Montrachet Domaine Leflaive	115.00		1990
322.	Auxey-Duresses Domaine Battault	29.00		1986

AUSTRALIA
White Wine

		Bottle	Half	Vintage
639.	Pooles Rock Chardonnay Hunter Valley	27.50		1995
640.	Rosemount Chardonnay "Show Reserve" Hunter Valley	32.00		1995
641.	Shaw & Smith Sauvignon Blanc Adelaide Hills	20.00		1996
642.	Bannockburn Vineyards Chardonnay Victoria	32.00		1994
643.	Smithbrook Chardonnay Western Australia	30.00		1993
651	Shaw&Smith "Reserve Chardonnay" South Australia	33.00		1992

Red Wine

		Bottle	Half	Vintage
644.	Rothbury Shiraz South Australia	21.00		1993
645.	Wynn's Cabernet Sauvignon John Riddoch Estate, Coonawarra	39.00		1993
646.	Rosemount Cabernet Sauvignon Show Reserve Coonawarra	32.50		1993

AMERICA
White Wine

		Bottle	Half	Vintage
626.	Mondavi Chardonnay Napa Valley, California	34.50		1994
628.	Calera Chardonnay Central Coast, California	36.00		1994

Red Wine

		Bottle	Half	Vintage
630.	Firestead Pinot Noir Oregon	28.50		1995
631.	Fetzer Barrel Select Pinot Noir North Coast, California	34.00		1993
632.	Bearboat Pinot Noir Russian River, California	37.00		1994
635.	Acacia Pinot Noir Carneros, California	38.00		1993
636.	Raymond Cabernet Sauvignon Napa Valley, California	29.00		1991
637.	Calera Pinot Noir Central Coast, California	36.00		1992

SOUTH AFRICA
White Wine

		Bottle	Half	Vintage
619.	Thelema Chardonnay Mountain Vineyards	24.50		1995
620.	Klein Constantia Chardonnay Constantia	27.50		1993
621.	Thelema Sauvignon Blanc Mountain Vineyards	26.50		1996
622.	Wildekrans Sauvignon Blanc Walker Bay	22.50		1993

Red Wine

		Bottle	Half	Vintage
627.	Stellenryck Cabernet Sauvignon Stellenbosch	27.00		1991
625	Meerlust "Rubicon" Stellenbosh	31.50		1992

NEW ZEALAND
White Wine

	Bottle	Half	Vintage
634. Cloudy Bay Sauvignon Blanc Marlborough	34.50		1996
650. Nautilus Sauvignon Blanc Marlborough	26.00		1996
652. Nobilo Gisbourne Chardonnay Dixon Vineyard, Huapai, Auckland	28.50		1994

Red Wine

	Bottle	Half	Vintage
655. Stoneleigh Cabernet Sauvignon Marlborough, Auckland	29.50		1986
656. Lincoln Vineyards Cabernet/Merlot Auckland	26.50		1995

GERMANY
White Wine

	Bottle	Half	Vintage
602. Piesporter Michelsberg Riesling Qualitätswein, Mosel	15.00		1993
604. Johannisberger Erntbringer Riesling Rheingau	17.00		1994
606. Niersteiner Riesling Rheinhessen	16.00		1991
609. Flonheimer Adelberg Sylvaner Eiswein, Rheinhessen	64.50		1985

PORTUGAL
White Wine

	Bottle	Half	Vintage
610. Grao Vasco "Blanco" Dao Vinicola do Vale do Dao	17.50		1991

Red Wine

	Bottle	Half	Vintage
612. Grao Vasco "Tinto" Dao Vinicola do Vale do Dao	18.50		1990

SPAIN
White Wine

	Bottle	Half	Vintage
580. Gran Vina Sol Reserva Torres, Penedés	18.50		1993
582. Ygay Marqués de Murrieta, Rioja	21.00		1988
583. Enate Chardonnay Somontano - Alto Aragon	28.00		1995

Red Wine

	Bottle	Half	Vintage
586. Marqués de Grinon "Reserva Privada" Rioja	26.50		1990
588. Gran Coronas Reserva Torres, Penedés	24.00		1991
589. Enate Reserva Cabernet Sauvignon Somontano - Alto Aragon	29.50		1992

ITALY
White Wine

	Bottle	Half	Vintage
560. Pinot Grigio Vigneti Le Monde	20.00		1996
561. Pomino "Il Benefizio" Marchesi de' Frescobaldi	28.00		1993
562. Poggio Alle Gazze "Ornellaia" Lodovico Antinori	26.50		1995
564. Chardonnay "Vigneto Marino" Estate Batasiolo La Morra	22.00		1994

Red Wine

	Bottle	Half	Vintage
565. Sassicaia "Marchesi Incisa della Rocchetta"	68.00		1992
566. Barolo "Serralunga d'Alba" Fontanafredda	29.50		1989
567. Brunello di Montalcino "Col D'Orcia"	38.00		1991
568. Chianti Classico "Riserva di Fizzano" Estate Rocca delle Macie	26.50		1990

SMOKED CHICKEN AND AVOCADO ON CASSIS DRESSING

GERÄUCHERTES HÜHNERFLEISCH UND AVOCADO AN CASSISDRESSING

For 4 - 6 persons:

1 smoked chicken,
2 avocados, juice of ¹/₂ lemon

For the cassis dressing:
250 ml/8 fl oz/1 cup red wine,
120 ml/4 fl oz/¹/₂ cup cassis syrup,
2 tbsp blackcurrants,
10 shallots, finely chopped, 2 tbsp English mustard,
150 ml/5 fl oz/³/₅ cup olive oil, salt, pepper

Mixed leaf salads,
white-wine vinegar, olive oil, salt and pepper,
2 tbsp saffron mayonnaise,
4 - 6 thin slices of Parma ham, fried crispy in
a little oil, a few sprigs of chervil

Für 4 - 6 Personen:

1 geräuchertes Huhn,
2 Avocados, Saft einer halben Zitrone

Für das Cassisdressing:
250 ml Rotwein,
120 ml Cassissirup,
2 EL schwarze Johannisbeeren,
10 Schalotten, fein gehackt, 2 EL englischer Senf,
150 ml Olivenöl, Salz, Pfeffer

Gemischte Blattsalate,
Weißweinessig, Olivenöl, Salz und Pfeffer,
2 EL mit Safran gewürzte Mayonnaise,
4 - 6 dünne Scheiben Parmaschinken, in etwas Öl
knusprig gebraten, einige Kerbelzweige

Remove the bones from the meat. Peel the avocados, cut into thin wedges and dip briefly in lemon water.

For the cassis dressing: Boil the red wine with the syrup, the blackcurrants and the shallots until the liquid thickens. Stir in the mustard and when the crème has cooled down stir in the olive oil and season with salt and pepper.

Wash and dry the salad leaves. Dress the salad with a little white-wine vinegar, olive oil, salt and pepper and distribute on the plates. Lay the chicken meat and avocado wedges all around. Add a few blobs of saffron mayonnaise and encircle with the cassis dressing. Lay a slice of Parma ham on each serving, garnish with chervil and serve.

Von dem Huhn das Fleisch auslösen. Die Avocados schälen, in dünne Spalten schneiden und kurz in Zitronenwasser tauchen.

Für das Cassisdressing: Den Rotwein mit dem Sirup, den Johannisbeeren und den Schalotten kochen, bis die Flüssigkeit eindickt. Den Senf unterrühren, wenn die Creme abgekühlt ist, mit dem Olivenöl verrühren und mit Salz und Pfeffer abschmecken.

Salatblätter waschen und trocknen. Mit etwas Weißweinessig, Olivenöl, Salz und Pfeffer den Salat würzen und auf Teller verteilen. Hühnerfleisch und Avocadospalten rundherum legen. Einige Klekse Safranmayonnaise dazugeben und mit dem Cassisdressing umgießen. Je eine Scheibe Parmaschinken darüber legen, mit Kerbel garnieren und servieren.

DEVONSHIRE APPLE CAKE

APFELKUCHEN NACH ART VON DEVONSHIRE

For the cake: *250 g/8 oz/1 cup flour, pinch of salt,* *125 g/4 oz/¹/₂ cup soft butter,* *125 g/4 oz/¹/₂ cup sugar,* *500 g/16 oz/2 cups peeled and coarsely grated apples,* *2 eggs*	*Für den Kuchen:* *250 g Mehl, 1 Prise Salz,* *125 g weiche Butter,* *125 g Zucker,* *500 g Äpfel, geschält und grob gerieben,* *2 Eier*
For the sauce: *125 g/4 fl oz/¹/₂ cup milk,* *125 g/4 fl oz/¹/₂ cup cream,* *65 g/2 oz/¹/₄ cup sugar, 1 vanilla pod, split,* *4 egg yolks, beaten*	*Für die Sauce:* *125 g Milch,* *125 g Sahne,* *65 g Zucker, 1 Vanillestengel, aufgeschnitten,* *4 Eigelb, verquirlt*
For the ice-cream: *3 egg yolks, 2 eggs, 225 g/7 oz/1 cup sugar,* *500 g/16 oz/2¹/₆ cups milk,* *250 g/8 oz/1 cup cream*	*Für das Eis:* *3 Eigelb, 2 Eier, 225 g Zucker,* *500 g Milch,* *250 g Sahne*
Apple crisps: *1 apple, cored and very thinly sliced*	*Apfelchips:* *1 Apfel, entkernt, in sehr dünne Scheiben geschnitten*

For the cake: Stir the flour, salt, butter and sugar together to form a crumbly texture. Stir in the grated apples and the eggs. Grease a 6 cm/2 ²/₅ in deep cake mould with butter and sprinkle with sugar. Pour in the cake mixture; bake in the preheated oven at 180° C/360° F for thirty to forty minutes. The cake is done when a knife poked into the middle comes out dry.

For the sauce: Bring the milk to the boil with the cream, sugar and vanilla. Stirring vigorously, pour over the beaten eggs. Return the mixture to the saucepan and heat, stirring, until the sauce thickens. Pass through a sieve and allow to cool.

For the ice-cream: Whip the eggs, egg yolk and sugar until fluffy. Bring the cream and milk to the boil. Stirring briskly, pour over the eggs and heat in a saucepan until the mixture is creamy. Pass through a sieve, allow to go cold and freeze in the ice-cream maker.

For the apple crisps: Lay the apple slices on a baking tray. Paint with egg white and bake in the oven preheated to 150° C/300° F until golden brown and crispy.

To serve: Place a piece of cake and some ice-cream on the plate. Encircle with a little sauce and finally decorate with the apple crisps.

Für den Kuchen: Mehl, Salz, Butter und Zucker verrühren, bis eine bröselige Masse entsteht. Die geriebenen Äpfel und die Eier unterrühren.
Eine 6 cm tiefe Kuchenform mit Butter auspinseln und mit Zucker bestreuen. Kuchenmasse einfüllen; im auf 180° C vorgeheizten Ofen dreißig bis vierzig Minuten backen. Der Kuchen ist gar, wenn ein in die Mitte gestochenes Messer trocken herauskommt.
Für die Sauce: Milch mit Sahne, Zucker und Vanille zum Kochen bringen. Unter kräftigem Rühren über die verquirlten Eier gießen. Die Masse zurück in den Topf gießen und unter ständigem Rühren erhitzen, bis die Sauce bindet. Durch ein Sieb passieren und abkühlen lassen. Für das Eis: Eier, Eigelb und Zucker schaumig rühren. Sahne mit der Milch zum Kochen bringen, unter kräftigem Rühren über die Eier gießen und im Topf erhitzen, bis die Masse cremig wird. Durch ein Sieb streichen, erkalten lassen und in der Eismaschine gefrieren.
Für die Apfelchips: Apfelscheiben auf einem Blech auslegen. Mit Eiweiß bepinseln und im auf 150° C vorgeheizten Ofen backen, bis sie goldbraun und knusprig sind.
Zum Servieren: Je ein Stück Kuchen und Eis auf Teller geben; mit etwas Sauce umgießen, zum Schluß mit den Apfelchips dekorieren.

CHOCOLATE BROWNIE WITH GLAZED BANANAS

SCHOKOLADENKUCHEN MIT GLACIERTEN BANANEN

For 12 - 15 persons:

For the brownie:
250 g/8 oz/1 cup soft butter,
250 g/8 oz/1 cup brown sugar,
4 eggs, beaten,
300 g/10 oz dark chocolate,
melted in the bain-marie,
250 g/8 oz/1 cup flour, 1 tsp baking powder,
4 tbsp thinly peeled lemon and orange zest from
untreated fruit, finely chopped

Sauce:
500 g/16 fl oz/2 cups water, 150 g/5 oz/³/₅ cup sugar,
250 g/8 oz dark chocolate, 3 tbsp cocoa powder,
2 tsp arrowroot

Sorbet:
125 g/4 fl oz/¹/₂ cup water, 250 g/8 oz/1 cup sugar,
1 vanilla pod, split, 250 g/8 oz/1 cup natural yoghurt

Bananas:
2 bananas, 200 g/7 oz/⁴/₅ cup sugar,
100 g/3¹/₂ fl oz/²/₅ cup orange juice

For the brownie: Cream the butter and sugar together with a whisk, fold in the eggs and melted chocolate, then work in the flour with the baking powder. Pour the mixture into a buttered deep tin. Smooth with a palette knife and bake in the preheated oven at 180° C/360° C.
Remove from the oven and allow the brownie to cool on the tray.
For the sauce: Put the water and sugar in a pan and boil. Dissolve the chocolate and the cocoa in the pan, then stir in the arrowroot, previously mixed with a little water. Reboil until the sauce starts to thicken. Pass through a sieve and allow to cool.
For the sorbet: Bring the water to the boil with the sugar and scraped vanilla. Allow to go cold. Stir in the yoghurt and freeze the crème in the ice-cream maker.
Peel the bananas, slice and place in a small bowl. Melt the sugar in a small saucepan over a low heat until completely caramelised, of medium brown colour, and free from lumps. Quench with the orange juice (beware of splashing) and boil until the hardened caramel has dissolved again. Pour the hot liquid over the slices of banana and allow to cool.
To serve: Cut the cake into slices or stamp out round "brownies", distribute onto plates and cover with slices of banana. Using a small spoon, decorate with ice-cream and encircle with a little sauce.

Für 12 - 15 Personen:

Für den Kuchen:
250 g weiche Butter,
250 g brauner Zucker,
4 Eier, verquirlt,
300 g dunkle Schokolade (zartbitter),
im Wasserbad geschmolzen,
250 g Mehl, 1 TL Backpulver,
4 EL dünn abgeschälte Zitronen- und Orangenschale
von unbehandelten Früchten, fein geschnitten

Sauce:
500 g Wasser, 150 g Zucker,
250 g dunkle Schokolade (zartbitter),
3 EL Kakaopulver, 2 TL Pfeilwurzmehl

Sorbet:
125 g Wasser, 250 g Zucker,
1 Vanillestengel, aufgeschnitten, 250 g Naturjoghurt

Bananen:
2 Bananen, 200 g Zucker,
100 g Orangensaft

Für den Kuchen: Butter und Zucker mit dem Schneebesen schaumig rühren. Eier und geschmolzene Schokolade einrühren, dann das Mehl mit dem Backpulver einarbeiten. Den Teig auf ein gebuttertes, tiefes Blech geben, flachstreichen und im auf 180° C vorgeheizten Ofen backen. Herausnehmen und abkühlen lassen.
Für die Sauce: Das Wasser mit dem Zucker in einem Topf zum Kochen bringen. Die Schokolade und den Kakao darin schmelzen, dann das in wenig Wasser angerührte Pfeilwurzmehl einrühren. Erneut zum Kochen bringen, bis die Sauce leicht bindet. Durch ein Sieb passieren, erkalten lassen.
Für das Sorbet: Wasser, Zucker und ausgeschabtes Vanillemark zum Kochen bringen. Erkalten lassen, mit dem Joghurt verrühren und die Creme in der Eismaschine gefrieren.
Bananen schälen, in Scheiben schneiden und in eine kleine Schüssel geben. Den Zucker in einem kleinen Topf bei geringer Hitze schmelzen, bis er mittelbraun karamelisiert und klümpchenfrei ist. Mit dem Orangensaft ablöschen (Vorsicht vor Spritzern) und kochen, bis sich der erhärtete Karamel wieder aufgelöst hat. Die heiße Flüßigkeit über die Bananenscheiben gießen und erkalten lassen.
Zum Servieren: Den Kuchen in Stücke schneiden oder runde „Brownies" ausstechen. Auf Teller verteilen und mit Bananenscheiben belegen. Mit je einem kleinen Löffel Eis dekorieren und mit etwas Sauce umgießen.

Giorgio Locatelli's dark, Hush-Puppy eyes stare calmly but wide awake at an imaginary spot on the light ochre wall of the Zafferano, his hands holding back his leonine mane of hair: "I cook for the mouth and for the stomach, I am not a stylist who paints pictures on the plate. The guests must feel content. You must let them live and experience, present the best products. That is what we Italians require of a good restaurant. Basta". This is what he calls a food-driven restaurant. A short time later in the kitchen. Locatelli's eyes are screwed up, sparkle, hurling flashes of lightning across the room. "Who hasn't sieved this stock properly? Where the devil are the vegetables for the minestrone? Bring some oil, avanti, avanti, avanti!" In the kitchen, Locatelli is in his element and is like a man possessed. He adjusts seasoning, arranges, discards, praises and curses. He is 34 years old and drives himself and his young team to supreme efforts. No-one can dispute any more that among the innumerable Italian restaurants in London he has made the Zafferano one of the best, if not the best.

Locatelli comes from northern Italy, where his family have for years run a famous restaurant near Lake Maggiore. His cuisine is also northern Italian in character, using no butter or cream, but olive oil and Italian vinegar and the freshest and best ingredients. He thanks Gualtiero Marchesi, with whom he has worked, for some important stimuli. The tomato salad, made partly with lightly braised, partly fresh fruit, and seasoned with the finest particles of dried tuna proves once again just one thing: the pure, uncompromising tomato taste is an experience in itself. The grissini made on the premises, barely finger-thick sticks of crispy bread dough originally from Piedmont, are addictive. The stuffed baby squid melt in the mouth. And Locatelli demonstrates with style the heights to which an expert can bring a simple dish like gnocchi with mozzarella. Sommelier Enzo Cassini presides over a wine cellar that with 133 of the best Italian wines leaves nothing to be desired.

Giorgio Locatellis tiefdunkle Hush-Puppy-Augen fixieren ruhig aber hellwach einen imaginären Punkt im hellem Ocker der Wände des Zafferano, seine Hände bändigen die Löwenmähne: „Ich koche für den Mund und für den Magen, ich bin kein Stylist, der Bilder auf Teller malt. Die Gäste müssen sich wohlfühlen, man muß sie mitleben und miterleben lassen, ihnen die besten Produkte präsentieren, das ist unser italienischer Anspruch an ein gutes Restaurant. Basta". Food-driven Restaurant nennt er das. Kurze Zeit später in der Küche: Locatellis Augen funken, schleudern Blitze durch den Raum: „Wer hat hier den Fond nicht richtig passiert? Wo zum Teufel ist das Gemüse für die Minestrone? Öl her, avanti, avanti, avanti!" Locatelli ist in der Küche und damit in seinem Element, und da ist er ein Besessener. Er schmeckt ab, arrangiert, verwirft, lobt und flucht. Er ist 34 Jahre alt und treibt sich selbst und seine junge Mannschaft zu Höchstleistungen. Daß er unter den unzähligen italienischen Restaurants in London das Zafferano zu einem der besten, wenn nicht gar zum allerbesten Italiener gemacht hat, bestreitet niemand mehr.

Locatelli kommt aus Norditalien, wo seine Familie in der Nähe des Lago Maggiore seit Jahren ein renommiertes Restaurant betreibt. Norditalienisch geprägt ist auch seine Küche; Butter- und Sahne-frei, gekocht wird mit Olivenöl und italienischem Essig und mit frischesten und besten Zutaten. Gualtiero Marchesi, mit dem er zusammengearbeitet hat, verdankt er wesentliche Impulse. Der Tomatensalat, teils aus angedünsteten, teils aus frischen Früchten und mit feinsten Partikeln von getrocknetem Thunfisch gewürzt, beweist wieder einmal nur das Eine: ein ultimativer Tomatengeschmack ist ein Erlebnis für sich. Die selbst-gebackenen Grissini, knapp fingerdicke, knusprige Brotteigstangen, die im Piemont ihre Heimat haben, machen süchtig. Die gefüllten Tintenfischchen zergehen auf der Zunge. Auf welche Höhen ein Könner das Einfachgericht „Gnocchi mit Mozzarella" führen kann, beweist Locatelli mit seltener Bravour. Sommelier Enzo Cassini wacht über einen Weinkeller, der mit 133 besten Italienern keine Wünsche offen läßt.

"Sundried Tomatoes"

"Pesto"

Insalate selvatiche ai carciofi e parmigiano
Artichokes and wild salad with parmesan

Insalata di polipo, patate novelle e sedano
Octopus salad with new potatoes and celery

Insalata di spinaci al vino rosso e ricotta salata
Baby spinach salad with red wine vinaigrette and ricotta cheese

Caponata di melanzane e tonno
Pickled aubergine and tuna salad with pine nuts and basil

Insalata mosciame di tonno, fagiolini e pomodori
Wind dried tuna salad with french beans and tomato

Calamari ripieni al pomodoro
Chargrilled stuffed squid with tomato

Carpaccio di manzo all'olio tartufato
Beef carpaccio with truffle oil

Mozzarella di bufala alle melanzane   Supplement £2.00
Buffalo mozzarella with baked aubergine and oregano

Insalata gemma al parmigiano
Cos salad with parmesan vinegar

———

Tortelli di ricotta di bufala e asparagi
Asparagus and ricotta parcels

Ravioli ai gamberi
Prawn parcels with basil and tomato sauce

Linguine alle vongole   Supplement £2.50
Flat spaghetti with sweet chilli, garlic and clams

Pappardelle alle fave e rucola
Pasta ribbons with broad beans and rocket

Gnocchi di semolino con scamorza affumicata
Semolina dough baked with smoked cheese

Gnocchi di patate al pepe nero, salsa al caprino e erba cipollina
Potato dumplings with black pepper, goat's cheese sauce

Tagliolini alle zucchine e bottarga
Home made egg pasta with courgette and dried tuna roe

Minestrone primaverile agli scampi e pesto
Spring vegetable soup with dublin bay prawns and basil pesto

Tortellini in brodo
Meat and black truffle parcels in clear broth

Risotto con Asparagi
Asparagus risotto

Fetta d'agnello primaverile alla griglia con peperonata
Chargrilled spring leg of lamb with peppers and aubergine

Anatra arrosto al balsamico e farro   Supplement £2.50
Roast duck with balsamic vinegar and spelt

Paillarde di pollo con spinaci
Chargrilled chicken breast with spinach

Filetti di maiale all'aglio novello
Pork fillet and new season garlic

Rognone di vitello ai carciofi e lenticchie
Veal kidneys with artichoke and lentils

Filetti di san pietro con patate e olive
Pan fried fillet of John Dory with potatoes and olives

Filetti di passera in crosta di basilico
Pan fried fillet of plaice in a basil crust

Trancio di spada alla griglia   Supplement £2.50
Chargrilled Swordfish with rocket and tomato salad

Filetti di triglia all'anconetana   Supplement £2.50
Red Mullet with parma ham and sage

Trancio di Salmone al balsamico
Panfried salmon with balsamic vinegar

———

Yogourt congelato ai frutti di bosco
Frozen yoghurt with spring berries

Torta di limone al mascarpone
Lemon and mascarpone tart

Tiramisú

Torta al cioccolato e mandorle
Chocolate and almond tart

Composizione di frutta e sorbetti
Fresh fruits and sorbet composition

Cannoli siciliani in salsa all'arancia
Brittle pastry tubes filled with ricotta, candied fruit, pistacchio nuts and orange coulis

Babá al rhum e frutta
Rum-babá with cream and fruits

Tortino di rabarbaro e amaretto yogurt congelato
Rhubarb and amaretto tartlette with frozen yoghurt

Mango e frutti della passione con sorbetti
Fresh passion fruit and mango with sorbet

Semifreddo di torrone salsa al cioccolato
Nougat parfait, chocolate sauce

Two Courses   £21.50   Three Courses   £25.50   Four Courses   £28.50
As our produce is purchased freshly each day, please be understanding if certain dishes are not available
SERVICE NOT INCLUDED

Bresaola di manzo al caprino
Thinly sliced cured beef with rocket salad and goats cheese dressing

Insalata di polipo, patate novelle e sedano
Octopus salad with new potatoes and celery

Insalata gemma salad al parmigiano
Cos salad with parmesan vinegar

Insalata mosciame di tonno, fagiolini e pomodori
Wind dried tuna salad with french beans and tomato

Insalate di spinaci al vino rosso e ricotta salata
Baby spinach salad with red wine vinaigrette and ricotta cheese

Caponata di melanzane e tonno
Pickled aubergine and tuna salad with pine nuts and basil

Carpaccio di legumi
Chargrilled vegetables with basil

Calamari ripieni al pomodoro
Chargrilled stuffed squid with tomato

Mozzarella di bufala e melanzane   Supplement £2.00
Buffalo mozzarella with baked aubergine and oregano

Carpaccio di manzo all'olio tartufato
Beef carpaccio with truffle oil

Culatello alle zucchine
Thin slices of cured ham with courgettes

———

Tortelli di ricotta di bufala e asparagi
Asparagus and ricotta parcels

Gnocchi di patate al pepe nero, salsa al caprino
Potato dumplings with black pepper, goat's cheese sauce

Tagliolini alle zucchine e bottarga
Home made egg pasta with courgette and dried tuna roe

Gnocchi di semolino con scamorza affumicata
Semolina dough baked with smoked cheese

Pappardelle alle fave e rucola
Pasta ribbons with broad beans and rocket

Ravioli ai gamberi
Prawn parcels with basil and tomato sauce

Linguine alle vongole   Supplement £2.00
Flat spaghetti with sweet chilli, garlic and clams

Minestrone primaverile agli scampi e pesto
Spring vegetable soup with dublin bay prawns and basil pesto

Fetta d'agnello primaverile alla griglia con peperonata
Chargrilled spring leg of lamb with peppers and aubergine

Filetti di maiale all'aglio novello
Pork fillet and new season garlic

Antra arrosto al balsamico e farro   Supplement £2.50
Roast duck with balsamic vinegar and spelt

Paillarde di pollo con spinaci
Chargrilled chicken breast with spinach

Filetti di san pietro con patate e olive
Panfried fillet of John Dory with potatoes and olives

Trancio di spada alla griglia   Supplement £2.50
Chargrilled Swordfish with rocket and tomato salad

Trancio di Salmone al balsamico
Panfried salmon with balsamic vinegar

Muggine alla griglia con pomodoro fresco
Chargrilled grey mullet with fresh tomatoes

Filetti di passera in crosta di basilico
Panfried fillet of plaice in a basil crust

———

Tiramisú

Yogourt congelato ai frutti di bosco
Froxen yoghurt with spring berries

Composizione di frutta e sorbetti
Fresh fruits and sorbet composition

Tortino di rabarbaro e amaretto yogurt congelato
Rhubarb and amaretto tartlette with frozen yoghurt

Semifreddo di torrone salsa al cioccolato
Nougat parfait, chocolate sauce

Babá al rhum e frutta
Rum-babá with cream and fruits

Mango e frutti della passione con sorbetti
Fresh passion fruit and mango with sorbet

Cannoli siciliani in salsa all'arancia
Brittle pastry tubes filled with ricotta, candied fruit, pistacchio nuts and orange coulis

———

Two Courses   £16.50

Three Courses   £19.50

As our produce is purchased freshly each day, please be understanding
if certain dishes are not available
SERVICE NOT INCLUDED

VINI BIANCHI

					Bottle
20.	Sette Soli, *Sicilia*	1995	Glass £2.70 125 ml		£10.70
21.	Breganze Bianco, Breganze, *Veneto*	1996			£12.50
22.	Frascati Superiore S. Teresa, Fontana Candida, *Lazio*	1996			£14.00
23.	Orvieto del "Vigneto Torricella" Classico, Bigi, *Umbria*	1995			£15.50
24.	Verdicchio Classico "Casal di Serra", Umani Ronchi, *Marche*	1995			£16.00
25.	Colomba Platino, Salaparuta, *Sicilia*	1996			£18.00
26.	Le Vaglie Verdicchio, Santa Barbara, *Marche*	1995			£19.80
27.	Le Arenaie, Sella e Mosca, *Sardinia*	1996			£18.70
28.	Vigna dei Pini , D'Angelo, *Basilicata*	1994			£19.00
29.	Erbaluce di Calusso, Orsolani, *Piemonte*	1996			£19.50
30.	Pomino Bianco, Frescobaldi, *Toscana*	1996			£19.50
31.	Soave Classico "La Rocca", Pieropan, *Veneto*	1995			£22.00
32.	Francia Corta Bellavista, Bellavista, *Lombardia*	1995			£24.00
33.	Sauvignon, Villa Berthenau, *Alto Adige*	1995			£23.50
34.	Pinot Grigio, Franz Haas, *Alto Adige*	1995-96			£25.00
35.	Pinot Grigio,Felluga, *Friuli*	1996			£29.00
36.	Gavi di Gavi "La Minaia", N. Bergaglio, *Piemonte*	1995			£27.00
37.	Serena, Sauvignon, Banfi, *Tuscana*	1994			£29.00
38.	Villa Margon Chardonnay, Lunelli, *Veneto*	1994			£31.50
40.	Terre Alte, Felluga, *Friuli*	1993-94			£37.80
41.	Vintage Tunina, Jermnan, *Friuli*	1993-95			£45.00
42.	Bianca di Valguarnera, Salaparuta, *Sicilia*	1992			£39.50
43.	Cabreo "La Pietra del Muschio", Ruffino, *Toscana*	1990			£39.50
44.	Uccellanda Chardonnay, Bellavista, *Lombardia*	1994			£45.00
45.	Where Dreams Have No End Chardonnay, *Jermann, Friuli*	1995			£61.00
46.	Ca del Bosco, Chardonnay, *Zanella*	1993			£63.00
47.	Chardonnay - Gaja & Rey, Gaja, *Piemonte*	1995			£89.00

HALF BOTTLES BIANCHI

48.	Vigneto Torricella, Orvieto Classico, Bigi, *Umbria*	1995		£9.50
49.	Soave Classico Pieropan, *Veneto*	1995		£12.50
50.	Pinot Grigio, Puiatti, *Friuli*	1996		£14.00

HALF BOTTLES ROSSI

140.	Chianti Classico, Brolio, *Toscana*	1994-5		£10.50
141.	Corvo Rosso, Salaparuta, *Sicilia*	1994		£ 9.80
142.	Barolo, Villa Doria, *Piemonte*	1992		£15.80

VINI ROSSI

					Bottle
51.	Montepulciano D'Abruzzo, *Abruzzo*	1995	Glass £2.70 125 ml		£10.70
52.	Merlot Breganze di Breganze, Breganze, *Veneto*	1995			£12.50
53.	Salice Salentino Riserva, Candido, *Puglia*	1993			£14.50
54.	Rosso Conero 'San Lorenzo', Umani-Ronchi, *Marche*	1994			£16.00
55.	Marzemino, Tarczal, *Trentino*	1994-5			£19.00
56.	Dolcetto D'Asti, Alasia, *Piemonte*	1995			£19.00
57.	Rosso Piceno Superiore, Cocci Grifoni, *Marche*	1995			£19.50
58.	Pignocco Rosso, Santa Barbara, *Marche*	1995			£18.50
59.	Riserva del Carignano 'Rocca Rubia', Santadi, *Sardinia*	1993			£22.00
60.	Aglianico del Vulture Riserva, D'Angelo, *Basilicata*	1991			£23.00
61.	Pinot Nero, Vigna Barthenau, Hofstatter, *Alto Adige*	1994-95			£25.00
62.	Campovecchio Rosso, Castel de Paolis, *Lazio*	1994			£25.00
63.	Vino Nobile di Montepulciano, Le Casalte, *Toscana*	1993			£29.00
64.	Sassoalloro, Biondi Santi, *Toscana*	1994			£29.50
65.	Cumaro Rosso, Umani Ronchi, *Marche*	1993			£28.50
66.	Cumaro Rosso, Umani Ronchi, *Marche*	1988-90			£45.00
67.	Chianti Classico, Felsina, *Toscana*	1993-94			£27.00
68.	Chianti Classico Riserva Castell'in Villa, *Toscana*	1988			£39.00
69.	Rubesco Riserva Monticchio, Lungarotti, *Umbria*	1986			£33.00
70.	Sfursat 5 Stelle, Valtellina, *Lombardia*	1994			£37.00
71.	San Leonardo di Vallagarina, Gonzaga, *Trentino*	1991			£41.00
72.	Il Latini, Il Vivaio, *Toscana*	1993			£36.50
73.	San Giorgio, Lungarotti, *Umbria*	1986			£39.00
74.	Cepparello, Isole e Olena, *Toscana*	1991			£43.00
75.	Fontalloro, Felsina, *Toscana*	1990			£61.00
76.	Fontalloro, Felsina, *Toscana*	1993			£45.00
77.	Pinot Nero, Marchese Pancrazi, *Toscana*	1990			£40.00
78.	Duca Enrico, Salaparuta, *Sicilia*	1992			£53.00
79.	Flaccianello del Pieve, Fontodi, *Toscana*	1990			£53.00
80.	Flaccianello del Pieve, Fontodi, *Toscana*	1991			£38.50
81.	Pinot Nero, Ca'del Bosco, Lombardia	1987-88			£49.00
82.	Marchese di Villamarina, Sella e Mosca, *Sardinia*	1992			£49.50
83.	Summus, Banfi, *Toscana*	1993			£46.00

SPUMANTI & CHAMPAGNE

					Bottle
1.	Prosecco Ombra Gregoletto	N.V.	Glass £4.00 125 ml		£19.50
2.	Ronco Monpiano Spumante	1991			£27.00
3.	Ferrari Spumante Brut	N.V.			£31.00
4.	Ferrari Spumante Rosé	N.V.			£33.00
5.	De Horsay Champagne	N.V.	Glass £5.50 125 ml		£29.80
6.	De Horsay 35cl	N.V.			£15.00
7.	Laurent Perrier Brut	N.V.			£41.00
8.	Laurent Perrier Rosé	N.V.			£44.00
9.	Moet & Chandon	1992			£46.00
10.	Moet et Chandon Rosé	1990			£51.00
11.	Veuve Clicquot Ponsardin	1989			£55.00
12.	Louis Roederer Cristal	1989			£120.00
13.	Dom Perignon	1988			£98.00

VINI ROSATI

15.	Chiaretto de Bardolino L'Infinito, Santi, *Veneto*	1996		£15.00
16.	Vin Ruspo, Capezzana, *Toscana*	1996		£19.50
17.	Oleandro, Sella e Mosca, *Sardinia*	1996		£16.50

RISERVE

TOSCANA

91.	Brunello di Montalcino, Castello Banfi	1992		£35.00
92.	Brunello di Montalcino Riserva, Col D. Orcia	1990		£49.00
93.	Brunello di Montalcino, Riserva Argiano	1991		£46.00
98.	Brunello di Montalcino, Vigna del Fiore, I Barbi	1991		£59.50
94.	Brunello di Montalcino, Castello Banfi	1990		£85.00
95.	Brunello di Montalcino, Fattoria I Barbi	1991		£52.00
96.	Brunello di Montalcino, Poggio alle Mura, Mastropaolo	1975		£85.00
97.	Brunello di Montalcino, Biondi Santi	1983		£149.00
99.	Ornellaia, Tenuta dell'Ornellaia, *Bolgheri*	1988		£180.00
100.	Ornellaia, Tenuta dell'Ornellaia, *Bolgheri*	1986		£130.00
101.	Ornellaia, Tenuta dell'Ornellaia, *Bolgheri*	1992		£56.00
102.	Sassicaia, Tenuta S. Guido, Rochetta	1993		£84.00
103.	Sassicaia, Tenuta S. Guido, Rochetta	1982		£270.00
104.	Tignanello, Antinori	1994		£60.00
105.	Tignanello, Antinori	1978		£150.00
106.	Tignanello, Antinori	1986		£130.00
111.	Tignanello, Antinori	1987		£75.00
107.	Masseto, Tenuta dell'Ornellaia, *Bolgheri*	1993		£90.00
108.	Solaia, Antinori	1993-94		£98.00
109.	Solaia, Antinori	1988		£180.00
110.	Solaia, Antinori	1978		£205.00

PIEMONTE

112.	Barolo, Vigna Scarrone, Cesari	1992		£35.00
113.	Barolo, Rocche dei Manzoni	1990		£41.00
114.	Barolo, Vigna La Raul, Rocche dei Manzoni	1993		£61.00
115.	Barolo, Riserva Borgogno	1982-85		£89.00
116.	Barolo, Cerequio, Gromis	1989		£90.00
117.	Barolo, Granbussia, Aldo Conterno	1989-90		£130.00
118.	Barolo, Sperss Gaja	1990		£170.00
119.	Barolo, Sperss Gaja	1991		£120.00
120.	Barolo, Pio Cesare	1961		£180.00
123.	Barbaresco Gaja	1991		£80.00
124.	Barbaresco il Bricco, Pio Cesare	1990		£65.00
125.	Barbaresco, Gaja	1989		£150.00
126.	Barbaresco, Sori Tildin	1989		£190.00
127.	Barbaresco, Costa Russi, Gaja	1982-83		£240.00
128.	Barbaresco, Gaja	1964		£220.00
129.	Barbaresco, Gaja	1971		£270.00
130.	Barbaresco, Gaja	1958		£380.00

VENETO

132.	Amarone Classico, Allegrini	1990		£41.00
133.	Amarone Superiore, Le Ragose	1990		£45.00
134.	Amarone Superiore, Bertani	1986-87		£61.00
135.	Amarone Il Bosco Riserva, Cesari	1990		£40.00
136.	La Poja, Allegrini	1990		£72.00
137.	La Poja, Allegrini	1985		£110.00
138.	La Poja, Allegrini	1988		£105.00

SEMOLINA GNOCCHI WITH SCAMORZA SMOKED CHEESE

GRIESSGNOCCHI MIT GERÄUCHERTEM SCAMORZA KÄSE

For 4 persons:

1 litre/1 pint 14 oz/4 cups milk,
200 g/6¹/₂ oz/⁴/₅ cup wheat semolina,
2 egg yolks,
50 g/1²/₃ oz/¹/₅ cup grated Parmesan,
a pinch of nutmeg,
salt, pepper,
2 whole Scamorza smoked cheeses

Bring the milk to the boil in a thick-bottomed pan. Stir in the semolina and cook slowly for half an hour, stirring frequently.
Remove the pan from the stove, then stir in the egg yolk, the Parmesan and the nutmeg, and season with salt and pepper. Spread the semolina mixture onto a flat tray. Cover with clingfilm and allow to cool.
Slice the cheeses. Stamp out round pieces of semolina of the same size and arrange in an ovenproof dish. Cover with cheese slices and bake in a 200° C/390° F preheated oven until the cheese has melted and the semolina is golden brown.

Für 4 Personen:

1 Liter Milch,
200 g Weizengrieß,
2 Eigelb,
50 g geriebener Parmesan,
eine Prise Muskat,
Salz, Pfeffer,
2 geräucherte Scamorza Käselaibchen

Die Milch in einem Topf mit dickem Boden zum Kochen bringen. Den Grieß einrühren und bei kleiner Hitze eine halbe Stunde köcheln lassen, dabei immer wieder umrühren. Den Topf vom Herd nehmen, dann die Eigelb, den Parmesan und den Muskat einrühren, mit Salz und Pfeffer abschmecken. Die Grießmasse auf eine flache Platte streichen und mit Frischhaltefolie bedeckt erkalten lassen.
Den Käse in Scheiben schneiden. Aus der Grießmasse gleichgroße, runde Stücke ausstechen und in eine feuerfeste Form legen. Mit Käsescheiben bedeckt im auf 200° C vorgeheizten Ofen backen, bis der Käse geschmolzen und der Grieß goldbraun ist.

POTATO GNOCCHI WITH BLACK PEPPER AND GOATS' CHEESE SAUCE

KARTOFFELGNOCCHI MIT SCHWARZEM PFEFFER UND ZIEGENKÄSESAUCE

For 4 - 6 persons:

1 kg potatoes,
375 g/12 1/2 oz/1 1/2 cups flour,
1 egg,
1 tsp freshly ground black pepper,
3 tsp salt

100 g/3 1/2 oz goats' cheese,
100 ml/3 1/2 fl oz/ 2/5 cup milk,
75 ml/2 1/2 fl oz/ 1/3 cup double cream

Boil the potatoes in their jackets. When cooked, peel them and cut into quarters and spread on a baking sheet.

Place in the hot oven at 200° C/390° C to dry for about five minutes. Squeeze the potatoes through a potato press and mix well with the flour, eggs, salt and pepper.

When the mixture is cool, shape it into long thin rolls. Cut into 2 cm/ 4/5 inch pieces and hand-shape them into gnocchi by rolling them with the thumb over the back of a fork. Put them into boiling salted water, lower the heat and cook the gnocchi for five minutes.

For the sauce: Heat the goats' cheese with the milk and the cream until melted. Season with salt and black pepper. Mix the well-drained gnocchi with the hot sauce and transfer to plates. Serve sprinkled with chives.

Für 4 - 6 Personen:

1 kg Kartoffeln,
375 g Mehl,
1 Ei,
1 TL frisch gemahlener, schwarzer Pfeffer,
3 TL Salz

100 g Ziegenkäse,
100 ml Milch,
75 ml Doppelrahm

Kartoffeln in der Haut weichkochen. Wenn sie gar sind, schälen, vierteln und auf einem Backblech auslegen. Im heißen Backofen bei 200° C ca. fünf Minuten trocknen lassen. Durch eine Kartoffelpresse drücken und mit dem Mehl, dem Ei, Salz und Pfeffer gut vermischen. Mit einem Tuch bedecken und erkalten lassen. Aus dem abgekühlten Teig lange, dünne Rollen formen. Daraus ca. 2 cm lange Stücke schneiden und von Hand Gnocchi daraus formen, in dem die Teigstücke mit dem Daumen über einen Gabelrücken gerollt werden. In kochendes Salzwasser geben, Hitze zurückstellen und die Gnocchi fünf Minuten sieden.

Für die Sauce: Ziegenkäse in der Milch mit der Sahne erhitzen und schmelzen lassen. Mit Salz und schwarzem Pfeffer abschmecken. Die abgetropften Gnocchi mit der heißen Sauce vermengen und auf Teller anrichten. Mit Schnittlauch bestreut servieren.

MINESTRONE OF LANGOUSTINES WITH PESTO

MINESTRONE MIT GARNELENSCHWÄNZEN UND PESTO

For 6 persons:

For the consommé:
1 kg/2 lb 3 oz unshelled langoustines,
a small piece each of celery, carrot and fennel,
roughly chopped,
1 tbsp tomato purée, 1 bayleaf,
salt, pepper, 50 g/1 2/3 oz/1/5 cup egg white,
1.5 litres/2 pints 12 fl oz/6 cups fish stock

For the soup filling:
1 small onion, 1/2 leek, 1 small carrot,
1 stick of celery, 1/2 courgette,
1 medium-sized potato, 50 g/1 2/3 oz mange-tout,
12 asparagus spears, 2 tbsp olive oil

pesto:
1 bunch basil, 1 garlic clove,
100 ml/3 1/2 fl oz/2/5 cup olive oil

Shell the langoustine tails and keep in the refrigerator. Grind the heads and tails in a large mortar. Add the chopped vegetables, tomato purée, bayleaf and a little salt and pepper. Then pour over the egg white and stir until all ingredients are bound. Place in a saucepan with a heavy base and pour on the cold fish stock.

Bring to the boil and simmer over a low heat for two and a half hours. Then pass the consommé through a muslin.

Cut the vegetables for the soup filling into cubes or diamond shapes. Heat the olive oil in a saucepan. Gradually add the vegetables and sauté – onions first, followed by the leeks, carrots, celery and finally the courgettes. Cover the pan and sweat for five minutes.

Add the consommé and cook for a further ten minutes. Add the potato and cook for a further ten minutes. Last of all, add the mange-tout and asparagus spears and cook for five minutes. Fry the langoustines in a little olive oil.

For the pesto: Finely purée the basil and garlic in the blender, gradually adding the olive oil.

To serve: Pour the minestrone into soup plates. Distribute the langoustines and finally top with a small spoonful of pesto.

Für 6 Personen:

Für die Consommé:
1 kg ungeschälte Garnelen,
je ein kleines Stück Sellerie, Karotte und Fenchel,
grob gehackt,
1 EL Tomatenmark, 1 Lorbeerblatt,
Salz, Pfeffer, 50 g Eiweiß,
1,5 Liter Fischbrühe

Für die Suppeneinlage:
1 kleine Zwiebel, 1/2 Lauchstange, 1 kleine Karotte,
1 Stange Staudensellerie, 1/2 Zucchini,
1 mittlere Kartoffel, 50 g Zuckerschoten,
12 Spargelspitzen, 2 EL Olivenöl

Pesto:
1 Bund Basilikum, 1 Knoblauchzehe,
100 ml Olivenöl

Garnelenschwänze auslösen und kühlstellen. Die Köpfe und Schalen in einem großen Mörser zerstampfen. Gehacktes Gemüse, Tomatenmark, Lorbeerblatt und etwas Salz und Pfeffer dazu geben, dann die Eiweiß darübergeben und umrühren, bis alle Zutaten gut vermischt sind. In einen Topf mit dickem Boden geben und die kalte Fischbrühe zugießen. Zum Kochen bringen und bei kleiner Hitze zweieinhalb Stunden sieden, dann die Consommé durch ein feines Tuch passieren.

Die Gemüse für die Suppeneinlage in Würfel oder Rauten schneiden. In einem Topf das Olivenöl erhitzen. Nach und nach die Gemüse zugeben und anschwitzen. Zuerst die Zwiebel, dann den Lauch, die Karotte, den Sellerie und zum Schluß die Zucchini. Zudecken und 5 Minuten dünsten lassen. Die Consommé zugießen und weitere 10 Minuten köcheln lassen. Die Kartoffel zugeben, 10 Minuten kochen lassen und zum Schluß die Zuckerschoten und Spargelspitzen hinzufügen und 5 Minuten mitkochen. Die Garnelen in etwas Olivenöl anbraten.

Für das Pesto: Basilikum und Knoblauch im Mixer fein pürieren, nach und nach das Olivenöl zugießen.

Zum Servieren: Die Minestrone in Teller füllen, die Garnelen verteilen und zum Schluß je einen Löffel Pesto darübergeben.

GRILLED STUFFED SQUID

GEFÜLLTE TINTENFISCHE VOM GRILL

For 4 persons:

500 g/1 lb 2 oz fresh baby squid

For the stuffing:
5 slices white bread, without crust,
milk for soaking,
2 anchovy fillets from the tin,
1 large bunch of flat-leaf parsley,
2 tsp freshly grated Parmesan cheese, 1 tsp garlic oil,
about 100 g/3 1/2 oz freshly crumbled
white bread without crust,
sea salt and freshly ground black pepper

For the sauce:
150 ml/5 fl oz/3/5 cup extra virgin olive oil,
3 ripe tomatoes, cut into eighths and seeded,
6 large, fresh basil leaves

12 slices of ciabatta bread,
3 tbsp chopped parsley,
1 fat clove of garlic, finely chopped

Preparation: Thoroughly wash the squid. Cut off the head and tentacles, remove the eyes, teeth and skin, and dab dry. Skin the bag-like bodies, turn inside out, and remove all entrails, then dab dry.
For the stuffing: Soak the slices of bread in milk. Then squeeze dry and place in the blender. Add the squid heads and tentacles, anchovies, parsley, Parmesan, and garlic oil, and purée to a smooth mousse.
Gradually add the fresh bread crumbs, season with salt and pepper, and continue blending until you have a smooth farce that will hold its shape.
Stuff the farce into the squid and close them with wooden cocktail sticks. Paint the squid with olive oil and lightly season with salt and pepper.
For the sauce: Heat the olive oil in a frying pan; add the tomatoes and basil, season with salt and pepper. Sweat for about five minutes until the tomatoes start to cook down but still retain some shape. Keep warm.
Grill the stuffed squid for about two minutes on each side. Likewise toast the ciabatta bread on the grill.
Remove the skewers from the squid and mix the squid well with the tomatoes. Transfer to plates, sprinkle with parsley and garlic and serve immediately. Serve toasted bread separately.

Für 4 Personen:

500 g frische kleine Tintenfische

Für die Füllung:
5 Scheiben Weißbrot ohne Kruste,
Milch zum Einweichen,
2 Sardellenfilets aus der Dose,
1 großes Bund glatte Petersilie,
2 TL frisch geriebener Parmesan,
1 TL Knoblauchöl,
ca. 100 g frisch geriebenes Weißbrot ohne Rinde,
Meersalz und schwarzer Pfeffer aus der Mühle

Für die Sauce:
150 ml Olivenöl „Extra Vergine",
3 reife Tomaten, in Achtel geschnitten und entkernt,
6 grosse, frische Basilikumblätter

12 Scheiben Ciabattabrot,
3 EL gehackte Petersilie,
1 grosse Knoblauchzehe, fein gehackt

Vorbereitung: Tintenfische gründlich waschen, Kopf mit Fangarmen abschneiden, Augen, Kauwerkzeuge und Haut entfernen, trockentupfen. Die sackartigen Körper enthäuten, umstülpen und die gesamten Innereien entfernen, alles trockentupfen.
Für die Füllung: Brotscheiben in Milch einweichen, anschließend ausdrücken und in einen Mixer geben. Tintenfischköpfe und -tentakel, Sardellen, Petersilie, Parmesan und Knoblauchöl zugeben, dann das Ganze zu einer feinen Creme pürieren. Nach und nach die frischen Brotkrumen zugeben, mit Salz und Pfeffer würzen und pürieren, bis die Masse an Konsistenz gewinnt. Die Farce in die Tintenfische füllen und diese mit Holzspießchen verschließen. Die Tintenfische mit Olivenöl bepinseln, mit Salz und Pfeffer leicht würzen.
Für die Sauce: Olivenöl in einer Pfanne erhitzen; Tomaten und Basilikum zugeben, mit Salz und Pfeffer würzen. Ungefähr 5 Minuten dünsten, bis die Tomaten weich sind, aber noch nicht zerfallen. Warmstellen. Gefüllte Tintenfische auf dem Grill von jeder Seite 2 Minuten rösten. Das Ciabattabrot ebenfalls auf dem Grill rösten. Die Holzspießchen aus den Tintenfischen nehmen und diese gut mit den Tomaten vermengen. Auf Teller anrichten, mit Petersilie und Knoblauch bestreuen und sofort servieren. Das geröstete Brot separat dazu reichen.

ROAST PORK FILLET WITH NEW SEASON GARLIC

SCHWEINEFILET MIT JUNGEM KNOBLAUCH

For 4 persons:

*8 slices of pork fillet of about 50 g/1²/₃ oz each,
carefully trimmed of all fat,
8 thin slices of Italian lardo,
2 heads of new season garlic,
1 tbsp butter, 150 g/5 oz/³/₅ cup goose fat*

*For the chicken jus:
Carcass of 1 chicken,
2 tbsp peanut oil, 1 tbsp butter,
1 garlic clove, crushed, 2 shallots, chopped,
1 carrot, cut into pieces,
1 sprig rosemary, 2 bayleaves,
1 tsp tomato purée, 1 tsp flour,
250 ml/8 fl oz/1 cup chicken stock,
60 ml/2 fl oz/¹/₄ cup white wine*

*200 g/7 oz cooked saffron risotto, cooled,
a little flour, 2 tbsp peanut oil*

Wrap each of the pork medaillons in a slice of lardo and tie with string. Cut the garlic cloves in half and sauté in butter for five minutes on all sides. Transfer to a small ovenproof dish, half-cover with goose fat; place in a 200° C/390° F oven and cook for about one hour until very soft.

For the chicken jus: Fry the carcass in hot oil. Add the butter. Lower the heat and brown the carcass. Add the garlic, shallots and carrot, and continue frying. Then add the rosemary, bayleaf, tomato purée and flour.

Fry everything, stirring, then quench with the chicken stock. Simmer on a low heat for two hours, stirring occasionally. When finished, pass the jus through a fine sieve.

Cut the saffron risotto into 5 cm/2 in diamond shapes, dip in flour and fry in oil until golden brown.

To assemble the dish: Seal the pork medaillons in a little oil on all sides. Remove from the pan and bake in the 200° C/390° F oven for five minutes. Then remove the string. Deglaze the frying pan with white wine. Reduce a little. Then add the chicken jus and adjust seasoning. Heat the garlic and risotto diamonds in the hot oven. Arrange on warmed plates and encircle with the jus.

Für 4 Personen:

*8 Scheiben Schweinefilet von je ca. 50 g,
sorgfältig von allem Fett befreit,
8 dünne Scheiben italienischer Speck,
2 Knollen junger Knoblauch,
1 EL Butter, 150 g Gänseschmalz*

*Für die Geflügeljus:
Karkassen von einem Huhn,
2 EL Erdnußöl, 1 EL Butter,
1 Knoblauchzehe, zerdrückt, 2 Schalotten, gehackt,
1 Karotte, in Stücke geschnitten,
1 Zweig Romarin, 2 Lorbeerblätter,
1 TL Tomatenmark, 1 TL Mehl,
250 ml Hühnerbrühe,
60 ml Weißwein*

*200 g fertig gekochtes, abgekühltes Safranrisotto,
etwas Mehl, 2 EL Erdnußöl*

Die Schweinemedaillons in je eine Scheibe Speck wickeln und mit Bindfaden zubinden. Knoblauchknollen halbieren und in Butter rundum 5 Minuten braten. In einer kleinen, feuerfesten Form mit Gänseschmalz halb bedeckt im Ofen bei 200° C ungefähr eine Stunde sehr weich garen.

Für die Geflügeljus: Karkassen im Öl heiß anbraten. Butter zugeben und bei reduzierter Hitze die Karkassen bräunen. Knoblauch, Schalotten und Karotte zugeben, weiterbraten, dann den Rosmarin, Lorbeer, das Tomatenmark und das Mehl zugeben.

Das Ganze unter Rühren braten und mit der Brühe ablöschen. Bei kleiner Hitze zwei Stunden köcheln lassen, von Zeit zu Zeit umrühren. Zum Schluß die Jus durch ein feines Sieb passieren.

Von dem Risotto ca. 5 cm große Rauten formen, diese in Mehl wenden und im Öl goldbraun braten.

Fertigstellung: Die Schweinemedaillons in einer Pfanne in wenig Öl rundum braten. Herausnehmen, im 200° C heißen Ofen fünf Minuten fertig garen, Bindfaden entfernen.

Die Pfanne mit Weißwein ablöschen, etwas einkochen lassen, dann die Geflügeljus zugießen und abschmecken. Knoblauch und Risottorauten im heißen Ofen erwärmen. Auf vorgewärmte Teller anrichten, mit der Jus umgießen.

LEMON AND MASCARPONE TART

ZITRONENTORTE MIT MASCARPONE

For 6 - 8 persons:

Pastry:
270 g/9 oz soft butter,
240 g/8 oz caster sugar,
2 eggs, 500 g/1 lb 2 oz flour

Filling:
2 egg yolks, 2 whole eggs,
120 g/4 oz caster sugar,
40 g/1 1/3 oz butter,
2 tbsp cornflour, 1/2 tsp honey,
400 g/13 oz mascarpone cheese,
180 ml/6 fl oz lemon juice,
grated zest of 2 untreated lemons

For the pastry: Beat the butter with the sugar until light and airy. Then stir in the eggs. Work in the flour, cover, and place the pastry in the refrigerator for one hour. Roll out the pastry on a floured work surface and use it to line a round, buttered and floured cake or spring mould. Blind bake in the oven at 190° C/375° F.

For the filling: Beat the eggs and sugar in a pan with a whisk until fluffy.

Then add the butter, lemon juice and the grated lemon zest, and beat vigorously. Work in the cornflour, honey and mascarpone. Stirring constantly, slowly heat and simmer until the mixture becomes thick.

Pour the mixture into the baked pastry case and bake in the oven for ten minutes. Allow to cool before cutting.

Für 6 - 8 Personen:

Teig:
270 g weiche Butter,
240 g Grießzucker,
2 Eier, 500 g Mehl

Füllung:
2 Eigelb, 2 ganze Eier,
120 g Grießzucker,
40 g Butter,
2 EL Maisstärke, 1/2 TL Honig,
400 g Mascarpone,
180 ml Zitronensaft,
geriebene Schale von 2 unbehandelten Zitronen

Für den Teig: Butter mit Zucker schaumig rühren, dann die Eier einrühren. Das Mehl einarbeiten und den Teig zugedeckt eine Stunde in den Kühlschrank stellen. Auf einer bemehlten Arbeitsfläche den Teig ausrollen und eine runde, mit Butter eingefettete und mit Mehl ausgestäubte Kuchen- oder Springform damit auskleiden. Im Ofen bei 190° C blind backen.

Für die Füllung: Eier und Zucker in einem Topf mit dem Schneebesen schaumig rühren. Dann die Butter, den Zitronensaft und die geriebene Zitronenschale zugeben und kräftig schlagen. Maisstärke, Honig und Mascarpone einarbeiten. Unter ständigem Rühren langsam erhitzen und köcheln lassen, bis die Masse bindet. In den vorgebackenen Kuchenteig füllen und im Ofen zehn Minuten fertig backen. Vor dem Aufschneiden erkalten lassen.

AMARETTI BISCUITS WITH RHUBARB AND STRAWBERRY COMPOTE

AMARETTIKÜCHLEIN MIT RHABARBER-ERDBEERKOMPOTT

For 4 persons:

For the biscuits:
250 g/8 oz almond flour,
250 g/8 oz caster sugar,
60 g/2 oz bitter almonds, peeled and finely chopped,
125 g/4 oz icing sugar,
2 tsp honey, 5 egg whites

For the compote:
2 sticks of rhubarb, cleaned,
4 tbsp sugar,
150 g/5 oz strawberries

Mix together all the ingredients except the egg white, then fold in the egg whites one after another and vigorously beat with a wooden spoon. Dust a baking sheet with icing sugar.

Using a piping bag, squirt the mixture onto the sheet in 5 cm/2 in piles, leaving sufficient gaps between them. Dredge with icing sugar and leave overnight in a dry place.

Before baking, dust once again with icing sugar, then bake for about ten minutes in a 200° C/390° F oven.

For the compote: Cut the rhubarb into small pieces and heat in a saucepan with the sugar until the juice begins to run. Sweat until soft on a low heat. Cut the strawberries into small pieces. Add and briefly cook. Allow to cool.

To serve: Distribute the amaretti biscuits on plates and encircle with the compote. If desired, serve with a ball of blueberry-and-yoghurt ice-cream.

Für 4 Personen:

Für die Kuchen:
250 g Mandelmehl,
250 g Grießzucker,
60 g geschälte, feingehackte Bittermandeln,
125 g Puderzucker,
2 TL Honig, 5 Eiweiß

Für den Kompott:
2 Stangen Rhabarber, geputzt,
4 EL Zucker,
150 g Erdbeeren

Alle Zutaten außer Eiweiß miteinander vermengen, dann die Eiweiß eines nach dem andern unterrühren. Mit einer Holzkelle kräftig den Teig schlagen. Ein Backblech mit Puderzucker bestäuben. Von dem Teig mit einem Spritzsack ca. 5 cm große Häufchen spritzen, genügend Abstand dazwischen lassen. Mit Puderzucker bestreuen und über Nacht an einem trockenen Ort aufbewahren.

Vor dem Backen nochmals mit Puderzucker bestäuben, dann im 200° C heißen Ofen ca. zehn Minuten backen.

Für den Kompott: Den Rhabarber in kleine Stücke schneiden und in einem Topf mit dem Zucker erwärmen, bis er Wasser zieht. Bei kleiner Hitze weichdünsten. Erbeeren kleinschneiden, zugeben und kurz mitkochen. Erkalten lassen.

Zum Servieren: Amarettiküchlein auf Teller verteilen und mit dem Kompott umgießen. Nach Belieben mit einer Kugel Blaubeer-Joghurteis servieren.

AUBERGINE

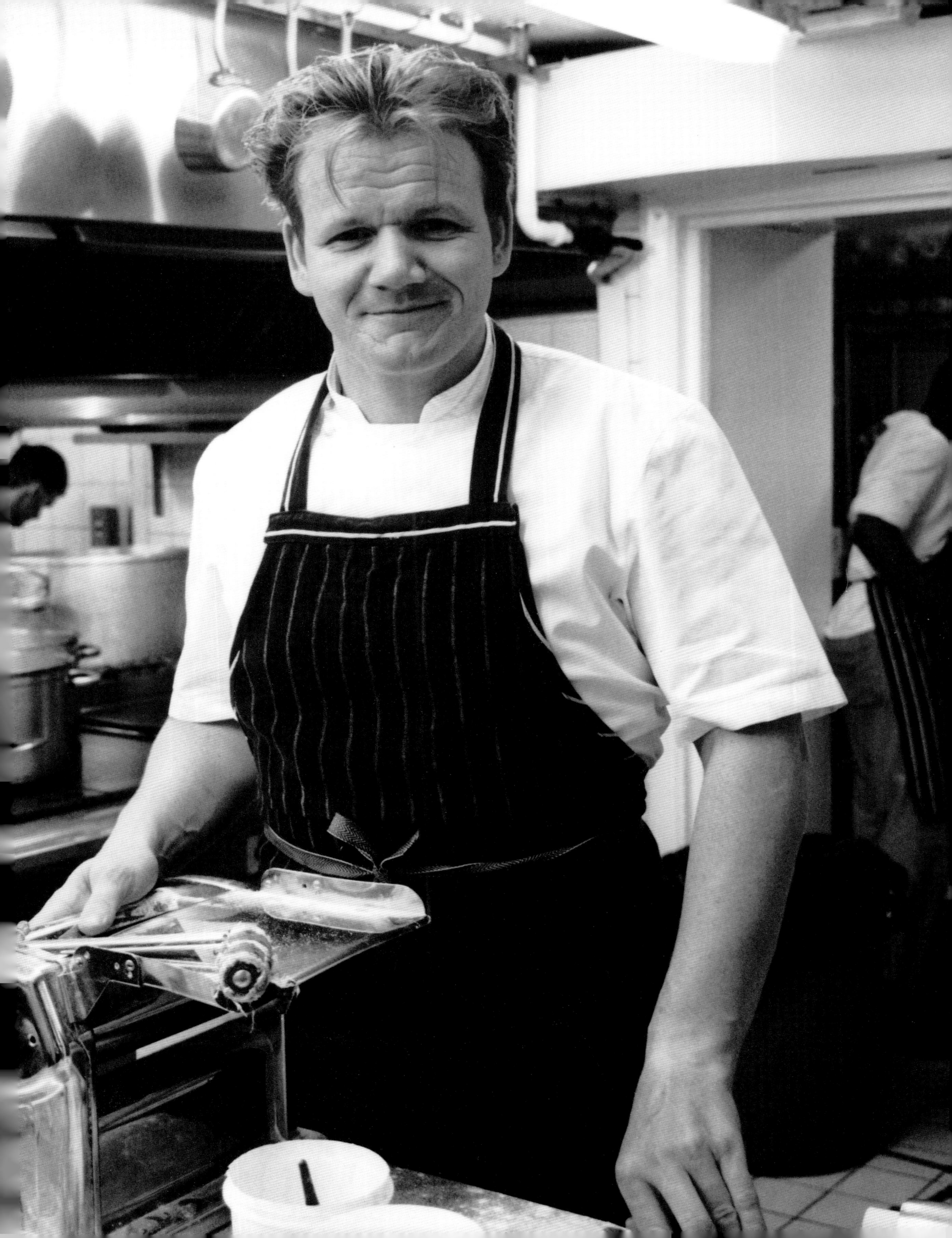

The restaurant is intimate and charming; expressionist paintings and yellow color tints suggest a Provençal light, bringing a southern atmosphere to the room. It is plain that this ambience must have the French name "Aubergine" and not the English "Eggplant". The mere difference in the sound of the words! Gordon Ramsay, 30 years old, has a cuisine that meets all the expectations aroused by the first impression. "A Passion for Flavour" is the name of his cookery book, and this program is present on every plate, just as are the charactistic signatures of his masters Guy Savoy and Joël Robuchon.

The truffled white-bean soup christened "Cappuccino" is one of these taste miracles, a "Passion for Flavour": it is not served in a large soup dish, but in a small cup, and the spoon to match is also small, namely a coffee spoon. But with one spoonful one has more of a mouthful of taste than other cooks can pack into a whole soup tureen. Minimum use of butter and cream, but rich stocks and aromatic oils make his cuisine so intensive, yet so light and carefree, as does his tendency away from meat and more toward fish. Fried bass with braised salsify and vanilla flavors was no small contribution to winning his first Michelin star, awarded in 1995. Fillets of red mullet on aubergine puree with scampi fritters and lemon-grass vinaigrette, together with his tortellini with poached quail formed the basis for the second star in 1997. Thierry Beron, the youthful sommelier, watches over one of the largest London collections of wines from the Côtes-du-Rhône and Alsace.

By the way – up to the age of 19, Gordon Ramsay had a career in soccer with Glasgow Rangers. Then his life took a dramatic turn – he signed on with the still young, but today almost legendary Marco Pierre White at Harvey's Restaurant and learned to cook. Bad luck for football, fortunate for us gourmets!

*D*as Restaurant ist intim und charmant, expressionistische Bilder und gelbe Farbtöne zaubern provenzalisches Licht und südliches Flair in den Raum. Klar, daß es bei diesem Ambiente französisch „Aubergine" und nicht englisch „Eggplant" heißen muß. Alleine schon der Unterschied im Klang der Wörter! Gordon Ramsay, 30 Jahre alt, erfüllt mit seiner Küche alle Erwartungen, die der erste Eindruck hier weckt. „A Passion for Flavour" heißt sein Kochbuch, und dieses Programm ist auf jedem Teller gegenwärtig, ebenso wie die Grundzüge der Handschrift seiner Lehrmeister Guy Savoy und Joël Robuchon.

Die getrüffelte Suppe aus weißen Bohnen, „Cappuccino" getauft, ist ein solches Geschmackswunder, eine solche „Passion for Flavour": Sie kommt nicht im großen Suppenteller, sondern im kleinen Tässchen auf den Tisch, und der Löffel dazu ist ebenso klein: ein Kaffeelöffel eben. Aber mit einem einzigen davon hat man mehr Geschmack im Mund als andere Köche in einer ganzen Suppenterrine unterbringen. Minimaler Einsatz von Butter und Sahne, dafür satte Fonds und aromatische Öle, das macht seine Küche so intensiv und so leicht und unbeschwert, ebenso wie seine Tendenz, die weg vom Fleisch und hin zu mehr Fisch geht. Gebratener Wolfsbarsch mit geschmorten Schwarzwurzeln und Vanillearomen waren an der Verleihung des ersten Michelin-Sternes im Jahre 1995 nicht unwesentlich beteiligt. Filets von der roten Meerbarbe auf Auberginenpüree mit Langoustinen-Beignets und Zitronengras-Vinaigrette waren neben Tortellini mit pochierter Wachtel Grundlage für den zweiten im Jahr 1997. Thierry Berson, der jugendliche Sommelier, wacht über eines der größten Londoner Angebote an Weinen von der Côtes-du-Rhône und aus dem Elsaß.

Übrigens: Gordon Ramsay machte bis zum 19. Lebensjahr Karriere als Fußballer bei Glasgow Rangers. Dann nahm sein Lebenslauf eine dramatische Wende – er heuerte beim zwar noch immer jungen, heute aber fast schon legendären Marco Pierre White in Harvey's Restaurant an und lernte kochen. Pech für den Fußball, ein Glück für uns Feinschmecker!

Braised fillet of turbot with a tortellini of herbs and sauté lettuce,
served with sea urchin sauce

Fillets of red mullet roasted on purée of aubergine with beignet
of langoustine, lemon grass vinaigrette

Sautéd tranche of seabass served with boulangère potatoes
seasoned with thyme flowers, braised fennel and a sauce niçoise

Fillet of halibut poached in a court bouillon, served with courgettes
farcies and a velouté of broad beans

Canon of lamb roasted with herbs with a couscous ratatouille,
sauté courgettes, served with a tarragon sauce

Ballottine of poulet de Bresse cooked in its own stock,
served with a light morel sauce
(£10 supplement - 2 persons)

Fillet of venison with braised baby turnips and girolles
à la crème, sauce Saint Emilion

Pot au Feu of pigeon from Bresse poached in a bouillon of ceps,
served with choux farci

•

Passion fruit soufflé served with chocolate sorbet amer

Tarte tatin of pineapple caramelised with vanilla

Assiette de l'Aubergine
(for two)

La saveur de chocolate with a mandarin sorbet

Pyramid of chocolate and lime parfait with fromage blanc sorbet

French cheeses

Three-course menu £45
Coffee and petits fours £4.00

Foie gras three ways; sauté, pressé and
mi-cuit, served with an Earl Grey consommé (£6 supplement)

Salad of roasted sea scallops with new potatoes
and truffle vinaigrette

Ravioli of lobster and langoustine with a confit of tomatoes
and asparagus, in a vinaigrette of lobster

Cappuccino of haricots blancs with sauté girolles and grated truffle

Tartare of sea scallops with crème fraiche and caviar,
served in a basil consommé

Salad of caramelised calf's sweetbreads with sauté ceps

Beignets of grenouilles served with a velouté of fennel

Terrine of ham knuckle, calf's tongue, foie gras,
calf's sweetbread pressé, served with a salad of herbs

•

As our produce is purchased freshly each day,
please be understanding if certain dishes
are not available.

No cigar smoking. If you smoke,
please do so with consideration for other guests.

We recommend Taxis are ordered at least
thirty minutes before you wish to leave.

	Bottle	Half

CHAMPAGNE

#				Bottle	Half
1	Alain Thiénot Brut		NV	31.00	16.00
2	Mumm de Cramant		NV	42.00	
3	Bruno Paillard		NV	49.00	25.00
4	Veuve Clicquot Brut Ponsardin, Yellow Label		NV	54.00	
5	Jacquesson Blanc de Blanc		1990	48.00	24.00
6	Veuve Clicquot Brut Ponsardin, Gold Label		1989	65.00	34.00
7	Perrier Jouët Belle Époque		1989	85.00	
8	Perrier Jouët Belle Époque		1988	79.00	
9	Perrier Jouët Belle Époque		1983	119.00	
10	Louis Roederer Cristal		1989	154.00	
11	Krug Grande Cuvée		NV	149.00	
12	Krug Vintage		1985	190.00	
13	Krug Vintage		1982	209.00	
14	Krug Vintage		1976	248.00	
15	Duval Leroy Cuvée des Roys		1986	73.00	
16	Dom Pérignon		1990	120.00	
17	Dom Pérignon		1988	139.00	280.00(Mag)
18	Dom Pérignon		1985	160.00	
19	Alain Thiénot Grande Cuvée		1985	82.00	
20	Mumm Reneé Lalou Cuvée Prestige		1985	75.00	
21	Bollinger R D		1982	125.00	
22	Dom Pérignon Rosé		1985	248.00	
23	Laurent Perrier Rosé	Rosé	NV	49.00	
24	Alain Thiénot Rosé	Rosé	1989	38.00	
25	Perrier Jouët Belle Époque	Rosé	1982	119.00	

1

SWEET WHITE WINES

BORDEAUX

#			Bottle	Half
29	Château de Ricaud, Loupiac	1990	36.00	
30	Château de Ricaud, Loupiac	1989	39.00	
31	Château Broustet, Barsac 2ème Cru	1988	48.00	26.00
32	Château Guiraud, Sauternes 1er Cru	1988	85.00	
33	Château Filhot, Sauternes 2èmes Cru	1988	68.00	
34	Château Suduiraut, Sauternes 1er Cru	1983		49.00
35	Château Rieussec, Sauternes 1er Cru	1983	135.00	
36	Château Gilette, Sauternes	1975	335.00	
37	Château Gilette, Sauternes	1970	243.00	
38	Château d'Yquem, Sauternes Grand 1er Cru	1980	210.00	
39	Château d'Yquem, Sauternes Grand 1er Cru	1983	371.00	
40	Château d'Yquem, Sauternes Grand 1er Cru	1989		145.00
41	Château d'Yquem, Sauternes Grand 1er Cru	1967	960.00	
42	Château d'Yquem, Sauternes Grand 1er Cru	1955	878.00	

FRENCH REGIONAL WINE

#			Bottle	Half
45	Pacherenc du Vic Bilh Moelleux, Domaine Frédéric Laplace	1993	27.00 (50cl)	
46	Gaillac Doux grains de Folie, Domaine de Causses Marine	1995	24.00 (50cl)	
47	Saussignac Jean Marie Huré, Château de Tourmentine	1993	32.00 (50cl)	
48	Muscat de Beaumes de Venise , Domaine de Durban	1995	28.00	14.00
49	Muscat Domaine des Hautes Lausses	1994	25.00	
50	Maury - Mas Amiel, Charles Dupuy	1994	35.00	
51	Vin de Paille, Daniel Chalandard, Le Vernois	NV	28.00	
52	Jurancon Vendange Tardive, Domaine Cauhapé	1994	39.00	

NEW WORLD

#			Bottle	Half
60	Botrytis Semillon, Mc Guigan Australia	1994		35.00
61	Late Harvest Riesling, Brown Brothers, Australia	1982		18.00
62	Muscat Vin de Glacière, Bonny Doon, Californie	1995		27.00
65	Klein Constantia, Vin de Constance, South Africa	1990	69.00(50cl)	
66	Tokaji Aszú, 5 Puttonyos, Royal Tokay Wine Company, Hungary	1991	29.00(50cl)	
67	Eiswein, A. Fisher, Austria	1992	31.00 (25cl)	

2

FRENCH REGIONAL WINE

#			Bottle	Half
76	Corbières, Château Etang des Colombes, Henri Gualco	1995	18.00	
77	Cassis, Sainte Magdelaine, François Sack	1994	27.00	
78	Prieuré Saint Jean de Bedian, Côtes du Roussillon	1995	30.00	
79	Palette, Château Simone	1994	39.00	
81	Gaillac, Vin de Voile Robert Plageoles, Gauby	1983	86.00	

RHôNE VALLEY WHITE

#			Bottle	Half
90	Châteauneuf du Pape Vieilles Vignes, Domaine de Beaucastel	1989	78.00	
91	Condrieu, Louis Cheze	1994	38.00	
92	Condrieu Doriane, Guigal	1995	71.00	
93	Château Grillet, Neyret Gachet	1986	98.00	
94	Hermitage, Chave	1988	69.00	

ALSACE

#			Bottle	Half
100	Muscat, Louis Sipp	1992	16.00	
101	Sylvaner, Vieilles Vignes, André Ostertag	1994	18.00	
102	Pinot Blanc, Léon Beyer	1995	19.00	
103	Tokay Pinot Gris, Réserve, Jean Trimbach	1994	27.00	
104	Tokay Pinot Gris Lerchenberg, Marc Kreydenweiss	1994	32.00	
105	Tokay Pinot Gris, Clos Jebsal, Domaine Zind Humbrecht	1993	54.00	
106	Gewurztraminer, Charles Schléret	1993	23.00	
107	Gewurztraminer Fleur de Guebwiller, Domaine Schlumberger	1993	25.00	
108	Gewurztraminer Vendange Tardive, Léon Beyer	1989		39.00
109	Gewurztraminer Vendange Tardive, Hugel	1976	98.00	
110	Gewurztraminer Cuvée Anne, Domaine Schlumberger	1976	129.00	
111	Riesling Grand Cru Geisberg, André Kientzler	1992	35.00	
112	Riesling Princes Abbés, Domaine Schlumberger	1994		13.00
113	Riesling, Cuvée Frédéric Emile, Jean Trimbach	1992	39.00	
114	Riesling Grand Cru Kiterle, Domaine Schlumberger	1991	42.00	
115	Riesling Grand Cru Kiterle, Domaine Schlumberger	1986	55.00	
116	Riesling, Clos Sainte Hune, Jean Trimbach	1986	64.00	32.00
117	Riesling Cuvée des Comtes D' Eguisheim, Léon Beyer	1989	39.00	

3

WHITE BORDEAUX

GRAVES

#			Bottle	Half
120	Château Rahoul	1990	34.00	
121	Château Haut Gardére	1989	25.00	

LOIRE VALLEY

VIN DU PAYS DE NANTES

#			Bottle	Half
130	Muscadet de Sèvre et Maine "Sur Lie", Domaine de la Huperie	1995	16.00	

VIN D'ANJOU dry

#			Bottle	Half
134	Chardonnay, Vin de Pays, Jardin de la France, Domaine Gachère	1996	15.00	
135	Anjou Blanc, Vincent Lecointre	1992	17.00	
136	Saumur Blanc, Vieilles Vignes Pierre de Bruyn	1993	26.00	
137	Savennières, Coulée de Serrant Nicolas Joly	1990	58.00	
138	Savennières, Clos du Papillon Pierre-Yves Soulez	1989	28.00	
139	Savennières, Roches aux Moines Pierre-Yves Soulez	1994	23.00	

VIN D'ANJOU sweet

#			Bottle	Half
146	Côteaux du Layon Chaume "Vieilles Vignes" Patrice Achard	1985	42.00	
147	Quarts de Chaume Château de Bellerive	1978	58.00	
148	Bonnezeaux, Domaine Mark Angeli, Cuvée Mathilde	1994	74.00	

TOURAINE dry

#			Bottle	Half
155	Sauvignon Touraine, Domaine du Vieux Poirier	1995	15.00	
156	Vouvray Sec, Marc Bredif	1993	20.00	

TOURAINE sweet

#			Bottle	Half
160	Vouvray, Marc Bredif	1959	86.00	

NIÉVRE-BERRY

#			Bottle	Half
164	Pouilly Fumé Grande Cuvée, Pascal Jolivet	1990	59.00	
165	Pouilly Fumé, Baron de L, Domaine de Ladoucette	1992	52.00	
166	Pouilly Fumé, "Les Griottes", Mr. Pascal Jolivet	1995	28.00	
167	Sancerre Jean Max Roger Vieilles Vignes	1995	38.00	
168	Sancerre, Les Caillottes, Jean-Max Roger	1995	26.00	13.00
169	Menetou-Salon, Domaine de Chantenoy Mr Clément	1996	22.00	11.00
170	Quincy, Mr Jaumier	1995	18.00	

4

WHITE BURGUNDY

Vignobles de L'Yonne

#			Bottle	Half
176	Chablis, Jean Defaix	1995	22.00	11.00
177	Chablis 1er Cru Vaillons, Jean Defaix	1994	28.00	15.00
178	Chablis 1er Cru Côte de Lechet, Domaine Daniel Etienne Defaix	1991	39.00	
179	Chablis Grand Cru Blanchots, Domaine Vocoret	1988	62.00	
180	Chablis Grand Cru "Les Clos", Domaine Dauvissat	1994	71.00	

Côte Chalonnaise

#			Bottle	Half
183	Montagny 1er Cru Bonneveaux, Arnoux	1994	25.00	
184	Rully "Gresigny" 1er Cru, Domaine Jacqueson	1995	32.00	17.00

Maconnais

#			Bottle	Half
188	Pouilly Fuissé, Michel Delorme	1993	26.00	
189	Mâcon VillageVieilles Vignes La Roche Vineuse, Olivier Merlin	1995	18.00	12.00
190	St. Véran, Domaine des Valanges	1994		13.00
191	St Véran Vieilles Vignes, Jacques Saumaize	1996	26.00	
192	Mâcon Clessé Cuvée Tradition, Jean Thevenet	1993	42.00	

La Côte d'Or

#			Bottle	Half
193	Pernand Vergelesses 1er Cru, Laleure Piot	1993	35.00	17.00
194	Bourgogne Blanc, Eric Boigelot	1993	25.00	
195	Auxey Duresses, Jean Pierre Diconne	1993	34.00	
196	Saint Aubin 1er Cru Les Pucelles, Lamy Pillot	1993	36.00	
197	Chorey Les Beaune, Domaine Maillard	1995	32.00	
198	Puligny Montrachet Les Grands Champs, Dupont Fahn	1995	62.00	
199	Puligny Montrachet, Jean Pillot	1995	44.00	
200	Puligny Montrachet 1er Cru Les Perrières, Etienne Sauzet	1990	119.00	
201	Puligny Montrachet 1er Cru Clavoillons, Domaine Leflaive	1989	112.00	
202	Puligny Montrachet 1er Cru Clavoillons, Domaine Leflaive	1992	92.00	
203	Puligny Montrachet, 1er Cru Les Perrières, Louis Carillon	1993	69.00	
204	Puligny Montrachet, Jean Pascal	1994		27.00
205	Puligny Montrachet 1er cru "Les Pucelles", Domaine Leflaive	1986	143.00	

5

#			Bottle	Half
206	Meursault "Sous Velle", Mr Buisson	1992	52.00	
207	Meursault "Les Vireuils", Domaine Dupont-Fahn	1994	58.00	
208	Meursault Clos de La Barre, Domaine des Comtes de Lafon	1993	91.00	
209	Meursault 1er Cru Les Perrières, Domaine des Comtes de Lafon	1993	175.00	
210	Meursault Clos de La Barre, Domaine des Comtes de Lafon	1992	109.00	
211	Meursault Clos de La Barre, Domaine des Comtes de Lafon	1989	150.00	
212	Meursault Clos de La Barre, Domaine des Comtes de Lafon	1988	125.00	
213	Meursault Rougeot, Coche-Dury	1986	193.00	
214	Meursault Rougeot, Coche-Dury	1988	159.00	
215	Meursault Charmes, Leroy	1976	119.00	
216	Chassagne Montrachet 1er Cru les Champs Gains Domaine Verget	1992	122.00	
217	Chassagne Montrachet "Masures, Jean Noël Gagnard	1994	58.00	
218	Chassagne Montrachet 1er cru "Les Caillerets"Jean Noël Gagnard	1991	78.00	
219	Chassagne Montrachet 1er cru "Les Caillerets"Jean Noël Gagnard	1993		36.00
220	Chassagne Montrachet 1er Cru Les Ruchottes, André Ramonet	1993	84.00	
221	Chassagne Montrachet 1er Cru Les Chaumées, Pierre Jouard	1994	52.00	

Grands Crus

#			Bottle	Half
222	Corton , Domaine Maillard	1994	77.00	
223	Corton Charlemagne, Marius Delarche	1990	84.00	
224	Batard Montrachet , Jean-Noël Gagnard	1991	159.00	
225	Batard Montrachet, Louis Latour	1988		78.00
226	Chevalier Montrachet, Henri Clerc	1989	172.00	
227	Montrachet, Louis Latour	1988	279.00	
228	Montrachet, Marquis de Laguiche	1983	419.00	
229	Montrachet, Domaine des Comtes de Lafon	1993	382.00	
230	Montrachet, Comte de Lafon	1981	630.00	
231	Criots Batard-Montrachet, Roger Belland	1992	120.00	
232	Musigny, Comte George de Vogié	1992	169.00	
233	Bienvenue Batard Montrachet, André Ramonet	1993	124.00	

6

WHITE ITALIAN

			Bottle	Half
235	Casal di Serra Ronchi	1994	17.00	
236	Poggio Alle Gazze, Sauvignon Blanc	1995	26.00	
237	Soave Classico Calverino, Pieropan	1995	23.00	
238	Terre di Tufi, Teruzzi e Puthod	1995	32.00	
239	Pinot Griggio, Piuatti	1996	28.00	

NEW WORLD WHITE WINES

SOUTH AFRICA

245	Sauvignon Blanc, Thelema Montain Vineyards	1996	32.00	
246	Chardonnay, Thelema Montain Vineyards	1995	35.00	
247	Neil Ellis Chardonnay	1995	24.00	

AUSTRALIA

250	Mc Guigan Brothers Verdehlo	1995	17.00	
251	Cape Mentelle, Margaret River, Semillon Sauvignon	1996	23.00	
252	Mc Guigan Réserve Chardonnay	1995	35.00	
253	Shaw and Smith Chardonnay Réserve	1993	32.00	
254	Shaw and Smith Sauvignon Blanc	1994	26.00	

NEW ZEALAND

255	Cloudy Bay, Marlborough, Sauvignon Blanc	1996	32.00	
257	Martinborough, Sauvignon Blanc	1995	25.00	
258	Martinborough, Chardonnay	1995	26.00	

CALIFORNIA

265	Bernardus, Sauvignon Blanc	1994	26.00	
267	Au Bon Climat Talley Reserve, Chardonnay	1994	42.00	
268	Monterey Chardonnay, Central Coast	1994	18.00	

CHILE

270	San Pedro, Sauvignon	1995	16.00	
271	Carmen, Chardonnay	1996	20.00	

ROSÉ WINE

275	Rosé de Loire, Domaine de la Gachère	1996	28.00	
276	Tavel Rosé, Château D' Aquèria	1995	24.00	

RED WINES

FRENCH RÉGIONAL WINES

			Bottle	Half
282	Madiran, South Ouest, Domaine Crampilh	1990	19.00	
283	Saint Chinian, Cuvée Sélection, Languedoc Roussillon, Château de Creissan, Bernard Réveillas	1993	21.00	
284	Côte du Roussillon, Languedoc Roussillon Château Canterrane, Mr Maurice Conte	1986	21.00	
285	Corbières, Languedoc Roussillon, Cuvée Helène de Troie	1993	24.00	
286	Prieuré Saint Jean de Bédian, Côtes du Roussillon	1991	28.00	
287	Vin de Pays de L'Herault, Daumas de Gassac	1989	38.00	

LOIRE VALLEY

TOURAINE

296	Bourgueil, Cuvée Les Busardières, Domaine de la Chevalerie	1986	26.00	
297	Chinon, Vieilles Vignes, Michel Page	1989	32.00	
298	Bourgueil, Cuvée Réserve, Domaine de la Chevalerie	1985	32.00	
299	Chinon Clos de l' Echo, Couly Dutheil	1986	28.00	
300	Chinon Vieilles Vignes, Michel Page	1993		8.00

NIÈVRE BERRY

305	Sancerre, Moulin Bèle, Mr Vatan	1994	31.00	

BEAUJOLAIS

309	Morgon, Domaine du Vieux Cèdres, E. Loron	1995	26.00	
310	Beaujolais Cuveé Tradition Vieilles Vignes, Domaine de Vissoux	1995	18.00	
311	Fleurie, Domaine de Vissoux, Poncié	1996	25.00	

PROVENCE

315	Bandol, Château de Pradaux	1985	34.00	
316	Côteaux des Baux, Trévallon, Mr. Durbach	1991	35.00	
317	Palette, Château Simone	1990	32.00	

RHÔNE VALLEY

			Bottle	Half
320	Côte Rôtie, Robert Jasmin	1975	98.00	
321	Côte Rôtie, Robert Jasmin	1985	75.00	
322	Côte Rôtie, Robert Jasmin	1988	145.00 (Magnum)	
323	Côte Rôtie, Emile et Joël Champet	1989	49.00	
324	Côte Rotie Brune and Blonde, Guigal	1985	86.00	
325	Côte Rôtie La Turque, Guigal	1992	157.00	
326	Côte Rôtie La Turque, Guigal	1986	214.00	
327	Côte Rôtie Landonne, Guigal	1987	195.00	
328	Côte Rôtie Landonne, Guigal	1982	314.00	
329	Côte Rôtie Mouline, Guigal	1985	360.00	
330	Côte Rôtie Mouline, Guigal	1983	440.00	
331	Côte Rôtie Mouline, Guigal	1978	470.00	
332	Cornas, La Geynale Mr. Robert Michel	1988	61.00	
333	Cornas, Domaine De Rochepertuis, Jean Lionnet	1990	46.00	
334	Hermitage, Chave	1988	260.00 (Magnum)	
335	Hermitage, Chave	1985	92.00	
336	Hermitage, La Chapelle Paul Jaboulet Aîné	1992	65.00	
337	Gigondas Grand Montmirail, Domaine Chéron	1990	29.00	
338	Châteauneuf du Pape Chante Cigale, Noël Sabon	1974	82.00	
339	Châteauneuf du Pape, Château de La Nerthe	1991	35.00	
340	Châteauneuf du Pape, Château de Beaucastel	1994		25.00
341	Châteauneuf du Pape, Château de Beaucastel	1989	115.00	
342	Châteauneuf du Pape, Château de Beaucastel	1988	57.00	
343	Châteauneuf du Pape, Château de Beaucastel	1983	110.00	
344	Châteauneuf du Pape, Château de Beaucastel	1978	171.00	
345	Croze Hermitage, Alain Graillot	1995	26.00	13.00
346	Saint Joseph Cuvée Caroline, Domaine Chèze	1993	32.00	
347	Côtes du Rhone Villages, Mr Perrin	1994	18.00	
348	Côtes du Rhone Villages Cairanne, Domaine Rabasse Charavin	1993	22.00	
349	Côtes du Rhône Villages Rasteau, Domaine Saint Gayan	1993	24.00	

BURGUNDY

La Côte de Nuits

			Bottle	Half
359	Marsannay, Domaine Louis Trapet	1994	26.00	
360	Gevrey Chambertin 1er Cru Les Cazetiers, Mr Sérafin	1989	110.00	
361	Gevrey Chambertin, Mr Serafin	1989	49.00	
362	Gevrey Chambertin, Réserve Personnel, Domaine Trapet	1978	88.00	
363	Gevrey Chambertin 1er Cru Les Cazetiers, Louis Jadot	1985	92.00	
364	Vosne Romanée, Domaine Confuron Cotetidot	1992	46.00	
365	Vosne Romanée, 1er Cru Les Gaudichots	1994	52.00	26.00
366	Vosne Romanée Magnum, Mr. Forey	1990	109.00 (Magnum)	
367	Nuits St Georges 1er Cru, Domaine Michel Chevillon	1989	45.00	
368	Nuits Saint Georges 1er Cru, Michel Chevillon	1987	54.00	
369	Nuits Saint Georges, Leroy	1985	86.00	
370	Nuits Saint Georges 1er Cru de l'Arlot	1989		28.00

Grands Crus

374	Chambertin, Domaine Louis Trapet	1992	72.00	
375	Latricière Chambertin, Domaine Louis Trapet	1991	85.00	
376	Chapelle Chambertin, Domaine Louis Trapet	1992	79.00	
377	Charmes Chambertin, Domaine Serafin	1985	135.00	
378	Charmes Chambertin, Armand Rousseau	1990		52.00
379	Charmes Chambertin G Lignier	1985	149.00	
380	Echezeaux, Mongeard Mugneret	1991	144.00	
381	Grand Echezeaux, Mongeard Mugneret	1989	118.00	
382	Clos Vougeot, Renée Engel	1987	95.00	
383	Clos Vougeot, Faiveley	1985	162.00	
384	Musigny, Vieilles Vignes F. Mugnier	1989	145.00	
385	Musigny, Vieilles Vignes F. Mugnier	1986	171.00	
386	Musigny, Vieilles Vignes F. Mugnier	1988	310.00 (Magnum)	
387	Clos de la Roche, Domaine Ponsot	1987		84.00
388	Clos de la Roche Vieilles Vignes Domaine Ponsot	1989	129.00	
389	Clos de la Roche, Domaine Dujac	1989		68.00

Domaine Romanée Conti

			Bottle	Half
402	Richebourg	1991	210.00	
403	La Tâche	1991	385.00	
404	La Tâche	1982	250.00	
405	La Tâche	1959	990.00	
406	Echezeaux	1991	150.00	
407	Echezeaux	1988	310.00	
408	Echezeaux	1985	367.00	
409	Grand Echezeaux	1991	191.00	
410	Romanée Conti	1991	1450.00	
411	Romanée Saint Vivant	1991	180.00	
412	Romanée Saint Vivant	1985	446.00	

La Côte de Beaune

415	Chassagne Montrachet 1er Cru Morgeot, Jean Pillot	1993	41.00	22.00
416	Aloxe Corton, Château de Corton André	1985	74.00	
417	Blagny La Pièce sous Bois, Robert Ampeau	1981	85.00	
418	Beaune 1er Cru Theurons, Régis Rossignol Changarnier	1990	52.00	
419	Volnay Clos d'Audignac 1er Cru, Domaine La Pousse d'Or	1992	59.00	
420	Volnay 1er Cru, Régis Rossignol Changarnier	1990	68.00	30.00
421	Pommard 1er Cru Les Rugiens, Domaine de Courcel	1991	49.00	
422	Pommard 1er Cru Grand Clos des Epenots, Domaine de Courcel	1989	82.00	
423	Pommard, Régis Rossignol Changarnier	1988	52.00	25.00
424	Pommard, Leroy	1980	96.00	
425	Côte de Beaune Villages, Domaine Arnoux	1993	24.00	
426	Savigny les Beaune Les Bourgeots, Domaine Simon Bize	1993	35.00	
427	Chorey les Beaune, Domaine Maillard	1994	32.00	65.00(Mag)
428	Bourgogne Rouge, Leroy	1990	28.00	

			Bottle	Half
429	Mercurey Les Sazenay 1er Crus, Genot-Boulanger	1993	28.00	
430	Santenay 1er Cru Gravières, Roger Belland	1993	25.00	
431	Saint Aubin 1er Cru sur le Sentier du Clos, Henri Prudhon	1993		18.00
432	Macon-Azé, Domaine de Rochebin	1995		12.00
433	Pernand Vergelesses 1er Cru Iles de Vergelesses	1992	46.00	

Grands Crus

438	Le Corton, Marius Delarche	1991	58.00	
439	Corton Renardes, Maillard	1990	89.00	
441	Corton Clos des Corton Faiveley	1985	166.00	

BORDEAUX

			Bottle	Half
MÉDOC ET HAUT MÉDOC				
450	Château Cantemerle, 5ème Cru	1985	64.00	
451	Château Beaumont Cru Bourgeois	1986	41.00	
452	Château Sociandot Mallet	1988	38.00	
453	Château La Cardonne Cru Bourgeois	1988	24.00	
454	Château de la Lagune, 3ème Cru	1986	72.00	
455	Château Bel Orme Tronquoy de Lalande Cru Bourgeois	1982	64.00	
456	Château Cissac, Cru Bourgeois	1990	35.00	
ST. JULIEN				
461	Château Gruaud Larose 2ème Cru	1989	62.00	
462	Château Talbot, 4ème Cru	1989	75.00	
463	Château Ducru Beaucaillou, 2ème Cru	1983	86.00	
464	Château Langoa Barton, 3ème Cru	1989		34.00
465	Château Léoville Las-Case, 2ème Cru	1978	125.00	
466	Château Léoville Las-Case, 2ème Cru	1981	85.00	
467	Château Lagrange, 3ème Cru	1970	135.00	
468	Château Beychevelle, 4ème Cru	1982	139.00	
469	Les Fiefs de Lagrange, 2nd Wine	1992	27.00	
470	Château Gloria	1989	42.00	
MARGAUX				
480	Château Labergoce Zédé, 5ème Cru	1992	44.00	
481	Château Cantenac Brown, 3ème Cru	1989	66.00	
482	Château d'Issan, 3ème Cru	1989	64.00	
483	Château Segonnes, 2ème Vin	1993	28.00	
484	Château Lascombes, 2ème Cru	1961	190.00	
485	Château du Tertre, 4ème Cru	1985		28.00
486	Château Boyd-Cantenac, 3ème Cru	1982		44.00
489	Château Siran, Cru Exceptionnel	1990	41.00	
490	Château Giscours, 3ème Cru	1975	92.00	
491	Château Malescot St Exupéry, 3ème Cru	1983	52.00	
493	Château Margaux 1er Cru	1978	330.00	

			Bottle	Half
PAUILLAC				
495	Château d'Armailhac, 5ème Cru	1989	59.00	
496	Château Batailley, 5ème Cru	1989		29.00
497	Château Pichon Longueville 2ème Cru	1991	57.00	
498	Château Latour, 1er Cru	1983	145.00	
499	Château Latour, 1er Cru	1981	132.00	
500	Château Latour, 1er Cru	1978	280.00	
501	Château Latour, 1er Cru	1976	120.00	
502	Château Latour, 1er Cru	1962	416.00	
503	Château Grand Puy Lacoste 5ème Cru	1983	73.00	
504	Château Lafite Rothschild, 1er Cru	1986		228.00
505	Château Lafite Rothschild, 1er Cru	1982	675.00	
506	Château Lafite Rothschild, 1er Cru	1978	410.00	
507	Château Lafite Rothschild, 1er Cru	1970	460.00	
508	Château Haut Bages, Libéral 5ème Cru	1986	54.00	
509	Château Haut Bages, Libéral 5ème Cru	1990		28.00
510	Les Forts de Latour, 2ème Vin	1991	44.00	
511	Les Forts de Latour, 2ème Vin	1989	75.00	
512	Les Forts de Latour, 2ème Vin	1981	75.00	
513	Les Forts de Latour, 2ème Vin	1978	96.00	
514	Château Lynch Bages, 5ème Cru	1985	145.00	74.00
515	Château Lynch Bages, 5ème Cru	1978	120.00	
516	Château Mouton Rothschild, 1er Cru	1967	141.00	
517	Château Mouton Rothschild, 1er Cru	1975	230.00	
518	Château Mouton Rothschild, 1er Cru	1970	498.00	
519	Château Mouton Rothschild, 1er Cru	1990	222.00	
520	Château Mouton Rothschild, 1er Cru	1989	257.00	
521	Château Mouton Rothschild, 1er Cru	1988	218.00	
522	Château Mouton Rothschild, 1er Cru	1985	350.00	
523	Château Mouton Rothschild, 1er Cru	1983	205.00	

			Bottle	Half
LISTRAC				
525	Château Clarke, Cru Bourgeois	1989	38.00	
526	Château Fourcas Dupré	1989	26.00	
ST ESTEPHE				
530	Château Calon Segur, 3ème Cru	1989	88.00	
531	Château Cos Labory, 5ème Cru	1985	54.00	
532	Château Cos d'Estournel, 2ème Cru	1990		55.00
533	Château Cos D'Estournel, 2ème Cru	1981	144.00	
534	Château Cos D'Estournel, 2ème Cru	1957	228.00	
GRAVES				
540	Château Rahoul	1989		15.00
541	Château Haut Brion, 1er Cru	1983	154.00	
542	Château Haut Brion, 1er Cru	1966	345.00	
543	Château La Mission Haut Brion, Grand Cru	1979	159.00	
544	Château La Mission Haut Brion, Grand Cru	1989	342.00	
545	Château Pape Clément Grand Cru	1970	187.00	
MOULIS				
547	Château Chasse Spleen, Cru Bourgeois	1982	86.00	
ST EMILION				
564	Latour Figeac Grand Cru	1988		38.00
565	Château Ausone 1er Grand Cru	1985	159.00	
566	Château Cheval Blanc, 1er Grand Cru	1988	214.00	
567	Château Cheval Blanc, 1er Grand Cru	1981	190.00	
568	Château Cheval Blanc, 1er Grand Cru	1978	260.00	
569	Château Cheval Blanc, 1er Grand Cru	1959		
570	Château La Dominique Grand Cru	1985	57.00	
571	Château Pavie Grand Cru	1983	75.00	
572	Château Figeac Grand Cru	1983	110.00	
573	Château Figeac Grand Cru	1982	243.00	
574	Château Villemaurine Grand Cru	1986	48.00	

			Bottle	Half
POMEROL ET LALANDE POMEROL				
580	Château Vieux Certan	1992	42.00	
581	Château Marsan	1991	52.00	
582	Château des Annereaux	1990		12.00
583	Château L'Enclos	1990/89	68.00	35.00
584	Château Feytit Clinet	1989	52.00	
585	Château Plince	1986	46.00	
586	Clos de La Vieille Eglise	1983	81.00	
587	Château Trotanoy	1983	114.00	
588	Château Trotanoy	1981	98.00	
589	Château La Conseillante	1976	139.00	
590	Château La Conseillante	1961	600.00	
591	Pétrus	1987	310.00	
592	Pétrus	1978	424.00	
593	Pétrus	1955	938.00	
594	La Fleur Pétrus	1970	290.00	

			Bottle	Half
ITALY				
600	Chianti Classico, Tenuta Fontodi	1992	22.00	
601	Valpolicella Classico, La Grola, Allegrini	1993	26.00	
602	Cepparello, Isole e Olena	1990	52.00	
603	La Poja, Allegrini	1990	44.00	
604	Amarone Classico della Valpolicella, Allegrini	1990	35.00	
605	Barolo, Aurelio Settimo	1986	46.00	
606	Brunello Di Montalcino, Costanti	1991	39.00	
SPAIN				
610	Viña Tondonia Tinto Grand Reserva, Rioja, R. López de Heredia	1978	59.00	
611	Caroixa de Scala del Priorat, Gran Reserva	1987	26.00	
612	Rioja Viña Tondonia Reserva	1988	28.00	
613	Viña Cubillo Crianza, Rioja, R López de Heredia	1990	22.00	
614	Clos Mogador, Priorat René Barbier	1992	42.00	
615	Bodegas Alion	1992	49.00	
NEW WORLD				
AUSTRALIA				
620	Cape Mentelle Margaret River, Cabernet Sauvignon	1992	24.00	
621	Cape Mentelle Margaret River, Zinfandel	1993	28.00	
622	Peter Lehmann, Shiraz	1994	22.00	
623	Tyrell's, Shiraz Cabernet VAT no 8	1994	32.00	
CALIFORNIA				
630	Napa Valley Long Vineyards, Cabernet Sauvignon,	1988	59.00	
631	Frog's Leap, Zinfandel, Napa Valley	1993	24.00	
632	Pinot Noir, Firesteed Oregon	1995	24.00	
633	La Cagoule, Pinot Noir, Oregon	1993	45.00	
634	Qupe Winery, Syrah, Central Coast	1994	25.00	
635	Syrah, Réserve Bien Nacido Qupé Winery	1994	46.00	

			Bottle	Half
PORT				
636	Cockburn's	1963	129.00	
637	Taylor's	1963	189.00	
638	Colheita, Quinta Do Noval	1963	143.00	42.00
639	Colheita, Quinta Do Noval	1971		42.00
640	Colheita, Quinta Do Noval	1976		32.00
641	Colheita, Quinta Do Noval	1982		26.00
642	Ramos Pinto, Quinta da Ervamoira	10 years	28.00	
643	Sandeman Late Bottle Vintage	1989	32.00	
644	Warre's	1977	78.00	

TERRINE OF DUCK FOIE GRAS WITH DUCK MEAT

TERRINE VON DER ENTENSTOPFLEBER MIT ENTENFLEISCH

For 8 - 10 persons:

4 medium-sized duck legs, carefully cleaned,
salt, pepper,
2 sprigs thyme, 1 sprig rosemary,
200 g/7 oz/⁴/₅ cup duck fat

2 fresh duck foie gras of about 750 g/1 lb 10 oz each,
1 tbsp white port, 1 tbsp Armagnac, 1 tbsp Madeira,
sea salt and freshly ground black pepper

Accompaniments (optional):
4 slices of fresh duck foie gras, fried in a little butter,
fresh brioche bread, briefly toasted

Für 8 - 10 Personen:

4 mittelgroße Entenbeine, sauber geputzt,
Salz, Pfeffer,
2 Zweige Thymian, 1 Zweig Rosmarin,
250 g Entenfett

2 frische Entenstopflebern von je ca. 750 g,
1 EL weißer Portwein, 1 EL Armagnac, 1 EL Madeira,
Meersalz und schwarzer Pfeffer aus der Mühle

Beilagen (nach Belieben):
4 Scheiben frische Entenstopfleber, in etwas Butter gebraten,
frisches Briochebrot, kurz geröstet

Salt and pepper the duck legs and sprinkle with the plucked thyme and rosemary needles. Cover and place in refrigerator for two hours to allow the flavours to soak in.

Put the duck legs in a small casserole and pour over the melted duck fat. Cover tightly with aluminium foil so that no air can enter. On the stove, bring the fat to the boil, then carefully place the casserole in the oven preheated to 170° C/340° F. Cook for two hours; the meat should be tender and fall from the bones. Allow to go cold in the fat.

Cut open the duck livers with a sharp knife and carefully remove by hand all veins and sinews that can be felt without the lobes of the liver collapsing. Place in a deep frying pan. Season with salt and pepper and pour over the port wine, Armagnac and Madeira. Marinate for one hour.

Preheat the oven to 190° C/375° F. Roast the duck livers for about twelve minutes. Carefully take out the livers saving any fat that has seeped out. Strip the duck meat from the bones and mix with a little of the fat in which it was cooked.

Line a terrine mould about 1.5 litres/2 pints 12 fl oz/6 cups in volume with cling film. Cut the foie gras into 1 cm/²/₅ in thick slices and layer them in the mould alternately with the duck meat, finishing with a layer of foie gras. Fold the cling film over the top to keep airtight and weight the terrine with a measuring weight. Leave overnight in the refrigerator.

Open the foil and pour some melted fat left over from cooking the livers over the terrine. Allow to set in the refrigerator.

To serve: Unmould the terrine onto a platter, remove the foil, cut into thick slices, and distribute on plates. If desired, serve with a piece of fried duck liver. Circle with a little fat and serve with toasted hot slices of brioche.

Entenbeine salzen, pfeffern und mit den gezupften Thymian- und Rosmarinblättchen bestreuen. Die Aromen im Kühlschrank zugedeckt zwei Stunden einziehen lassen.

Entenbeine in eine kleine Kasserolle legen, mit dem geschmolzenen Entenfett übergießen. Mit Alufolie dicht bedecken, so daß keine Luft mehr hinzu kommt. Auf dem Herd das Fett zum Kochen bringen, dann die Kasserolle vorsichtig in den auf 170° C vorgeheizten Ofen stellen. Zwei Stunden garen, das Fleisch soll zart sein und sich vom Knochen lösen. Im Fett erkalten lassen. Die Entenlebern mit einem scharfen Messer aufschneiden und von Hand vorsichtig von allen fühlbaren Sehnen und Adern befreien, ohne daß die Leberlappen zerfallen. In eine tiefe Pfanne legen. Mit Salz und Pfeffer würzen, mit dem Portwein, Armagnac und Madeira übergießen, dann während einer Stunde marinieren.

Den Ofen auf 190° C vorheizen. Die Entenlebern ca. 12 Minuten braten, danach vorsichtig herausnehmen, das ausgetretene Fett aufheben. Von den Entenbeinen das Fleisch ablösen und mit etwas Kochfett vermischen. Eine Terrinenform von ca. 1,5 Liter Volumen mit Frischhaltefolie auskleiden. Entenlebern in 1 cm dicke Scheiben schneiden und abwechselnd mit dem Entenfleisch in die Terrine schichten. Zum Schluß mit einer Lage Entenleber zudecken. Die Frischhaltefolie oben luftdicht zusammenschlagen und die Terrine mit einem regelmäßigen Gewicht beschweren. Im Kühlschrank über Nacht ruhen lassen. Die Folie öffnen und die Terrine mit etwas geschmolzenem Fett, das vom Garen der Lebern übriggeblieben ist, übergießen. Im Kühlschrank fest werden lassen.

Zum Servieren: Die Terrine auf eine Platte stürzen, Folie entfernen, in dicke Scheiben schneiden und auf Teller verteilen. Nach Belieben mit einer Scheibe gebratener Entenleber servieren. Mit etwas Fett umgießen, geröstete, warme Briochescheiben dazu reichen.

RAVIOLI OF LOBSTER

HUMMERRAVIOLI

For 4 persons:

2 small lobsters of about 500 g/1 lb 2 oz each,
100 g/3 1/2 oz salmon fillet,
1/2 tsp each of chopped basil, tarragon and chervil,
200 g/7 oz pasta dough,
sea salt, freshly ground black pepper,
1/2 a Savoy cabbage,
50 g/1 2/3 oz/1/5 cup butter,
1 carrot,

200 ml/7 fl oz/4/5 cup lobsters stock,
5 tbsp olive oil,
1/2 tsp each of chopped basil, tarragon and chervil

Boil the lobsters in fast boiling water for about one minute. Remove and refresh with cold water.
Break out the meat from the tails and claws, dab dry with kitchen paper and chop finely. Place in the refrigerator.
Finely chop the salmon fillet and blend in a food processor to a smooth purée together with the lobster meat, the herbs, sea salt and pepper.
With completely dry hands, roll the mixture into 8 balls. Place them on a plate and refrigerate. Roll out the pasta dough thinly and, using a 10 cm/4 in cutter, stamp out 16 discs. Fill them with the chilled balls, paint the edges with a little egg white and cover with the second dough disc, and press the edges together, making sure that all air is excluded.
Blanch the ravioli in boiling salted water for two minutes. Pour through a sieve and allow to drain.
Chop the Savoy cabbage finely and sauté it in half of the butter until it collapses. Peel the carrot, cut into thin strips, and sauté in the remaining butter until wilted but still crisp.
For the vinaigrette: Reduce the lobster stock to about two thirds of its volume. Allow to cool, then mix with the olive oil and herbs.
To serve: Boil the ravioli in salted water for two minutes, then drain. Pile a bed of Savoy cabbage on each warmed plate, place the ravioli on top and decorate with the carrot strips. Drizzle everything with lukewarm vinaigrette and serve.

Für 4 Personen:

2 kleine Hummmer von je ca. 500 g,
100 g Lachsfilet,
je 1/2 TL gehackter Basilikum, Estragon und Kerbel,
200 g Nudelteig,
Meersalz, schwarzer Pfeffer aus der Mühle,
1/2 Wirsing,
50 g Butter,
1 Karotte

200 ml Hummerfond,
5 EL Olivenöl,
je 1/2 TL gehackter Basilikum, Estragon und Kerbel

Die Hummer in sprudelnd kochendem Wasser eine Minute kochen, dann herausnehmen und kalt abschrecken. Fleisch aus den Schwänzen und Scheren brechen, mit Küchenpapier trockentupfen und fein hacken. Kühlstellen. Lachsfilet feinschneiden und mit dem Hummerfleisch, den Kräutern, Meersalz und Pfeffer im Mixer fein pürieren. Die Masse mit trockenen Händen zu 8 Kugeln formen, auf einen Teller legen und kühlstellen.
Den Nudelteig dünn ausrollen und 16 runde, ca. 10 cm große Teigplatten ausstechen. Mit der Füllung belegen, Ränder mit etwas Eiweiß bestreichen, dann mit dem zweiten Teigkreis belegen und die Ränder festdrücken, daß alle Luft ausgeschlossen ist. Die Ravioli in kochendem Salzwasser zwei Minuten blanchieren, durch ein Sieb abgießen und abtropfen lassen. Den Wirsing fein schneiden und in der Hälfte der Butter dünsten, bis er zusammenfällt. Die Karotte schälen, in dünne Streifen schneiden und in der restlichen Butter knackig-weich dünsten.
Für die Vinaigrette: Den Hummerfond auf etwa zwei Drittel der Menge einkochen lassen. Erkalten lassen, dann mit dem Olivenöl und den Kräutern verrühren.
Zum Servieren: Die Ravioli in Salzwasser zwei Minuten kochen, dann abgießen. Auf jeden vorgewärmten Teller ein Bett von Wirsing häufen, die Ravioli darüberlegen und mit den Karottenstreifen dekorieren. Das Ganze mit der lauwarmen Vinaigrette begießen und servieren.

CAPPUCCINO OF HARICOTS BLANCS WITH MORELS

CAPPUCCINO VON WEISSEN BOHNEN MIT MORCHELN

For 6 persons:

250 g/8 oz small white, dried haricot beans,
steeped overnight,
1 small onion, 1 carrot,
1 bouquet garni of leek, celeriac, thyme,
parsley and bayleaf,
800 ml/1 pint 8 fl oz/3 ⅓ cups chicken stock,
100 g/3 ½ oz fresh morels, cleaned and cut in half,
50 g/1 ⅔ oz/⅕ cup butter,
1- 2 tsp truffle oil,
150 ml/5 fl oz/⅗ cup double cream,
sea salt, freshly ground, black pepper,
1 tbsp ice-cold butter,
a few fine slices of truffle to decorate (optional)

Drain the beans through a sieve and place in a saucepan. Pour in water until they are covered by 5 cm/ 2 in, salt lightly, then add the onion, carrot and bouquet garni. Bring to the boil, cook vigorously for ten minutes, then reduce the heat and cook the beans for about thirty minutes until soft.

Using a slotted spoon, remove about 100 g/3 ½ oz of the beans and continue cooking the remainder for ten minutes more until very soft. Drain, discard the vegetables, and blend the beans to a fine purée in a liquidiser.

Reduce the chicken stock in a saucepan for five minutes. Sauté the morels in the butter until soft, then stir in half of the truffle oil.

Blend the beans with the reduced stock, the double cream and the remaining truffle oil until smooth. Divide the reserved 100 g/3 ½ oz white beans and the morels between six cappuccino cups. Adjust the seasoning of the soup and bring to the boil again. Stir in the ice-cold butter, using a hand blender, and froth up the soup.

Pour into the cups, making sure that some froth settles on the surface; decorate, if desired, with slices of truffle and serve immediately.

Für 6 Personen:

250 g kleine weiße Bohnen,
über Nacht in Wasser eingeweicht,
1 kleine Zwiebel, 1 Karotte,
1 Bouquet garni mit Lauch, Sellerie, Thymian,
Petersilie und Lorbeer,
800 ml Hühnerbrühe,
100 g frische Morcheln, geputzt und halbiert,
50 g Butter,
1 - 2 TL Trüffelöl, 150 ml Doppelrahm,
Meersalz, schwarzer Pfeffer aus der Mühle,
1 EL eiskalte Butter,
einige feine Trüffelscheiben zum Dekorieren
(nach Belieben)

Die Bohnen durch ein Sieb abießen und in einen Topf geben. Mit Wasser aufgießen, bis sie 5 cm hoch bedeckt sind, leicht salzen, dann die Zwiebel, die Karotte und das Bouquet garni zugeben.
Zum Kochen bringen, 10 Minuten stark kochen lassen, dann die Hitze reduzieren und die Bohnen ca. 30 Minuten weich garen. Mit einer Lochkelle ungefähr 100 g der Bohnen herausnehmen, den Rest noch weitere zehn Minuten sehr weich kochen lassen. Durch ein Sieb abgießen, die Gemüse herausnehmen und die Bohnen im Mixer sehr fein pürieren.
Die Hühnerbrühe in einem Topf fünf Minuten einkochen lassen. Die Morcheln in der Butter weich dünsten, dann die Hälfte des Trüffelöls unterrühren. Die Bohnen mit der reduzierten Brühe, dem Doppelrahm und dem restlichen Trüffelöl schaumig mixen. Die reservierten 100 g weißen Bohnen und die Morcheln in sechs Cappuccinotassen verteilen. Die Suppe abschmecken und nochmal zum Kochen bringen. Die eiskalte Butter mit dem Pürierstab einrühren und erneut schaumig mixen. In die Tassen füllen. Darauf achten, daß obenauf etwas Schaum zu liegen kommt, nach Belieben mit Trüffelscheiben dekorieren und sofort servieren.

SCALLOP SALAD WITH TRUFFLE VINAIGRETTE

JAKOBSMUSCHELSALAT MIT TRÜFFELVINAIGRETTE

For 4 persons:

12 fine new potatoes,
12 scallops, removed from shells,
olive oil for frying

Mixed leaf salads

1 tbsp white-wine vinegar,
3 tbsp olive oil,
salt, pepper

For the truffle vinaigrette:
2 tbsp white-wine vinegar,
6 tbsp olive oil,
1 tbsp peanut oil,
salt,
1 tbsp chopped truffle,
4 tbsp cream

Für 4 Personen:

12 schöne, neue Kartoffeln,
12 Jakobsmuscheln, ausgelöst,
Olivenöl zum Braten

Gemischte Blattsalate

1 EL Weißweinessig,
3 EL Olivenöl,
Salz, Pfeffer

Für die Trüffelvinaigrette:
2 EL Weißweinessig,
6 EL Olivenöl,
1 EL Erdnußöl,
Salz,
1 EL gehackter Trüffel,
4 EL Sahne

Scrub the potatoes vigorously under running water, slice and fry golden brown in olive oil over a medium heat.

Cut the scallops in half horizontally and likewise fry in olive oil until they change colour. Drain on kitchen paper and, alternating with the potato slices, lay a rosette on the plates.

Mix the leaf salads well with a dressing of white-wine vinegar, olive oil, salt and pepper and place a small pile in the middle of each rosette. Purée all the ingredients for the truffle vinaigrette, except the cream, in the blender to make a smooth sauce, then fold in the cream.

Adjust the seasoning and pour the sauce around the rosettes.

Die Kartoffeln unter fließendem Wasser kräftig abbürsten, in Scheiben schneiden und in Olivenöl bei mittlerer Hitze goldbraun braten.

Jakobsmuscheln flach halbieren und ebenfalls in Olivenöl braten, bis sie Farbe annehmen.

Auf Küchenpapier entfetten und abwechselnd mit den Kartoffelscheiben jeweils eine Rosette auf die Teller legen.

Blattsalate mit einem Dressing aus Weißweinessig, Olivenöl, Salz und Pfeffer gut vermischen und in die Mitte der Rosetten kleine Häufchen anrichten. Alle Zutaten für die Trüffelvinaigrette ausser die Sahne im Mixer zu einer homogenen Sauce pürieren, zum Schluß die Sahne einrühren. Abschmecken und die Rosetten mit der Sauce umgießen.

CRÈME BRÛLÉE WITH DRIED APPLE

GEBRANNTE CREME MIT GETROCKNETEM APFEL

For 6 persons:

2 vanilla pods, 350 ml/12 fl oz/1¹/₂ cups double cream,
125 ml/4 fl oz/¹/₂ cup milk, 6 egg yolks,
75 g/2¹/₂ oz/¹/₃ cup sugar

For the sauce:
2 green apples (Granny Smith),
juice of ¹/₂ lemon, 1 tbsp sugar

For the decoration:
2 green apples (Granny Smith),
110 g/4 oz/²/₅ cup sugar,
200 ml/7 fl oz/⁴/₅ cup water,
¹/₂ tsp grated lemon zest, juice of ¹/₂ lemon

Line the bases of six ramekin dishes with discs of greaseproof paper. Slit open the vanilla pods lengthways, scrape out the marrow, and stir into the cream.
In a saucepan, bring to the boil the milk and the scraped pod husks, stirring. Beat the egg yolks in a bowl with a whisk until a paler shade of yellow. Stirring vigorously, slowly pour the boiling cream-milk mixture onto the yolks. Stir in the sugar until it has all dissolved. Strain the mixture through a sieve; remove the vanilla pods. Pour the crème into the ramekins, place them on a baking tray and cook in the oven preheated to 120° C/250° F for about one hour until firm. Allow to cool, then chill properly in the refrigerator.
For the sauce: Cut the apples in half, remove the core, and cut into large pieces. Slightly warm the lemon juice and dissolve the sugar in it. Allow to cool.
Purée the apple pieces finely with the lemon juice in the blender and pass through a sieve.
In a saucepan, bring the sugar with water and lemon zest to the boil and keep at a fast boil for five minutes. Allow to cool and stir in the lemon juice. Hollow out the apples with the corer, then slice as thinly as possible. Turn them in lemon syrup and lay them flat on a tray covered with greaseproof paper. Dry in the oven at 80° C/175° F for about two hours.
If desired, hang the warm apple rings over a wooden rod to cool which gives them a semi-circular shape.
To serve: To unmould run a small, sharp knife around the edge of the ramekins. Invert onto the hand, remove the greaseproof paper, and place on dessert plates with the baked side up.
Surround with apple sauce and decorate with the dried apple rings shortly before serving.

Für 6 Personen:

2 Vanillestengel, 350 ml Doppelrahm,
125 ml Milch, 6 Eigelb,
75 g Zucker

Für die Sauce:
2 grüne Äpfel (Granny Smith),
Saft einer halben Zitrone, 1 EL Zucker

Für die Dekoration:
2 grüne Äpfel (Granny Smith), 110 g Zucker,
200 ml Wasser,
¹/₂ TL geriebene Zitronenschale,
Saft einer halben Zitrone

Die Böden von sechs Keramikförmchen mit je einem runden Stück Backfolie auskleiden. Vanillestengel längs aufschneiden, das Mark herauskratzen und mit der Sahne verrühren. Mit der Milch und den ausgekratzten Stengeln in einem Topf unter Rühren zum Kochen bringen. Die Eigelb in einer Schüssel mit dem Schneebesen hellgelb schlagen. Die kochende Sahne-Milchmischung unter kräftigem Rühren langsam einarbeiten. Zucker zugeben und rühren, bis er sich vollständig aufgelöst hat. Masse durch ein Sieb passieren; Vanillestengel entfernen. Die Creme in die Förmchen füllen, diese auf ein Backblech stellen und im auf 120° C vorgeheizten Ofen ca. eine Stunde fest werden lassen. Abkühlen lassen, dann im Kühlschrank richtig durchkühlen.
Für die Sauce: Äpfel halbieren, Kernhaus entfernen und in grobe Stücke schneiden. Zitronensaft leicht erwärmen und den Zucker darin auflösen. Erkalten lassen. Apfelstücke mit dem Zitronensaft im Mixer fein pürieren und durch ein Sieb passieren.
Zucker mit Wasser und Zitronenschale in einem Topf zum Kochen bringen, während 5 Minuten stark kochen, abkühlen lassen und mit dem Zitronensaft verrühren. Die Äpfel mit einem Kernhausentferner aushöhlen und dann in möglichst dünne Scheiben schneiden. Im Zitronensirup wenden und auf einem mit Backpapier begelegten Blech flach auslegen. Bei 80° C im Ofen ca. zwei Stunden trocknen lassen. Die noch warmen Apfelringe nach Belieben über einen Holzstiel gehängt erkalten lassen, um ihnen eine halbrunde Form zu geben.
Zum Servieren: Die Flans mit einem kleinen scharfen Messer etwas vom Rand lösen, auf die Hand stürzen, Backfolie entfernen und auf Dessertteller legen, mit der Backseite nach oben. Mit Sauce umgießen und mit den getrockneten Apfelringen kurz vor dem Servieren dekorieren.

TARTE TATIN WITH PINEAPPLE

TARTE TATIN MIT ANANAS

For 6 persons:

1 pineapple, 300 g/10 oz/1 1/4 cups sugar,
120 ml/4 fl oz/1/2 cup water,
200 g/7 oz Gordon's puff pastry (recipe see page 466)

For the sorbet:
300 g/10 oz pineapple flesh,
cut into small cubes,
300 ml/10 fl oz/1 1/4 cups water,
125 g/4 oz/1/2 cup sugar

Decorate as desired:
prepared dried pineapple (as for dried apples,
see page 462), vanilla pod

Cut away the skin of the pineapple, remove the hard inner part and cut into slices so that they will fit into small individual-portion baking tins. Boil the sugar with the water to form a dark caramel. Carefully immerse the pineapple in this and cook, turning occasionally, until the slices are coated all over with caramel. Rinse out the baking tins with a little caramel and layer the pineapple slices in the tins about 3 cm/1 1/5 in deep. Roll out the puff pastry to a thickness of about 5 mm/1/5 in and cut out discs the same size as the pineapple. Cover the pineapple with the pastry and bake in the oven preheated to 250° C/485° F until they begin to change colour. Then turn down the oven to 160° C/320° F and bake until ready. Remove from the oven and allow to cool.

For the sorbet: Bring the water and sugar to the boil, stirring. Reduce over a strong heat for five minutes. Poach the pineapple cubes in this for about ten minutes until soft. Purée in the blender and pass through chinois. Freeze into sorbet in the ice-cream maker.

To serve: Carefully unmould the tarte tatin onto plates. Place a ball of pineapple sorbet on top and decorate as desired.

Für 6 Personen:

1 Ananas, 300 g Zucker,
120 ml Wasser,
200 g von Gordons Blätterteig (Rezept siehe Seite 466)

Für das Sorbet:
300 g Ananas-Fruchtfleisch,
in kleine Würfel geschnitten,
300 ml Wasser,
125 g Zucker

Dekoration nach Belieben:
getrocknete Ananas (wie getrocknete Äpfel
herstellen, siehe Seite 462), Vanillestengel

Die Schale von der Ananas wegschneiden, den inneren, harten Teil entfernen und in Scheiben so zurechtschneiden, daß diese in kleinen Portions-Backblechen Platz haben. Zucker mit Wasser zu dunklem Karamel kochen. Ananas vorsichtig einlegen und unter Wenden kochen, bis die Scheiben rundum mit Karamel überzogen sind.

Die Backbleche mit etwas Karamel ausgießen und die Ananasscheiben ca. 3 cm hoch einschichten. Den Blätterteig etwa 5 mm dick ausrollen und davon Scheiben in der Größe der Ananas ausschneiden. Die Ananas damit belegen und im auf 250° C vorgeheizten Ofen backen, bis sie beginnen Farbe anzunehmen. Dann den Ofen auf 160° C zurückschalten und fertig backen. Herausnehmen und abkühlen lassen.

Für das Sorbet: Das Wasser mit dem Zucker unter Rühren zum Kochen bringen. Bei starker Hitze fünf Minuten einkochen lassen. Die Ananaswürfel ungefähr zehn Minuten darin weichkochen. Im Mixer pürieren und durch ein Sieb passieren. In der Eismaschine zu Sorbet gefrieren.

Zum Servieren: Die Tarte Tatin vorsichtig auf Teller stürzen. Mit einer Kugel Ananassorbet belegen, nach Belieben dekorieren.

GORDON'S PUFF PASTRY

GORDONS BLÄTTERTEIG

For about 1 kg of pastry:
500 g/1 lb 2 oz/2 1/2 cups flour,
good pinch of salt,
500 g/1 lb 2 oz/2 1/2 cups butter, cut into pieces,
1 tsp white-wine vinegar,
about 300 ml/10 fl oz/1 1/4 cups ice-cold water

Für ca. 1 kg Teig:
500 g Mehl,
eine gute Prise Salz,
500 g Butter, in Stücke geschnitten,
1 TL Weißweinessig,
ca. 300 ml eiskaltes Wasser

Weigh out 450 g/1 lb/2 cups of the flour and sift into a bowl. Add the salt and rub by hand with 50 g/1 2/3 oz/ 1/5 cup of butter until crumbly. Add the vinegar and ice-water (the quantity of water required may vary slightly) and, using a table-knife or a pastry mixer, work into a soft dough. Wrap in cling film. Mix the remaining flour and butter in the blender. Spread this mixture on a large piece of cling film in a rectangle of 14 x 20 cm/5 1/2 x 8 inches. Pack in foil and place together with the pastry in the refrigerator for twenty minutes.

On a lightly floured work surface, carefully roll out the pastry into a triangle twice the size of the butter mixture, pulling into an exact shape by hand. Lay the butter mixture on one half and fold over the other half. Seal the edges well and roll out the pastry to three times the length. Fold in the outer thirds so that the rectangle is again a third of the size. With a little flour, roll out again and fold as described. Wrap in cling film and lay in the refrigerator for twenty minutes.

Take out and roll twice more, folding as described, and making sure that the pastry is always folded, turned and rolled in the same manner.

The butter now lies in very thin layers between the layers of pastry which allows the airy, crispy, mille-feuille effect to develop during baking. Wrap the pastry again and cool in the refrigerator for twenty minutes.

In view of the work involved it is not worth making a small quantity. The finished puff pastry can be readily deep-frozen after dividing into portions of an appropriate size.

Von dem Mehl 450 g abwägen und in eine Schüssel sieben. Salz zugeben und von Hand mit 50 g Butter zu Bröseln zerreiben. Essig und Eiswasser zugeben (die benötigte Menge Wasser kann leicht variieren) und mit einem Tischmesser oder mit einer Teigrühr-maschine zu einem weichen Teig verarbeiten. In Frischhaltefolie wickeln. Restliches Mehl und rest-liche Butter im Mixer zusammen verrühren. Diese Masse auf Frischhaltefolie in Form eines 14 x 20 cm Rechtecks streichen. In Folie einpacken und mit dem Teig für 20 Minuten in den Kühlschrank legen. Auf der leicht bemehlten Arbeitsfläche den Teig vor-sichtig zu einem doppelt so großen Rechteck wie die Buttermasse rollen, von Hand in eine exakte Form ziehen. Den Butterteig auf eine Hälfte legen und die andere Hälfte darüberklappen. Die Ränder gut ver-schließen und den Teig auf die dreifache Länge aus-rollen. Die äusseren Drittel einklappen, so daß das Rechteck wieder ein Drittel so groß ist. Erneut mit wenig Mehl ausrollen und falten wie beschrieben. In Frischhaltefolie wickeln und 20 Minuten in den Kühlschrank legen. Herausnehmen und noch zwei-mal ausrollen und einklappen wie beschrieben, dar-auf achten, daß der Teig immer in der gleichen Weise gefalten, gedreht und ausgerollt wird. Die Butter liegt jetzt sehr dünn zwischen den Teigschichten, was beim Backen die luftige knusprige Millefeuille-Wir-kung ergeben wird. Den Teig eingewickelt im Kühl-schrank 20 Minuten kühlen. Angesicht des Arbeits-aufwandes lohnt es sich nicht, eine kleinere Menge zuzubereiten. Der fertige Blätterteig kann problemlos tiefgekühlt werden, zuvor sollte er in die voraus-sichtlich benötigten Mengen portioniert werden.

Hütte Station

~ PIED - À - TERRE ~

A huge frosted-glass window in London's Charlotte St. evidently arouses curiosity. What could possibly be hidden behind it? In short: one of the best cooks of his current, and maybe also of the next generation, as Tom Aikens was once acclaimed by a British restaurant critic. Indeed, like scarcely any other of the jeunes fauves on London's exciting gastronomy scene, Aikens has developed a sparkling style all of his own. A super-class cook with a perfect foundation in the craft, with infectious ideas and creative courage. Two Michelin stars at the tender age of 26 – even higher-ranking cook Marco Pierre White has to admit having been beaten by a year. By the way, the team comprising cook Tom Aikens, restaurant manager David Moore and sommelier Bruno Asselin is a complete offshoot of Raymond Blanc's "Le Manoir aux Quat' Saisons". An extra compliment from here to the likeable Frenchman in Oxford. Anyone who trains restaurateurs like these deserves a medal.

What makes Aiken's cooking so fascinating? It is not (only) his faultless handling of the noble products of great cuisine, such as foie gras and pigeon breasts, which one can take for granted in man like him. He ventures into simple dishes and makes great achievements out of them. Pigs' jowls with deep-fried pigs' ears and broad beans – all with strong flavors, perfectly cooked, basic products without a flaw or blemish, served with a sauce basis and an extra plateful to feast on – such great cooking we have rarely experienced, and not for a long time. Or confit de canard, the hearty, simple dish from south-western France. From this he makes a clever ballottine with a markedly sour accent, places it upon potato salad, and thus refines everything to a delicate lightness. This is more than the jazzed-up regional cuisine freed from ballast that one can find in many places these days – and very tasty it is too. This is a complete gustatory reinterpretation of well-known products.

Concentrating so hard on the plate, we almost run the risk of not taking in the restaurant, which would be a pity, for it is impressive in its artistic simplicity and worth more than a fleeting glance up from the highly concentrated quail consommé being served as an amuse-gueule. The great British artist, Richard Hamilton, a promoter and friend of this establishment decorated it with modern art with much fineness of feeling. And the chairs shipped in specially from Milan provide a comfort rarely found in restaurant seating – not a decisive factor, but further proof that we here have young experts with whom one feels – including the competent and uncomplicated service – quite simply at ease.

*E*ine gewaltige Milchglasscheibe in Londons Charlotte Street weckt erkennbar Neugier. Was sich dahinter wohl verbergen mag? Machen wir`s kurz: einer der besten Köche seiner jetzigen, vielleicht auch schon der nächsten Generation, wie Tom Aikens von einem englischen Restaurantkritiker schon einmal attestiert wurde. In der Tat: wie kaum ein anderer der jungen Wilden in Londons aufregender Koch-Szene hat Aikens einen fulminanten und eigenständigen Stil entwickelt. Ein Koch der Extraklasse, mit perfekter handwerklicher Grundlage, mit mitreißenden Ideen und kreativem Mut. Zwei Michelin-Sterne im zarten Alter von 26 Jahren – da mußte sich selbst Überflieger Marco Pierre White um ein Jahr geschlagen geben. Die Mannschaft, Koch Tom Aikens, Restaurant-Manager David Moore und Sommelier Bruno Asselin ist übrigens ein komplettes Gewächs aus Raymond Blancs „Le Manoir Aux Quat'Saisons". Ein Extra-Kompliment von hier aus an den sympathischen Franzosen in Oxford. Wer solche Gastronomen ausbildet, ist reif für einen Orden.

Was macht Aikens Küche so faszinierend? Es ist nicht (nur) der fehlerfreie Umgang mit den Edelprodukten der großen Küche wie Gänseleber und Taubenbrüstchen, der bei einem wie ihm als selbstverständlich vorausgesetzt werden kann. Er wagt sich an die einfachen Dinge und macht Großes daraus. Schweinebäckchen mit fritierten Schweineohren und Saubohnen dazu – das alles mit starken Aromen, perfekt gegart, Grundprodukte ohne Fehl und Tadel, dazu eine Sauce zum Reinsetzen und ein Teller voll davon zum Schlemmen – so haben wir große Küche selten und lange nicht mehr erlebt. Oder Confit de Canard, das deftige Einfachgericht aus dem Südwesten Frankreichs.

Er macht eine raffinierte Ballotine daraus mit einer deutlich säuerlichen Betonung, plaziert sie auf etwas Kartoffelsalat und veredelt so alles zu delikater Leichtigkeit. Das ist mehr als aufgepeppte und von Ballast befreite Regionalküche, wie man sie mittlerweile vielerorts – und durchaus lecker – findet. Das ist eine komplette geschmackliche Neuinterpretation von bekannten Produkten.

Bei so viel Konzentration auf den Teller läuft man beinahe Gefahr, das Restaurant selbst gar nicht wahrzunehmen, was schade wäre, ist es doch in seiner künstlerischen Schlichtheit beeindruckend und mehr wert als nur

einen flüchtigen Augenaufschlag von der hochkonzentrierten Wachtel-Consommé, die als Amuse-gueule gereicht wird. Richard Hamilton, der große englische Künstler, ein Förderer und Freund des Hauses, hat es mit viel Einfühlungsvermögen mit moderner Kunst ausgestattet. Und daß man auf den eigens aus Mailand herbeigeschafften Stühlen so gut sitzt wie sonst kaum auf einem Restaurantgestühl, ist zwar nicht entscheidend, aber ein weiterer Beweis dafür, daß man es hier mit jungen Könnern zu tun hat, bei denen man sich – einschließlich dem ebenso kompetenten wie unkomplizierten Service – ganz einfach wohlfühlt.

WINE LIST

July 1997

CHAMPAGNE

			Bt.	Hf.
099	Henri de Navarre *Cuvée Réservée*		33.00	
100	Joseph Perrier NV		36.00	
101	Perrier Jouët NV		38.00	
102	De Venoge *Cordon Bleu*		39.00	
103	Jacquart NV		39.00	
104	Jacquart 199		41.50	
105	Joseph Perrier *Rosé*		43.00	22.50
107	Jacquart Rosé 1990 *Cuvée Mosaïque*		45.00	
108	Veuve Cliquot 1989		50.00	
109	Mumm Cordon Rouge 1988		50.00	
110	Mumm de Cramant *Blanc de Blancs*		55.00	
111	Louis Roederer 1989		60.00	
112	Perrier Jouët Belle Epoque 1988		75.00	
113	Joseph Perrier NV *Blanc de Blancs*	**Magnum**	80.00	
114	Mumm Cuvée René Lalou 1985		80.00	
115	Louis Roederer 1989 *Cristal*		115.00	
116	Dom Perignon 1985		155.00	
117	Dom Perignon 1982 *Rosé*		275.00	
118	Krug 1985 *Clos du Mesnil*		295.00	

SPARKLING WINE

140	Cuvée Napa by Mumm	24.00

WHITE

House White Wine

Vin de Pays Des Coteaux de Murviel 1994
Domaine de Coujan (Rolle) 15.00

LOIRE, ALSACE & RHONE

300	Touraine 1995 *Sauvignon Blanc* *Domaine de Marcé*	14.00
301	Bergerac 1995 *Château Mallevieille*	14.50
302	Côtes du Rhone 1995 *Domaine de la Bécassonne*	17.50
303	Muscat 1993 *Reserve* *Trimbach*	19.25
304	Menetou-Salon 1996 *Domaine de Chatenoy*	20.50
305	Sablet 1995 *Domaine de Piaugier*	21.00
306	Pouilly-Fumé 1995 *Les Chicottes* *Charles Dupuy*	23.50
307	Sancerre Chavignol 1996 (half 95) *Vincent Delaporte*	24.50
308	Gewürztraminer 1994 *Des Princes Abbés* *Domaine Schlumberger*	24.50
309	Riesling 1991 *Grand Cru Saering* *Domaine Schlumberger*	27.50
310	Pouilly-Fumé 1995 *Les Griottes* *Pascal Jolives*	33.00
311	Gewürztraminer 1990 *Seigneurs de Ribeaupierre* *Trimbach*	--,--
312	Sancerre 1994 *La Poussie*	39.00
313	Pinot Gris 1994 *Grand Cru Kitterlé* *Domaine Schlumberger*	42.00
314	Gewürztraminer 1994 *Grand Cru Kitterlé* *Domaine Schlumberger*	45.00

WHITE
FROM THE REST OF THE WORLD

315	Savennieres 1989 *Clos de Papillon* *Domaine du Closel*	44.00
316	Sancerre 1994 *La Grande Cuvée* *Pascal Jolives*	44.00
317	Gewürztraminer 1989 *Grand Cru Kessler* *Domaine Schlumberger*	47.00
318	Condrieu 1996 *Pierre Gaillard*	48.00
319	Condrieu 1994 *René Rostaing*	57.00
320	Pouilly-Fumé 1992 *Baron de L* *Ladoucette*	70.00
321	Pouilly-Fumé 1994 *Silex* *Didier Dagueneau*	75.00
322	Riesling 1982 *Clos Sainte Hune* *Trimbach*	--,-- 49.00
323	Riesling 1983 *Clos Sainte Hune* *Trimbach*	--,-- 55.50

400	Sauvignon Blanc 1995 *Maipo De Martino* *Chile*	14.50
401	Sauvignon Blanc 1995 *Aconcagua Villard* *Chile*	15.50
402	Torrontes 1995 *Norton* *Argentina*	16.50
403	Vina Esmeralda 1995 *Penedes Torres* *Spain*	18.50
404	Orvieto Classico 1995 *Deccugnano Del Barbi* *Italy*	19.50
405	Pinot Bianco 1995 *Rodaro* *Italy*	21.50
406	Rioja 1988 *Lopez de Heredia* *Spain*	24.00
407	Chardonnay 1994 *Cape Charlotte* *Barossa Valley Western Australia*	24.50
408	Roero Arneis 1995 *Vigna Elisa* *Italy*	24.00
409	Chardonnay 1994 *J. Lohr Estates* *Monterey, California, U.S.A.*	25.00
410	Sauvignon Blanc 1995 *Shaw & Smith* *South Australia*	29.50

411	Chardonnay Elston 1995 *Te Mata* *New Zealand*	29.50
412	Chardonnay Augustus 1995 *Puig & Rocca* *Penedes Spain*	30.00
413	Sauvignon Blanc 1994 *Spottswoode* *Napa, California, U.S.A.*	31.00
414	Chiarandà del Merlo 1994 *Donna Fugata* *Italy*	31.50
415	Sauvignon Blanc 1996 *Cloudy Bay* *New Zealand*	33.00
416	Chardonnay 1994 *Leeuwin Estate, Art Series* *West Australia*	49.50
417	Chardonnay 1994 *Kistler, Vine Hill Vineyard* *Russian River Valley, California, U.S.A.*	70.00
418	Chardonnay 1994 *Kistler, Durell Vineyard* *Son, California, U.S.A.*	70.00

WHITE
BURGUNDY

330	Beaujolais 1994 *Domaine Pivot*	18.0
331	Sauvignon de Saint Bris 1994 *Domaine Goisot*	18.5
332	Petit Chablis 1995 *Thierry Hamelin*	23.5
333	Saint-Veran "En Crèche" 1996 *Vieilles Vignes* *Jacques Saumaize*	25.5
334	Pouilly-Fuissé 1995 *Georges Duboeuf*	27.5
335	Montagny 1993 *1er Cru, Les Coères* *Domaine Bertrand*	28.0
336	Mâcon-Viré 1994 *Vieilles Vignes* *Domaine Bonhomme*	30.5
337	Bourgogne Aligote 1994 *Domaine Coche-Dury*	35.0
338	Chablis 1993 *1er Cru, Vau de Vey,* *Jean Durup*	33.5
339	Marsannay 1993 *Bruno Clair*	36.
340	Savigny-Les -Beaune 1994 *Jean-Marc Pavelot*	41.
341	Meursault 1992 *Paul Garaudet*	42.

342	Bourgogne Chardonnay 1994 *Domaine Coche-Dury*	45.00
343	Chassagne-Montrachet 1993 *1er Cru, Chaumées* *Colin-Deleger*	--,-- 29.50
344	Chassagne-Montrachet 1994 *Colin-Deleger*	49.00
345	Chassagne-Montrachet 1994 *Les Masures* *Jean-Noel Gagnard*	52.00 27.00
346	Chassagne-Montrachet 1994 *1er Cru, Morgeots* *Colin-Deleger*	55.00
347	Aloxe-Corton 1993 *Daniel Senard*	64.00
348	Chablis 1993 *1er Cru, Vaillons* *Jean-Marie Raveneau*	72.00
349	Chablis 1993 *1er Cru, Butteaux* *Jean-Marie Raveneau*	72.00
350	Meursault 1994 *Domaine Coche-Dury*	74.00
351	Meursault 1993 *1er Cru, Poruzot* *Domaine Jobart*	75.00
352	Chassagne-Montrachet 1994 *Les Caillerets* *Jean-Noel Gagnard*	75.00 40.00
353	Meursault 1994 *Les Téssons, Clos de mon Plaisir* *Domaine Roulot*	77.00 41.00
354	Nuits-St-Georges 1993 *1er Cru* *Clos de l'Arlot*	77.00

355	Chablis 1992 *Grand Cru, Grenouilles* *Jean-Paul Droin*	80.00
356	Meursault 1992 *1er Cru, Genevrieres* *Domaine Michelot*	82.50
357	Meursault 1985 *Leroy*	85.00
358	Chassagne 1988 *1er Cru, Chenevottes* *Leroy*	90.00
359	Meursault 1994 *Les Chevalières* *Domaine Coche-Dury*	90.00
360	Puligny-Montrachet 1989 *1er Cru Champ Canet* *Domaine Etienne Sauzet*	--,-- 52.00
361	Corton-Charlemagne 1989 (half 1990) *Bonneau du Martray*	98.50 55.00
362	Corton-Charlemagne 1985 *Bonneau du Martray*	99.00
363	Puligny-Montrachet 1992 *1er Cru Champ Canet* *Domaine Sauzet*	99.00

364	Meursault 1988 *1er Cru Charmes,* *Lafon*	100.00
365	Meursault 1990 *1er Cru Perrier,* *Lafon*	160.00
366	Meursault 1990 *1er Cru, Genevrieres,* *Lafon*	150.00
367	Bienvenue-Batard-Montrachet 1986 *Domaine Leflaive*	175.00
368	Batard- Montrachet 1985 *Domaine Leflaive*	175.00
369	Chevalier-Montrachet 1986 *Domaine Leflaive*	180.00
370	Chevalier- Montrachet 1985 *Domaine Leflaive*	190.00
371	Le Montrachet 1994 *Domaine Ramonet*	325.00
372	Batard-Montrachet 1990 *Jean-Noel Gagnard* **Magnum**	400.00
373	Le Montrachet 1986 *Marquis de Laguiche*	425.00

RED

House Red Wine

Vin de Pays Des Coteaux de Murviel 1990
Domaine de Coujan 15.00

REGIONAL , LOIRE & BEAUJOLAIS

501	Beaujolais-Villages 1994 *Domaine Pivot*	--,--
502	Beaujolais-Villages 1995 50cl. *Georges Duboeuf*	--,--
503	Minervois 1993 *Château D'Oupia*	20.50
504	Saumur Champigny 1994 *Domaine Filliatreau*	23.00
505	Fleurie 1995 *La Madone* *Georges Duboeuf*	23.50
506	Madiran 1993 *Château D'Aydie*	29.00
507	Chinon 1986 *Clos de L Echo* *Couly-Dutheil*	35.00
508	Bourgueil 1985 *Cuvée Réservée* *Pierre-Jacques Druet*	37.00
509	Sancerre 1994 *La Poussie*	39.00
510	Chinon 1981 *Couly-Dutheil*	42.00

RED
COTE DU RHONE

520	Côte du Rhone 1994 *Jean-Luc Colombo*	21.50
521	Côte du Rhone 1993 *Rasteau* *Domaine Rabasse Charavin*	22.50
522	Gigondas 1991 *Domaine Saint Gayan*	29.00
523	Crozes-Hermitage 1994 *Domaine Du Colombier*	31.00
524	Côte-Rôtie 1988 *Michel Mourier*	35.00
525	St. Joseph 1994 *Grippat*	37.50
526	Cornas 1993 *Terres Brules* *Jean-Luc Colombo*	40.00
527	Côte-Rôtie 1992 (Half 1986) *Etienne Guigal*	42.00
528	Côte-Rôtie 1994 *Brune et Blonde* *M. Chapoutier*	49.50
529	Hermitage 1991 *Monier De La Sizeranne* *M. Chapoutier*	52.00
530	Hermitage 1990 *Etienne Guigal*	--,--
531	Côte-Rôtie 1993 *Côte Blonde* *René Rostaing*	54.00
532	Chateauneuf du Pape 1978 *Clos du Mont-Olivet*	55.00

RED WINES
FROM THE REST OF WORLD

630	Cabernet-Sauvignon 1993 *Villard* *Chile*	16.50
631	Malbec 1994 *Norton* *Argentina*	17.50
632	Barbera 1990 *Norton* *Argentina*	22.00
633	Tancredi 1992 *Donna Fugata* *Italy*	23.50
634	Ylleras 1991 *Los Curros* *Spain*	24.00
635	Pinot Noir 1995 *Coldstream Hill* *Australia*	27.00
636	Douro 1994 *Quinta Do Crasto* *Portugal*	28.00
637	Cabernet-Sauvignon 1992 *Prelude, Leeuwin Estate* *Australia,*	29.00
638	Zinfandel Dry Creek 1992 *Nalle* *Sonoma, USA*	30.50
639	Ratti 1993 *Villa Pattono* *Italy*	34.00
640	Shiraz 1993 *Old Block, St Hallet* *Australia, Barossa Valley*	35.00

641	Vina Ardanza 1989 *Reserva, Rioja Alta* *Spain*	36.00	19.00
642	Matarromera 1994 *Ribera del Duero, Vinedos Y Bodegas* *Spain,*	36.00	
643	Pinot Noir 1995 *Martinborough Ata Rangi* *New Zealand*	42.00	
644	Zinfandel, Geyserville 1994 *Ridge* *California, USA*	43.00	22.50
645	Cabernet Merlot 1989 *Goldwater* *Waiheke Island, New Zealand*	44.00	
646	Pinot Noir 1994 *Bearboat* *Russian River, California, USA*	45.50	
647	Priorat 1991 *Clos Mogador* *Spain*	45.00	
648	Barbaresco 1986 *Reserva, La Spinono, Beruffi Piefro* *Italy*	46.00	
649	Pinot Noir 1994 *Etude* *Carneros, California, USA*	47.50	25.00
650	Chianti Classico 1988 *Reserva Riecine* *Italy*	49.50	
651	Cabernet-Sauvignon 1992 *Art Series, Leeuwin Estate* *Australia,*	52.00	
652	Cabernet Sauvignon 1992 *Spottswoode* *Napa California, USA*	55.50	
653	Cabernet Merlot 1994 *Te Motu , Dunleavy* *Waiheke Is. New Zealand*	59.00	33.50
654	Sassicaia 1993 *Tentuta San Guido Marchesi* *Italy*	77.00	
655	Monte Bello 1992 *Ridge* *California, USA*	105.00	55.50
656	Cabernet Sauvignon 1989 *Beringer, Reserve* *California, USA*	110.00	

RED
BURGUNDY

539	Bourgogne Pinot Noir 1993 *Domaine Parent*	26.00
540	Mercurey 1992 *Clos Tonnerre 1er Cru* *Michel Juillot*	32.00
541	Chorey-Les-Beaune 1993 *Tollot-Beaut*	34.00
542	Bourgogne Pinot Noir 1994 *Domaine Coche-Dury*	35.00
543	Savigny-les-Beaune 1992 *Tollot-Beaut*	36.00
544	Marsannay 1992 *Les Grasses Têtes* *Bruno Clair*	37.00
545	Saint-Aubin 1993 *1er Cru* *Marc Colin*	40.00
546	Savigny Lavières 1993 *1er Cru* *Tollot-Beaut*	--,--
547	Aloxe-Corton 1994 *Tollot-Beaut*	--,--
548	Nuits-St-Georges 1990 *1er Cru Vaucrains* *Henri Gouges*	--,--
549	Nuits-St-Georges 1990 *1er Cru Clos Des Porrets* *Henri Gouges*	49.00
550	Nuits-St-Georges 1990 *1er Cru Les Pruliers* *Henri Gouges* (halfs 1992)	49.00
551	Savigny-Les -Beaune 1990 *Jean-Marc Pavelot*	47.00

552 Volnay 1989
   J.M. Boillot — 50.00
553 Santenay 1985 *1er Cru Clos de Tavannes*
   Domaine Remoisenet — 58.00
554 Chambolle-Musigny 1992
   Domaine Roumier — 52.00
555 Gevrey-Chambertin 1992 *1er Cru Lavaux-St-Jacques*
   Domaine Vachet-Rousseau — 56.00
556 Savigny-les-Beaune 1985 *1er Cru Les Gravains*
   Domaine Remoisenet — 57.00
557 Santenay 1985 *1er Cru Clos de Tavannes*
   Domaine Remoisenet — 58.00
558 Nuits-St-Georges 1990 *1er Cru Les St Georges*
   Henri Gouges — 60.00
559 Beaune 1989 *1er Cru Montrevenots*
   J.M. Boillot — 60.00
560 Auxey-Duresses 1985 *Les Ecusseaux*
   Domaine Ampeau — 64.00
561 Volnay 1989 *Carelle Sous La Chapelle*
   J.M. Boillot — 68.00
562 Gevrey-Chambertin 1990 *1er Cru les Gazetiers*
   Armand Rousseau — 71.00
563 Savigny-Les -Beaune 1985 *Lavieres*
   Domaine Ampeau & Fils — 79.00
564 Nuits-St-Georges 1990 *1er Cru Clos des Forets*
   Clos de l'Arlot — 85.00
565 Bonnes-Mares 1992
   Domaine Roumier — 90.00
566 Chambolle Musigny 1990
   Domaine Dujac — 90.00

567 Gevrey-Chambertin 1992 *1er Cru Clos St-Jacques*
   Armand Rousseau — 92.00
568 Corton 1990 *Clos des Meix*
   Domaine Senard — 94.00
569 Volnay 1991 *Clos du Chateau des Ducs*
   Michel Lafarge — 96.00
570 Chambolle Musigny 1990 *1er Cru "Fuesselotes"* — 97.00
571 Gevrey-Chambertin 1985 *Vieilles Vignes*
   Denis Bachelet — 99.00
572 Nuits-St-Georges 1985 *1er Cru Les Cailles*
   Domaine Michelot — 110.00
573 Corton-Bressandes 1990 *Grand Cru*
   Tollot-beaut & Fils — 115.00
574 Beaune-Greves 1985 *1er cru Vigne de l'Enfant Jesus*
   Bouchard Pere & Fils — 118.00
575 Gevrey-Chambertin 1985 *1er cru les Gazetiers*
   Domaine Jadot — 125.00
576 Corton 1985 *Clos du Roi*
   Domaine Senard — 110.00
577 Nuits-St-Georges 1967 *1er Cru Les Corvées Paget*
   Domaine Vienot — --.--
578 Chambertin 1985
   Louis Trapet — 111.00
579 Nuits-St-Georges 1992 *Aux Lavieres*
   Leroy — 115.00
580 Vosne-Romanée 1988 *Genevrieres*
   F. Esmonin — 120.00

581 Clos de la Roche 1986
   Armand Rousseau — 120.00
582 Echezeaux 1989
   Domaine Henri Jayer — 120.00
583 Pommard 1985 *1er Cru Rugiens*
   Domaine Hubert de Montille — 125.00
584 Vosne-Romanée 1990 *1er Cru Aux Brulées*
   Domaine Méo-Camuzet — 130.00
585 Echezeaux 1988
   Domaine Henri Jayer — 135.00
586 Griottes-Chambertin 1990
   F. Esmonin — 135.00
587 Mazis-Chambertin 1990
   F. Esmonin — 135.00
588 Ruchottes-Chambertin 1990
   Domaine Georges Mugneret — 140.00
589 Echezeaux 1990
   Domaine Henri Jayer — 150.00
590 Vosne-Romanée 1992 *Les Beaux Monts*
   Leroy — 150.00
591 Echezeaux 1985
   Domaine Dujac — 170.00
592 Richebourg 1992 *Grand Cru*
   Alain Hudelot-Noellat — 175.00
593 Vosne-Romanée 1990 *Cros Parantoux*
   Emmanuel Rouget — 180.00
594 La Tache 1976
   D.R.C. — 399.00

BORDEAUX

580 Domaine Du Galet 1994
   Bordeaux — 8.50
581 Château La Haye 1993 *Cru Bourgeois,
   St. Estephe* — 29.50 15.0
582 Baron Villeneuve de Cantemerle 1993
   Haut-Médoc — 24.50
583 Château Cartillon 1990 *Cru Bourgeois,
   Haut Medoc* — 25.00
584 Château Cissac 1993 *Cru Bourgeois,
   Haut Medoc* — 27.50
585 Château D'Angludet 1993
   Margaux — 29.00
586 Château Clarke 1993
   Listrac Medoc — 30.00
587 Les Fiefs de Lagrange 1989
   St.Julien — 36.00
588 Château Leoville Poyferre 1993
   2 ème Cru, St. Julien — 39.00

589 Château De Castelot 1993
   Grand Cru Classé, St. Emilion — --.-- 25
590 Château Clerc Milon 1993
   5 ème Cru, Pauillac — 41.00
591 Château Chasse Spleen 1993
   Cru Bourgeois Moulis — 42.00
592 Château Grand Puy Lacoste 1993
   5ème Cru, Pauillac — 47.50
593 Château Lynch-Bages 1993
   5ème Cru, Pauillac — 60.00
594 Château Clerc Milon 1989
   5ème Cru, Pauillac — 63.00
595 Château Meyney 1970
   Cru Bourgeois St. Estephe — 65.00
596 Château Talbot 1988
   4ème Cru, St. Julien — 66.00
597 Château D'Angludet 1983
   Margaux — 72.00

598 Château Haut-Batailley 1985
   5ème Cru, Pauillac — 75.00
599 Château Cantemerle 1964
   5ème Macau — 79.50
600 Château Talbot 1989
   4 ème Cru, St. Julien — 81.00
601 Château La Croix 1989
   Pomerol — 89.00
602 Château Chasse Spleen 1982
   Cru Bourgeois Moulis — 99.00
603 Château Talbot 1970
   4 ème Cru, St. Julien — 90.00
602 Château Batailley 1970
   5ème Cru, Pauillac — 90.00
604 Château Ducru Beaucaillou 1983
   2ème Cru, St. Julien — 95.00
605 Château Lynch-Bages 1964
   5ème Cru, Pauillac — 100.00
606 Château Beychevelle 1970
   4 ème Cru, St. Julien — --.-- 62.00

607 Château Cheval Blanc 1993
   1er Cru, St. Emilion — 120.00
608 Château Pichon-Longueville-Contesse 1970
   2ème Cru, Pauillac
609 Château Cheval Blanc 1978
   1er Cru, St. Emilion — 240.00
610 Château Cheval Blanc 1983
   1er Cru, St. Emilion — 260.00
611 Château Haut Brion
   1ère Cru, Graves — --.-- 140.00
612 Château Cheval Blanc 1970
   1er Cru, St. Emilion — 287.00 150.00
613 Château Margaux 1966
   1ère Margaux — --.-- 180.00
614 Château Leoville Poyferre 1975
   2ème Cru, St. Julien — Imperial 480.00
615 Château Haut-Batailley 1975
   5ème Cru, Pauillac — Imperial 525.00
616 Château Petrus 1970
   Pomerol — 1180.00

WINES

		Bt.	Hf.	Gl.
199 Muscat de Mireval 1995				
Domaine de La Capelle		--.--	16.00	4.50
200 Pacherenc Du Vic Bilh 1991				
MoelleuxChâteau d'Aydie		29.50	--.--	6.50
201 Muscat de Beaumes de Venise 1994				
Domaine de Durban		--.--	18.00	6.50
202 Coteaux du Layon Rablay 1990				
Domaine des Sablonnettes		--.--	17.00	
203 Ben Ryé 1992 Passito Di Pantelleria				
Donna Fugata Italy		--.--	27.50	
204 Riesling Botrytis 1994 Australia				
Hollick		--.--	30.00	
205 Loupiac 1994				
Château La Bertrande	50 CL	--.--	30.00	
206 Banyuls 1989				
Domaine de la Casa Blanca		--.--	--.--	4.00
207 Vouvray 1990 *Réserve Personnelle*				
Château Gaudrelle	50 CL	--.--	48.00	
208 Gewürztraminer 1989 Selection de Grains Nobles				
Trimbach		--.--	51.00	

All wines sold by glass are 125 ml

		Bt.	Hf.	Gl.
209 Coteaux du Layon Rablay Quintessence 1995				
Domaine des Sablonnettes	50 CL	--.--	55.00	
210 Château Filhot 1983				
2ème Cru Sauternes		57.50	--.--	
211 Brown Muscat 1986				
Brown Brothers		60.00	--.--	
212 Château Filhot 1986				
2ème Cru Sauternes		65.00	--.--	
213 Château Suduiraut 1983				
1er Cru Sauternes		100.00	--.--	
214 Weisser Welschriesling 1994				
Trockenbeerenausle Willi Opitz		115.00	--.--	
215 Weisser Welschriesling Eiswein 1993				
Willi Opitz Austria		122.50	--.--	
216 Eltviller Rheinberg Riesling Spatlese 1934				
GermanyJean Iffland		150.00	--.--	
217 Gewurztraminer 1990 Cuvée Anne				
Domaine Schlumberger		99.00	45.00	
218 Pino Gris 1989 Cuvée Clarisse				
Domaine Schlumberger		110.00	60.00	
219 Tokaji 1973 Hungary 50 CL.				
5 Puttonyos		115.00	--.--	

		Bt.	Hf.
220 Vouvray 1976 *Le Mont*			
Gaston Huet		120.00	--.--
221 Tokaji 1983 Hungary 50 Cl			
6 Puttonyos		145.00	--.--
222 Coteaux du Layon 1959			
Domaine de Moulin de Tigné		150.00	--.--
223 Riesling Ice Wine 1992 *Canada*			
Brights		--.--	175.00
224 Flonheimer Adelberg Beerenausle 1976			
Germany		180.00	--.--
225 Geierslay Beerenausle 1976 *Germany*			
Adolph Huesgen		200.00	--.--
226 Wintricher Grober Herrgott Riesling Beerenausle			
1976 Germany Ewald Theod Drathen		210.00	--.--
227 Vouvray 1947 *Le Haut-Lieu*			
Gaston Huet		220.00	--.--
228 Château Yquem 1989			
1er Cru, Sauternes		--.--	177.00
229 Château Yquem 1967			
1er Cru, Sauternes		850.00	--.--

ROSE

430 Bourgueil 1992 Pierre-Jacques Druet — 19.50
431 Marsannay 1993 Bruno Clair — 26.00
432 Sancerre 1994 La Poussie — 38.00
433 Etude 1995 Carneros
   California Anthony Sother — 45.00

MAGNUMS AND IMPERIALS

113 Joseph Perrier NV
   Blanc de Blancs — 80.00
578 Savigny-les-Beaune 1990 *1er Cru La Dominode*
   Jean-Marc Pavelot — 165.00
579 Nuits-Saint-Georges 1990 *1er cru Chaignots*
   Domaine Michelot — 199.00
373 Batard-Montrachet 1990
   Jean-Noel Gagnard — 400.00
611 Château Leoville Poyferre 1975
   2ème Cru, St. Julien — Imperial 480.00
612 Château Haut-Batailley 1975
   5ème Cru, Pauillac — Imperial 525.00

The Web Site
www.pied.a.terre.co.uk

E-mail
p-a-t@dircon.co.uk

TERRINE OF GOOSE FOIE GRAS AND ARTICHOKES

TERRINE VON DER GÄNSESTOPFLEBER UND ARTISCHOCKEN

For 8 - 10 persons:

2 goose livers of about 750/1 lb 8 oz each,
150 g/5 oz/³/₅ cup coarse sea salt

16 fresh artichoke hearts, soaked in lemon water,
4 shallots, chopped, 200 ml/6²/₃ fl oz/⁴/₅ cup olive oil,
2 heads of garlic, split, 1 sprig of thyme, 6 bayleaves,
2 tsp sea salt, 1 tsp white pepper corns,
150 ml/5 fl oz/³/₅ cup white-wine vinegar,
200 ml/6²/₃ fl oz/⁴/₅ cup white wine

butter, 150 ml/5 fl oz/³/₅ cup double cream,
7 gelatine sheets, soaked in cold water,
1 tbsp white truffle oil, salt, freshly ground white pepper

Für 8 - 10 Personen:

2 Gänselebern von je 750 g,
150 grobes Meersalz

16 frische Artischockenherzen, in Zitronenwasser eingelegt,
4 Schalotten, gehackt, 200 ml Olivenöl,
2 Knoblauchknollen, auseinandergedrückt,
1 Thymianzweig, 6 Lorbeerblätter,
2 TL Meersalz, 1 TL weiße Pfefferkörner,
150 ml Weißweinessig, 200 ml Weißwein

Butter, 150 ml Doppelrahm,
7 Gelatineblätter, in kaltem Wasser eingeweicht,
1 EL weißes Trüffelöl, Salz, weißer Pfeffer aus der Mühle

To prepare the livers: Remove the goose livers from the refrigerator an hour before use. Slit the lobes crossways and, with a small knife, carefully remove all veins and membranes. Lay the livers on clingfilm. Cover with a second layer of clingfilm and, using a rolling pin, roll out 1 cm/²/₅ in thick. Allow to set in the refrigerator, then remove the clingfilm and sprinkle the liver thickly on both sides with sea salt. Chill thoroughly for 3 hours in the refrigerator. Then cut into 4 strips to the size of the terrine mould. Wash of the salt in cold water. Then dab dry with kitchen paper.

For the artichokes: Sweat the shallots in the olive oil. Add the garlic, thyme, bayleaves, sea salt and pepper corns, and sweat. Quench with vinegar and white wine, add the artichoke hearts and cover with water. Bring to the boil and cook the artichokes for twenty minutes until soft. Leave to go cold in the liquid. Remove any traces of choke from the artichoke hearts. Set 4 hearts aside and cut the rest into flat squares for the terrine. Coarsely chop the 4 hearts and cook, together with the off-cuts, in a frying pan with the butter and a little water until they collapse. Stir in the cream, add the squeezed gelatine and dissolve. Then purée until smooth in the blender.

Season with truffle oil, salt and white pepper and pass the purée through a sieve.

For the terrine: Line the mould with a strong foil. Place a strip of liver in the mould and coat with one-sixth of the artichoke purée. Top with a alyer of artichoke pieces. Coat with purée, then repeat the process until all ingredients are used up and the terrine is covered with a final strip of liver. Wrap the foil over the top and weight the terrine evenly with a heavy weight. Chill for 36 hours in the refrigerator.

To serve: Unmould the terrine and slice with a sharp knife. An excellent accompaniment would be remoulade sauce mixed with celeriac and truffle mayonnaise.

Vorbereitung der Leber: Die Gänselebern eine Stunde vor der Verarbeitung aus dem Kühlschrank nehmen. Die Lappen über Kreuz aufschneiden und mit einem kleinen Messer sorgfältig alle Adern und Häutchen entfernen. Die Lebern auf eine Lage Frischhaltefolie legen. Mit einer zweiten Folie zudecken und mit einem Wallholz 1 cm dick ausrollen. Im Kühlschrank festwerden lassen, dann die Folie entfernen und die Leber auf beiden Seiten dick mit Meersalz bestreuen. Drei Stunden im Kühlschrank durchkühlen lassen. Die Masse dann in 4 Streifen in der Größe der Terrinenform schneiden. Mit kaltem Wasser das Salz abwaschen, mit Küchenpapier trockentupfen.

Für die Artischocken: Schalotten im Olivenöl anschwitzen. Knoblauchknollen, Thymian, Lorbeerblätter, Meersalz und Pfefferkörner zugeben und mitdünsten. Mit Essig und Weißwein ablöschen, die Artischockenherzen zugeben und mit Wasser aufgießen, bis sie bedeckt sind. Zum Kochen bringen und die Artischocken 20 Minuten weich kochen. In der Flüssigkeit erkalten lassen. Die Artischockenherzen von eventuellen Heuresten befreien. Vier Herzen zur Seite legen, den Rest für die Terrine in eckige flache Stücke schneiden. Die vier Herzen grob hacken und mit den Abschnitten in einer Pfanne mit der Butter und etwas Wasser kochen, bis sie zerfallen. Den Rahm unterrühren, die ausgedrückte Gelatine darin auflösen und im Mixer fein pürieren. Mit Trüffelöl, Salz und weißem Pfeffer würzen und das Püree durch ein Sieb streichen.

Für die Terrine: Die Form mit einer festen Folie auslegen. Einen Streifen Leber einlegen und mit einem Sechstel des Artischockenpürees bestreichen. Eine Lage Artischockenstücke einlegen, mit Püree bestreichen. Den Vorgang wiederholen, bis alle Zutaten aufgebraucht sind und die Terrine mit dem letzten Leberstreifen zugedeckt ist. Die Folie oben zusammenschlagen und die Terrine mit einem schweren Gewicht gleichmäßig beschweren. Im Kühlschrank 36 Stunden durchkühlen lassen.

Zum Servieren: Die Terrine aus der Form nehmen und mit einem scharfen Messer in Scheiben schneiden. Dazu paßt ausgezeichnet eine mit Sellerie und Trüffelmayonnaise gewürzte Remouladensauce.

STEAMED PIGEON BREAST WITH CABBAGE ROULADES

GEDÄMPFTE TAUBENBRÜSTCHEN MIT KOHLWICKEL

For 4 persons:

For the cabbage roulade:
1 onion, finely chopped, 200 g/7 oz/⁴/₅ cup duck fat,
200 g/7 oz smoked bacon, finely chopped,
1 small white cabbage, 1 bottle white wine,
1 tbsp coarse sea salt,
80 g/2²/₃ oz/¹/₃ cup goose foie gras

For the potatoes:
2 large potatoes, 200 g/7 oz/⁴/₅ cup duck fat,
6 slices smoked bacon

4 squab pigeons, gutted, with neck,
wings and legs removed,
1 tbsp butter, 2 tbsp olive oil, 8 sprigs thyme,
150 ml/5 fl oz/³/₅ cup brown chicken stock,
1 sprig rosemary,
salt, freshly ground pepper, 1 tbsp cold butter

Für 4 Personen:

Für die Kohlwickel:
1 Zwiebel, feingehackt, 200 g Entenschmalz,
200 g geräucherter Speck, fein gehackt,
1 kleiner Weißkohlkopf,
1 Flasche Weißwein,
1 EL grobes Meersalz, 80 g Gänsestopfleber

Für die Kartoffeln:
2 große Kartoffeln, 200 g Entenschmalz,
6 Scheiben geräucherter Speck

4 junge Tauben, küchenfertig,
ohne Flügel und Keulen,
1 EL Butter, 2 EL Olivenöl,
8 Thymianzweige,
150 ml brauner Hühnerfond, 1 Rosmarinzweig,
Salz, Pfeffer aus der Mühle, 1 EL kalte Butter

Cook the onion with the bacon in duck fat on low heat until soft. Remove four fine leaves from the cabbage. Finely chop the rest and blanch in boiling salted water. Drain, then add to the onions. Add the wine and sea salt and cook on a low heat for three hours. Boil the cabbage leaves in salted water for about four minutes, drain and refresh in iced water.

Line four small round moulds first with clingfilm, then with a cabbage leaf. Fill with the cooked choucroute and top each one with a slice of foie gras. Then fold the cabbage leaves and clingfilm over the top of each mould.

For the potatoes: Peel the potatoes and cut into cylinders with a round cutter, approximately 4 cm/ 1¹/₂ in across. Slice the cylinders thinly. Heat the duck fat in a frying pan and add the potato slices. Cook on a low heat for about 10 minutes until soft. Pour off the fat and layer the potatoes with the bacon into four stacks on a non-stick baking sheet. Preheat the oven to 160° C/320° F and bake for fifteen to twenty minutes.

Fry the pigeons in oil and butter until golden brown. Place one sprig thyme on each breast and wrap the pigeons in foil. Steam for eight to ten minutes. Bring the chicken stock to the boil with the rosemary. Unwrap the pigeons and add the cooking juices and thyme to the sauce. Cut the breasts off the pigeons and keep warm. Pass the jus through a sieve. Adjust the seasoning and whisk in the cold butter.

To serve: Remove the clingfilm from the cabbage roulades and place them on plates. Lay the pigeon breasts on top and place the potato stacks beside them. Pour the sauce around.

Zwiebel im Entenschmalz mit dem Speck bei kleiner Hitze weich braten. Vom Kohlkopf vier schöne Blätter wegnehmen, den Rest fein hacken und in Salzwasser blanchieren. Durch ein Sieb abgießen, dann zu den Zwiebeln geben. Den Wein und das Meersalz zugeben und das Ganze bei kleiner Hitze drei Stunden schmoren lassen. Die Kohlblätter in Salzwasser ca. 4 Minuten kochen, abgießen und kalt abschrecken. Vier runde Förmchen erst mit Frischhaltefolie, dann mit je einem Kohlblatt auskleiden. Mit dem gekochten Kraut füllen, mit je einer Scheibe Gänsestopfleber belegen, dann die Kohlblätter und die Folie oben zusammenschlagen.

Für die Kartoffeln: Kartoffeln schälen und runde Stangen mit 4 cm Durchmesser ausstechen. Die Stangen in dünne Scheiben schneiden. Den Entenschmalz in einer Pfanne erhitzen. Die Kartoffelscheiben darin ungefähr 10 Minuten weich garen. Das Fett abgießen und die Kartoffeln abwechselnd mit dem Speck auf einem beschichteten Blech zu vier Türmchen schichten. Im auf 160° C vorgeheizten Ofen 15 - 20 Minuten backen.

Die Tauben in einer Pfanne im Öl-Buttergemisch goldbraun anbraten. Jede Brust mit einem Thymianzweig belegen und die Tauben in Folie wickeln. Über Dampf 8 - 10 Minuten garen. Den Hühnerfond mit dem Rosmarin zum Kochen bringen. Die Tauben aus der Folie nehmen, den ausgetretenen Saft und den Thymian zu der Sauce geben. Die Brüstchen auslösen, warmhalten. Die Jus durch ein Sieb passieren, abschmecken und die kalte Butter unterrühren. Zum Servieren: Die Kohlwickel aus der Folie nehmen und auf Teller verteilen. Die Taubenbrüste darüberlegen und die Kartoffeltürme daneben geben. Mit der Sauce umgießen.

SCALLOPS ON GAZPACHO WITH TOMATO CONFIT

JAKOBSMUSCHELN AN GAZPACHO MIT TOMATENCONFIT

For 4 persons:

Marinated scallops:
16 scallops, shells removed, without roe,
8 basil leaves, cut into strips, juice of 1 lemon,
2 tbsp olive oil,
salt, freshly ground pepper

For the gazpacho:
250 g/8 oz cherry tomatoes,
400 g/13 oz small cucumbers, 2 red bell peppers,
2 shallots, 6 garlic cloves, 1 bunch basil, 1 onion,
1 dash each of Tabasco and Worcestershire sauce,
juice of 1 lemon, 100 ml/3 1/2 fl oz/ 2/5 cup water,
250 ml/8 1/2 fl oz/1 cup olive oil

For the confit:
12 plum tomatoes, 2 tbsp icing sugar,
6 garlic cloves, sliced,
1/2 bunch thyme,
coarse sea salt, freshly ground black pepper,
8 basil leaves, sliced,
4 tbsp olive oil

To garnish:
frisée lettuce, basil

Für 4 Personen:

Marinierte Jakobsmuscheln:
16 Jakobsmuscheln, ausgelöst, ohne Corail,
8 Basilikumblätter, in Streifen geschnitten,
Saft von 1 Zitrone, 2 EL Olivenöl,
Salz, Pfeffer aus der Mühle

Für den Gazpacho:
250 g Kirschtomaten, 400 g Salatgurken,
2 rote Paprika, 2 Schalotten, 6 Knoblauchzehen,
1 Bund Basilikum, 1 Zwiebel,
je 1 Spritzer Tabasco und Worcestershire,
Saft von 1 Zitrone, 100 ml Wasser,
250 ml Olivenöl

Für das Confit:
12 Flaschentomaten, 2 EL Puderzucker,
6 Knoblauchzehen, in Scheiben geschnitten,
1/2 Bund Thymian, grobes Meersalz,
schwarzer Pfeffer aus der Mühle,
8 Basilikumblätter, in Streifen geschnitten,
4 EL Olivenöl

Garnitur:
Friséesalat, Basilikum

For the gazpacho: Chop all vegetables and herbs, then marinate overnight with the mixed spices, lemon juice, water and olive oil. The next day, purée in the blender and pass through a fine sieve.
For the confit: Blanch the tomatoes in salted water. Skin, cut into quarters lengthways and remove the seeds. Press the quarters flat and with a pastry cutter cut out 24 discs.
Place the discs and remnants on a baking tray, sprinkle with icing sugar, garlic, thyme, sea salt, basil and pepper, and drizzle with olive oil. Place in an 80° C/175° F oven and allow to dry slowly for three to four hours.
Save the tomato discs and finely chop the rest of the tomato confit.
Finely chop half of the scallops, stir together with basil, 100 ml/3 1/2 fl oz/ 2/5 cup of the tomato confit, a little lemon juice, olive oil, salt and pepper. Slice the rest of the scallops horizontally into three slices each. Fry in a little hot olive oil on both sides, season with salt, pepper, and a little lemon juice. Heat the prepared tomato discs in the oven.
To serve: Spread the scallop mix on 4 chilled plates. Add a generous saucing of the gazpacho in an exterior ring and garnish with a little frisée and basil leaves.
Interlayer the fried scallops with the tomato discs in the middle.

Für den Gazpacho: Alle Gemüse und Kräuter hacken, dann mit den Gewürzen, dem Zitronensaft, Wasser und Olivenöl vermischt über Nacht marinieren. Am nächsten Tag im Mixer fein pürieren und durch ein engmaschiges Sieb streichen.
Für das Confit: Die Tomaten in Salzwasser blanchieren, enthäuten, längs vierteln, dann die Kerne entfernen. Die Viertel flachdrücken und mit einem runden Ausstechförmchen 24 Scheiben ausstechen. Diese Tomatenscheiben mit den Abschnitten auf einem Blech ausbreiten. Mit Puderzucker, Knoblauch, Thymian, Meersalz, Pfeffer und Basilikum bestreuen, das Olivenöl darüberträufeln. Im Ofen bei ca. 80° C drei bis vier Stunden langsam ziehen lassen. Die Tomatenscheiben aufheben, den Rest des Tomatenconfits fein hacken. Die Hälfte der Jakobsmuscheln fein hacken. Mit Basilikum, 100 ml von dem Tomatenconfit, etwas Zitronensaft, Olivenöl, Salz und Pfeffer verrühren. Die restlichen Muscheln quer in je drei Scheiben schneiden. In etwas Olivenöl von beiden Seiten heiß anbraten, mit Salz, Pfeffer und etwas Zitronensaft würzen. Die vorbereiteten Tomatenscheiben im Ofen heiß werden lassen. Zum Servieren: Vier gekühlte Teller mit dem Muschelpüree bestreichen. Den Gazpacho großzügig rundherumgießen, mit Salat- und Basilikumblättern garnieren. Die gebratenen Jakobsmuscheln abwechselnd mit den Tomatenscheiben in der Mitte auftürmen.

TURBOT WITH LANGOUSTINES AND RED-WINE SAUCE

STEINBUTT MIT GARNELEN AN ROTWEINSAUCE

For 4 persons:

4 turbot fillets of about 150 g/5 oz each,
salt, pepper, finely ground star anise,
2 tbsp olive oil,
20 langoustines, shelled

1 fresh cucumber, 12 baby leeks,
200 g/7 oz chanterelles, cleaned and sliced,
5 tbsp butter, 4 punnets of watercress,
150 ml/5 fl oz/³/₅ cup langoustine stock,
215 ml/7 fl oz/1 cup double cream,
350 ml/11²/₃ fl oz/1¹/₂ cups red wine,
200 ml/6²/₃ fl oz/⁴/₅ cup port wine,
1 shallot, sliced, 2 sprigs of thyme,
150 ml/5 fl oz/³/₅ cup brown chicken stock,
1 tbsp chives, finely chopped, 1 lemon

Peel the cucumber and cut in half lengthways. Slice on a mandolin into thin ribbons. Cook in boiling salted water for two minutes. Boil the leeks in salted water for four minutes, drain and refresh. Cut into 2.5 cm/1 in lengths.

Sauté the chanterelles in two spoonfuls of butter, season, and add the plucked watercress leaves. Add the langoustine stock and reduce to half the volume. Stir in a spoonful of double cream and a spoonful of cold butter.

For the sauce: Place the red wine, port, shallot and thyme in a pan and reduce to a syrupy consistency. Add the chicken stock and cook for fifteen minutes more. Sift through a muslin cloth and stir in two spoonfuls of cold butter.

Reduce the remaining cream in a pan until thick. Add the leeks and the chives. Season and add a dash of lemon juice.

Season the turbot with salt, pepper and a little ground anise. Fry on all sides in hot olive oil. Add the langoustines and fry briefly.

To serve: Place the strips of cucumber in the centre of the plate with the turbot on top. Place 5 small piles of chanterelles around the fish with 2 pieces of leek between every 2 piles. Spoon the red-wine and white sauce all around.

Für 4 Personen:

4 Steinbuttfilets von je ca. 150 g,
Salz, Pfeffer, feingemahlener Sternanis,
2 EL Olivenöl,
20 Garnelen, ausgelöst

1 Salatgurke, 12 Stangen Minilauch,
200 g Pfifferlinge, geputzt, in Scheiben geschnitten,
5 EL Butter, 4 Körbchen Brunnenkresse,
150 ml Langustenfond,
215 ml Doppelrahm,
350 ml Rotwein, 200 ml Portwein,
1 Schalotte, in Scheiben geschnitten,
2 Zweige Thymian,
150 ml brauner Hühnerfond,
1 EL fein geschnittener Schnittlauch, 1 Zitrone

Salatgurke schälen, längs halbieren und in dünne Streifen hobeln. In Salzwasser 2 Minuten kochen. Lauchstangen vier Minuten in Salzwasser kochen, abgießen und kalt abschrecken. In 2,5 cm lange Stücke schneiden. Die Pfifferlinge in zwei Löffeln Butter anbraten, würzen, dann die gezupften Kresseblätter zugeben. Mit dem Langustenfond aufgießen und auf die halbe Menge einkochen lassen. Ein Löffel Rahm und ein Löffel kalte Butter unterrühren. Für die Sauce: Den Rotwein mit dem Portwein, der Schalotte und dem Thymian in einem Topf zu einer sirupartigen Konsistenz einkochen lassen.

Den Hühnerfond zugeben und weitere 15 Minuten kochen lassen. Durch ein Tuch abpassieren, zwei Löffel kalte Butter unterrühren. Den restlichen Rahm in einem Topf dick einkochen lassen. Den Lauch und den Schnittlauch unterrühren, würzen und einen Spritzer Zitronensaft zugeben. Den Steinbutt mit Salz, Pfeffer und etwas Anispulver würzen. In einer Pfanne mit Olivenöl rundum heiß anbraten. Die Garnelen zugeben und kurz mitbraten.

Zum Servieren: Die Gurkenstreifen auf Tellermitte anrichten und mit dem Steinbutt belegen. Je fünf Häufchen Pfifferlinge darum herum setzen, dazwischen je 2 Lauchstücke legen. Mit der Rotwein- und der weißen Sauce umgießen.

POACHED VEAL FILLET WITH GOOSE FOIE GRAS SAUCE
POCHIERTES KALBSFILET MIT GÄNSELEBERSAUCE

For 4 persons:

450 g/1 lb veal fillet, cut into 4 medaillons,
75 g/2 1/2 oz fresh goose foie gras,
175 g/6 oz/3/4 cup butter,
80 g/2 2/3 oz dried morels, soaked in Madeira,
150 ml/5 fl oz/3/5 cup double cream,
200 g/7 oz celeriac, diced,
200 ml/7 fl oz/4/5 cup milk,
100 g/3 1/2 oz smoked bacon, finely chopped,
4 tbsp duck fat, 1 small Savoy cabbage
2 tbsp parsley, finely chopped,
240 g/8 oz young broad beans, shelled,
100 g/3 1/2 oz fresh morels,
salt, freshly ground pepper

For the stock:
450 g/1 lb chicken wings, chopped,
1 bulb of garlic, split, 1 bunch thyme,
80 g/2 2/3 oz dried ceps, 6 shallots

For the stock: Cover the chicken wings with cold water in a pan and bring to the boil. Skim and add the garlic bulb, thyme, dried ceps and five coarsely chopped shallots. Simmer for two hours, season. Allow to cool in the pan. Then strain and reserve.

Press the soaked morels and chop finely. Fry in a spoonful of butter, then add 100 ml/3 1/2 fl oz/2/5 cup chicken stock and a spoonful of cream. Bring to the boil. Then stir in the cold foie gras-butter.

Simmer the celeriac with the milk and 100 ml/3 1/2 fl oz/2/5 cup double cream in a small saucepan on a low heat for about 40 minutes until the celeriac collapses and almost all the liquid has evaporated. Purée in the blender, pass through a sieve and season. Fry half of the bacon in the duck fat. Add the finely chopped Savoy cabbage. Cover and braise over a low heat until soft. Finally, stir in a spoonful each of cream and parsley.

Cook the broad beans in salted water for one minute. Refresh with cold water and remove the loosened skins.

Sauté the rest of the bacon and shallot in a little butter, add the broad beans, 70 ml/2 1/3 fl oz/1/3 cup of chicken stock and one tablespoon of double cream and reduce to half the volume. Finally stir in 70 g/2 1/3 oz/1/3 cup of cold butter and a spoonful of chopped parsley.

Fry the fresh morels in a spoonful of butter and season. Heat the remaining stock and poach the veal fillet over a low heat for five minutes.

To serve: Spread the celeriac purée in the middle of each plate. Lay the Savoy cabbage on top and then one poached veal medaillon. Surround with broad beans and morels. Pour a little sauce over the veal fillets and serve immediately.

Für 4 Personen:

450 g Kalbsfilet, in 4 Medaillons geschnitten,
75 g frische Gänsestopfleber,
175 g Butter,
80 g getrocknete Morcheln, in Madeira eingeweicht,
150 ml Doppelrahm,
200 g Sellerie, in Würfel geschnitten,
200 ml Milch,
100 g geräucherter Speck, fein gehackt,
4 EL Entenschmalz, 1 kleiner Wirsing,
2 EL feingehackte Petersilie,
240 g junge dicke Bohnen, ausgehülst,
100 g frische Morcheln,
Salz, Pfeffer aus der Mühle

Für die Brühe:
450 g Hühnerflügel, gehackt,
1 Knoblauchknolle, auseinandergedrückt, 1 Bund Thymian,
80 g getrocknete Steinpilze, 6 Schalotten

Für die Brühe: Hühnerflügel in einem Topf mit kaltem Wasser bedeckt zum Kochen bringen. Abschäumen, dann die Knoblauchknolle, den Thymian, die getrockneten Steinpilze und fünf grobgehackte Schalotten zugeben. Zwei Stunden sieden lassen, würzen, die Brühe im Topf erkalten lassen, dann durch ein feines Sieb passieren. Die Gänsestopfleber mit 75 g Butter im Mixer pürieren, durch ein Sieb streichen, kühlstellen. Die eingeweichten Morcheln ausdrücken, fein hacken, in einem Löffel Butter anbraten, dann 100 ml Hühnerbrühe und einen Löffel Rahm zugeben. Zum Kochen bringen, die kalte Stopfleber-Butter unterrühren.

Den Sellerie mit der Milch und 100 ml Doppelrahm in einem kleinen Topf bei kleiner Hitze ca. 40 Minuten köcheln lassen, bis das Gemüse zerfällt und nahezu alle Flüssigkeit eingekocht ist. Im Mixer pürieren, durch ein Sieb streichen und würzen. Die Hälfte des Specks im Entenschmalz anbraten. Den feingeschnittenen Wirsing zugeben und zugedeckt bei kleiner Hitze weichdünsten. Zum Schluß je einen Löffel Rahm und Petersilie unterrühren.

Die dicken Bohnen in Salzwasser eine Minute kochen, kalt abschrecken, abgelöste Häutchen entfernen. Restlichen Speck und Schalotte in etwas Butter dünsten, dicke Bohnen, 75 ml Hühnerbrühe sowie einen Löffel Doppelrahm zugeben und auf die Hälfte einkochen. Zum Schluß 70 g kalte Butter und einen Löffel gehackte Petersilie einrühren. Die frischen Morcheln in einem Löffel Butter anbraten und würzen. Die restliche Brühe erhitzen, das Kalbsfilet darin bei kleiner Hitze fünf Minuten pochieren.

Zum Servieren: Das Selleriepüree in die Mitte der Teller streichen. Den Wirsing darübergeben und mit je einem pochierten Kalbsmedaillon belegen. Dicke Bohnen und Morcheln rundherum verteilen. Die Kalbsfilets mit etwas Sauce überziehen; sofort servieren.

FILO PASTRY WITH CARAMELISED APPLES
PHILOTEIGGEBÄCK MIT KARAMELISIERTEN ÄPFELN

For 4 persons:

6 sheets filo pastry, 6 tbsp clarified butter, melted,
2 tbsp icing sugar, 1 tbsp ground cinnamon,
9 Granny Smith apples, washed

For the purée:
1 stick cinnamon, 1 tbsp butter, 1 tbsp sugar

Butter sauce:
200 g/6²/₃ oz/⁴/₅ cup sugar, 2 vanilla pods,
1 tsp lemon juice, 100 g/3¹/₂ oz/²/₅ cup cold butter

For the sorbet:
100 ml/3¹/₂ fl oz/²/₅ cup stock syrup, 1 tsp lemon juice

For the caramelised apples:
100 g/3¹/₂ oz/²/₅ cup sugar,
100 g/3¹/₂ oz/²/₅ cup butter, 1 tbsp Armagnac

To garnish:
120 ml/4 fl oz/¹/₂ cup crème anglaise (or vanilla crème),
diluted with a little milk

Take 1 sheet of filo and paint with the melted clarified butter. Then dust with icing sugar and cinnamon. Add a 2nd and 3rd sheet, buttering and dusting as before. Do the same again with the other 3 sheets of filo. From the pastry cut 12 rectangles, about 4 x 8 cm/1³/₅ x 3¹/₅ in. Heat the oven to 190° C/375° F and bake the pieces of pastry for about 5 minutes until caramelised and medium-brown. For the purée: Peel and core 3 apples, saving the peelings. Chop the apples and place in a pan with 1 cinnamon stick, 1 spoonful of butter and a spoonful of sugar and cook to a pulp on a low heat. Remove the cinnamon stick and purée in a blender. Then pass through a sieve and keep warm.

For the butter sauce: In a saucepan, heat 200 ml/6²/₃ fl oz/⁴/₅ cup water with the sugar until the sugar dissolves. Slit the vanilla pods and scrape out the seeds. Add the seeds and pods to the pan and reduce the syrup by a third. Pass the syrup through a sieve, add the lemon juice. Then whisk in 100 g/3¹/₂ oz/²/₅ cup of cold butter and a spoonful of apple purée. Keep warm.

For the sorbet: Peel the remaining apples and cut in half. Cut each half into 3 wedges and remove the core. Purée all apple peelings, also those from the purée, in the blender. Pass through a sieve to give a green apple juice. Mix with the syrup and add a squeeze of lemon juice to taste. Churn the sorbet in the ice-cream maker.

For the caramelised apples: Place the apple wedges in a hot frying pan with the sugar. Stir until the sugar is caramelised, then add the butter. Cook until the apples are soft. Then add the Armagnac and flambé.

To serve: Draw a ring of apple purée on each plate. Surround this with a little vanilla sauce and fill the ring with butter sauce. Lay 1 piece of filo pastry in the centre of each plate. Place 4 pieces of apple on the pastry and cover with another slice of filo, a 2nd layer of apple, and top with another layer of filo. Spoon small balls of apple sorbet onto the plates and serve immediately.

Für 4 Personen:

6 Blätter Philoteig, 6 EL geklärte Butter, geschmolzen,
2 EL Puderzucker, 1 EL Zimtpulver,
9 Granny Smith Äpfel, gewaschen

Püree:
1 Zimtstange, 1 EL Butter, 1 EL Zucker

Buttersauce:
200 g Zucker, 2 Vanillestangen,
1 TL Zitronensaft, 100 g kalte Butter

Sorbet:
100 ml Zuckersirup, 1 TL Zitronensaft

Karameläpfel:
100 g Zucker, 100 g Butter,
1 EL Armagnac

Garnitur:
120 ml Englische Creme (oder Vanillecreme),
mit Milch etwas verdünnt

Ein Philoteigblatt mit der geklärten Butter bepinseln, dann mit Puderzucker und Zimt bestäuben. Mit einem zweiten und dritten Blatt bedecken, beide buttern und bestäuben wie zuvor. Den Vorgang mit den anderen drei Teigblättern wiederholen. Aus dem Teig 12 Rechtecke von ca. 4 x 8 cm ausschneiden. Ofen auf 190° C vorheizen und die Teigstücke ungefähr fünf Minuten backen, bis sie mittelbraun karamelisiert sind. Für das Püree: Drei Äpfel schälen und entkernen, die Schalen aufheben. Die Äpfel hacken, dann mit einer Zimtstange, einem Löffel Butter und einem Löffel Zucker in einem Topf bei kleiner Hitze zu Brei kochen. Die Zimtstange entfernen, den Brei zu Püree verarbeiten und durch ein Sieb streichen. Warmhalten. Für die Buttersauce: In einem Topf 200 ml Wasser mit dem Zucker erhitzen, bis sich der Zucker auflöst. Die Vanillestangen aufschneiden und das Mark herauskratzen. Mark und Stengel in den Topf geben und den Sirup um einen Drittel einkochen lassen. Durch ein Sieb passieren, mit Zitronensaft würzen, dann 100 g kalte Butter und einen Löffel Apfelpüree unterrühren. Warmhalten. Für das Sorbet: Restliche Äpfel schälen, halbieren, die Hälften in drei Spalten schneiden, das Kernhaus entfernen. Alle Apfelschalen, auch die vom Püree, im Mixer fein pürieren. Durch ein Sieb streichen, so daß ein grüner Apfelsaft übrigbleibt. Mit dem Zuckersirup vermischen, und mit Zitronensaft abschmecken. In der Eismaschine zu Sorbet gefrieren. Für die Karameläpfel: Die Apfelspalten in einer heißen Pfanne mit dem Zucker bestreuen. Umrühren, wenn der Zucker karamelisiert ist, die Butter zufügen. Köcheln lassen, bis die Äpfel weich sind, dann den Armagnac zugeben und flambieren. Zum Servieren. Auf jeden Teller mit dem Apfelpüree einen Ring ziehen, diesen mit etwas Vanillesauce umranden und mit Buttersauce füllen. In die Mitte jeweils ein Stück Philoteig legen. Den Teig mit je vier Apfelspalten belegen, mit einem weiteren Teigstück bedecken, eine zweite Schicht Apfel und zum Schluß mit einem Teigstück zudecken. Mit je einer Kugel Apfelsorbet servieren.

Addresses · Adressen

HONG KONG

**Hong Kong
Tourist Association**
9th - 11th Floors,
Citicorp Centre
18 Whitfield Road
North Point, Hong Kong
Tel. (852) 2807 6543
Fax (852) 2807 6582
E-Mail sw@hkta.org
Internet: http://www.hkta.org

djpr
Public Relations-Consultants
Berger Straße 436
D - 60385 Frankfurt am Main
Tel. 069/46 55 66
Fax 069/46 87 55

Lauda-air
Luftfahrt AG - Wien
Rosental 8/III
D - 80331 München
Tel. (089) 2 36 60 70
Fax (089) 23 66 07 99

The Regent
18 Salisbury Road
Kowloon, Hong Kong
Tel. (852) 2721 1211
Fax (852) 2739 4546

The Peninsula
Salisbury Road
Kowloon, Hong Kong
Tel. (852) 2366 6251
Fax (852) 2722 4170

The Kowloon Hotel
19 - 21 Nathan Road
Kowloon, Hong Kong
Tel. (852) 2369 8698
Fax (852) 2739 9811

Island Shangri-La
Pacific Place
Supreme Court Road
Central, Hong Kong
Tel. (852) 2877 3838
Fax (852) 2521 8742

Forum Restaurant
485 Lockhard Road
Causeway Bay, Hong Kong
Tel. (852) 2891 2555
Fax (852) 2893 0756

Sun Tung Lok
Shark's Fin Restaurant Ltd.
17 - 19 Canton Road,
Tsim Sha Tsui
Kowloon, Hong Kong
Tel. (852) 2730 0288
Fax (852) 2736 5702

**East Ocean
Seafood Restaurant**
3/F, Harbour Centre
25 Harbour Road
Wanchai, Hong Kong
Tel. (852) 2827 8887
Fax (852) 2827 4794

Tai Woo Restaurant
27 Percival Street
Causeway Bay, Hong Kong
Tel. (852) 2893 0822
Fax (852) 2891 9564

Hunan Garden Restaurant
3/F, The Forum,
Exchange Square
8 Connaught Place
Central, Hong Kong
Tel. (852) 2868 2880
Fax (852) 2810 6650

Snow Garden Restaurant
4/F, Miramar Tower,
Miramar Shopping Centre
1 - 23 Kimberley Road,
Tsim Sha Tsui
Kowloon, Hong Kong
Tel. (852) 2377 1331
Fax (852) 2377 1361

Golden Island Bird's Nest
Chiu Chau Restaurant
2/F, East Half,
Star House
Salisbury Road,
Tsim Sha Tsui
Kowloon, Hong Kong
Tel. (852) 2736 6228

Yung Kee Restaurant
4/F, Yung Kee Bldg.
32 - 40 Wellington Street
Central, Hong Kong
Tel. (852) 2522 1624
Fax (852) 2840 0888

MOROCCO · MAROKKO

**Staatlich Marokkanisches
Fremdenverkehrsamt**
Graf-Adolfstraße 59
D - 40210 Düsseldorf
Tel. (0211) 37 05 51
Fax (0211) 37 40 48

Royal Air Maroc
Friedensstraße 9
D - 60311 Frankfurt am Main
Tel. (069) 23 61 20
Fax (069) 23 57 52

La Gazelle d'Or
B.P. 260
Taroudannt
Morocco
Tel. (08) 85 20 39
Fax (08) 85 27 37

La Roseraie
Val d'Ouirgane, Km 60,
Route Marrakech-Taroudannt
B.P. 769, Marrakech
Morocco
Tel. (04) 43 91 28
Fax (04) 43 91 30

Hotel Le Tivoli
Boulevard du 20 Août
Agadir
Morocco
Tel. (08) 84 76 40
Fax (08) 84 76 46

Villa Maroc
10, Rue Abdellah Ben Yassin
Essaouira
Morocco
Tel. (04) 47 31 47
Fax (04) 47 28 06

La Mamounia
Avenue Bab Jdid
Marrakech
Morocco
Tel. (04) 44 89 81
Fax (04) 44 46 60

Restaurant Yacout
79, Sidi Ahmed Soussi
Marrakech
Morocco
Tel. (04) 38 29 29
Fax (04) 38 25 38

LONDON

Mosimann's London
118 West Halkin Street
Belgrave Square
London SW1X 8JL
Tel. (0171) 235 9626
Fax (0171) 245 6354

The Dorchester
Park Lane
London W1A 2HJ
Tel. (0171) 629 8888
Fax (0171) 409 0114

The Stafford
Member of Small Luxury
Hotels of the World Ltd.
St. James Place
London SW1A 1NJ
Tel. (0171) 493 0111
Fax (0171) 493 7121

Restaurant Aubergine
11 Park Walk
London SW10 0AJ
Tel. (0171) 352 3449
Fax (0171) 351 1770

Zafferano
15 Lowndes Street
London SW1X 9ES
Tel. (0171) 235 5800
Fax (0171) 235 1971

Restaurant Pied-à-Terre
34 Charlotte Street
London W1P 1HJ
Tel. (0171) 636 1178
Fax (0171) 916 1171

Acknowledgements · Danksagung

In producing a book like THE CULINARY CHRONICLE
innumerable people have been directly and indirectly involved.
We therefore wish to express our gratitude to all who have in any way
contributed to its completion. Our special hearty thanks go to the
following persons and institutions for their cooperation and support:

An der Entstehung eines Buches wie THE CULINARY CHRONICLE
sind unzählige Menschen direkt und indirekt beteiligt. An dieser Stelle
möchten wir all jenen unseren Dank aussprechen, die in irgendeiner
Form dazu beigetragen haben, das Werk zu vollenden.
Bei den folgenden Personen und Institutionen möchten wir uns
besonders herzlich für ihre Mitarbeit und Unterstützung bedanken:

The Dorchester, London
Nabil Fenjiro
Hotel La Gazelle d'Or, Taroudannt
Katrin Holtkott, SLH
Hong Kong Tourist Association
Dieter Jacobs
Veronica Kay
The Kowloon Hotel, Hong Kong
Claire Lau
Lauda-air
Hotel La Mamounia, Marrakech
Moroccan State Tourism Office Düsseldorf
The Peninsula, Hong Kong
The Regent, Hong Kong
Ludwig Riepl
Hotel La Roseraie
Royal Air Maroc
Sabine Schramek
Dr. Barbara Schweighofer
John Smith
The Stafford, London
Hans-Albert Stechl
Adam Stevenson
Hotel Le Tivoli, Agadir
Stephen Wong
Lee Yeeman

... and all the cooks and their staff, the restaurants and hotels that are
presented in this volume.

... und allen Köchen und deren Mitarbeitern, den Restaurants und
Hotels, die im vorliegenden Band vorgestellt werden.

Illustration credits · Bildnachweis

RECIPE INDEX

REZEPTVERZEICHNIS

HONG KONG

SOUPS

Chicken-spinach crème "Yin Yang"	130
Won ton in crab bouillon	30

APPETIZERS

Deep-fried prawn rolls	97
Dumplings with prawns and lime	101
Goose foie-gras with ginger figs on sweet-and-sour sauce	192
Lobster cocktail with spicy lemon-horseradish vinaigrette	194
Mixed hors d'oeuvres "Delicious combination"	128
Prawn wasabi terrine with deep-fried prawn balls	40
Seafood plate	38
Smoked salmon rolls with caviar and champagne vinegar	174
Steamed dumplings with scallops	100
Steamed dumplings with squid	100
Stir-fried shrimps with spring onion	118
Tuna fish tartare on sesame oil sauce with white-radish salad	162

RICE, NOODLES, SPECIALITIES

Birds' nests	133
Fried bird's-nests with egg-white	150
Pizza Marco Polo	107
Seafood paella "Yü"	28
Sea snails (Abalone)	148
Shark's fin soup	64
Shark's fin in brown sauce	64
Shell noodles with grilled tiger prawns	34

VEGETABLES, SIDE DISHES

Fried green beans	112
Fried lotus root cakes in black-bean sauce	56
Vegetable platter with mushrooms	132
Vegetables with bamboo shoots	119

FISH, SHELLFISH

Braised grouper	52
Fried crab with ginger and bell pepper	94
Fried lobster with black-bean sauce	33
Fried lobster with noodles	95
Fried prawns with chili	113
Fried seafood on chili sauce in a taro basket	98
Fried squid	74
Giant crab in yellow rice-wine sauce	72
Prawns in lemon-grass chili sauce	32
Prawns with garlic and honey	50
Scallops with bell peppers	51
Scallops with vegetables	94
Sole with basil and tomato sauce	178
Steamed grouper	36
Steamed hung yau, lotus root and broccoli	42
Sweet-and-sour fried carp	116
Swordfish on fennel with taro gnocchi	190

POULTRY

Chicken and cashew nuts in soy sauce	112
Fried breast of duck in black-bean sauce	54
Glazed roast goose	138
Peking duck	76

MEAT

Braised brisket of beef 110

Calves' kidneys with sherry vinegar 177

Fried fillet of beef
on a potato-truffle rosette 176

Grilled Angus beef tournedos
with fried prawns and tomato sauce 188

Jiangnan Spare Ribs 75

Strips of fillet steak in a crispy basket 55

DESSERTS, PASTRY

Coconut mousse
with sago on pineapple 42

Iced Mango Dessert 102

Lotus soup with dates 152

Steamed doughballs
with coconut-egg cream 99

Stuffed glazed tomatoes
with orange syrup 164

MOROCCO

SOUPS, APPETIZERS, VEGETABLES, SALADS

Brined lemons 230

Fasting soup "Harira" 334

Fish brochettes 274

Mixed salad with couscous 232

Stewed white beans 234

Stuffed pastry envelopes (Brewattes) 245

Tajine with vegetables and olives 264

Vegetable soup "Chorba" 274

FISH, SHELLFISH

Oven-braised sea bream "M'Chermel" 262

Pastilla with seafood 242

Sea bass with dates, Tafilalet style 291

Stuffed sea bream, Fes style 241

Tuna tajine with brined lemons 238

POULTRY

Braised chicken with lemon and olives 342

Chicken with almonds "M'Qalli" 276

Cinnamon pigeon with noodles 294

Moroccan layered pastry
with chicken "Beldi" 292

Pigeons with almonds and raisins 346

Turkey tajine
with couscous and almonds 239

MEAT

Braised lamb Marrakech style 290

Couscous with lamb and vegetables 277

Knuckle of beef with artichokes and peas 235

Lamb tajine with artichokes and peas 348

Lamb tajine with onions 236

Lentil stew 240

Meatballs "Kefta" with eggs 244

Shoulder of lamb "Méchoui" 288

Tajine with lamb and olives 264

DESSERTS, PASTRY

Gazelle horns 246

Pastilla with milk 296

Pastilla with rice pudding 276

Sesame and honey pastries 248

RECIPE INDEX 491

LONDON

SOUPS

Cappuccino of haricots blancs
with morels   458

Minestrone of langoustines with pesto   436

APPETIZERS, SALADS

Anton's Caesar salad   366

Leek terrine
with horn of plenty mushrooms   368

Potato gnocchi with black pepper
and goats' cheese sauce   434

Ravioli of lobster   456

Risotto with wild mushrooms   370

Salmon and halibut sashimi
with spring onion and toasted sesame   372

Scallop salad with truffle vinaigrette   460

Semolina gnocchi
with Scamorza smoked cheese   432

Smoked chicken and avocado
on cassis dressing   417

Terrine of duck foie gras with duck meat   454

Terrine of goose foie gras and artichokes   474

FISH, SHELLFISH

Baked salmon on potato gnocchi
with lime and basil   400

Fillet of sea bass with Chinese greens   402

Grilled stuffed squid   438

Pan-fried scallops on tomato confit   398

Scallops on gazpacho
with tomato confit   478

Turbot with langoustines
and red-wine sauce   480

POULTRY

Chicken breast wrapped
in Parma ham on asparagus salad   396

Steamed pigeon breast
with cabbage roulades   476

MEAT

Lamb noisettes
with a mustard and herb crust   374

Loin of lamb wrapped in noodle paste
flavoured with coriander   404

Poached veal fillet
with goose foie gras sauce   482

Roast pork fillet with new season garlic   440

DESSERTS, PASTRIES

Amaretti biscuits with rhubarb
and strawberry compote   444

Bread and butter pudding   376

Chocolate brownie
with glazed bananas   420

Chocolate tears with caramelised banana
and pistachio ice-cream   406

Crème brûlée with dried apple   462

Devonshire apple cake   418

Filo pastry with caramelised apples   484

Gordon's puff pastry   466

Lemon and mascarpone tart   442

Summer pudding   378

Tarte tatin with pineapple   464

HONG KONG

SUPPEN

Hühnerfleisch-Spinatcreme „Yin Yang"	130
Won-Ton in Krebsbouillon	30

VORSPEISEN

Fritierte Garnelenröllchen	97
Gänsestopfleber mit Ingwerfeigen an süßsaurer Sauce	192
Garnelen-Wasabi-Terrine mit fritierten Garnelenbällchen	40
Gemischte Vorspeise „Delicious combination"	128
Hummercocktail an würziger Zitronen-Meerrettich Vinaigrette	194
Kurz gebratene Krabben mit Frühlingszwiebeln	118
Meeresfrüchte-Platte	38
Räucherlachsröllchen mit Kaviar und Champagneressig	174
Teigtaschen im Dampf mit Tintenfisch	100
Teigtaschen mit Garnelen und Limone	101
Teigtaschen mit Jakobsmuscheln	100
Thunfischtatar an Sesamölsauce mit Rettichsalat	162

REIS, NUDELGERICHTE, SPEZIALITÄTEN

Gebratenes Schwalbennest mit Eiweiß	150
Haifischflossensuppe	64
Haifischflosse in brauner Sauce	64
Meeresfrüchte-Paella „Yü"	28
Meeresschnecken (Abalone)	148
Muschelnudeln mit gegrillten Riesengarnelen	34
Pizza Marco Polo	107
Schwalbennester	133

GEMÜSE, BEILAGEN

Gebratene grüne Bohnen	112
Gebratene Lotoswurzelkuchen in Bohnensauce	56
Gemüsetopf mit Bambusschote	119
Gemüseplatte mit Pilzen	132

FISCH, MEERESFRÜCHTE

Fritierte Garnelenröllchen	97
Garnelen in Zitronengras-Chilisauce	32
Garnelen mit Knoblauch und Honig	50
Gebratene Garnelen mit Chili	113
Gebratener Hummer in Bohnensauce	33
Gebratener Hummer auf Nudeln	95
Gebratener Krebs mit Ingwer und Paprika	94
Gedämpfter Hung Yau, Lotos und Broccoli	42
Gedämpfter Zackenbarsch	36
Geschmorter Zackenbarsch	52
Jakobsmuscheln mit Gemüse	94
Jakobsmuscheln mit Paprika	51
Karpfen süßsauer	116
Meeresfrüchte an Chilisauce im Tarokörbchen	98
Seezunge mit Basilikum und Tomatensauce	178
Schwertfisch auf Fenchel mit Taro Gnocchi	190
Taschenkrebs in gelber Reisweinsauce	72

GEFLÜGEL

Gebratene glacierte Gans	138
Gebratene Entenbrust mit Chili in Bohnensauce	54
Hühnerfleisch und Cashewnüsse in Sojasauce	112
Peking Ente	76

FLEISCH

Gebratene Rinderlende auf einer Kartoffel-Trüffelrosette	176
Gegrillte Anguslende mit gebratenen Garnelen und Tomatensauce	188
Geschmorte Rinderbrust	110
Jiangnan Spare Ribs	75
Kalbsnierchen an Sherryessig	177
Rinderfiletstreifen im knusprigen Körbchen	55

DESSERTS, GEBÄCK

Lotossüppchen mit Datteln	152
Gefüllte glacierte Tomaten an Orangensirup	164
Gedämpfte Teigbällchen mit Kokosnuß-Eiercreme	99
Geeister Mango Pudding	102
Kokosnuß-Mousse mit Sago auf Ananas	42

MAROKKO

SUPPEN, VORSPEISEN, GEMÜSE, SALATE

Bunter Salat mit Couscous (Taboulet)	232
Eingelegte Zitronen	230
Fastensuppe „Harira"	334
Fischspießchen	274
Gefüllte Teigtaschen (Brewattes)	245
Gemüsesuppe „Chorba"	274
Geschmorte weiße Bohnen	234

FISCH, MEERESFRÜCHTE

Dorade im Ofen geschmort „M'Chermel"	262
Gefüllte Goldbrasse nach Art von Fes	241
Pastilla mit Meeresfrüchten	242
Thunfisch-Tagine mit eingemachten Zitronen	238
Wolfsbarsch mit Datteln nach Art von Tafilalet	291

GEFLÜGEL

Geschmortes Zitronenhuhn mit Oliven	342
Huhn mit Mandeln „M'Qalli"	276
Marokkanische Pastete mit Huhn „Beldi"	292
Tauben mit Mandeln und Rosinen	346
Truthahn-Tagine mit Couscous und Mandeln	239
Zimt-Taube mit Nudeln	294

FLEISCH

Couscous mit Lamm und Gemüse	277
Geschmortes Lamm nach Art von Marrakesch	290
Hackfleischbällchen „Kefta" mit Eiern	244
Lammschulter „Méchoui"	288
Lamm-Tagine mit Artischocken und Erbsen	348
Lamm-Tagine mit Zwiebeln	236
Linseneintopf	240
Rinderhaxen mit Artischocken und Erbsen	235
Tagine mit Gemüse und Oliven	264
Tagine mit Lammfleisch und Oliven	264

DESSERTS, GEBÄCK

Gazellenhörnchen	246
Pastilla mit Milch	296
Pastilla mit Milchreis	276
Sesam-Honiggebäck	248

LONDON

SUPPEN

Cappuccino von weißen Bohnen
mit Morcheln — 458

Minestrone mit Garnelenschwänzen
und Pesto — 436

VORSPEISEN

Antons Cäsarsalat — 366

Geräuchertes Hühnerfleisch
und Avocado an Cassisdressing — 417

Griessgnocchi
mit geräuchertem Scamorza Käse — 432

Hummerravioli — 456

Jakobsmuschelsalat mit Trüffelvinaigrette — 460

Kartoffelgnocchi mit schwarzem Pfeffer
und Ziegenkäsesauce — 434

Lauchterrine mit Herbsttrompeten — 368

Risotto mit Waldpilzen — 370

Sashimi von Lachs und Heilbutt
mit Frühlingszwiebeln und Sesam — 372

Terrine von der Entenstopfleber
mit Entenfleisch — 454

Terrine von der Gänsestopfleber
und Artischocken — 474

FISCH, MEERESFRÜCHTE

Gebratene Jakobsmuscheln
auf Tomatenconfit — 398

Gefüllte Tintenfische vom Grill — 438

Jakobsmuscheln an Gazpacho
mit Tomatenconfit — 478

Lachs auf Kartoffelgnocchi
mit Limone und Basilikum — 400

Steinbutt mit Garnelen an Rotweinsauce — 480

Wolfsbarschfilet mit Chinagemüse — 402

GEFLÜGEL

Gedämpfte Taubenbrüstchen
mit Kohlwickel — 476

Hühnerbrust in Parmaschinken
auf Spargelsalat — 396

FLEISCH

Lammlendchen im Nudelteig
mit Koriander — 404

Lammnüßchen
mit Senf- und Kräuterkruste — 374

Pochiertes Kalbsfilet
mit Gänselebersauce — 482

Schweinefilet
mit jungem Knoblauch — 440

DESSERTS, GEBÄCK

Amarettiküchlein
mit Rhabarber-Erdbeerkompott — 444

Apfelkuchen nach Art von Devonshire — 418

Brot- und Butterpudding — 376

Gebrannte Creme mit getrocknetem Apfel — 462

Gordons Blätterteig — 466

Philoteiggebäck mit karamelisierten Äpfeln — 484

Schokoladenkuchen
mit glacierten Bananen — 420

Schokoladentränen mit karamelisierter
Banane und Pistazieneis — 406

Sommerpudding — 378

Tarte Tatin mit Ananas — 464

Zitronentorte mit Mascarpone — 442

THE
CULINARY
CHRONICLE